# GOD ON THREE SIDES

# GOD ON THREE SIDES

*German Pietists at War in Eighteenth-Century America*

Jonathan M. Wilson

☙PICKWICK *Publications* · Eugene, Oregon

GOD ON THREE SIDES
German Pietists at War in Eighteenth-Century America

Copyright © 2019 Jonathan M. Wilson. All rights reserved. Except for brief quotations in critical publications or reviews, no part of this book may be reproduced in any manner without prior written permission from the publisher. Write: Permissions, Wipf and Stock Publishers, 199 W. 8th Ave., Suite 3, Eugene, OR 97401.

Cascade Books
An Imprint of Wipf and Stock Publishers
199 W. 8th Ave., Suite 3
Eugene, OR 97401

www.wipfandstock.com

PAPERBACK ISBN: 978-1-5326-6318-5
HARDCOVER ISBN: 978-1-5326-6319-2
EBOOK ISBN: 978-1-5326-6320-8

*Cataloguing-in-Publication data:*

Names: Wilson, Jonathan Mark, author.

Title: God on three sides : German pietists at war in eighteenth-century America / Jonathan M. Wilson.

Description: Eugene, OR: Pickwick Publications, 2019 | Includes bibliographical references and index.

Identifiers: ISBN 978-1-5326-6318-5 (paperback) | ISBN 978-1-5326-6319-2 (hardcover) | ISBN 978-1-5326-6320-8 (ebook)

Subjects: LCSH: Pietism—North America | Pietism—United States—History—18th century | United States—Religion—18th century | Pietism—United States | Christian sects—United States.

Classification: BR1652.U6 W55 2019 (print) | BR1652.U6 (ebook)

Manufactured in the U.S.A.             SEPTEMBER 25, 2019

Dedication

In memory of Joel, whose personal walk with God took him on a journey from one political party to another and back again, and who thought his younger brother should write more.

# Table of Contents

Preface ix

Acknowledgments xii

Introduction 1

1 His Glorious Protestant Majesty and His Rebelling Colonies 19

2 The Holder of the Heavens: Conrad Weiser 51

3 The Pennsylvania Ministerium: Heinrich Melchior Mühlenberg 85

4 Serving God from Three Sides: The Moravians in Bethlehem 115

5 Crossing Over: A Lutheran Chaplain Discovers America 140

6 The Time to Fight: The Career of Peter Mühlenberg 181

7 Loving the Enemy: The Moravian Missionary David Zeisberger 220

8 The Halle Hessian 246

Conclusion, God on All Sides 279

Bibliography 287

Index 305

# Preface

ETHNIC GERMANS WERE THE largest non-Anglophonic settler group by far in North America in the eighteenth century. Historical societies, along with institutions descended from immigrant German founders such as the Moravian Archives in Bethlehem, the Abdel Ross Wentz Library in Gettysburg, and local churches, continue to store copious amounts of German-language material from the eighteenth century: minutes, diaries, letters, contracts, sermons, books, etc. In addition, beginning in the middle of the twentieth century thousands of pages of these primary materials have been translated into English. With the onset of digital technologies, many archives and libraries have made increasing shares of their collections available online. In mining such resources scholars in social and religious history have produced a comprehensive mosaic of ethnic German life in colonial America.

This study brings to the surface the perspectives of ethnic Germans on the partisan issues of the eighteenth century in America, building towards and including the War of Independence. This study proposes that the ethical conundrums of the ethnic German immigrant in the eighteenth century can have bearing on contemporary discussions in faith and politics. *God on Three Sides* falsifies the popular axiom that religious affinity predicts political alignment, and establishes that adherents to the same fervent, personal religious experience are often found to be at odds with each other over socio-economic and political issues. Partisan factions are much more likely to adhere around other demographic descriptors such as one's community affinity, social status, and personal economic opportunity, rather than one's religious affinity. The connection between religious affinity and political alignment is probed, and suggestions are made for a more generous engagement between people who share a common faith but who hold disparate political views.

This study is guided by the matters of concern which were committed to paper by ethnic Germans during the eighteenth century. Thus while the experience of Black slaves owned by ethnic Germans is touched on and is a project worthy of consideration, it is not part of this study's focus. Issues relating to North America's indigenous peoples figure prominently in this story but not from the perspectives of Native Americans as such. The part taken by German settlers in slavery and territorial expansion make it clear that their roles in colonial America are ethically ambiguous. Female perspectives are notably under-represented as well; a study focusing on the stories of ethnic German women in the War of Independence would be a difficult path of research in terms of discursive material but well worth pursuing nevertheless.

In the case of *God on Three Sides*, the specific religious experience under examination is the Pietistic element in German Protestant Christianity. Pietists believed that spiritual regeneration, in which a portion of God's very own Spirit indwells the repentant sinner, was essential to one's power to live in God's will. The immigrant German Pietists given focus in the study belonged to two distinct ethnic German Pietist communities: Lutheran congregations served by missionary pastors trained at the pietist Halle Institutes in the Kingdom of Prussia; and, the Renewed Unity of the Brethren which, by the 1740's, had established the communitarian town of Bethlehem, Pennsylvania.

German Pietists each laid claim to an intimate life with God yet were found on all three sides of the American Revolution, patriot, royalist, and neutral, and many chose arms to assert their convictions over and against their co-religionists. In the eighteenth century, when much of the Euro-ethnic cultural context was nominally Christian, that sharers in the same faith often found themselves on opposite sides of a war was no impediment to one's military duty. Royalist Highland regiments of Scottish Presbyterians fought to suppress devout Presbyterian patriots, and German Lutherans from Braunschweig marched in the royalist auxiliaries to suppress the revolt of German American co-religionists against England's King.

It is not this project's purpose to argue for or against the merits of pietist doctrine, but rather to make the case that adherents to a shared and highly particular religious vocabulary and orientation may harbor and in the past have harbored political views that set them in opposition to each other. It is too simplistic to assert that Pietists on two of these three sides had to have been in error, and it is unhelpful to dismiss their own testimonies of personal faith as misguided. Found on all three sides of the war are those who shared the premise that as regenerate believers in Christ they each possessed God's Spirit within their own souls. On the terms of faith set by these pietists themselves, it follows that through these conscious spiritual and ethical agents *God was personally active on all three sides of the War of Independence.*

# Acknowledgments

Much of chapters 3 and 5 of this study, *God on Three Sides*, are drawn from the author's doctoral dissertation, "Switching Sides: A Hessian Chaplain in the Pennsylvania Ministerium," which tells the story of a German chaplain's journey from captivity and into the Pennsylvania Ministerium. The bibliography also lists articles published by the author which have been recast for this study. *God on Three Sides* incorporates subsequent research and notes corrections or updates to findings in the previous publications. However, *God on Three Sides* is not a reproduction of the dissertation, nor does it reprint formerly published articles, nor does it replace them; it is a stand-alone study.

    I am grateful for the help, patience, and flexibility of my wife, Amy, and my daughters, Hope and Holly, so that I could see this project through. I am also grateful to the legion of archivists, research and circulation librarians, and those in their employ who quietly and anonymously do the work of scanning documents to build online resources. Without them this project could never have been imagined, much less executed. I am grateful to James Leroy Wilson, MA (Political Theory), for his suggestions, to Amy Wohl Wilson for proofing, and for other peer readers known and unknown to me whose feedback helped bring this work to final form. I am grateful to my dissertation advisor Kurt Hendel, and to the history faculties at the Lutheran School of Theology at Chicago and North Park Theological Seminary who extended collegiality, opportunity, and encouragement. I am grateful to the editors and staff at Pickwick for extending this opportunity. I am especially grateful to the Evangelical Covenant Church and its partners in the International Federation of Free Evangelical Churches which carry the torch of pietism and shine its light around the world and in my own soul.

# Introduction

At least as far back as the eighteenth century there has been a popular assumption that one's religious faith will predict one's political views. This assumption was shared by the royalist Governor of New Jersey William Franklin (1731–1813), the son of the wealthy printer, scientist, and international celebrity Benjamin Franklin. In a letter to his father, William Franklin surmised that the unrest over the Stamp Act had been fomented by New England's Presbyterians.[1] This opinion gained circulation when the unrest of the 1760s boiled into a revolutionary war for independence, which was called by many royalists a "Presbyterian Rebellion."[2]

The assumption that one's political views are predicted by one's religious faith has taken on the force of an axiom in the discourse of the twenty-first century. In the United States, for example, it is popularly assumed that evangelical Christians hold conservative views on social and economic philosophy and constitute a base for the Republican Party.

If one's faith determines one's politics, it should follow that the more that the particulars of a faith are shared by adherents, the more those adherents should conform to the same political ideals. This is why some descriptors of faith alignment are too broad to predict socio-political views: In Governor Franklin's eighteenth-century context, the terms "Christian" or "Protestant" are not precise enough to predict political alignment; Anglicans, assumed to be partisans for the royalists, were both Christian and Protestant just as much as were patriot Presbyterians. Thus a more defined level of faith alignment, such as a denomination, is needed for the axiom to ring true. William Howe, supreme commander of the royalist forces in North America from 1776–1778, reflected the assumption that denominational affinity equaled political sympathy by using New

1. Kidd, *God of Liberty*, 33.
2. Allen, *Tories*, 147–48.

York City's Anglican churches for worship, and its Presbyterian churches as stables.[3]

An embarrassment to Howe's generalization is that George Washington, his enemy counterpart as the patriot commander-in-chief, was no less an Anglican than Howe himself. Meanwhile many in the Scots regiments deployed under Howe's command in the British forces in America were both Presbyterians and Royalists. It is obvious therefore that the axiom that shared religious faith predicts conformity of political views, even at the particular level of denomination, fails to be generally descriptive even in the setting where Howe applied it.

Yet the axiom has continued to be applied whenever Americans have contended with each other across partisan divides: Evangelicals are striped as pro-South in the Civil War but stripped of credit for their leadership in the Abolition Movement. Similar broad strokes are applied to historiographies of the Temperance Movement, Civil Rights, peace efforts, and the politics of abortion and women's health. Political movements in the early twenty-first century that self-consciously recovered themes and memes from the American War of Independence, such as the Tea Party Movement, came to be associated with conservative evangelicals. This so-called evangelical constituency bloc has been variously denigrated or credited, depending on the journalist's or blogger's point-of-view, for playing a key role in propelling Donald Trump to his first term as president in 2016.

That the axiom is problematized, even in Howe's context, has already been shown. Perhaps if the religious alignment is even more precise and particular, it then becomes predictive. Evangelicalism speaks to a precise and particular understanding of Christian faith, which is, that one must be "born again" to be a true follower of Jesus Christ. In the conversion experience the Holy Spirit is sent from Christ to dwell in the life of the believer, both sealing the relationship with God and bringing that divine holiness into the inner life which is needful for the person's soul to inherit eternal life. For many adherents, such conversion is credited with bringing a change of values and aspirations and of changing the course of one's life. It might therefore follow that a personal conversion experience esteemed as both typical and essential by all adherents, through which God's Spirit occupies the mind and will of a person, might foster a unity of political idealism and a conformity of political action.

---

3. Allen, *Tories*, 148.

Put another way: One God with One Spirit should evince One Opinion in all these minds and hearts that have a personal relationship with God such as evangelicals self-describe. If such a case is proven in this instance, the axiom stands. If, however, there is discovered to be a wide divergence of *political views* among adherents to conversion and a personal relationship with God, the axiom is shown to be misleading at best, and nonsense in fact.

This study submits the axiom to the historical case of a particular religious expression rooted in personal conversion that was operative during the American Revolutionary War. The faith priorities of the eighteenth-century adherents to this expression are well-documented through extant letters, diaries, and formal exposition. Unlike the proto-evangelicals that were the Methodists and Puritan Baptists of the eighteenth century, this study's proto-evangelicals in Colonial America were not only non-English, they did not even take to the English language with much enthusiasm.

The proto-evangelicals featured in this study are two ethnic German religious groups who shared Pietism as their common religious expression. Pietism insisted both upon the experience of personal conversion and on the necessity of that conversion showing forth in lifestyles and actions that conformed to the demands of the Christian scriptures. One group is a subset of German Lutheran clergy in colonial America called the Pennsylvania Ministerium, constituted of pastors who were supported as missionaries by the pietist Halle Institutes headquartered in the German kingdom of Prussia. This support took the forms, first, of being vetted and then sent to colonial American congregations in answer to the request of colonial church officials, and second, in an annual disbursement of gifts and cash supplements.[4]

The second group of German Pietists included in this study was officially called the Renewed Unity of the Brethren, but in common parlance its members were variously styled Herrnhuters, Zinzendorfers, and Moravians. The focus in this study is on those Moravians who maintained a distinctive communitarian lifestyle bounded by disciplines that limited contact beyond their towns, but which served to undergird a thriving

---

4. Cash, books, and pharmaceuticals were shipped from the Halle Institutes in Prussia and disbursed at annual Synod meetings of the Pennsylvania Ministerium. Although interrupted by the War of Independence, these shipments were resumed and continued to the end of the century. See Spaeth et al., *Documentary History*, 288.

holistic cross-cultural mission to indigenous peoples based on replicating the pattern of these communities.

These two groups, the Halle Pietists and the Moravians, were rivals in Germany and in colonial America. The rivalry has its origins in what they shared as theological priorities, which in turn led to distinctions in doctrinal minutiae and to personality conflicts between those at the head of each hierarchy.[5] What the Halle Pietists and the Moravians shared is crucial to the case at hand, not to mention to the development of evangelicalism on American soil.[6]

That faith came alive by being consciously appropriated in a conversion experience was a singular doctrine held by both groups. Both also held as a necessary corollary that the life of faith has an impact on the individual believer's ethics and convictions. Among the Lutheran Pietists it was the clergy, more than the laity, who were subject to the accountability of visible fruits; in the Moravian communities all residents submitted to a discipline that fostered conformity. Both Lutheran Pietists and Moravians believed that in one's walk with God, one carried God's Spirit personally within oneself. God's own Spirit was the gift sent by Jesus Christ as the seal of salvation, so that one could directly speak with God through prayer, and God could also speak through various means including, very often, the promptings of the conscience.

These doctrines of a personal relationship with God continue to be foundational to Evangelical Christian faith. To support the axiom that shared faith alignment predicts shared political alignment, we should find that in the American Revolution, German Pietists were in agreement with each other over which side to support.

However, there is a sharp and particular distinction in the religious experience of those who lived in Moravian towns from the average Lutheran laity. Whereas Moravians lived under a conforming discipline,

---

5. The patron who reestablished the Renewed Unity of the Brethren, Nicholas Ludwig Count von Zinzendorf, had boarded as a student at the Halle Institutes during the tenure of the founder, August Hermann Francke. Zinzendorf later received ordination by one of Francke's protégé's, J. Albrecht Bengel, at the pietist University of Tübingen. A short biography of Zinzendorf for lay readers is Anderson, *Lord of the Ring*.

6. The Moravians were direct influences on John Wesley, who later became a key figure in Great Britain's Evangelical Awakening. His colleague, George Whitefield, was the most popular evangelist in the First Great Awakening in colonial America, and he befriended both Lutheran Pietist and Moravian leaders. The Methodist movement which Wesley and Whitefield founded grew quickly on American soil during the Second Great Awakening after 1800.

the typical Lutheran layperson exercised considerable independence from the strictures that governed their Halle-sponsored clergy. It is thus begging the question to compare Lutheran Pietist laypeople with Moravian community residents in their responses to the political questions of American independence. This study further narrows the particulars and presents two cases: One focusses on the responses to the issues of American independence in the Pennsylvania Ministerium Clergy, as opposed to ethnic German laypeople, and compares Lutheran Pietist pastors with each other. The other case focusses primarily on Moravian community leaders in comparing their decisions with each other.

The discursive and documentary evidence conclusively shows that German Lutheran Pietist pastors were divided in their political views between patriots, royalists, and those holding to neutrality. German Moravians were more uniformly neutral based both on their shared and particular convictions of nonviolence, and on the socio-economic reality of living under a community discipline where pacifism was enforced. This dynamic narrowed the range of divergence among the communitarian Moravians, yet divergence is still present, most acutely in the various ways the obligations to pacifism were understood as absolutes or were relativized. By dwelling personally, through the Holy Spirit, in the hearts of communitarian Moravians and Lutheran Pietist pastors, God is found in the hearts of patriots, royalists, and neutrals; in short, God is found on all three sides of the American War of Independence.

The study of German Pietism in the American Revolution shows us that even a religious experience as particular as conscious conversion to life in Christ *does not predict that person's alignment* with political sides and partisan causes. This has implications for those who find it convenient to tar all evangelicals with broad strokes, and it has implications for those evangelicals (especially those self-appointed leaders with a media profile) who find those broad strokes convenient for their own purposes. Adherents of various Christian communions are no less vulnerable to stereo-typing than are evangelicals, as this study shows in penetrating the virile anti-Catholicism at work in the patriot agenda before and during the War of Independence.

The implications may also apply to other faiths in their own particular varieties of expression and community. Sweeping statements about the partisan choices of religious adherents are made incautiously in popular discourse, often smearing many convinced and faithful observers of their own traditions with assumptions about their politics that are distasteful and even offensive. American Muslims, American Jews, American Hindu, American Buddhists, American followers of Earth religions and of animism, and Americans of no faith at all, are each vulnerable to the broad strokes of politicized stereo-type and polarized misunderstanding that enter public conversation. The generalizations become broader still and even less nuanced in the popular discourse on global politics and international relations where violent conflicts have religious overtones, such as the War on Terror.

The personalities under examination in this study of the eighteenth century are not household names; George Washington and Benjamin Franklin appear throughout the narratives but are not the subject of this study. Neither are these household names in the story of American religion; Jonathan Edwards and George Whitefield are referred to only a few times. The ethnic German story in early America is an accomplished field of scholarship, a sample of which appears in this study's bibliography, but it is not a story that figures into the popular discourse of either early American religion or of early America's eighteenth-century wars.

Even so, the figures whose stories are told in this study were not obscure in their time. Heinrich Melchior Mühlenberg was the founding superintendent of the first permanent Lutheran synod in North America. G. A. Freylinghausen, to whom he reported, headed up the global operation which was the Halle Institutes. Mühlenberg's father-in-law Conrad Weiser was the leading German American citizen of his generation, and Mühlenberg's eldest son J. Peter Mühlenberg was a brigadier general on George Washington's staff. Among the Moravians Nicholas Ludwig von Zinzendorf, August Spangenberg, and Johann Ettwein were known to European royalty, to dignitaries of the Continental Congress, and to officers of the Continental Army. David Zeisberger is a leading figure in Moravian missionary discourse. The Hessian chaplain who deserted to serve a church in the pietist Pennsylvania Ministerium, Friedrich Melsheimer, pioneered the science of entomology, joined the American Philosophical Society, and was featured in the 1930s publication *Dictionary of American Biography*. The Halle Missionary to Georgia, Christopher Triebner, became the personal enemy of the patriot Governor of Georgia, who also happened to be his own ethnic German Lutheran parishioner, John Treutlen. With one exception these ethnic German figures have been subjects of secondary, critical academic study, some more exhaustive than others. This author's modest contribution to the field is critical research and analysis of the life and discourse of Friedrich Melsheimer.[7]

These narratives shed light on other, more nuanced aspects of the relationship between religious alignment and political action. One's religious convictions do indeed act as constraints on one's political actions, and it is this truth that may have led to the false assumption that since faith modifies political action it also predicts political opinion. Furthermore, certain demographic indicators do predict political views far more reliably than religious affinity; here the parsing out of the factors is complex and must be precise. The range of political opinion and action has a far narrower divergence among communitarian Moravians than it does among heads of private Lutheran Pietist households. That indicates that what one identifies as one's primary community is more predictive of political alignment than what one identifies as a particular faith experience.

The German Lutheran Pietists did not identify the local church congregation as their primary community; rather it was their own nuclear families which were primary. Widespread aspirations for the freedom and means to provide for their families had most German immigrants interested in negotiating the socio-economic and legal-political spheres of colonial American society, and the Lutheran Pietist subset was no exception.[8] For the Lutheran Pietist God was still at the center of one's life as it was for the Moravian, but the several aspects of life were not governed directly by the Church as it was in a closed Moravian community. For those for whom the nuclear family was the primary community, the family's economic ties and prospects were much more predictive of political alignment than was their faith.

In this study the phrase "God on Three Sides" refers to the patriots, the royalists, and the neutrals in the American War of Independence, where this study finds the starkest contrasts in conflicting choices by persons who otherwise shared in a particular experience of God. However, these convictions and choices evolved through a series of conflicts in North America in the eighteenth century. The American Revolution and the partisan choices with which it confronted the public cannot be

---

7. Wilson, "Switching Sides." See also an article by Wilson reconsidering the importance of Gottlieb Anastasius Freylinghausen in his own life-time as the Director of the Halle Institutes during the American War of Independence (Wilson, "Civil Unrest and the Pastoral Vocation," 7–17).

8. This theme is exhaustively treated in Roeber, *Palatines, Liberty, and Property.*

understood apart from the crucible of struggle against rival colonial powers and their allied Native Nations. The progression of the ethnic German settler from friendship with the Mohawk to radicalized, racial violence against all indigenous peoples is perhaps the most tragic of the narrative arcs captured in this study. Even so, this drift in social and political perspective concerning the Native Nations must be taken into account for the emergence of patriotism among ethnic Germans to be understood. The narrative studies, therefore, begin early in the eighteenth century, and trace the ethnic German distinctives to the politics of military rivalry and warfare in early America. This background culminates in the focus of the better part of this study, including this introduction, on the partisan choices that the issues of revolution presented to German Lutheran Pietists.

## Minority Voices

Outside of those fields committed to the study of ethnic Germans in early America, one is hard-pressed to find more than passing references to the ethnic German experience in survey volumes on early America, early American religion, or the American Revolution. Whether geared for academic or general audiences, in the wide selection of social and military histories of the War of Independence most of the German point-of-view is given to the German Auxiliaries ("*Hessians*") who are treated as parenthetical to the royalist effort and who became foils for an exotic "otherness" in patriot propaganda. On the patriot side there are a couple of famous Germans, two nobles who emigrated in order to enlist themselves as generals in the patriot army: Johannes de Kalb, killed at Camden while his regiment covered a retreat, and Friedrich von Steuben, arriving during the winter at Valley Forge and given credit for unifying the drill of the Continental Army.[9] In these histories German American patriots are paid scant attention.

Although their interests certainly overlapped with those of Anglophone patriots, ethnic German patriots were not eager to assimilate into the majority culture or to adopt its causes, and the list of priorities that had them embrace independence is ordered in a different way. In setting the context for the choices that Pietists made, this study will establish that

---

9. For a biography of the colorful Prussian officer, see Lockart, *Drill Master at Valley Forge*.

the motivating concern across the larger German American culture was the sense of mutual obligation between a government and the governed. Duty to functioning sovereign governments was expected and even cheerfully rendered, but when government failed to function, loyalties shifted toward those powers whose claims of sovereign authority proved to be effective and enforceable. While Anglophone patriots rallied to the causes of representative government, taxes, resistance to parliamentary over-reach, and fear of an expanding Anglican Church establishment, the ethnic German patriots rallied first to the issue of the common defense. Where ethnic German patriots had the most common cause with Anglophone patriots was on the frontier, where settlers of all ethnic backgrounds shared in the aspirations of westward expansion.

A subset of the ethnic German community was the Lutheran Pietist Pennsylvania Ministerium, comprised of Lutheran churches served by Halle-sponsored clergy. Pietists claimed to be regenerated by the personal, indwelling Holy Spirit who transformed them into active, ethical agents of Christ's divine personality. Pietists on the whole were opposed to rationalism, which was making deep inroads into many mainline Euro-ethnic Christian denominations by the late eighteenth century. For Pietists in the ethnic German Lutheran clergy, sympathy for one side or other in the War of Independence was not a matter of political ideology grounded in a rational, philosophical system; rather it was a matter of deep, heart-searching reflection. The issues of the 1770s were new and distinct from what had gone before; finding themselves adrift on a sea of uncharted ethical issues, they could not rely on experience to steer them.

To wit, the civil war occasioned by patriot rebellion created partisan options in the War of Independence that were not present in the earlier conflicts in North America. King George's War of the 1740s, and the French and Indian Wars of the 1750s, were conventional wars in the sense that rival European empires and their allied Native Nations invaded each other's territories in bids of conquest. Partisanship was a non-issue, one was either a friend and ally or an enemy national. Some Native Nations held themselves neutral in those conflicts in the conventional sense afforded by their own sovereignty; but with every colonial province involved in hostilities the classification of "neutral" did not exist for North America's Euro-ethnic populations.

In those conflicts at mid-century there were non-combatant civilians in the conventional sense, and there were pacifist religious communities. Among the pacifists, including the Moravians, some asserted their convictions of non-violence as disciplines over their own adherents, while others asserted their ideals in order to shape public policy, especially in Pennsylvania. The range of political action narrows considerably when rival sovereign powers are engaged in a conventional war: in the wars against France the Lutheran Pietists were wholly on the side of the British Empire. This loyalty has nothing to do with religion and everything to do with one's own government engaged in a war with a hostile foreign government. Even so, diversity in pacifist ethics emerged among the Moravians themselves; they did not hold uniform opinions as to how best to reduce violence and witness to peace even in their own highly particular communities.

The American Revolutionary War was not a conventional war between rival sovereignties as much as it was a civil war fought between partisan factions, the patriots and the royalists. So radical were the partisan oppositions by the 1770s, in fact, that when France again engaged with its own forces in North America, they did so as allies to the patriots against the sovereign government of Great Britain. Now redcoats on American soil were considered the invaders, and those who aided and abetted them were "unpatriotic" partisans. Caught between these two were numerous additional factions that formed around a third pole of political concerns: the neutrals. These were the three "sides" in the War of Independence.

Sources describing the Anglophonic majority estimate that one-fifth of the Euro-ethnic population of the Colonies were avowed royalists, perhaps one-third were patriots, and around half were neutral in the conflict, with the sympathies in many shifting with the fortunes of war.[10] Whether this partisan alignment was mirrored in the ethnic German minority is disputed: Some see the ethnic Germans in parallel to the Scots-Irish Ulster Presbyterians as a predominantly patriot community,[11] while others have contended that the pietist influence among Germans had the effect that the German American community under-contributed to the patriot cause.[12]

Both the Halle-allied Lutheran clergy and the Moravians publicly held to a position of neutrality. For the Lutheran Pietists neutrality was a constraint only upon the clergy; congregants chose sides without fear of ecclesial discipline. In Pennsylvania the partisanship of choice was with

---

10. Allen, *Tories*, xx.
11. Roeber, *Palatines, Liberty, and Property*, 306.
12. Atwood, *Hessians*, 32.

the patriots. In New York, especially in the city on Manhattan Island and its environs, Lutheran laity were self-described loyalists. Radical partisanship led some Halle Lutheran pastors to serve in patriot regiments, and led others to settle in Canada or England at war's end. For the Moravians, neutrality rose from a commitment to pacifism that was binding on all members of the community. Thus the spectrum of partisan involvement for German Moravians falls on a narrower band than that of the Halle Lutherans, and carries more resemblance to their own behaviors during the earlier French wars. At that, Moravian attitudes towards royalism or independence were by no means uniform, and the help that their largest community, Bethlehem in Pennsylvania, rendered to the patriot cause was of vital importance to the Continental Army.

The Renewed Unity of the Brethren had come about in part as the result of an alienation of some German Pietists from the Halle Lutherans, to be described in chapter 4. The Moravians, headquartered in Herrnhut, Saxony, leapt ahead of the Halle Lutherans to reach out to German emigrants to Pennsylvania. This actually spurred the Halle Institutes to sponsor its own missionary activity in the province by sending Heinrich Mühlenberg. The relations between the Moravians, centered in Bethlehem, and Mühlenberg and his supporters headquartered in Philadelphia, were conflicted from the outset. While these rivalries mellowed over the course of Mühlenberg's career, they did not disappear.

## A Day in the Life of German Pietists during the War of Independence

One date has been selected to illustrate the variety of political viewpoints and ethical responses of German Pietists during the War of Independence: Saturday, September 27, 1777, when the Continental Congress convened in the courthouse of Lancaster, Pennsylvania, in the heart of what continues to be "Pennsylvania German" country. On this day only, Lancaster was the capital city of the United States. This event makes this day remarkable in history, though at the time few people other than members of Congress took note of it. Royalist and patriot armies were squared off at two fronts: The larger front in terms of numbers of troops involved was north and west of Philadelphia in Pennsylvania, from which the Continental Congress had fled; the smaller front which turned out to be of much greater strategic importance to the war's outcome, though none predicted so at the time, was near the tiny hamlet of Saratoga in western New York. On September 27 no pitched battle took place on either front.

Diaries and correspondence as well as official logs, records and registers describe September 27, 1777 as more or less remarkable if they take note of it at all. These materials also demonstrate the breadth of private opinion regarding the struggle. This study samples discourse from across the span of the sea-board colonies either at the hand of, or pertaining to, the Christian missionary David Zeisberger in a Native American town on the Ohio Frontier, to Friedrich Melsheimer, billeted as a prisoner of war in a private home in Brimfield, to a town in Georgia that was being torn in half by the opposed allegiances of its citizens. On this day a singular episode was recorded by Heinrich M. Mühlenberg (1711–1787), a semi-retired elderly pastor, who copiously recorded many details of his life in journals that, in turn, helped him prepare reports to his missionary supervisors, the "Reverend Fathers" at the pietist Halle Institutes in Frederick the Great's Kingdom of Prussia.[13]

September 27 was a day fraught with tension for the opposed armies. After occupying Philadelphia the day before, the British were consolidating their posts in and around Philadelphia, while the patriots watched their movements and debated counter-measures. The patriots could not strike back until they were reinforced, and this was the mission of the Cumberland County Militia's First Battalion. On September 27, in their march from Carlisle in Pennsylvania, they paused in the town of Providence (modern day Trappe), Pennsylvania, to rest and eat. The town sits 24 miles northwest of Philadelphia as the crow flies and 32 miles distant on modern roads.

Organized on January 1, 1777, the First Battalion had shortly thereafter come under the command of Col. James Dunlap, an elder at a Scots-Irish Presbyterian Church in Middle Spring.[14] Cumberland County had become active in the cause of resistance in 1774 when committees formed in response to the British parliament's "Intolerable Acts" against Boston. The County boasted James Wilson as a signer of the Declaration of Independence and the promotion of Edward Hand to Brigadier General. Many Cumberland men were already at the front, serving in

---

13. Mühlenberg, *Journals*, 3:80–81. Dunlap is identified in the text, Cumberland County is not.

14. *History of Cumberland and Adams Counties*, 89. For the Scots-Irish background of Dunlap (also Dunlop) cf. 344.

Pennsylvania's Continental line. By contrast militia enlistments were short-term, and by that September many in the First Battalion were veterans of earlier enlistments raised for actions in Canada and New York. In their various campaigns many of these men had lost friends to disease, battle, and capture over two years of war. Now their own state had been invaded.

The aging Lutheran pastor in the town, Heinrich Melchior Mühlenberg (1711–1787) had first arrived in the town in 1743. On September 27 the reverend walked the half-mile from his home to his church, Augustus Lutheran, to prepare for the funeral of a child. When he arrived he found the sanctuary occupied by the Cumberland County militia. The floor was littered with horse manure and straw, a soldier accompanied raucous songs on the organ, and the altar was strewn about with dishes and drinking vessels. When the pastor reacted to the mess, soldiers jeered at him and called up to their organist, "Play a Hessian march." Personal insult was added to the injury to the church, for the Rev. Heinrich Melchior Mühlenberg was an ethnic German immigrant. After thirty-five years in the colonies of British North America he was fluent in four languages including English. Yet the accent he retained as a native German speaker set him apart for suspicion and ridicule as a "Hessian," the epithet applied to all auxiliary soldiers in the service of several German princes who had hired out their regiments to the King of England. His complaints to Col. Dunlap brought no satisfaction, only the excuse that it was impossible to keep discipline in a militia.[15]

Mühlenberg wrote: "In short I saw, in miniature, 'the abomination of desolation in the temple.'"[16] Mühlenberg was quoting both the Gospel of Matthew and the Book of Daniel. "The abomination of desolation" is an apocalyptic figure which biblical scholars and theologians came to associate with the Anti-Christ. One might suppose that only a loyalist to King George can have compared patriot soldiers to the biblical Anti-Christ. Yet this pastor's oldest son John Peter Mühlenberg (1746–1807) had been raised to Brigadier General on George Washington's staff and was at that moment, on September 27, helping to rally the Continental Army outside Philadelphia as scouts reported the extent of Howe's lines. The reverend's second son Friedrich Mühlenberg (1750–1801) would soon be elected to the Pennsylvania Assembly; the third son, Gotthilf

---

15. Mühlenberg, *Journals*, 3:80–81.
16. Mühlenberg, *Journals*, 3:81.

Heinrich Ernst Mühlenberg (1753–1815), that very day was fleeing Philadelphia.[17] One tradition holds that Heinrich Ernst crossed through British lines in the darkness disguised as a Native American warrior, and arrived in Providence that same night.[18]

Notwithstanding, for this elderly Lutheran pastor the patriots were guilty of desecrating a sanctuary of the Lord in a behavior he attributes to the Antichrist. The scene in the Augustus Lutheran Church therefore upends several myths which many Americans cherish about our Revolution. One myth is that virtue rested on the patriot side to the exclusion of all others. A second myth is that the patriot revolutionaries, in affirming that "all men are created equal," had in mind that they were fostering a culturally diverse, multi-ethnic society.[19]

Augustus Church was the first permanent sanctuary built under Mühlenberg's leadership in North America,[20] and he named it in honor of the founder of Halle Pietism and the Halle Orphan Institutes, August Hermann Francke. Seeing manure on the floor and the altar desecrated, and then mocked as a Hessian, the elderly pastor canceled the funeral and went home depressed.[21] The disquieting truth regarding Pennsylvania's Cumberland County militia is that their own behavior, and not any partisanship or factionalism on Heinrich Mühlenberg's part, provoked his judgment on their characters, spirits, and eternal destinies.

## The Place of Religion in the American Revolution

Despite the abundance of German language material left by religious leaders who witnessed the War of Independence, such as Heinrich Mühlenberg, critical studies of the religious dimensions of the American Revolution view the ethnic German experience as falling outside their scope. In Thomas Kidd's study *God of Liberty,* published in 2015, the omission of ethnic Germans is nearly total.[22] No mention is made of chaplains for the royalist German Auxiliaries, yet primary discursive and documentary

---

17. Mühlenberg, *Journals*, 3:81.
18. Richards, *Pennsylvania German*, 431.
19. Griffin, *America's Revolution*, 72–73.
20. Mühlenberg, *Journals*, 1:84. The structure still stands and continues to be used occasionally by the Augustus congregation of Trappe in addition to its main facility.
21. Mühlenberg, *Journals*, 3:81.
22. Kidd, *God of Liberty*.

resources are clear that most regiments were served by chaplains of either Reformed or Lutheran faith, that religious services were mandatory, and that many units entered battle singing hymns.[23] Kidd's treatment of ethnic German patriots is limited to two references to Brigadier General J. Peter Mühlenberg, who is introduced as "a Lutheran turned Anglican" with no explanation of his ethnic German background.[24] General Mühlenberg's father Heinrich and others of the Pennsylvania Ministerium do not appear at all.

Kidd's volume is valuable in confirming that religious sentiments were key motives for ethical action among the majority Anglophone colonists. In addition, Kidd documents that many issues that sparked revolution touched on religious questions: whether to expand the Anglican establishment, the degree to which Catholicism should be tolerated, and the connection or separation of church and state. Much of this will be surveyed in chapter 1. Yet religious sentiment, essential as it is to understanding motives for ethical and political action, is not shown to be coterminous with religious alignment. English-speaking Baptists were profoundly motivated by their sentiments, yet are found on all sides of the American Revolution. As Kidd indicates, a revival among Baptists is documented in Nova Scotia in 1780, fomented among committed Baptist loyalists.[25]

How American colonists chose sides defies religious generalization, yet religion was enormously important in the motives of many of the revolution's participants. Kidd argues that the First Great Awakening had helped to forge an American identity that moved across provincial borders and tied the regions of the Atlantic Seaboard together as never

---

23. In the mid-to-late nineteenth century, William Leete Stone and William Wood translated and published numerous primary sources of German auxiliaries. The late twentieth and early twenty-first centuries have seen renewed interest in translating and publishing the diaries and letters of German auxiliary soldiers, officers, quartermasters, and medical and religious personnel who were attached to regiments as civilian contractors. Bruce E. Burgoyne (d. 2011) has published over thirty volumes. Other sources, such as *The Diary of Stephan Popp* have been published by family descendants. Hessian Studies remains an undeveloped field with relatively few critical translations and treatments of the primary sources. One such critical translation is Helga Doblin's publication of the journals of Braunschweig company surgeon Julius Wasmus. See Wasmus, *Eye-Witness Account.*

24. Kidd, *God of Liberty,* 115.

25. Kidd, *God of Liberty,* 190.

before.[26] German language sources show that many German Pietist leaders approved of the revival movement on the whole and enjoyed collegial relationships with the evangelist George Whitefield (d. 1770).[27] The documents and discourse of the revolutionary period are clear that on all three sides of the war Christian religion and Protestant identity were very much in view. From a German Auxiliaries chaplain in New York joyfully reporting the number of soldiers he communed, to the fiery speech of a patriot chaplain before leading a charge with sword drawn, to a letter from a Moravian pastor enjoining patriot legislators to make allowance for a refusal to fight on religious grounds, to repeated Acts of Congress calling on special days of fasting or of thanksgiving depending on the fortunes of a campaign, it is clear that participants on all sides of the War of Independence were conscious of God.[28]

That said, there may never be a way to measure the depth to which one's private motives and opinions are influenced by one's public religious affinity. Heinrich Mühlenberg expressed pessimism about the overall spiritual condition of his congregations;[29] this is turn might indicate that a majority of the German Lutheran laity in the Pennsylvania Ministerium churches were scarcely Pietist at all, at least according to the strict self-understandings of the Halle Institutes' directors.[30] In their frequent comments on the torpid spiritual condition of their congregants, Heinrich Mühlenberg and his Halle-Lutheran missionary colleagues were under no illusions that the heart religion espoused by the Halle Institutes held sway in the Lutheran congregations of North America.[31] This is why the case focuses on the pastors that were loyal to Halle's mission directors, and who were part of planting and sustaining the first successful,

26. Kidd, *God of Liberty*, 21–25.

27. Mühlenberg, *Journals*, 1:688–89.

28. On communion for royalist troops, see Waldeck, *Eighteenth-Century America*, 57; on a patriot chaplain in combat, see Thompson, *From its European Antecedents*, 162; on the Moravian protest, see Hamilton, *John Ettwein and the Moravian Church*, 234; on Congress calling feast days, see Mühlenberg, *Journals*, 3:270.

29. Mühlenberg, *Journals*, 3:683.

30. Halle Pietists carried forward the personal experience of regeneration according to the conversion paradigm modeled in the personal testimony of August Hermann Francke, the movement's founder. See Francke, "From the Autobiography," 99–107.

31. Mühlenberg, *Journals*, 1:136–37.

long-term synodal experiment for German Lutherans in North America, the Pennsylvania Ministerium.[32]

Through connections to Halle and the royal chaplains in London, these clergy fostered a network of vetted missionary pastors in regular calls to the pulpits and circuits of the middle colonies. The more that the Pennsylvania Ministerium took root and flourished, the more that preachers with incomplete credentials, irregular ordinations and unsavory reputations were phased out of Lutheran pulpits.[33] Long after the deaths of its founders and into the nineteenth century the synod gathered by Heinrich Mühlenberg regulated its member clergy by pietistic values embedded in its constitution. In the middle colonies, the community of Pennsylvania Ministerium clergy outlasted the War of Independence and continued for generations despite its clergy landing at three different partisan poles during the years of the conflict.

The Moravians, known officially in the eighteenth century as the Renewed Unity of the Brethren, are also prominent in this study despite their much smaller numbers. The foci is centered on two Moravian communities: in chapter 4 the focus is on the town of Bethlehem and two of its leaders, August Spangenberg during the French wars and Johann Ettwein during the War of Independence, and in chapter 7 the focus shifts to the missionary towns that were under the protection of the Delaware Nation and under the direction of the Moravian David Zeisberger.

The unusual impact on the course of the American Revolution despite their small numbers and official neutrality lends particular weight to the case of Moravian pietism and political action. Their narratives suggest the interpretation that it is how one identifies one's primary community that is more predictive of one's political actions than is the identification of one's religion as such, even if the community is itself formed on the basis of religious beliefs and efforts. Even so, the Moravian communities did not escape the war unscathed and unchanged.

---

32. "The Pennsylvania Ministerium" refers to the body of clergy and congregations constituted as a governing body by Heinrich Mühlenberg for those Lutheran churches loyal to the Halle Institutes. First formed in 1748, this organization was not given an official constitution and name until 1781. It was re-constituted in 1792 and 1817, its name changing each time. Its geographic and population center was Pennsylvania, as acknowledged in 1792. The term "Pennsylvania Ministerium" to cover these various institutional incarnations is taken from the cover title of a translation of the minutes of its meetings and related documents. See Spaeth et al., *Documentary History*.

33. Glatfelter, *Pastors and People*.

Finally, the community that the Halle Institutes sponsored in Ebenezer, Georgia, discussed in chapter 8, did not hold up under the stresses of partisan conflict. Factions formed around the two leading pastors in the late 1760s, and the alignments around these personal animosities did much more to predict partisan political action than did Ebenezer's shared religious faith.

Although Lutheran Pietists and Moravians made important contributions to the American Revolution, ethnic Germans as a whole were under-represented in Congress, local patriot governments, and among the officers in the militia and Continental Army. This under-representation may be due in part to the outlook of the Lutheran Pietist clergy. From the time of the Augsburg Confession in 1530 the pastoral office was considered the highest of all callings, and Lutheran clergy were not to mix or combine their pastoral vocation with the offices of secular rule.[34] For the Halle missionary clergy in America this deep tradition meant that whatever sympathies were held privately, the clergy and their congregations—as public entities—were officially neutral. For Bethlehem's elders a different and deeper tradition dating to the Hussite Unity of the fifteenth century meant that, whatever desires were held privately, the residents of their closed communities were officially pacifist.

---

34. See *Augsburg Confession*, esp. art. 28.

*1*

# His Glorious Protestant Majesty and His Rebelling Colonies

As ETHICAL AGENTS MOTIVATED by their faith, pietists involved themselves in the political struggles of the eighteenth century. From the letters and memoirs they left behind—an enormous amount of material—it is clear that ethnic Germans had their own socio-cultural and religious reasons, distinct from the Anglophone majority, for participating on any one of the American Revolution's three sides. It is also clear that these views evolved with their experience in America through the course of the eighteenth century. "When they became involved in colonial politics and, eventually, in the imperial crisis, they did so on their own terms."[1]

### The Frontier Wars with France

During the frontier conflicts with the French the sympathies of the ethnic Germans did not split three ways. In these conventional wars with foreign powers, ethnic Germans were subjects of the British king, to whom they swore oaths when they naturalized.[2] German Pietists were involved at various levels in civic shows of support, in military rank-and-file, and in the case of the Moravians in the advocacy of non-violence.

1. Fogleman, *Hopeful Journeys*, 12.
2. That God was present in the hearts or the hosts of devout French Catholics may be taken for granted from an ecumenical point-of-view, but for the purpose of this study the argument of co-religionists dividing on political-ethical issues is based on a much narrower stripe of religious affinity, German Pietism.

In the aftermath of these conflicts Germans in Pennsylvania, including Halle-sponsored clergy, rallied to make themselves felt in that province's political alignments as never before.

Open war between France and Great Britain took place twice at mid-century. In King George's War from 1744–1748, the French operated at a distinct disadvantage as the Native Nations either aided the British or held themselves neutral. This policy among the indigenous peoples owed much to the "Chain of Friendship" that agents of British colonies had forged with the Native Nations beginning with the Iroquois Confederacy. This chain linked the indigenous peoples of the Great Lakes and Ohio regions through the Iroquois to the colonial governments of Pennsylvania and New York. In this linkage British agents and traders had the reputation of offering better prices for furs than their French counterparts. Conrad Weiser, an ethnic German frontiersman, became the agent of Pennsylvania's proprietary government and was key in forging the chain of friendship. His story is told in chapter 2.

Into the 1750s the colonies of Pennsylvania and New York continued the policies pioneered by William Penn in the late 1600s. Colonial agents engaged with dignitaries of the Native Nations, forged treaties and alliances, and secured land by purchase. These policies are excoriated by modern scholars as conniving, in that consumable goods were offered at costs far below the land's value. Even so, in the eighteenth century these approaches were by far more principled than the alternatives of violence and expansion by conquest that were more quickly resorted to by the southern colonies, especially Virginia and the Carolinas. Georgia is a singular exception, following Pennsylvania's pattern in its early relations with the indigenous peoples, for reasons discussed in chapter 8.

After peace was concluded in 1748 the French pursued a more assertive policy of generosity towards the Native Nations on the Ohio and Great Lakes, hoping to break the Chain of Friendship asunder. The British colonial governments were slow to respond to the French maneuvers, with the result that by the mid 1750s several populous and powerful Native Nations were openly declaring for the French. When the British effort to drive the French from Fort Duquesne in western Pennsylvania ended in a catastrophic defeat, this emboldened a widespread uprising of Native Nations against the British and against Iroquois hegemony. In 1755 open war on a scale hitherto unknown in North America was visited on Euro-ethnic settlers on the Great Lakes and Ohio frontiers.

The government of Pennsylvania responded with gridlock. Quaker pacifists dominating the Assembly resisted the efforts to take defensive measures on the frontier, by imposing conditions on the appropriations that the proprietors in London could not accept. The German Pietist Conrad Weiser was looked to both as an architect of policy and as a translator. Once the Native Nations were persuaded to bury their hatchets, the French were quickly defeated.

## Euro-ethnic Attitudes toward Indigenous Peoples and Westward Settlement

Conrad Weiser's impact was felt even more acutely in the vacuum of competence that was caused by his death in 1760. British agents and administrators were unable to correctly interpret the meaning of their victory in North America, and their blunders alienated the indigenous peoples. One catalyst for the growing hostility was Jeffrey Amherst, Great Britain's military commander-in-chief in North America in 1760. Amherst swept in after the issue with the French had been decided, and held the view that France's allied Native Nations had also been vanquished. William Johnson, who had been Conrad Weiser's counterpart and rival as the agent to the Native Nations for New York, disagreed with Amherst categorically and fervently.

Like Weiser, Johnson had been adopted into the Mohawk nation. He had then received a knighthood for his service against the French in the capture of Fort Niagara.[3] Through the early 1760s Sir William, getting nowhere in his frequent confrontations with Sir Jeffrey, wrote often to the Board of Trade to warn them of the outcomes of Amherst's destructive policies.[4] The Board took measures in 1762 to assert control over land purchases, but the lag in communication across the ocean meant that policies and enforcement continually ran behind events.

Peace was concluded with France in 1763. On the frontiers in North America, however, a war captain of the French-allied Ottawa Nation named Pontiac was aggrieved by Amherst's high-handedness, and plotted a general uprising of Native Nations across the span of the frontier. One of the tragedies of Pontiac's War was in the time-lapse required for communication, for in the august halls of London the Board of Trade was

3. Flexner, *Lord of the Mohawks*, 200–210.
4. Flexner, *Lord of the Mohawks*, 247.

crafting a policy which was enlightened for its time: On October 7 the Crown announced the Proclamation Line to limit colonial settlement to the Atlantic watershed. A chain of forts, some already existing and some to be built, would block the path of settlers while safeguarding the interests of, and commerce with, the indigenous peoples. However, no Native Nations delegates were included in those conversations in London. Had they been, their restive suspicions might have been allayed. At all events decisions were being made for Native Nations and for Euro-ethnic settlers rather than in collaboration with these disparate constituents. Five months before the Proclamation Line was declared, the Native Nations, following Pontiac's plan, attacked many of those same forts that were to have been garrisoned for their protection. This uprising, called Pontiac's War, was the result of their mistrust of Amherst. He was recalled on November 18, and Thomas Gage took his place.[5]

It is a significant revelation of Amherst's own blind-spots that he called the uprising an unprovoked betrayal.[6] Yet the violence by Pontiac and his allies in 1763 occasioned a more permanent and bitter alienation with Euro-ethnic settlers than had occurred in the 1750s. To the German, Scots-Irish, and English settlers streaming westward after France's defeat, the tactics in Pontiac's War represented an unforgiveable escalation in treachery and barbarism. A new, virulent race consciousness was evolving on the frontier.

Racial solidarity had begun to be articulated by the Native Nations in the 1740s, as described in a speech by the Iroquois spokesman Canasatego:

> What is one hundred years in comparison to the length of time since our claim began?—Since we came out of the ground? For we must tell you that long before one hundred years our ancestors came out of this very ground, and their children have remained here ever since. You came out of the ground in a country that lies beyond seas, there you may have a just claim, but here you must allow us to be your elder brethren, and the lands too belonged to us long before you knew anything of them.[7]

---

5. Griffin, *American Leviathan*, 22–27.

6. Griffin, *American Leviathan*, 22–27.

7. Starna, "Diplomatic Career of Canasatego," 145. See also Harper, "Delawares and Pennsylvanians," 167–79.

In this Native American "Two Creations" myth, the White Person was created from the ground across the seas, and the indigenous peoples of the Americas came from the ground in America. This view was not compatible with the Biblical view held or taught by most European Christians at the time, which was that all people in the whole world are descended from the sons and daughters of Noah after the great global flood. Two Creations speaks of distinctions, of humankinds rather than of humankind.

For Euro-ethnic settlers, Christian explanations of the kinship of all humankind under Noah's lineage were obviated by the curse Noah pronounced on Ham's son Canaan. This curse came to be interpreted racially as applying to the Bantu and other peoples of Africa as justification for taking them captive and selling them into slavery. For some settlers and officials the Bible contained no explanation of the origins of America's indigenous peoples, since even their humanity was manifestly suspect.[8] Among British Whigs and intellectuals two "scientific" models of anthropology competed with each other, both of them framed by the European Enlightenment.[9]

1) *The stadial model* of cultural development was developed by leading intellectuals of the mid-eighteenth century including Fran Hutcheson, Adam Smith, David Hume and William Robertson. The stadial model held that a culture existed in one of three discrete states: The savage state, the barbaric state, or the civilized state. There was fluidity between these states in some places as a culture was either advancing to higher states or regressing to lower states. However, all civilized cultures had passed through savage and barbaric states. There was nothing *inherently superior* in the *humanity* of the civilized; the main differentiation between cultures was in the environment of their germination. All human beings belong to one extended family. It was incumbent upon the civilized, therefore, to assist in elevating those at lower states. This "stadial" anthropology appears to match the assumptions of Moravian missionaries in the 1700s, as is detailed in chapter 7.

2) The *race model* was an alternative to the stadial model, and it developed by applying the philosophies of John Locke and Thomas Hobbes to non-European contexts. Locke proposed that human beings were

---

8. Griffin, *American Leviathan*, 25–26.
9. Griffin, *American Leviathan*, 28–37.

differentiated from lower forms by their reasoning capabilities.[10] This led to summary conclusions regarding cultures where human behavior appeared "irrational" to Europe's intellectuals. Locke's model predicted that societies ascended out of the "state of nature" propelled by motives where reason was used to address areas of common interest, such as crime and punishment, social order, and barter.

> What naturally leads us to seek communion and fellowship with other people is the fact that on our own we haven't the means to provide ourselves with an adequate store of things that we need for the kind of life our nature desires, a life fit for the dignity of man.[11]

Hence the premise on which human societies form is the motive of private property. "Our" human nature desires "an adequate store of things that we need" for a "life fit for the dignity of man." This premise carries many corollary assumptions, such as, that it is naturally human to endeavor to exploit resources in an intensive, industrial manner in order to dominate the ecology and the environment for human advantage and profit. Although Locke did not speak to racial distinctions, and his statements concerning humankind nearer the "state of nature" appear generous, many readers of Locke concluded that the more improvements made on nature that were found in a society, the more self-evident it was that such a society must have been constructed by superior human beings. Inferior societies, self-evident by their primitive technologies and a seemingly irrational accommodation of nature, were constructed by inferior human beings.

For Thomas Hobbes, writing forty years earlier than Locke, humankind's state of nature was depraved. The rational drive towards self-preservation made it natural for human beings both to amass private property and to create systems of government designed to protect the rights of property, otherwise human avarice and envy would keep society in a state of violent anarchy.[12] Thus, for Hobbes, notions of private property differentiated the human being from the animal, since a system for private property was the surest indication of human reason. By applying the theories of Hobbes and Locke to cultures established on wholly different world-views and aspirations, Eurocentric elites, military officers,

---

10. Locke, *Essay Concerning Human Understanding*.
11. Locke, *Second Treatise on Government*, 7.
12. Herman, *Scots Invented the Modern World*, 70–71.

and colonial administrators concluded that cultures with no concept of private property and little notion that one's environment had to be improved upon must have been constructed by less-than-human beings. If this was the case, then the Family of Humanity taught by the Bible did not apply, and the value of evangelizing "savage" peoples was denigrated. Race theory appealed to rational Lockean or Hobbesian principles, emphasized difference rather than commonality, and became an academic, intellectual rationale to excuse the enslavement or extermination of natives of sub-Saharan Africa, of Asian rain forests, of Australia, of the Pacific islands, and of the Americas.

The effort of the royal government to placate the Native Nations was based on the stadial assumption that the indigenous peoples in their "savage" condition would be ungovernable until such time, generations into the future, that continued peaceful contact with the British agents in trade gave them a hunger for the gentler manners of civilization. The Proclamation Line is about as enlightened and liberal a policy as any Euro-ethnic government could have been expected to devise in the middle of the eighteenth century. However, the King and his Board of Trade were removed from the violence of the frontier. With or without philosophical reflection settlers were escalating their reprisals, putting into grim practice the racial models of cultural alienation and conflict which reckoned other solutions: namely, race warfare and extermination.[13]

As it happened, the combination of the Board of Trade's pro-Native Nations policy and Gage's military and diplomatic competence brought the chiefs in Pontiac's conspiracy to peace talks in 1764. The negotiations were conducted by the two men long associated with Conrad Weiser as protégés and rivals: Sir William Johnson and his deputy George Croghan.[14] In that Pontiac's War ended with the indigenous nations once again coming to a tacit acceptance of Euro-ethnic presence on the continent, it was a victory for the colonial Atlantic Seaboard provinces. In that Pontiac's War ended by reaffirming the Proclamation Line as a

---

13. Griffin, *American Leviathan*, 154.

14. O'Toole, *White Savage*, 253–65. At the Niagara Conference of July, 1764, over two thousand delegates attended, some from as far as Hudson Bay. Pontiac was absent, but Johnson succeeded in dividing his coalition, putting Pontiac and those who remained hostile on the defensive. Croghan, sent by Johnson into the Illinois Country to seek out Pontiac for negotiations in 1765, took a hatchet to the head but survived the blow. This seemed to impress Pontiac, who accepted negotiations. A treaty conference with elaborate rituals and courtesies was held in Oswego in July, 1766, where Pontiac gave up the war belt.

concession to the concerns of the indigenous peoples of the Great Lakes and Ohio Country, it ended in a victory for the Native Nations.

The indigenous peoples enjoyed a victory doomed to be as short-lived as Pontiac's resort to violence had been short-sighted. The embittered settlers were scarcely mollified when concessions were made to the war parties with little for themselves. The royal government's terms respecting the rights of the Native Nations chafed at the twin ambitions of the settlers for land and for reprisal. The settlers, isolated and vulnerable on the frontier, thought of themselves as victims. They did not understand their own power or the mortal threat they represented to indigenous cultures. What for the Euro-ethnic settlers was just a trickle of westward movement by brave pioneers risking life and limb on the fringes of civilization, was for the Native Nations an intolerable population pressure at the center of their own world. The only feasible alternative to extend the survival of indigenous cultures, was for Euro-ethnic ambitions to steer away from settler expansion and look instead towards facilitating a denser population in the proprietary and crown colonies already secured. This was one of the theories underpinning the Proclamation Line as conceived by William Johnson himself in a letter to the Board of Trade.[15] But the boundary was not to be a wall of separation between settlers and indigenous peoples. Peace depended on friendship, and that meant ongoing treaty conferences with the gifts and favors that went along with it, as well as a fair exchange of goods in a sustainable fur trade.[16]

The Native Nations of the Ohio, Great Lakes and east Mississippi basin, who in their uprisings had proven themselves to be ungovernable, were to remain semi-autonomous, nominal subjects to the King of Great Britain. Trade would foster indigenous dependence on manufactured goods, which would in turn inspire friendly interest in Euro-ethnic lifestyles. Trade in rum and fire-arms would be greatly restricted. The licensing of Anglican missionaries through the Society for Propagating the Gospel (SPG) would expose indigenous proselytes to the civilizing benefits of Protestant faith while correcting any Catholic errors instilled in them by their former French allies. All of this working together would prepare the way for a peaceful assimilation which would finally open the regions of the interior to good government, settlement, and the

---

15. Flexner, *Lord of the Mohawks*, 260.
16. O'Toole, *White Savage*, 258.

uplifting benefits of civilization. This far-sighted policy was predicted by Hutcheson's stadial model and was intended to span generations.

The premise on which the Proclamation Line stood was that a long-term optimistic and non-coercive gradualism would win over indigenous cultures while preserving and expanding the prosperity and strength of the British Empire: The colonies of the Atlantic seaboard would continue intensive agriculture and industry while providing a market of 2.5 million and growing for British goods; meanwhile the massive interior, beginning on the west slope of the Appalachians, would provide a lucrative fur trade monopoly with the Native Nations that had the simultaneous benefit of keeping them appeased.[17]

Brilliant as the Proclamation Line strategy is, it was entirely incompatible with the aspirations of hundreds of thousands of English, German, and Scots-Irish immigrants answering a siren call to settle the provinces and find opportunity and freedom hitherto unknown in Europe. These settlers cared little for the abstractions of Whig economic philosophy which made the personal advantages of the Lords of Trade synonymous with imperial greatness. These settlers were looking for farms on productive land where they would have the opportunity, by their toil, to prosper themselves. These aspirations were fostered in their recruitment to emigrate. The Proclamation Line was thus nothing less than a betrayal of an enormous constituency of British subjects. The Whig elites' military-mercantile complex of the eighteenth-century Hanoverian Empire lost the loyalty of the settlers through the same measures and policies that secured the friendship of the Native Nations.

William Johnson had been side-lined by Amherst, but was looked to again to represent Crown interests in the wake of Pontiac's uprising. He continued in conferences with Pontiac and other indigenous leaders of the Great Lakes and Ohio regions into the late 1760s, with the Treaty of Stanwyx his *tour de force* in 1768, in which boundaries further west were negotiated and, as far as Johnson was concerned, fixed. Thomas Gage, Amherst's successor as commander of royal forces in British North America, was more circumspect. Agreeing with Johnson's philosophy, he spotted at once its glaring weakness: that settler pressures would compromise the entire effort, and that the terms were unenforceable by British arms in the frontier posts.[18]

17. Griffin, *American Leviathan*, 37–41.
18. O'Toole, *White Savage*, 273–79; Griffin, *American Leviathan*, 82–88.

The Euro-ethnic settlers and the indigenous peoples each formed a constituency for two competing sets of elite interests who sought to exploit the aspirations of one group over and against the other. One set of elites were the members of the London Board of Trade who designed the Proclamation Line. One of the benefits of this policy was that partnerships represented on the Board would continue profiting for the foreseeable future from a lucrative fur trade with the Native Nations of the continent's interior. Their rival elites were colonial investors in land companies, including George Washington, who were risking fortunes on the future of western expansion.[19] These two visions for the land and the lifestyles it would support could not co-exist. Deforestation and farming for surplus is incompatible with the lifestyle of hunting and horticulture. The agents of the Board of Trade were the fur traders such as William Johnson. The agents of the land companies were the surveyors. One surveyor, Christopher Gist, spoke of the risks if a compass were seen when in the company of Native Americans.[20]

To the settlers it seemed clear enough that the sympathies of the royal agents of government lay with the indigenous peoples at the expense of their own interests and safety. Forts once occupied by the French to guard against squatters and maintain trade routes to the Native Nations were now garrisoned by British regulars with missions seemingly identical to that of their erstwhile enemies, the French. Neither Anglophone nor ethnic German immigrants had any interest in heeding the Proclamation Line. In Pennsylvania and New York as much as in Virginia settler interests, and those of the land companies, lay in the boundary's subversion. The Crown's agents soon found that they could no more control the settlers on the frontier than they had been able to control Pontiac and his allies. Long after the peace, settlers avenged themselves scalp for scalp with grisly prejudice, paying little attention to distinctions between the indigenous peoples that had formerly been hostile and those that had never been hostile to Euro-ethnic settlers.

As the royal policy depended on docile adherence to settle within treaty limits, the policy was doomed to fail. The crown's intensification of its settler policy with the Quebec Act of 1774, and the "intolerable" Boston Port acts, galvanized the settlers to a unity of purpose with the

---

19. Ellis, *His Excellency, George Washington*, 55–57.
20. Calloway, *Indian World of George Washington*, 5.

colonists in the coastal cities.²¹ Committees of correspondence formed in Pennsylvania in such towns as Lancaster and Carlisle and, west of the Alleghenies, in Westmoreland County. In 1775 open war returned to Great Britain's colonial interests in North America. Many Native Americans west of the Appalachians, together with Britain's traditional Iroquois allies, saw that common cause with the royal government against the revolutionary patriots was their only hope at achieving cultural survival and a just peace for themselves.

## Majority Culture and Minority Adjustment

Under the pressure of uprisings on the frontier, the ethnic German community coalesced around the issues of common defense and sensible military appropriations. They were also gaining competence in leveraging their interests with a political establishment dominated by the Anglophone majority of English, Welsh, Scots, and Scots-Irish. To set the context for ethnic German options and priorities for socio-political action, it is necessary to outline how such options and aspirations were framed in the Anglophone majority, and the extent to which their religious affinities may have either predicted their evolving views or modified their political actions, or both.

A look at England's time-line from 1300 forward shows that when the Anglo-British are not fighting France than civil war among themselves, often in the form of a dynastic uprising aided by France, becomes a distinct historical likelihood. Wars in Ireland tell a saga of revolts and re-conquest as England sought to impose its rule. Those who emigrated from the British Isles in the eighteenth century hoping to escape the incessant warfare brought by adventures in Ireland and Jacobite rebellions in Scotland, were disabused of their illusions in the 1770s. Anglophones continued to face each other across fields of fire, but now in America.

In terms of religion, in early America to the end of the 1700s, the largest Anglophonic denominations were Congregationalists, Anglicans, Presbyterians, Quakers, and Baptists. A few English Catholics settled in Maryland in the seventeenth century when it was a proprietary colony of the Catholic Lord Baltimore.²² English settlers were responsible for

---

21. Calloway, *Indian World of George Washington*, 6, 498n21.

22. In 1775 the total Protestant presence in what became the continental United States was relegated to the Atlantic seaboard. Catholic claims west of the Appalachians

the only churches to be established by provincial policy: The Anglican and the Congregationalist. The Congregationalists, descended from the Puritans, were established with government support in Massachusetts, Connecticut, and New Hampshire, and constituted the largest Church body on the Atlantic Coast. The Anglican Church was established in Virginia from its founding, in South Carolina, in Maryland after it was chartered as a crown colony in 1729, and in Georgia. The Anglican provinces tended to be more tolerant of dissenting denominations, whereas the Congregationalist provinces were less tolerant of non-conformity.

From the early 1600s the march of 150 years saw two important developments among Puritans in America. First, the Enlightenment made inroads. The Salem Witch Trials were recanted by those responsible and became essentially unrepeatable. Harvard College, established in Cambridge in 1636 to train Puritan clergy, had Deists on the faculty by its fourth generation. Although the New England culture still valued moral rigor, its intellectuals in the pulpits and classrooms had begun to incorporate rationalism and criticism in their sermons. This helped to catalyze the second development, which was a current of revivalism that rose up partly in protest to the rationalizing influence. During the Great Awakening New Light Puritans split from Old Light, and new churches were formed.

Denominational rifts caused by the Great Awakening were less important than the revival's galvanizing influence on creating a common culture across the Atlantic Seaboard. Whether envied or lauded, the evangelizing preacher George Whitefield was a celebrity in all the provinces. Yet the Great Awakening had run its course by the 1770s; it is a chimera to try to associate royalism with Old Lights and patriotism with New Lights, or vise-versa. The rhetoric of Massachusetts Puritanism pervades the public discourse of John Adams, but it is the common core of the New England culture which is found in his speeches, and nothing about them suggests that Adams had a personal sympathy with New Light religion. New England's Old and New Light Churches were both recruiting grounds for the Minute Men at the war's beginning.

Anglo-American Baptists were small in number in the 1770s but their importance grew as the issue of disestablishment became more prominent in the patriot cause. Devolving from the Separatist Puritans, these Baptists retained strict Calvinist doctrines even while insisting on

---

were established by the Quebec Act under British rule in addition to the Spanish possessions west of the Mississippi to the Pacific, and on both sides of the Rio Grande.

the sole validity of a confessing believer's baptism by immersion. Puritan Baptists did not move towards the German and Dutch Anabaptist traditions which adhered to communitarianism and pacifism, but are a wholly separate movement and theological tradition. With the Second Great Awakening beginning in 1800 the Baptists exploded numerically, and the largest Baptist conventions in the United States today trace their origins to these Puritan Baptists. In the Revolutionary period many Baptists became patriots out of concern that the crown was plotting to force an episcopal see upon America.[23]

The Great Awakening that split Congregationalists and Presbyterians into "New" and "Old" did not spare the Anglican Church. John Wesley and George Whitefield were both Anglican preachers, and yet their revival efforts led to the eventual formation of numerous new denominations split off from the Church of England: Whitefield's brand of Calvinist Methodism took root especially in Wales, while Methodist and later Wesleyan Churches began to spring up on both sides of the Atlantic. At length, after the American Revolution, the African Methodist Episcopal Church (AME) took shape in the United States. Like the Baptists, the Methodists expanded in American society with the Second Great Awakening after 1800.

The early Methodist evangelists of the eighteenth century found their base among the "Low Church" Anglicans, those less disposed to liturgical trappings, vestments, and episcopal government. Low Church Anglicanism tended to draw the southern planters into its fold, including George Washington. When royalist officers spoke of the war as coming about from a Presbyterian rebellion against Anglicans, it was likely understood that "High Church" Anglicans were meant. This narrative was that Presbyterians, with whom were lumped Cromwellian republicans acting in the vein of their ornery ancestors, were rebelling against the establishment-conscious Anglican Whigs for whom George III was rightful head of both State and Church.

For the Anglican establishment in England, any other religious group was "non-conformist." Starting with the rule of William and Mary and continuing through the eighteenth century there was a good deal of toleration for non-conforming Protestant groups, especially when compared to other realms and empires. In the Atlantic colonies the Congregationalists were the largest ethnic-English non-conforming Protestant

---

23. Kidd, *God of Liberty*, 63–66.

group. However, in establishing Congregationalism in their provinces they had not been able to enforce the perfect conformity envisioned by the earliest founders. Baptists sprung up from among them, and were sometimes savagely persecuted.[24] The issue of religious freedom became a hallmark of Baptist adherents, who protested the injustice of clergy taxes in the Congregationalist provinces. The Baptists had better luck addressing the relationship of Church and State in Anglican Virginia, where they had the sympathy of the Deists and rationalists Thomas Jefferson and James Madison.[25]

Quakers also arrived in the New World, and found a chill and often hostile spiritual climate in the New England provinces in the 1600s. The Quakers have their origin in the seventeenth-century Puritan George Fox, who experienced a new insight into the spiritual relationship between the human being and God. This insight shaped Fox's attitude towards organized violence, class distinction, and church establishment and liturgy. The followers that gathered around him were called Quakers, and throughout the 1600s they were persecuted by Jacobite Catholics, establishment Anglicans, and republican Puritans. Quakers were barely tolerated anywhere although the Welsh, a Celtic people, were more receptive to the Quaker faith than their counterparts in Scotland and Ireland.

A new opportunity was presented to Quakers when Charles II issued a land grant on the west bank of the Delaware River to one of his large creditors, the Quaker William Penn, in order to retire a debt. By the late 1600s the colonies had already seen a low-church form of Anglicanism established in Virginia and Puritan congregationalism established in New England. Roger Williams had received a charter for Rhode Island in 1636 and devised a policy of religious toleration, offering his colony as a refuge to exiles from the New England provinces. Penn founded his colony in 1681 on a similar experiment of disestablished religion and toleration of non-conforming Protestant groups, including non-Anglophonic Peace Churches and Anabaptist groups that had led very contingent existences in central and northern Europe. In Pennsylvania, however, Quakers predominated in government and society as a *de facto* establishment. A large segment of Pennsylvania Quakers were of Welsh heritage.

William Penn curried the favor of James II/VII, the successor to Charles II, in order to keep secure his charter for Pennsylvania.

---

24. Kidd, *God of Liberty*, 172.
25. Kidd, *God of Liberty*, 52.

Unfortunately this put him under suspicion when parliament deposed James II in favor of his daughter Mary, the wife of William of Orange, in 1688. Hoping to gain favor with the new crown, the Penn family conformed, converting to the Anglican faith.[26] That the Penns thus forsook Quaker disciplines for power and ambition set in motion a long-standing rivalry between the proprietary heirs of the Penn family and the Quaker-dominated assembly of Pennsylvania. This tension would last until revolutionary governments and republican constitutions permanently swept both factions from power.

Numerous Quakers were wealthy merchants and tradesmen who made their homes in Philadelphia and corresponded with the Quaker Society of Friends in England throughout the war. By virtue of their nonviolent stance the Quakers are best classified as neutrals, however their refusal to take notice of American victories and to observe province-wide and union-wide days of thanksgiving or fasting put them under suspicion of being royalist sympathizers, as many were. As fervent pacifists, the Quakers also devised methods for positive ethical action that have inspired protest movements since. Among their scruples they refused to contribute any taxes, fines or donations that might be used to support any dimension of the war effort even indirectly. This included an embargo on food and medical supplies, and withholding their wagons from use in supply trains.[27] Even so the Quakers were not uniform in their pacifist stance. Regionalism shaded Quaker attitudes. Proximity to Philadelphia predicts the fervency of loyalty to Quaker peace doctrines and, by extension, loyalty to the disciplines of conscientious objection. A New England chapter of Quakers broke with the pacifist discipline, insisting that whether to take up arms or not was a matter for one's conscience and was not to be dictated by the church.[28] Some of Quaker background who became patriot leaders include the philosopher and pamphleteer Thomas Paine, and the patriot Brigadier General Nathaniel Greene.[29]

In politics, by the mid-1770s both the majority Anglophone and the ethnic German minority were split three ways, into Loyalism (supporting the royalists), Neutrality, and Patriotism (eventually supporting independence). As the war progressed many people shifted between these poles.

26. Brock, *Pacifism in the United States*, 214.
27. Brock, *Pacifism in the United States*, 209.
28. Brock, *Pacifism in the United States*, 231.
29. Brock, *Pacifism in the United States*, 207.

The partisan divides were not aligned in this way in the 1760s, when almost everyone on the Atlantic Seaboard considered themselves loyal subjects to their sovereign, King George III, and considered their protests against new taxes and settler policies to be directed against England's parliament.[30] As the three partisan poles emerged in the 1770s, many people who had participated in the protests of the 1760s retreated from the momentum that was spinning the colonies toward outright independence. For some this was a retreat to neutrality, for others it was a hardening of their conviction that George III remained their rightful sovereign, and these "loyalists" would prefer to endure parliamentary over-reach rather than declare independence outright. One stand-out example of loyalism is Joseph Galloway, who accompanied Howe's army into Philadelphia. He had participated in the First Continental Congress and helped draft the "Olive Branch" petition to reconcile the King and the colonies. Others who saw themselves as devout subjects in the 1760s found themselves radicalized in their opposition to the crown's increasingly coercive policies, and were ardent patriots by the mid-1770s. These include Benjamin Franklin, who had lived many of those years in London.

In terms of political office royalists held crown-appointments as, for example, provincial governors with their staffs, agents and underlings. By the mid-1770s those elected into offices and representative seats who sympathized with the "royalists" were "loyalists." Opposing them were the patriots, whose insistence that parliament respect the local authority of the provincial assemblies evolved into a commitment to sovereign independence. Patriots took to forming alternative governments with committees of safety which coordinated militia efforts and sought to enforce measures such as economic boycotts, and committees of correspondence by which patriots could network from town to town and across provincial boundaries. With the onset of violent rebellion in 1775, many provincial elections swept patriots into power. A loyalist assembly in Philadelphia elected in 1776 convened only once before adjourning in the face of a coup d'état. Several royalist governors and their administrations fled to ships off-shore.

Patriots included some who had more moderate goals than winning sovereign independence; however, they saw their grievances as cause enough to take up arms. Some of these pre-independence causes included: protest against Parliament's imposition of taxes in disregard of the local province's legislative authority; resentment toward the requirement for

---

30. Griffin, *America's Revolution*, 35.

billeting British soldiers in private homes; fear of a clerical establishment through an Anglican prelature in North America; resentment toward the British policy of appeasement to the Native Nations in the Ohio Valley—territory comprised today by the states of Ohio, West Virginia, Kentucky, and Indiana—the patriot core in the German American population was rallied to that last concern. Here primary sources make a clear association between two prominent "back-country" populations who seemed to be hand-in-glove in their joint distrust of royalist policy and opposition to royalist interference: Germans, and Scots-Irish (also "Ulster Irish.")

Those who held a neutral opinion, meanwhile, had no partisan option in their choices for representation. With the issues being presented in such stark ways one ponders the reasons why fully half the public, whether Anglophone or German, would choose to sit on the fence. That puzzlement continues among American party ideologues in the twenty-first century, who every four years present the current presidential election as the most important since the birth of the country, and yet cannot persuade even half of registered voters to turn out to the polls.

Neutrals, whether Anglophone or ethnic German, preferred not to join the fight or to advance one cause against the other in any way: Some remained neutral hoping for negotiated settlement; some because of complicated relational networks of marriage, family and business tied to partisans on each side; some out of religious duty to pacifism. As will be seen in chapter 3, leaders at the Halle Institutes in Prussia, while not pacifist in outlook, coached their clergy in Pennsylvania to remain neutral. Some scholars place all neutrals, including pacifists, with the royalists/loyalists, since neutrality raised *de facto* objections to the violent methods of revolution, and revolution only succeeds on the rank-and-file strength and fervor of its supporters.[31]

Economically the top tier was divided on the issue of independence. Many of the wealthiest colonials were tied to the royalists. There was a "new money" class that emerged in the colonies, and this elite provided much of the leadership in the patriotic movement.[32] John Hancock was a shipping magnate, John Adams a farmer and barrister, Thomas Jefferson and George Washington owned plantations, Benjamin Franklin made a vast fortune as a printer and newspaper publisher. This rung of the economic and political ladder was closed to the ethnic German throughout

31. "By one estimate, half of the colony's two hundred thousand people were Loyalists, *most of whom kept their allegiance to themselves*" (Allen, *Tories*, 160, italics mine).

32. Allen, *Tories*, 73–74, 93–94; Ellis, *His Excellency, George Washington*, 40–65.

the 1700s; as the war progressed there were some ethnic Germans who advanced in leadership, but at the outset their exclusion from senior rank was total.

Provincial militias tended to be recruited from the second position on the economic strata, the "middle class." In the towns these were tradesmen and business owners, and in rural settings these were yeomen farmers. Militias were highly democratic in organization; a colonel was often separated from his troops by virtue of a popular election held when the regiment first assembled. The early successes of the New England militias confirmed a prejudice that the war was winnable on the virtue of its cause and the virtue of the enfranchised citizen-soldiers doing their duty on a rotation of thirty-day enlistments.[33] Of course back-country yeomen also formed loyalist "ranger" companies, while a great number, perhaps most, enfranchised farmers and tradesmen tried to stay out of the fighting altogether.

As the war lengthened the Continental Army began to parallel European formations in its demographic make-up, in that its "regulars" were recruited from the lowest rungs of society, were enlisted for extended periods, and were professionalized by their drills and discipline. These men formed a class of soldier over which the officers could assert a hierarchy based not only on rank but on status, and enforce the hierarchy by corporal punishment. By contrast the red-coat army of British regulars was closed to the poor American male because it excluded enlistment by provincials, and the loyalist volunteers were drawn from the higher economic strata whose men were incentivized by motives other than cash inducements. As a result the royalist cause did not offer the same opportunities to the non-enfranchised wage laborer, farm-hand, indentured servant, and apprentice, as did the patriot cause.

Socially, in dynamics that parallel those Anglophone colonists with the redcoat British soldiers, ethnic German colonists found themselves face to face with uniformed royalists who shared their language and religion. The great majority of German Auxiliary regiments were served by either Reformed or Lutheran chaplains, and the soldiers in the rank and file were co-religionists with those whom they were sent to suppress. As was true for Anglophone colonists concerning the redcoats, the presence of the German auxiliaries inspired a range of responses among ethnic German colonists, from bitter hostility to romantic interest

33. On discursive connections made by New England preachers between morality and the vindication of "provincial privileges," see Bailyn, *Ideological Origins*, 7.

In another social dimension, relating to German involvement as a share of the population, the depth of the commitment of ethnic Germans to the patriot cause is a point of disagreement among scholars. In the nation's memory there is little made of the contributions of ethnic German patriots. One reason may be that given their numbers the German Americans were proportionately under-represented in the top tiers of affluence and, consequently, were underrepresented in the seats of Congress and in the command positions in army and militia leadership. This is a feature of the eighteenth-century ethnic German experience that is shared with modern immigrant minority populations.[34]

Regionally, ethnic Germans were concentrated in the Middle Colonies, comprising over one-third the population of Pennsylvania with other heavy concentrations in Maryland, New York, and Virginia, but reaching as far as Georgia and New England. As was true for Anglophones, German loyalists were especially numerous in New York. Across the colonies there were likely more patriots than loyalists, but, as was true of Anglophones, it appears that, all told, a plurality and perhaps a small majority of ethnic Germans were neutral. The chief aims of most neutral colonists whether Anglophone or ethnic German were, first, to survive the war with families and economic prospects intact, and second, where possible, to profit from the passage of armies or at least be spared their depredations.

The radical German pietists and peace churches, concentrated in Pennsylvania, had their counterparts as well in the English Quakers. As Quakers experienced division over how best to maintain their pacifist testimony in the midst of a civil war, so the Moravians, Mennonites, Dunkers and various sectarian offshoots in the German immigrant milieu struggled with similar questions and faced similar suspicions from the warring sides. Moravian experiences, some of which are detailed in this study, do not exactly replicate Quaker experiences, since the Quakers had held political power for generations in the province, but there are important parallels as will be described in chapters 2, 4, and 7.

North to south the regions of the Atlantic seaboard are delineated as New England, the mid-Atlantic, and the south. Distinctions between these regions may be attributed to their unique settlement patterns:

---

34. Heinrich Mühlenberg's son, John Peter Mühlenberg, is the only ethnic German American to attain the rank of general, one of thirty-six not including Washington, the commander-in-chief. Ethnic German Americans, with this sole representative, were outnumbered by European mercenaries and adventurers on Washington's staff.

Militant Puritans established their Congregationalist Church in the New England colonies, while Pennsylvania was chartered to a Quaker—the Quakers were a sect of mystical pacifists for whom the Puritans felt particular antipathy. The southern colonies were established with closer ties to the motherland, including the Anglican establishment.

If regionalism can be predictive of choices made for one faction or another, perhaps it is better to gauge affinities by directional compass than by provincial boundary. Loyalists seem to have been concentrated on the coast where the largest cities were situated. Up and down the Atlantic Seaboard it seems to be the case that the further west one settled, the greater the likelihood of sympathy with the patriots, given two mitigating factors: First, if the western settler belonged to a Peace Church, that person's spiritual and ethical motives for pacifism tended to trump their other interests. Second, if the westerner had a history of diplomatic and trade relations with Native Nations, their personal interests tended to be more in step with the royalists, that is, the Board of Trade's, Parliament's, and the Crown's. These tended to be loyalist partisans, but they were far fewer in numbers than the optimistic projections given by loyalist provincial governors to bureaucrats in London.

For those aligned with mainstream churches, whether Anglican, Presbyterian, Congregationalist, Reformed or Lutheran, affinity seems still to be better determined by the compass rather than by one's denomination. Frontier Anglicans, such as those served by Peter Mühlenberg in the Shenandoah Valley, were more likely to be patriots than their urban counterparts in Williamsburg and Charleston. Even Boston became an enclave for loyalist refugees in late 1775, and hundreds of New Englanders took themselves into exile and sailed with the redcoats to Halifax when Howe withdrew from the city in April 1776.

The east-to-west banding of loyalist to patriot sympathies may be explained by the Royal Navy's dominion on the ocean. Control of the seas gave loyalists on the coast continued access to European goods and oceanic travel, particularly before France entered the war. The Atlantic World interests of the urban elite were distinct from the interests of those pushing westward into North America's interior in pursuit of independent living on inexpensive land. Settlement policies that privileged the fur trade over farming, that in October 1763 created the barrier along the Appalachian divide called the Proclamation Line, and seemed to favor Native Americans over settlers, soured many on the frontier against the crown.

Consideration of the south as a third direction on the compass combines the features of elite interests and frontier interests in the plantation, or planter, class. That in Virginia this class produced Washington and Jefferson is an indication of its sympathies. By the 1760s the provincial planters found themselves at a disadvantage with the British mercantile firms that extended them credit but with exorbitant interest rates. Debt became a mark of distinction among the planters including Jefferson, although that was a feature of the lifestyle Washington studiously avoided.[35]

Southern interests lay in being fairly treated in the Atlantic economy, in speculation on expansion westward, and in the preservation of slavery. This last was justified on the intensive labor needed to cultivate the number of acres devoted to a cash crop in order to return a profitable margin. Free labor, meaning the wages of free workers, was cost-prohibitive. The southern planters were almost exclusively Anglican, yet on the whole came to support the patriot cause. In 1775 Virginia's royal governor, Lord Dunmore, promised freedom to any slaves of patriot masters who escaped to royalist lines. This policy, pursued later by other royalist generals, only served to alienate the planters and harden their resolve.

Beyond the plantations small freeholders in the south are most notorious for choosing partisan alignments based on personal animosity with creditors or others with whom disputes had become bitter. Among the southern freeholders there is the least ability to find a demographic indicator of partisan alignment. Romantic notions of poor backwoods patriots rising up against the rich loyalist elite break down in the face of the alignment of the elite patriot planters. Mirroring this dynamic among southern English speakers, chapter 8 discusses how a close-knit settlement of German Lutherans in Ebenezer, Georgia, served by Halle missionaries, unraveled under the partisan pressures of the American Revolution.

## Anglophone Diversity: Celtic Groups in North America

A vast host of non-Anglo Saxon people also migrated from the British Isles. Many of these Welsh, Irish and Scots were bi-lingual, with English having replaced their Celtic hearth-languages in the law, marketplace, and Protestant liturgies. By the 1770s these Celtic peoples were Anglophonic

---

35. Ellis, *His Excellency, George Washington*, 48–53.

quite apart from any feelings of affection for England, yet as immigrants this fluency gave them an advantage in American society.

The impact of the Welsh as a distinct demographic group during the American Revolution is felt most in their representation among the Quakers as already discussed. The Welsh in Wales were predominantly Anglican and, later, Methodist. Welsh regiments were mustered for royalist service in the American Revolutionary War, and a company was deployed from Boston to protect the last stage of the British column's retreat from Lexington.

Similarly, native highland Scots were most notably present in the American Revolutionary War when they took the field as redcoats in plaid trousers or kilts. The more recent the Scots immigrant the more they tended toward loyalism, although several outstanding individuals achieved fame as patriots, including James Wilson who signed the Declaration of Independence, and the Rev. John Witherspoon, a Presbyterian cleric and Edinburgh professor who emigrated to accept the office of President of the College of New Jersey (Princeton). Like Wilson and Witherspoon, the vast majority of immigrant Scots in the eighteenth century were Presbyterian and Whig.

Catholic Irish immigration to the Atlantic Seaboard was practically unknown in the eighteenth century. Some who arrived moved to the margins of society at the outset, living on the frontiers as Indian agents and fur traders, and taking wives from the Native Nations. With both the toleration of religious dissent and the disestablishment of the Church confirmed after the Revolutionary War, the United States of the nineteenth century became a more attractive destination for Catholics throughout Europe, including those in Ireland and in the Scottish highlands.

The largest Celtic Anglophone group in colonial politics and society was the Scots-Irish, a population of migratory Presbyterians with ancestral roots in Scotland. In the 1600s English Kings had settled them in Ireland in the region of Ulster in an attempt to consolidate Protestant, pro-British foot-holds. In the ongoing seasons of violence and recalcitrance in Ireland, English policy towards the Ulster settlers proved inconstant. As a result many, up to a quarter-million, streamed overseas to the Atlantic Seaboard provinces, bringing with them a distinct Ulster Presbyterian identity forged on a frontier between fiercely independent Irish Catholics and over-weaning English land-lords.

This group's experience of Ireland may be considered, by analogy, an extrapolation and intensification of the hurdles and embarrassments that were visited upon the Palatines in Livingston Manor, discussed in chapter 2. Just as these Celtic-heritage religious adherents are credited and blamed for a high incidence of patriotic fervor among them, so it is also the case that many tie the ethnic German frontier settlers together with them. It is upon these Presbyterian shoulders that the officers and ministers of government, High Church Anglicans, foisted the blame for the rebellion.

## Whigs More And Less

New England's Puritans and the Scotts-Irish Presbyterians of the middle and southern colonies described their patriot struggle as being against "Tories." William Howe and John Burgoyne would have chafed at this designation, as they were each committed Whigs.[36] In fact the Anglophone patriots were in a struggle against a distinctly different constellation of opponents from what their Puritan or Presbyterians ancestors had known.

Parliament's experiments did not follow traditional Tory politics, but were progressive Whig efforts to consolidate the gains for the Hanoverian sovereigns and the Protestant succession. The Whigs of Parliament initiated forward-thinking policies designed to elicit revenue from their colonies while at the same time pacifying the Native Nations. The American public, however, seized upon the most salacious rumors about the mother country's intentions. The rumors that spread fastest and burned hottest concerned threats to their core identities, causing them to draw parallels with the struggles of their ancestors. And so: The effort of parliament to assert its own authority to levy taxes while over-riding provincial assemblies smacked of old Stuart despotism. When the Quebec Act installed a Catholic bishop in Montreal whose diocese extended through the Ohio Country to the Gulf of Mexico, this was thought to be a popish (read "old Stuart") maneuver to establish Catholicism throughout the seaboard provinces. These fears fogged over the valid discussion of whether to establish an American See with a resident Anglican Bishop.

Those disposed to see conspiracy began to surmise that the King had secretly converted to Catholicism: This was the great fear held against the Stuarts one hundred years earlier. These fears are embarrassing to many Christians of a more ecumenical spirit in the twenty-first

36. Phillips, *Cousin's Wars*, 158–59.

century and are laughable to many shaped by post-religious assumptions. Considering the history of Stuart pretensions, which made Protestants in Scotland and England painfully aware that their gains in establishment were always contingent and reversible, these fears, however false, may at least be understood. These fears helped to craft the narratives of what the different partisan groups were fighting for, even if they were projecting misconstrued motives on the opposing side.

The term "Tory" was applied to American royalists as an epithet. Toryism, classically understood, referred to support for the Jacobites, and especially to the parliamentary faction that was sympathetic to the Stuart claimants to the throne of the United Kingdom of England and Scotland. Tories tended to be Catholic or more tolerant of them, to favor France as an ally against usurping Orange and Hanoverian dynasties, and to approve a more despotic mode of monarchial rule based on traditional feudalism.

In the 1770s very few people in any of the colonies, much less in Quaker-founded Pennsylvania, could be considered Tories in this classical sense. The label stuck to them referred to the constellation of fears which was galvanizing the patriot cause. These fears had their root in centuries of struggle by Scottish Presbyterians and English Protestants against establishment Catholicism; these were the fears that were stoked by the seeming appearance of autocratic rule and by the crown's establishment of the Catholic religion in Quebec. To be a loyalist to a King pursuing such policies as George III, made one a "Tory" in the eyes of the American "Whig."

Yet the "Whig," in the classical sense, was a proponent of the Glorious Revolution. An English or a Scottish Whig believed that the form of government devised by Great Britain's parliament in its invitation to William and Mary in 1688, and confirmed in 1715 when the "protestant succession" was secured at the accession of George I, balanced the needs of British subjects for a representative government with the symbolic power of a sovereign *and Protestant* head of state. The Whigs of parliament by and large sympathized with the complaints of their American counterparts, but they were by no means "republican," for England had dispensed with that experiment at the death of Oliver Cromwell and Whigs were not interested in reviving it.

Whigs were modernists, capitalists, progressives. In their view the Glorious Revolution of 1688 had brought an era of prosperity to the United Kingdom and advanced it to the pinnacle of civilization. In 1745, while the philosophers of the Scottish Enlightenment kept their profiles low and hid in taverns,[37] the Highland Jacobites made one more desperate attempt at the throne of the United Kingdom, and were decisively defeated.[38] Successive foreign wars into the middle of the eighteenth century demonstrated the strength of the United Kingdom's burgeoning industrial and mercantile enterprises. After the French were vanquished in the Seven Years War, religious apologists saw God smiling providentially upon Great Britain.[39]

For conservative Whigs anything that upset royal interests as they were represented in the Lords of the Board of Trade, in the shipyard magnates, coal mines, cigarette factories, textile manufacturers, and in the Protestant establishment, amounted to treason. Sometime early in the reign of George III the view was taken that the interests of prosperity and strength were best maintained by centralizing authority over the empire's colonies in Great Britain's parliament, yet in relation to that parliament, keeping the American provincials disenfranchised. Since that became the crown's governing point-of-view, conservative Whigs were willing to defend that view to the death.

Moderate Whigs, represented in Parliament by Edmund Burke and others, thought that the interests of the Crown were best served by the style of relationship that had pertained between the colonies and the United Kingdom until the death of George II. They disagreed with conservative Whigs that the defeat of France somehow changed the way the Mother Country must relate to her American provinces.[40] Moderate Whigs may have had a direct outcome on the war, in that several officers put in charge of the royalist forces in North America, the brothers William and Richard Howe, Henry Clinton, and John Burgoyne evinced moderate Whig sympathies. This orientation more than any other factor (although some Anglican piety might have played a part) may be the reason the British lost the colonies; their generals had little stomach to destroy the lives of America's Whigs. Demonstrations of the superiority of British arms were intended to bring the Americans to heel, rather than to conquer and destroy them.[41]

37. Herman, *Scots Invented the Modern World*, 139–43.
38. Herman, *Scots Invented the Modern World*, 150–55.
39. Griffin, *America's Revolution*, 35.
40. Kidd, *God of Liberty*, 75–76.
41. Phillips, *Cousins Wars*, 158–59.

Among the Americans themselves, the preponderance of a moderate Whig "common sense" philosophy may be why upwards of half of all English-speaking Americans remained neutral.[42] Arguments over taxes, issues of representation, and the crown's government of the Ohio Country were simply not reason enough to shed blood in the opinion of half, perhaps even most, Americans in the 1770s.

In political terms the revolution in the American colonies might best be considered a civil war between Whig factions. Conservative Whigs who linked America's greatness to the greatness of Great Britain's Glorious Protestant Majesty were loyalists (loyal royalists), but few, if any, could be classified as Tory except by epithet. Moderate Whigs like Edinburgh's intellectuals leading the charge of the Scottish Enlightenment, tilted to one side or the other in their sympathies. This leaves the patriots, the Radical Whigs for whom the ideals of a representative government trumped all other considerations, including loyalty to the Glorious Revolution and its Hanoverian representative. The Radical Whigs were even willing to return to an experiment in republican government. Cromwell's revolution had been more radical than the Glorious Revolution, and it is these two visions, each of them progressive and revolutionary, that clashed in America.

## A Presbyterian Rebellion?

The Radical Whigs of New England were descended from supporters of Cromwell's republican government, the Puritans of the mid-seventeenth century. The Puritans of the English Republic at that time had maintained ties with Presbyterian republicans in Scotland, though the Presbyterians did take a short-sighted nationalist course in supporting the final attempt of Charles I to win back the throne. Many Puritan leaders had been tutored in doctrine and government in the Calvinist Reformed republican cities of Switzerland and Holland. Although separated by an ocean, a

---

42. Thomas Reid, writing in 1764, presented Common Sense philosophy, a positivism that was sharply critical of David Hume's radical skepticism. Common Sense philosophy influenced such patriots as Thomas Jefferson and the Scottish emigrants John Witherspoon and James Wilson, and it inspired the title of Thomas Paine's pamphlet. Moderate Whig sensibilities also influenced by Common Sense philosophy would be found among the merchants of Glasgow and Edinburgh, who opposed the patriot revolution, and on those who, like Adam Smith, averred compromise on the British side as a preferable alternative to violence. See Herman, *Scots Invented the Modern World*, 254–57.

century, and a religious awakening dividing "new side" and "new light" from "old side" and "old light," the radicals were informed by Puritan visions of liberty and government in New England.

The Presbyterians were an older branch of Reformed faith, having taken root in Scotland nearly a century before the English Civil War. Their church government, while distinct in organization from the Congregationalists, was nevertheless also heavily influenced by Dutch and Swiss Calvinists and organized on republican principles, dispensing with bishops and democratizing the selection of leaders. When the Puritans were gaining prominence in England, the Scottish Presbyterians were at times invaluable and at times inconstant allies; the Stuarts were a Scottish dynasty, after all, and nationalist dreams die hard. Nevertheless from the Glorious Revolution and forward the Presbyterians became increasingly loyal to the Protestant succession, so that on Christmas Day in 1745 the Bonnie Prince had a chill reception in Glasgow.[43]

If by 1745 the Presbyterians of the Scottish lowlands were committed Hanoverian Whigs, their cousins in the Ulster County of Ireland and on into the middle and southern colonies of North America had a different, more radical outlook. Their history of disappointments in the promises of English masters had driven them towards more republican sympathies that were aroused when parliament began to over-reach itself.

The aggregation of these identities and antipathies led many Anglican royalist Whigs, conservative and moderate, to summarize the causes for the state of war in the phrase, "A Presbyterian Rebellion." As Thomas B. Allen writes, "Many loyalists believed that the Revolution itself had emerged from a conflict between Presbyterians and Anglicans." He then quotes a loyalist, and follows this up with a quote from German auxiliaries Captain Heinrich.[44]

Such prejudice was in evidence among the royalist Whigs, in that Howe used Anglican churches for worship and Presbyterian churches for stables.[45] The term "Presbyterian" in this context is most certainly intended to denote the full spectrum of republican-oriented Calvinist non-conformists and dissenters, including New England's Congregationalists and their Baptist off-chutes. However, being Presbyterian predicted conservative Whig politics as much as it did republican sympathy; other

---

43. Herman, *Scots Invented the Modern World*, 147.
44. Allen, *Tories*, 148.
45. Allen, *Tories*, 171.

demographic considerations must be accounted for in the prediction of partisan alignment. The moderate and conservative Whigs in Edinburgh and Glasgow would have been indignant to have their religious tradition so maligned by the royalist officers.

What is not to be forgotten is that a huge proportion, perhaps more than half, of all Anglophones wished to remain neutral in the conflict. Perhaps for many there was a religious dimension to the desire for peace: this was certainly true for Quakers. It is at least as likely that the typical colonial English-speaking American was at heart and in self-interest a moderate Whig. It is not that the typical farmer or tradesman was inclined to abstraction or did much reading in the Scottish Enlightenment, but rather that the philosophers in Edinburgh reflected the pulse of their times as they proposed their various philosophies. As these principles were distilled through the colleges to the pulpits, taverns, courtrooms, and newspapers, many common Americans were unselfconsciously immersed in a popular culture that was syncretizing Enlightenment philosophy with the spirited rhetoric of personal religious revival.

The Whiggery of American culture maintained the faith espoused in the civic religion, as for example practiced in the annual celebrations of the king's birthday and coronation, that God's providential design had been worked out through the protestant succession. God's favor on Britain was confirmed and consolidated through successive victories over Stuart pretenders and their meddling French sponsors. For moderate American Whigs holding these premises there would be confusion in the 1760s occasioned by parliament's change of policy after the French were defeated, and in 1774 a visceral anger that would be self-discerned as righteous indignation on hearing that a Catholic bishop was going to land in Montreal.

Above all, however, the moderate Whig understood war's impact on one's own prospects. Self-interested economic agency was the premise in Enlightenment Whig politics and in the American colonial tradition. Because war represented a severe trial and interruption to prosperity, almost any alternative was better than that resort. The wisdom in this attitude was proven as the war lengthened and inflation soared.

As the economy worsened, enthusiasm for the war diminished. There may have been fewer patriots by 1781 than there had been when the British had withdrawn from Boston in 1776. Washington made this decline in patriotic zeal synonymous with a decline in public virtue, an arguable hypothesis at best; he considered those actions of self-interest that trumped patriotic partisan interests to be the greatest threat to the revolution's success, which is certainly the case.[46] In 1779 Connecticut met only one-third its quota for the Continental line, and several other states were lagging, while many of the infant nation's brightest lights that had signed the Declaration of Independence were retiring themselves from public life. In a letter to George Mason, Washington wrote, "Where are our Men of abilities? Why do they not come forth to save their country?"[47]

## Ethnic German Distinctions

Ethnic German Pietists viewed themselves as ethical agents of the Divine will in the midst of the struggles of eighteenth-century America. They are also a subset of the ethnic German community, which began trickling into North America in the late seventeen century, and by 1775 numbered at least 200,000, fully 10 percent of the Euroethnic population of the colonies.[48] These immigrants hailed from many autonomous German-language states loosely organized under the auspices of the Holy Roman Empire.

As German Catholic homelands did not participate much in the population transfer to North America in the eighteenth century, the overwhelming majority of the German immigrants were Protestants belonging to either the Reformed tradition or the Lutheran tradition. A tiny fraction belonged to radical Protestant groups, although these achieved lasting notoriety for the distinctive lifestyles and pacifism of their communities. The radical traditions were not tolerated well in Europe, and their adherents found refuge in the welcoming attitude of Pennsylvania's disestablishment approach to church relations. From early in the century it was often the case that Lutheran, Reformed, and the radical communities of Moravians, Dunkers, and Anabaptists, found it in their interests to cooperate across lines of Protestant faith and German dialect in their New World, in supporting newspapers, in sponsoring immigrants, and in

46. Ellis, *His Excellency, George Washington*, 124–30.

47. Washington quoted in Ferling, *Almost a Miracle*, 348.

48. Chapter 8 of this study owes a debt to the work of Jones, *Salzburger Saga*. Tracing the evolution of colonial German political values and reasoning throughout the eighteenth century into the Revolution is the singular achievement of Roeber, *Palatines, Liberty, and Property*. The actual routes of colonial German migration in pursuit of personal and social success are described in Fogleman, *Hopeful Journeys*.

constructing and sharing worship spaces.[49] As they blended into a single distinctive socio-cultural minority, ethnic Germans by around 1760 had strength in numbers to both take an independent voice in Pennsylvania politics and also to resist assimilation into the English-speaking mainstream of majority culture.

This cooperation did not, however, include the ecumenical dissolution of confessional boundaries, although the Moravian visionary and patron Nicholas Ludwig von Zinzendorf tried to steer Pennsylvania's ethnic Germans in that direction in the 1740s. Although Reformed and Lutheran Germans often cooperated to build and share a church together, they held separate services, each using the building at their allotted times. In some cases unity evolved, in many cases each community found its way to build its own church, whether the process took only a few years or several decades.[50] If Moravian preachers insinuated themselves into the Lutheran side, a frequent source of complaint for the Halle Lutheran Heinrich Mühlenberg, this often created a conflict in the Lutheran adherents put at risk in their ability to retain their rights to the building they shared with the Reformed. Far from an ecumenical spirit prevailing as Zinzendorf had hoped, these divisions within congregations could become intense and even violent.[51]

Ethnic Germans settled side-by-side with Anglophones in large population centers such as New York City, Philadelphia and Lancaster. Close proximity sometimes occasioned ethnic-oriented strife, especially when candidates of ethnic German, English, and Scots-Irish background were vying against each other for elected positions.[52] To identify someone as a Palatine or as Pennsylvania Dutch meant recognizing an otherness in that person, one who stood outside the English-speaking majority of British migrants from England, Scotland, Wales, and Ireland's Ulster County.

The ethnic German experience, however, is distinct from all other large non-Anglophone Euro-ethnic populations in one crucial respect: No eighteenth-century German sovereign or prince ever established a crown colony, a proprietary colony, or an overseas trading company in North America. Colonization by Germans was solely in the service of

49. Roeber, *Palatines, Liberty, and Property*, 120–27; Fogleman, *Hopeful Journeys* 136–39; Wallace, *Conrad Weiser*, 102–3.

50. Mühlenberg, *Journals*, 1:86.

51. Mühlenberg, *Journals*, 1:152–58.

52. Silver, *Our Savage Neighbors*, 293–301.

British interests. This separates the German immigrant not only from the experience of the French and Spanish, but also from their own closest cultural and religious kin, the Dutch and the Swedes, both of whom were actively colonizing in the mid-Atlantic seaboard in the 1600s.

The German immigrant was an unconquered and wholly voluntary subject of the British crown; on landing in America the German immigrant foreswore all other former allegiances as part of naturalization. Even if the passage itself was to be paid off by years of indentured service, that in itself was an agreement entered into voluntarily before the immigrant embarked from Europe's wharves. At the same time, being voluntary in their subjection may have made them sensitive to the justice of their treatment. Conquered persons, whether French, Dutch, or Swedish, might expect difficulties at the hands of the victors, but the Germans were not conquered. As will be discussed in chapter 2, a riot by German women in New York in the early 1700s may be viewed as anticipating German settler response to royal policy in the 1770s.

Ethnic German interest in assimilating into the dominant English culture was by no means uniform. Swelling immigration through the 1750s allowed the pace of assimilation to slow down, and allowed ethnic Germans especially in Pennsylvania to consolidate and propagate their own subculture. Yet America did serve as a melting pot in important ways. Although Germans did not melt quickly into the Anglophone majority, they did melt together. While comment on the Holy Roman Empire's regional differences in culture and dialect do not disappear from ethnic German discourse entirely, the differences take on less importance. Beginning in the early 1700s the ethnic Germans, although representing a composite of diverse dialects, cultures, and Protestant faiths, were socially evolving into a demographic unit.[53] The key community pillars for the ethnic Germans were their newspapers and their churches.

To better promote their particular interests and protect their culture, ethnic Germans found it necessary to learn English law and to cultivate the judicial and political systems of democracy to their advantage.[54] Their visible cultural strength and emerging assertiveness in turn raised Anglophone fears by the 1750s that the Germans in their midst might overwhelm legal and social systems and convert majority society

---

53. Otterness, *Becoming German*, 72–84.
54. Roeber, *Palatines, Liberty, and Property*, 184–205.

into their own image.[55] By the 1770s the ethnic German Pietists, along with their fellow immigrants, had all grown in their cultural and legal fluency.[56] Whether as patriots, loyalists, or neutrals in the War of Independence, the choices of the Lutheran Pietists and of the Moravians were much informed, but were not uniform.

55. Roeber, *Palatines, Liberty, and Property,* 286.
56. Fogleman, *Hopeful Journeys,* 146–48.

## 2

# The Holder of the Heavens

## *Conrad Weiser*

WHEN CONRAD WEISER FIRST appears in the Tappert-Doberstein redaction of Mühlenberg's *Journals* he is already a leading citizen of Pennsylvania in middle-age. While Weiser takes just a minor supporting role in the *Journals,* the references do hint that young Pastor Mühlenberg was marrying into perhaps the leading family of ethnic Germans in North America.[1] Although on the margins of executive and legislative power, Weiser was a judge, a city planner, and a militia colonel. Above all he was the trusted negotiator of treaties with the Native Nations on behalf of Pennsylvania's proprietary governors. He was envied by the government and Indian Agents in New York, and coveted by the governments of Maryland, Virginia and South Carolina who commissioned him to serve their interests as well. Part of his effectiveness is that he was no mere peon for English interests; the Mohawk trusted him as one of their own. Weiser's influence with the English colonial administrations came as a result of skills he had learned in the Mohawk community at a time that his family was contending against English colonial powers.

   1. The first half of the twentieth century saw two comprehensive biographies on Conrad Weiser (Walton, *Conrad Weiser*; Wallace, *Conrad Weiser*). Walton, more critical than Wallace, includes fewer details of Weiser's life outside of treaty negotiations. Wallace includes lengthy translations from Weiser's own journals and other primary sources.

In his religious life he committed himself to ethnic German faith communities. His spiritual journey into mid-century is representative of the dilemmas and paths of many pietistic German believers who were caught between less than ideal alternatives: they could join tightly-controlled communitarian sects, or, remain in their mainstream Reformed and Lutheran denominations, both of which faced chronic shortages of competent pastoral leadership throughout the eighteenth century.

His roles in civil service combined with his religious proclivities uniquely position Conrad Weiser as a lynchpin in American history: He was a mentor in diplomacy to Pennsylvania Assemblyman Benjamin Franklin; his vision for securing the Ohio Valley for settler expansion kick-started the career of the young Virginia officer George Washington; he was a tutor to Moravian missionaries preparing to enter the Mohawk culture and served as a trail guide for their patron Nicholas von Zinzendorf; he became father-in-law to Heinrich Melchior Mühlenberg the Halle missionary and founder of the first enduring Lutheran synod in the Americas. Two of Weiser's grandchildren would take leadership as patriots, while a third would die from wounds sustained as a patriot at the Battle of Brandywine.

## A Palatine Prototype for Revolt

The role of magistrate ran in the Weiser family, extending back through Conrad Weiser's uncle to ancestors in the late Middle Ages. The family seat was Gross Aspach in Württemberg, but on November 2, 1696 Conrad was born in Affstät, a village where his father, Johann Weiser, was stationed as a corporal in a dragoons company. After leaving the regiment Johann brought the family back to Gross Aspach, where he joined the baker's guild.

In Conrad's childhood Württemberg suffered continually under a tax burden that supported the extravagance of its liege, Duke Eberhard Ludwig, who is said to have once covered the streets of Stuttgart with salt so that his wife could enjoy a summertime sleigh ride.[2] In 1707 a French army pillaged the duchy. Late frosts in the spring of 1709 ruined the Weiser's vineyard, and on May 1 the family buried Conrad's mother, Anna Magdalena, who had died of fever at the age of 43, pregnant with

---

2. Wallace, *Conrad Weiser*, 5.

her fifteenth child. Johann took his eight surviving younger children with him on a quest for a new life, departing Gross Aspach on June 24, 1709.[3]

By that spring thousands of Germans were leaving their homelands in southwestern Germany: the Electoral Palatinate, Württemberg, the Kraichgau, and other principalities and regions. Most journeyed north, following the Rhine for the coast, a channel-crossing to England and the promise of passage to North America. This opportunity had been marketed by British agents throughout southwest Germany. One pamphlet featuring Queen Anne's picture, called *The Golden Book,* advertised farming settlements to be had in the British colonies on the Atlantic seaboard. The marketers described a land that was plentiful and productive, a climate that promoted health, and indigenous neighbors who were peaceful and friendly.[4]

This optimistic picture appealed to Germans oppressed by the obverse: limited opportunity, recent losses due to climate and disease, and the incessant depredations of France's Sun King. However Queen Anne, her parliament, and the public were ill-prepared for the massive response, a tide of 15,000 Germans sweeping across the channel by the summer of 1709.[5] These immigrants were cordoned off into tent cities in London and its suburbs. Public and church charities were soon stretched and exhausted. As the public began to fret over the presence of these refugees, a plan for settlement was needed immediately to relocate these "Palatines," the collective appellation applied to the immigrants by their English hosts.[6] The "Palatines" actually hailed from many German states clustered near the Rhine and the frontier with France.

Catholic migrants were deported back to Germany. Of the refugees remaining, three thousand were settled in Ireland and six hundred were organized for a transport to Carolina. Another 3,000 German refugees were designated for the colony of New York. They were to serve under indenture at Livingston Manor working off the costs of their passage by preparing "Navy Stores," specifically, supplies of pitch and tar required by the ships of the Royal Navy. The enterprise centered on the extraction of

3. Wallace, *Conrad Weiser,* 5.
4. Otterness, *Becoming German,* 60.
5. Fogleman, *Hopeful Journeys,* 5–6.
6. Roeber, *Palatines, Liberty, and Property,* 8.

sap from the abundance of fir trees, the raw material from which tar was brewed.[7]

There is much to commend the plan, provided that the administrators of the plan had the requisite skills and experience in the navy stores industry. The speculators backing the tar-and-pitch enterprise had assumed that all fir trees were alike. Fir trees in Scandinavia were harvested for the sap used to make tar for the world's navies, and it was that species which formed the basis for their glowing projections of profitability. Such a species of fir tree was not to be found in New York. What is especially puzzling is that surveyors from the Royal Navy had already concluded that the fir trees near Livingston Manor were not going to yield the necessary raw materials. Somehow, the optimism of the speculators won out over the surveys.

Conrad was 13 years old when the Weisers joined the Palatine Transport bound for settlement camps in the woods of Livingston Manor, New York. Once embarked for America the dreams and hopes began to darken. The holds of the ships were over-crowded and unsanitary. One-fourth of the passengers died on the voyage, including up to a third of the children.[8] The inhumane conditions disillusioned the restless group who had first left Germany in response to *The Golden Book*'s vision of opportunity.

As returns in barrels of pitch came nowhere close to what was anticipated, the speculators, including Robert Hunter (1666–1734) the new Governor of New York colony, tried to cut costs by reducing the rations to the indentured workers.[9] This exacerbated the fiasco, and the more the English investors heaped the blame onto the victims, the more this led to protests and mutinies. Johann Weiser emerged as an advocate and spokesperson for the disaffected Palatines. In their third year in New York he led an exodus of 500 indentured Palatines from Livingston Manor to the Schoharie Valley. This was done at the invitation of the Mohawk Nation. This arrangement had not been concluded with English colonial rulers, but with an indigenous nation.[10]

From the first the German settlers found common ground with their Mohawk neighbors, acting toward them based on the promises in

---

7. Otterness, *Becoming German*, 60.
8. Roeber, *Palatines, Liberty, and Property*, 8; Otterness, *Becoming German*, 17.
9. Wallace, *Conrad Weiser*, 15.
10. Otterness, *Becoming German*, 62.

*The Golden Book* which had described the friendliness of the indigenous peoples.[11] This approach of open-handed trust was mutual; the Mohawk of the Schoharie were indeed disposed to hospitality toward their German neighbors. The community established between German and Mohawk would set the tone for a broader framework of settler and Native relations, and keep the Six Nations on the whole amenable to Euro-ethnic settlers into the 1770s.

Early in the period of the Schoharie settlement Johann Weiser arranged with Mohawk friends for his son Conrad to live for a year in the Mohawk village of Chief Quagnant, to be immersed in their culture and language. In Conrad's autobiographical reflections he noted moments of terror when he hid himself among the trees because the men had gotten drunk.[12] Weiser writes with the provincialism of the eighteenth century and the moral chauvinism of his German Pietist faith regarding the customs and manners of his indigenous hosts. These eighteenth-century conventions of discourse cannot hide, however, that by means of this cultural exchange Conrad Weiser won fast, lifelong friends among the Six Nations. This made all the difference to his later career as a diplomat and peacemaker.[13]

Pursuing their indentured Palatines, the Livingston Manor partners manipulated New York and English law to obtain title to the Schoharie land. This made the Schoharie Palatines the tenants of the very people they had meant to escape. The investors now sought to enforce their claims on the service of the indentured Palatines. One Sheriff Adams was sent by Governor Hunter to arrest Johann Weiser. The ethnic German women of the settlement mobbed the sheriff, destroying an eye and breaking two of his ribs.[14]

Governor Hunter lost his fortune on an enterprise the Royal Navy had already scuttled based on its own surveys. He was recalled to London and the navy stores project was cancelled. Two colonies invited the Palatines of Livingston Manor and the Schoharie to resettle. New York extended the Mohawk Valley to them, while Governor Keith of Pennsylvania invited them to settle in the Tulpehocken Valley. The Weisers,

---

11. Otterness, *Becoming German*, 62.

12. Wallace, *Conrad Weiser*, 18.

13. The Six Nations, from east to west, were the Mohawk, the Oneida, Onondaga, Tuscarora, Cayuga, and Seneca. The Tuscarora had been adopted into the union after their defeat in war by the colony of South Carolina.

14. Roeber, *Palatines, Liberty, and Property*, 11–12; Wallace, *Conrad Weiser*, 29–30.

however, continued to live and farm on the Schoharie, and Johann Weiser continued to resist the claims of Robert Livingston over his land and body, even travelling to London with his grievances.[15]

In 1720, while his father was absent in England, Conrad married a Palatine neighbor, Ann Eve Feg. The ceremony was performed by Johann Friedrich Heger, a Reformed pastor in the Mohawk Valley.[16] In 1728 Conrad's family emigrated to the Tulpehocken Valley in Pennsylvania. Johann Weiser did not join them, choosing instead to speculate in other land opportunities. At an advanced Johann age finally retired under Conrad's roof in Tulpehocken. He died in 1746 at the age of 86.[17]

The first half of Conrad's life was a crucible that molded him for a career in diplomacy and law as a mature adult. While still a child in Germany he had experienced firsthand the depredations of war, complex grieving, and family dislocation. As a teen he had found that the motives of English business adventurers were often duplicitous and their promises hollow. He immersed himself in the Mohawk culture, and saw its most dignified components along with its most unseemly aspects. He spent years farming side-by-side with Mohawk neighbors, establishing his reputation among them. He did not realize that his move to Tulpehocken in 1728 was the beginning of a new life that would raise him to fame, leadership, and notoriety.

## The Need for an Interpreter

By settling in strength in the middle colonies, New York first and then especially Pennsylvania, German settlers identified on the whole with the regional concerns of the middle colonies. The geography of Pennsylvania made it a gateway to the continent's interior, setting it apart from the seaboard-bound New England colonies.

In the first half of the eighteenth century English settlers, along with large numbers of Scots-Irish and Germans, were pushing the frontier to the Appalachian divide and the headwaters of the Atlantic seaboard. Here the undeveloped land was less expensive than that closer to the coast. The proprietors of Pennsylvania, the heirs of William Penn,

---

15. Wallace, *Conrad Weiser*, 30–31.
16. Wallace, *Conrad Weiser*, 33.
17. Wallace, *Conrad Weiser*, 240–41.

continued his policy of peaceful engagement with the Native Nations.[18] At first government agents negotiated land purchases and treaties with individual Native Nations in what is now Delaware, New Jersey, and southeastern Pennsylvania. However, as the displaced indigenous groups moved westward across the Delaware and Schuylkill rivers from the land they had sold, they came under the suzerainty of the Six United Nations, also known as the Iroquois League. Starting in the 1730s Pennsylvania changed tack and began to negotiate with the Iroquois, treating them as the masters of all Pennsylvania north and west of the Schuylkill.[19]

The Six United Nations of the Iroquois claimed imperial hegemony over all Native Nations as far south as Maryland and west to include most of the Great Lakes and the Ohio valley. Some of the larger "subject" nations under this nominal rule included the Delaware, Shawnee, Wyandot (Western Huron) and Miami.[20] As Pennsylvania looked to expand westward through the purchase of lands they had to settle terms with the Iroquois. The delicate matter of jurisdiction was an issue for the colonial agents as well, as the Six Nations center was in Onondaga, a palisaded Iroquois town in upstate New York.

Weiser was 34 years when he was introduced to Pennsylvania's Provincial Secretary, James Logan. A delegation of the Six Nations also approached Weiser, asking him to speak on their behalf. In the early negotiations at which he was present between Pennsylvanian colonial authorities and Iroquois delegates, Weiser served as an ambassador in both directions, representing the Iroquois interests as much as he represented the Proprietary government.

Being neither English nor Iroquois Weiser was uniquely qualified to mediate between them; once immersed in the Mohawk culture and fluent in their speech, he was able to coach other colonial agents in Six Nations

---

18. See Bruun and Crosby, *Our Nations Archive*, 67. Their editorial comment introduces a circular letter from the year 1681 from William Penn to the Native Nations, which includes this statement, "God hath been pleased to make me concerned in your parts of the world, and the King of the country where I live hath given unto me a great province therein; but I desire to enjoy it with your love and consent, that we may always live together as neighbors and friends" (Bruun and Crosby, *Our Nations Archive*, 67).

19. Harper, "Delawares and Pennsylvanians."

20. In many sources of the period the Miami are called the Twightwees. The term "Delaware" collectively encompasses a cluster of nations related by language and custom, although more properly distinguished by individual designations, such the Lene Lenape who were native to what is now New Jersey.

etiquette. This confirmed and deepened the trust of the Six Nations that Weiser would and could represent their interests faithfully to the colonial powers.

An indigenous counterpart to Weiser was selected, the Oneida Chief Shickillimy, a resident at Shamokin. This was a settlement of mixed indigenous peoples in western Pennsylvania, and Shickillimy functioned within it as something like an imperial viceroy on behalf of the Iroquois. Conrad Weiser, Provincial Secretary James Logan, and Oneida Chief Shickillimy anchored the policy of Pennsylvania's direct negotiations with the Iroquois at Onondaga. Many times Weiser and Shickillimy travelled together to the Council Fire at Onondaga, an arduous journey over the Blue Mountains. On one early trek, undertaken in winter in an emergency effort to avert a war among rival Native Nations, the team nearly starved.[21]

These shared hardships cemented the friendship of Weiser and Shickillimy. For as long as the Oneida chief lived, Pennsylvania's policy of recognizing Iroquois suzerainty was effective in keeping the peace with the Native Nations. For his skills in Mohawk etiquette and translation Weiser was promoted in both the government of Pennsylvania and in the Council Fire of the Six Nations. In 1737 Weiser was chosen by the Onondaga Council to sign treaties on behalf of the Mohawk. He was given a Mohawk name, Tarachiawagon, "The Holder of the Heavens."[22]

The Weiser-Logan-Shickillimy policy was tested in 1737 in the Walking Purchase of Delaware land, a project which Logan undertook himself. Since it did not concern the Iroquois directly both Weiser and Shickillimy were kept out of the particulars. Logan proceeded on the basis that the proprietary colony and its farmers were victims of extortion by Delaware chiefs who were demanding ongoing payments for land already purchased fifty years earlier during the time of the first proprietor William Penn. Logan proposed that one final deed and purchase be enacted to cover the west bank of the Delaware River.[23] It was agreed that a line west would be drawn for a distance that a man could walk in a day-and-a-half, and that territory would be squared with a north-south line to the Maryland frontier. However, ahead of the agreed upon date the government secretly cut a trail through the woods and then recruited two

---

21. Wallace, *Conrad Weiser*, 83–86.
22. Wallace, *Conrad Weiser*, 159.
23. Walton, *Conrad Weiser*, 20–21.

men trained for endurance to run along the track. This greatly extended the territory beyond the limits the Delaware chiefs had in mind.[24]

Despite the Delaware's protest the province proceeded with the surveys and the creation of townships. Bethlehem, Nazareth, Easton and Reading, each established by the early 1740s, all fell within the territory that had been obtained when Logan turned the Walking Purchase into a long-distance race. Yet Weiser took Logan's point of view, and argued against Delaware complaints on two grounds: First, even if setting up a runner was cheating, it was done in order to close out the claims of living Delaware chiefs to land that had already been relinquished by their ancestors. Second, due to the suzerainty of the Iroquois, the Delaware had no right to sell land in Pennsylvania. Clearly Weiser's loyalties were tied to the Mohawk among whom he had lived and been adopted, and by extension the Six Nations where he held an honored place at the Council Fire.

In July, 1742 a conference was held in Philadelphia. One of the goals of the proprietors was to settle the complaints of the Delaware over the Walking Purchase through the arbitration of the Iroquois. The Iroquois Chief, Canasatego, spoke for the Iroquois council fire of Onondaga. The day before the Walking Purchase was addressed, he presented a masterful oration on the perspective of Native peoples towards treaty obligations, pointing out that what seemed a fair price from the colonist's point-of-view did not take into account the long-term impact of the sale of land on the lives of the Native peoples.[25] The methods of settlement and of intensive agriculture by European colonists scattered the game and deprived Native peoples of their hunting grounds; meanwhile the goods traded for the land were consumed in a short time, but the settler claims were permanent. Then, acting as a suzerain, Canasatego also spoke on behalf of his Delaware "cousins" about complaints of squatters on land that all agreed had been set apart for their reservation.[26]

Logan responded by making larger gifts that the Iroquois delegates would be able to share in their towns. The next day, July 9, Canasatego rendered the verdict of the Iroquois chiefs: After review of the deeds not only from the Walking Purchase of 1737, but also from the prior purchases that had been made by the William Penn administration, the

24. Starna, "Diplomatic Career of Canastego," 145.

25. Wallace, *Conrad Weiser*, 126–29.

26. Canasatego's speech of July 8, 1742, appears verbatim in Wallace, *Conrad Weiser*, 127–29. See also Bruun and Crosby, *Our Nation's Archive*, 89–90.

Iroquois ruled that the proprietors of Pennsylvania had obtained the land fairly. Canasatego then berated the Delaware chiefs that were present, addressing their spokesman Teedyuscung, that the Delaware had no land in Pennsylvania to sell, and that they must remove to the Wyoming Valley on the orders of their uncles, the Six Nations.[27] In his rhetoric Canasatego reminded the Delawares that they were "women," meaning, they had no right to speak in council and no right to fight in battle.[28] The Delaware removed themselves from eastern Pennsylvania and settled on the Wyoming River in northern Pennsylvania.

Weiser's influence expanded as Maryland looked to conclude treaties with Native Nations under Iroquois rule, and as Virginia sought peace between their Cherokee allies and the Iroquois, who were Pennsylvania's allies. When miscommunication erupted in a skirmish and bloodshed between far-ranging Iroquois warriors and the Virginia militia, Weiser was called upon to see that the hatchet was buried "forever." By the same token, when Virginia or Pennsylvania traders were robbed by warriors in the Ohio country, even if the culprits came from subject nations such as the Wyandot or Miami, Weiser was called upon to pass the grievance along to Shickillimy with demands for satisfaction.[29]

## Weiser in Politics

After ten years of work with the Pennsylvania government Weiser ventured to publish a political opinion, in the hopes of steering the ethnic German constituency away from their solidarity with the Quakers in the Assembly, and towards those running for election who were friendlier to the Proprietors.[30] Ethnic German support of the Quakers was a long-standing tradition beginning with the newspaper publisher Christopher Sauer, whose closest religious affinity was with the Dunkers (German Baptists), a pacifist Church that had formed out of the pietist movement in Germany in the late seventeenth century. By the 1730s the polarization between the Quaker-dominated Assembly and the proprietary governors was increasing. Late in the decade the assembly defeated a bill for appropriations that would be ear-marked for military needs, a measure

27. Bruun and Crosby, *Our Nation's Archive*, 89–90.
28. Starna, "Diplomatic Career of Canasatego," 148.
29. Wallace, *Conrad Weiser*, 176–77, 183.
30. Fogleman, *Hopeful Journeys*, 136–37.

which had the growing tensions with France in view. The rejection of this proposal caused Weiser to enter the fray on behalf of the proprietaries.

An English copy of his open letter, dated to September 1741, warns the ethnic Germans of what awaited Pennsylvania if its government ran aground on the issue of providing for the defense of the province. Weiser had moved beyond the mistrust that had been fostered towards English colonial authorities in the Livingston Manor fiasco. Whereas in the early experience of the Palatine transport the English had been guilty of dereliction in the duty they owed their German subjects, by 1741 the English were doing their part, and meanwhile the ethnic Germans were meeting the private goals that had motivated their immigration:

> Permit me to put in your mind that as we for the most part retired in this country for peace and safety, and to get our living easier than in Germany, we have not only obtained our ends in all of this, but we have also been well-received and protected by the governor of this province.[31]

It was time for the Germans to do their part, and return an assembly that could work with the proprietary government. Weiser had a strategic vision for what was at stake, and he shared it. The French were in possession of the Mississippi, which put them and their allied Native Nations within striking distance of the province. He wrote, "It is an easy matter for the French with the help of these Indians to come this road [sic] and lay this province waste in a few days." He then quoted Christ himself: "As we are told in the gospel, a house divided against itself cannot stand."[32] Weiser was ahead of his time; the ethnic Germans were not ready to be cajoled to a new partisan commitment. Just prior to the election a rebuttal against the proprietary party went to press, which was probably composed by the publisher and editor Christopher Sauer. The Quaker faction won handily.[33]

When King George's War erupted in the 1740s the frontiers remained quiet, despite France's effort to sow distrust. As the war lengthened, more Native Nations from the west, in the Ohio country, asked to be included in the English chain of friendship. The French monopoly on trade in the Mississippi basin had depressed prices for fur, and the First Nations of the Ohio knew that the English were much more generous.

31. Weiser, "On Serious Advice."
32. Weiser, "On Serious Advice."
33. Fogleman, *Hopeful Journeys*, 137.

Only a war captain named Peter Chartiers and a small band of disaffected Shawnee caused trouble on behalf of the French.[34]

For the Onondaga Council, land was traded for friendship, and friendship meant meeting together for "treaties," conferences that met at least annually, complete with ceremonies and feasts at Pennsylvania's expense. More or less actual business might be concluded based on what needed to be discussed. Resolutions required ratification at the Onondaga council fire, where the triad of Weiser, Shickillimy and Logan were often sent. It was an endless cycle of communication which kept the parties trusting of each other and the chain of friendship strong. The more effective proprietors and governors tolerated this etiquette. Some short-sighted assembly members and governors groused at the expense of maintaining Iroquois friendship, but Weiser argued steadfastly that such were small prices to pay given the alternative.[35]

As Weiser ascended in reputation and authority, he became a target of intrigue among ambitious English administrators. Logan's successor as Provincial Secretary, the Rev. Richard Peters, was competent but envious of Weiser's status. A letter from Weiser written in 1746, during the course of King George's War, shows himself to be plainspoken in English. Whereas Peters wanted frequent reports, Weiser stated his preference on waiting to write until he had something to say, "good or bad."[36] His occasion for writing was the news that Brigadier General Gooch, formerly the governor of Virginia, might be forming an expedition, and wanted Weiser for a guide.

Weiser expressed personal doubts about Gooch. When Gooch had been governor Weiser had not been rewarded for his service to Virginia "as he would have wished," and if he joined the expedition he would do so as a free agent and not under Gooch's command. Meanwhile he was "very glad to hear the Mohawks are engaged against the French and I hope the Gov. of N. York with the assistance of the commissions of Boston will be able to engage the rest [sic]."[37]

Among the indigenous peoples New York was home almost exclusively to Six Nations settlements including Onondaga, the chief town in the league. The provincial agents of New York found their separate

---

34. Wallace, *Conrad Weiser*, 258–71.
35. Wallace, *Conrad Weiser*, 258.
36. Weiser, "Letter to Richard Peters."
37. Weiser, "Letter to Richard Peters."

pursuits with the Iroquois overshadowed by the bi-cultural competence of Pennsylvania's Holder of the Heavens. New York's Governor George Clinton (1686–1761) tried to find equals to the Logan-Weiser nexus, raising Col. William Johnson and the trader George Croghan to be his representatives. Both of these men, however, were self-interested in the outcomes of treaties for their own profit-making opportunities, and at first lacked the credibility among the Six Nations that Weiser enjoyed. Yet when they acted apart from or in contradiction to Weiser's advice, New York's agents blundered. As a result relations became chilly, and New York's government neglected the frequent conferences that were essential to the bonds of friendship.[38]

Weiser's duties as First Nations negotiator, his magistracy and the demands of his own farm and family, still did not exhaust his vocational résumé. Weiser was also a city planner for Reading, a town that rose out of the wilderness after the Walking Purchase secured the land and Berks County was formed. When Weiser appears in Mühlenberg's journals, he is frequently in the role of the judge in whose jurisdiction had come disputes between Lutheran and Moravian factions feuding over the ownership and control of church property.[39] This brings us to the religious dimension of Conrad Weiser, and his personal longing to bring expression to his faith in worship and community.

## Weiser the Pietist

Throughout the 1730s as Weiser took frequent journeys into the Native Nations he was also on a spiritual journey. His correspondence and diaries from the period reflect an earnest piety, while his autobiography from later in life is spiritually-oriented. His pilgrimage through the German denominations in Pennsylvania illustrates well the sectarian culture described by Heinrich Mühlenberg to his Halle superiors when he landed in Pennsylvania in 1742. In the German immigrant community, adherents in mainstream denominations were chronically under-resourced by clergy, but various pietist sects and peace churches offered radical alternatives in lifestyle, and/or mystical orientations, and/or messianic pretension.

38. Walton, *Conrad Weiser*, 234–35.
39. Mühlenberg, *Journals*, 1:189.

The Dunkers were split by a schism when the mystic Conrad Beissel departed from their community to establish a new, purer church at Ephrata. In 1735 Weiser, along with the German Reformed Pastor Peter Miller at Tulpehocken, came under the spell of Beissel's charismatic personality. Both submitted to Ephrata's baptism by immersion and became attached to the cloister of "pure believers." In their new zeal for purity they made a bonfire of books filled with error, sending both Luther's Catechism and the Heidelberg Catechism to the flames along with many other volumes.[40]

The perfectionism demanded by Beissel and the elders in the sect included marital celibacy, a renunciation the Weisers kept imperfectly as Ann Eve continued to bear children in the late 1730s. Weiser also avoided adopting the monastic appearance, such as cutting his hair into a tonsure, choosing instead to wear a long beard. Although Weiser never became a resident of Ephrata he was devoted to the community. In 1738 Weiser paid the printer Benjamin Franklin for the reams of paper required so that Christopher Sauer, who had been embarrassed by his shortage, could print *The Zionitic Hill of Incense*, a hymnal of 791 pages.[41]

In August of 1739 Ephrata raised Weiser into its priesthood.[42] After attaining this stature, the relationship with the cloister deteriorated rapidly. Weiser represented one type of pietistic approach to church government in the form of radical democratization. This, for a time, had appeared to be the direction Ephrata would take. Others surrounding Beissel in leadership began to blend mysticism with a personality cult to create an absolutist regime, coupled with the recovery of the trappings of high liturgy.

Weiser's musings about resigning as the government's negotiator and translator for the sake of purer devotion caught the attention of his colleague James Logan and was passed on to the proprietor John Penn. George Thomas, deputy Governor, was dispatched to Ephrata in 1741. A skillful diplomat himself, Thomas praised the community highly for its order and piety, and then offered Weiser a position in the magistracy as new counties were being drawn up in Pennsylvania. Weiser submitted

---

40. Wallace, *Conrad Weiser*, 60.
41. Wallace, *Conrad Weiser*, 102–6.
42. Wallace, *Conrad Weiser*, 106.

the government's offer to Ephrata's leadership, which was at first divided but then united in their acquiescence.[43]

Not long after, however, Weiser renounced his membership in the community. As a magistrate he was put in the predicament of having to protect an Ephrata woman who accused Beissel of promising marriage and sleeping with her; that issue was resolved when she recanted her charges. Surprisingly Peter Miller, the former Reformed Pastor, stayed with Ephrata.[44]

By the early 1740s the Moravians had begun to appear in Pennsylvania. Weiser was drawn to them for their heart-religion, simplicity and ecumenical spirit. He started to attend the series of ecumenical meetings assembled by the Moravian Church's patron and senior minister, Nicholas Ludwig von Zinzendorf, who was residing in Pennsylvania on an extended missionary visit. These ecumenical meetings were to be the first stage in an effort to unite Pennsylvania's German believers into a new, Pan-Protestant unity, and the first session, held January 1, 1742 in Germantown, inspired much enthusiasm. Lutherans and Reformed sent delegates, as did the German Baptists and the Seventh Day Ephrata cloister. Weiser had not been appointed by anyone, and his presence, as the only German judge in the colony, created a stir until he reassured the meeting that he was present only as a private citizen.

The organizational strength of the Moravians impressed Weiser, and he recognized possibilities for the ecclesiastically underserved Germans in his own town. Introducing himself to Count Zinzendorf, he raised the question of whether he might be able to help the Lutheran Church in Tulpehocken. Pastors styling themselves "Lutheran" but firmly in Zinzendorf's sphere began to aid the church. After the second ecumenical council he offered to host the fourth such council in his own home.[45]

Meanwhile the Moravians came to appreciate his importance to county zoning, town planning, relations to the Native Nations and fluency in indigenous culture. The Moravian mission to the Native Nations, first to the Iroquois and then to the Delaware, began with Weiser as a tutor to the missionaries in the Mohawk language and culture.[46]

---

43. Wallace, *Conrad Weiser*, 106–9.
44. Wallace, *Conrad Weiser*, 108.
45. Wallace, *Conrad Weiser*, 120.
46. Wallace, *Conrad Weiser*, 133.

Zinzendorf's third ecumenical council featured the baptisms of some of the first converts to faith by Moravian missionaries. Zinzendorf called these councils "synods" for the "Congregation of God in the Spirit," and they could only have gotten off the ground with someone like Zinzendorf leading the way in fervor and vision. Unfortunately, once having launched it, the zealous aristocrat also steered the ecumenical synod project back into the ground, as it became clear to all that the ecumenical unity was contingent upon his own leadership. Weiser withdrew support and another location was found for the fourth synod.

When Zinzendorf and a team of missionaries made a tour of Native villages, Weiser was their guide.[47] The wilderness excursion resulted in personal alienation between Weiser and Zinzendorf: The count was a blunt-spoken noble and autocrat; Weiser a blunt-spoken frontier magistrate and wilderness survivor. Among other things Weiser criticized the mystical Count's use of the lot as a dangerous fetish on matters of common sense and experience, such as, which wilderness trail to follow.[48] In Zinzendorf's method, the lot consisted of three pieces of paper which were shuffled and then concealed. One paper held the answer "Yes," one "No," and one was blank. A question was prayed up to God, and then one of the papers was withdrawn from the concealment as God's answer. Having been recently disenchanted with mystical rites in Ephrata, Weiser's patience may have worn thin at the insistence of yet more mystical performances. Zinzendorf's use of the lot, however, was not confined to the upper lofts of an Ephrata barn; Zinzendorf's resort to the lot had caused the entire party to breach various protocols of etiquette among the Native Nations. Weiser drew the line with the promise the party had made to Shickillimy, and Weiser refused to guide them on another course that would result in breaking that promise regardless of what the lot said. Zinzendorf relented but the relationship became frosty.

Despite the falling-out Weiser remained an impartial friend and judge for the townspeople of Bethlehem, and corresponded with Zinzendorf after the count's return to Europe in 1743. As Bethlehem and its outlying communities formed, Weiser's relations to the Moravian leaders alternated between warm and cold depending on when he, as magistrate, had to render a decision opposed to or favored by the Moravian interests. Weiser's consent to his daughter to marry the Halle Lutheran

47. Zinzendorf, referred to as "Brother Ludwig," calls Weiser his "guide and travelling companion." See *Bethlehem Diary*, 1:97.

48. *Bethlehem Diary*, 1:143.

Mühlenberg, who had himself possessed the audacity to talk back to the revered patron shortly after arriving in Philadelphia, did not improve his standing in Bethlehem.[49]

When Heinrich Melchior Mühlenberg presented his credentials in Tulpehocken Conrad Weiser, who was nearing fifty years old, shifted his religious allegiances for the final time, to the Lutheran Church represented by its Halle Pietist missionary. Although Mühlenberg had extended his circuit to bring occasional services to Tulpehocken, this long-established Palatine settlement was considered important enough for the placement of one of the pastors sent from Halle, William Kurtz, a catechist not yet ordained. In 1745 Weiser consented to the engagement of his daughter Anna Maria to Mühlenberg, perhaps recognizing a kindred spirit with his son-in-law to be: tireless effort, passionate belief, and blunt manners.

When Anna Maria Weiser married Heinrich Mühlenberg in 1745, Conrad's star was still ascendant. King George's War was agitating the frontier between French claims and rapidly expanding English settlements. However, the "chain of friendship" between Pennsylvania and the Six United Nations of the Iroquois, a chain forged by Weiser in the 1730s on the premise of Iroquois suzerainty all the way to the Ohio Valley, kept violence to a minimum.[50]

Weiser, on hearing that his friend Shickillimy's family was ill and many were dying, visited the Oneida chief in Shamokin in 1747. He brought condolences for those already dead, sent for a doctor to treat those who remained, and arranged for a settler-style house to be built.[51] Returning to Tulpehocken Weiser took ill himself, and the fear was that he would die. The two Halle Lutheran reverends Mühlenberg and Kurtz were with him in Tulpehocken when he offered himself for Lutheran baptism and then took communion. Weiser recovered from his illness and from that time remained a loyal Lutheran layman and elder of the church in Tulpehocken.[52]

---

49. On Muhlenberg's show-down with Zinzendorf in Philadelphia, see Mühlenberg, *Journals*, 1:76–80. On comment regarding Weiser and his daughter's marriage, see Wallace, *Conrad Weiser*, 211–12.

50. Wallace, *Conrad Weiser*, 186.

51. Wallace, *Conrad Weiser*, 252–54.

52. Wallace, *Conrad Weiser*, 256–57.

## The Anchor is Severed

With the defeat of the French in King George's War Weiser pushed a plan to extend Pennsylvania's trade relations to the Native Nations of the Ohio. He supposed this could be easily done since the nations on the Ohio were under Iroquois suzerainty and policed by the confederacy's westernmost nation, the Seneca. The move would consolidate Pennsylvania's position on the frontier, taking advantage of the British victory. Virginia entered the westward rush. The French viewed these as acts of aggression, and redoubled their efforts to keep the Native Nations on the Ohio in their own sphere of influence.

Shickillimy died in Shamokin in his new settler-style house in 1749. David Zeisberger the Moravian missionary was with him, and immediately sent word to Weiser.[53] Shickillimy's death upset the unity of the Onondaga Council. The loss of a sober, clear head in councils where white men freely poured the rum damaged Weiser's own efforts to maintain Iroquois unity and, with it, the peace they had long imposed on the Ohio frontier. Shickillimy's death was the end of the golden age of Pennsylvania's peace-oriented relations with the Native Nations.

Grievances among the subject nations, especially the Shawnee and Delaware, were mounting against their Iroquois masters and against the Euro-ethnic settlers, traders and governments. Rum dealers wreaked havoc on Native villages, often hauling away a year's worth of hunting pelts for a few gallons of alcohol, leaving drunkenness and destitution in their wake. The complaints of Native kings, chiefs and captains, and nominal efforts by the colonial governments, had little effect on the trade in rum.[54]

Meanwhile, squatters were appearing on lands still claimed by the Native Nations which the government had not yet secured by purchase and treaty. In 1750 Weiser participated in an effort to remove squatters from Native Nations hunting grounds. His tactics included burning houses to the ground, but little progress was made. He also begged leave from the expedition just half-way through, in part because some of the territory where settlers were squatting was being claimed by Maryland. He also knew that Native Nations reaction to forced removal would be mixed. Hospitality was part of the Native Nations etiquette, and many of the squatters were actually cooperative, peaceful neighbors. The settlers

---

53. Wallace, *Conrad Weiser*, 272–75.
54. Walton, *Conrad Weiser*, 15, 175–76, 271–72.

were not blamed for the failure of the government to prevent them from getting that far on their own, just as it was the government's responsibility to prevent rum traders from reaching the Native settlements.[55] It is an interesting ethical perspective, one which Weiser seemed to acknowledge and understand. Fines and taxes were possible means of discouragement, but there was little will to take deterrent measures at cost to the provincial governments.

Yet there were also grievances on the part of colonial agents and legislatures. There had been a long-standing feud between the Six Nations and the Catawbas, an indigenous people who lived in areas claimed by Virginia and South Carolina. The hostilities dated to 1713, when the enemies of the Catawbas, the Tuscaroras, joined the Iroquois League, turning the Five Nations into six. The movement of Iroquois war parties into these southern colonies had already caused fatal misunderstandings with Euro-ethnic settlers. In 1750 Weiser was urged to try to bring the Onondaga Council to bury the hatchet and make peace with the Catawbas.

On that journey he was accompanied by his son-in-law the Rev. Mühlenberg, and by an apprentice in diplomacy, Daniel Claus. The trip took them first to Bethlehem for any information Bishop Cammerhof might have received from the missionaries. They then journeyed to the old camp sites of Livingston Manor. A town had grown up, Rhinebeck, with a church that was served by a Halle-trained pastor, Johann Christian Hartwick. Mühlenberg had come that far to do a work of mediation in that congregation. Weiser journeyed on with Claus. Approaching Onondaga he received news of the death of another pillar in the diplomacy, Canasatego, the one who had so resolutely set down the Delaware in 1742. He also learned of the Onondaga Council's rebuff of the Moravian Bishop Cammerhof who had hoped to settle a missionary among them. From the Iroquois side of the story Weiser formed the impression that Cammerhof was trying to smear him personally and insinuate Moravian agents into the treaty process.[56]

Canasatego's death changed the dynamic of Weiser's meeting, which now included a ritual of condolence. The Onondaga Council was not prepared to promise peace with the Catawbas until Weiser's proposal had been bandied about among all their interested parties, a process that, Weiser knew, could take years. Moreover, Weiser received the

---

55. Wallace, *Conrad Weiser*, 294–97.
56. Wallace, *Conrad Weiser*, 314.

disconcerting news that the Six Nations were feeling increasingly slighted by the agents of the Governor of New York even though they had aided the English in King George's War during the 1740s. The French, for their part, had learned from their mistakes in King George's and were doing all they could to warm relations with the Native Nations. The Seneca, the furthest west of the Iroquois with responsibility for the Ohio Country, were responding to the overtures.[57]

In 1751 Weiser's agreement to have his own son Samuel live with the Brants, a Mohawk family, was complicated when Samuel ran away from their home. He was returned to the Mohawk village with apologies.[58] Also in 1751 Conrad made a gift of a beaver coat to Halle Institutes director Gotthilf August Francke, who sent him a letter of gratitude for the gift and for all that Weiser did to support the Pennsylvania Ministerium.[59]

Meanwhile, New York had turned to a fur trader, William Johnson, to take the lead in relations with the Iroquois starting in 1747. Johnson exemplified the free-wheeling lifestyles of the fur trade, and in his own ways identified himself with the indigenous peoples, including taking Iroquois wives and mistresses.[60] He commanded forces against the French in the Fort George campaign in the French and Indian War, and later distinguished himself as an advocate for the rights of the Six Nations before a series of indifferent and chauvinistic civil and military governors.

Johnson secured the services of both Daniel Claus and George Croghan for New York's interests. By 1756 Johnson was named the head of Indian Affairs for the northern colonies. Johnson raised Croghan to be his deputy in charge of Pennsylvania, marginalizing Weiser, who by that time was approaching 60 years of age. The verdicts of history bend between Johnson and Weiser according to the predilections of their biographers.[61] Weiser scarcely appears in two biographies of Johnson, which also take Claus and Croghan for granted as Johnson's protégés. One recent biographer sees the agents clustered around Johnson as "an Irish fiefdom," scarcely accounting for Claus's immigrant German

57. Walton, *Conrad Weiser*, 237–40.
58. Wallace, *Conrad Weiser*, 332.
59. Wallace, *Conrad Weiser*, 337.
60. O'Toole, *White Savage*, 233.
61. Wallace and Walton being the chief biographers of Weiser spanning the first fifty years of the twentieth century, Johnson had two biographies written over a fifty-year span into the twenty-first century: Flexner, *Lord of the Mohawks*; O'Toole, *White Savage*.

background.⁶² Biographers of Weiser pay more attention to Johnson, but are more critical of him.⁶³

A letter to Johnson from Weiser in 1751 reflects the new conditions under which negotiations were taking place. The letter demonstrates Weiser's skill in English, including his ability to be polite and deferential when he chose. Weiser does not dispute that, with the Six Nations homeland and council fire falling within New York's provincial boundaries, New York had a right to know of Weiser's movements. While giving a report of his recent journey to express condolences to the Council on the death of Canasatego, Weiser also asked Johnson's advice as to whether it might be better to meet next time with Six Nations delegates in Albany, or even at Johnson's home. The hint is that Six Nations etiquette demanded friendship and hospitality on the part of New York's governor, and Weiser was offering himself as a mediator.⁶⁴ Johnson was cold to the suggestion, and the Albany Conference of 1751 achieved little except to show the Six Nations that the British Provinces were skittish with each other.⁶⁵

New York's government found Weiser's influence at Onondaga inconvenient to its own negotiations with the Iroquois. On the pretext that he represented Pennsylvania Weiser was excluded from attending the Onondaga Council in 1753, being turned back on orders from Governor Clinton. This elicited a complaint from Pennsylvania's Proprietor, Thomas Penn in London, and Clinton was recalled. A new policy was set, by John Campbell (1705–1782), Fourth Earl of Loudon and commander of the royal forces in North America, for the provinces to unify negotiations with the Native Nations with Virginia in the lead. Virginia's traders did not trust Weiser, considering him also to be Pennsylvania's man. For the first time since his career had begun Weiser was relegated to the margins of diplomacy.⁶⁶

---

62. O'Toole, *White Savage*, 232. O'Toole's biography of Johnson lists four page entries for Conrad Weiser in the index. The index in Wallace's biography of Weiser has thirty-seven page entries for Johnson and fifteen subject headings.

63. Wallace, *Conrad Weiser*, 247–48.

64. Weiser, "Letter to William Johnson."

65. Wallace, *Conrad Weiser*, 331–32.

66. Wallace, *Conrad Weiser*, 542–52.

## Dealings with Franklin and Washington

The tide of German immigration throughout the reign of George II caused Benjamin Franklin to publish some caustic comments in 1751 in the pamphlet "On the Increase of Mankind."[67] He spoke of ill-mannered "Palatine boors" whose numbers were such they might never be fully integrated into the majority society of the province.[68] He would revise and temper his views, but these words would come back to hurt him politically.

When he wrote this in 1751 he had already had personal dealings with some, including a deal for paper that he had made with Conrad Weiser. It may be that he found the German immigrant and fellow publisher Christopher Sauer a competitive nuisance. It cannot be known to what degree Weiser and Franklin crossed paths when treaty conferences came as far as Philadelphia. It is the case, however, that it was not until 1753 that Franklin became a personal participant in these conferences, first in Carlisle, and saw the abilities of the Palatine Conrad Weiser from the front row. Weiser, who had no taste for wigs, finery, and airs, and seemed to prefer the etiquette of his Mohawk colleagues, may have indeed struck Franklin as boorish on the streets of Philadelphia, but on the frontiers he learned a different lesson. After the Declaration of Independence, Franklin was sent with the diplomatic team to France to seek arms, support, recognition, and alliance. In France he quickly adopted the persona of a rustic American frontiersman. This is in fact the wigless, powderless, plain-clothed Franklin that most Americans are accustomed to having pictured before them, although portraits exist from earlier of the much-dressed, powdered, bewigged Franklin. In France, at the same time presenting himself so unpretentiously, he was also unfailingly sensitive to the etiquette of his French hosts. Whether Franklin was conscious of it or not, he was using diplomatic lessons he had picked up over twenty years earlier from Conrad Weiser, a rustic "Palatine boor,"[69] whose conversance with Mohawk manners had held up the heavens for indigenous peoples and settlers alike.

---

67. Franklin, *Essays*, 367–74.
68. Franklin, *Essays*, 374.
69. Franklin published this caricature of ethnic Germans, and it was used against him years later in the 1760s as the surging ethnic German electorate asserted their clout. See Roeber, *Palatines, Liberty, and Property*, 286.

In the fall of 1753 a delegation of Pennsylvania dignitaries, independently of Virginia, met with Native leaders in Carlisle. With Conrad Weiser were: Isaac Norris, Speaker of the Assembly; Richard Peters, Provincial Secretary; Benjamin Franklin, member of the Assembly. At issue was the presence of the French forts. The Native Nations wanted the English to commit to a strong response. The dignitaries were not able to do so. Weiser, sharing the frustration of his Iroquois counterparts with the lack of vision in Pennsylvania's government, wrote privately to Virginia's Governor Dinwiddie. Since Pennsylvania, paralyzed by political intrigues and pacifist tradition, would be incapable of the actions required to maintain the allegiance of the Native Nations, it was up to Virginia to respond militarily to the French forts.[70] Virginia mobilized a militia under a young major named George Washington whose orders were to display a show of force against French interests. Conrad Weiser's letter and Virginia's response were together a kick-start to Washington's career.

George Washington's mission, undertaken in the summer of 1754, combined reconnaissance with diplomacy. While that was in motion New York hosted a treaty conference in Albany with representatives from several Native Nations and colonial governments. This conference is famous for being the showcase of Benjamin Franklin's plan to unite the colonies under a royal administrator. He envisioned a program of mutual defense and coordinated agreements in commerce and westward settlement.[71] Writing in 1789, Franklin remarks that, "after many days thorough discussion of all its parts in Congress it was unanimously agreed to, and copies ordered to be sent to the Assembly of each province for concurrence."[72] Unfortunately for thousands who would soon suffer violence, none of the Colonial assemblies signed on, seeing no need for stronger inter-colonial bonds. This allowed the crown to ignore the plan as well.[73] Meanwhile Pennsylvania's government remained indifferent to its own need for a militia and a strategic, coordinated defense. Weiser's prediction of 1741 in his "Serious Advice to the German People" was borne out by events.

It was Washington who precipitated these events, on May 28, 1754. On the trail to Fort Duquesne in western Pennsylvania Washington,

---

70. Walton, *Conrad Weiser*, 274–75.
71. Franklin, *Essays*, 378–401.
72. Franklin, *Essays*, 401.
73. Isaacson, *Benjamin Franklin*, 161.

thinking himself ambushed, opened fire on a delegation from the French that had been advancing under parlay. He killed several, and took some as prisoner. In a letter to the Governor of Virginia on May 29, 1754, he insisted that the French claims that they had come to parlay were false, and that they were clearly reconnoitering his positions.[74] Nevertheless this encounter changed the complexion of his mission. He dug himself in behind a palisade he dubbed "Fort Necessity." His position was untenable and on July 3 he surrendered to superior French forces. The inauspicious beginning of his military career shook the world. Tensions with France erupted in full scale war in the following year in North America, and in Europe the year after that.[75]

The Albany Conference of 1754 had a still more profound impact on history than Franklin's unity plan, in large part because its provincial participants had enlarged their ambitions without gaining competence in Native Nations etiquette. A series of vaguely-worded treaties of land purchase were ratified by Native chiefs who had been induced to drink. The Albany Conference of 1754 is widely agreed to have worsened the relations between the Native Nations and the provinces, making the resort to uprising and hostilities practically inevitable.[76] It may be unsurprising that biographers for Weiser and for Johnson issue different verdicts on each one's role in the proceedings.[77]

In his biography of Johnson *Lord of the Mohawk*, James Thomas Flexner describes Johnson as merely a delegate from New York, while the Iroquois implored the governor to reinstate Johnson as their agent. Flexner writes: "Only William Johnson had the influence with the Iroquois needed to save British America." He then depicts Weiser applying alcohol in his diplomacy to manipulate a land purchase in the Ohio Valley for Pennsylvania, which "created another cause of contention." Fintan O'Toole in his biography, *White Savage: William Johnson and the Invention of America,* passes over the conference with mention only of Johnson's attendance, while he credits Johnson with scoring the triumph of the Easton Conference in 1758, the accords which mollified most of the hostile Native Nations and led them to abandon their alliance with the French. Writing Weiser's story, Paul A. Wallace depicts Weiser as the one

---

74. Washington, "To Robert Dinwiddie."
75. Flexner, *Lord of the Mohawks,* 121–22.
76. Anderson, *Crucible of War,* 77–85.
77. Flexner, *Lord of the Mohawk,* 120–21.

trusted by the Six Nations delegates at Albany, and credits Weiser with following the same transparent and careful procedures that had made him esteemed as the Holder of the Heavens even when other agents and interests had far fewer scruples.[78] Wallace then assigns Weiser the credit as the architect of the terms that pacified the Native uprisings at Easton in 1758. The dynamics are complex enough for the biographers to have drawn these conclusions that on the surface appear mutually exclusive. Yet each verdict can be considered valid when considering the cross-purposes at which these colonial agents were working.

## The French and Indian War

While a shooting war was precipitated by Washington's inexperience and itching trigger finger, his mistake in opening fire by no means made inevitable the hostility of the Native Nations. On that, Washington's error pales in scale to three blunders made at the Treaty Conference in Albany that same week, which together ruined English interests among the Native Nations. Had Weiser been allowed to retain his former latitude it is doubtful these mistakes would have been made.

First, there was confusion caused by a land company from Connecticut which wanted to obtain the Delaware Reservation of the Wyoming Valley for settlement by New Englanders. This offer was rejected by the Onondaga Council.[79] One of the two agents from Connecticut, in the evening hours, circulated among numerous Iroquois chiefs, got them drunk, and had them sign a treaty document handing the Wyoming Valley over to the Connecticut company.[80] Second, there was an agreement to purchase land encompassing some of the Alleghenies range. Called the Albany Purchase, the western boundary of that purchase became semantically confused; the English supposed they were entitled to more than what the Native Nations thought they had traded away. Weiser's warnings on the matter fell on deaf ears.[81] Third, Pennsylvania persisted in its refusal to promise a show of strength against the French. Among the colonies, initiative to deal with the hostile forts lay with Virginia, but this

---

78. Wallace, *Conrad Weiser*, 357–63.
79. Wallace, *Conrad Weiser*, 359–60.
80. Wallace, *Conrad Weiser*, 360.
81. Walton, *Conrad Weiser*, 297.

was not enough.[82] Due to the lack of a unified policy among the colonies, bitterness and mistrust fostered by the Connecticut company and by the "Albany Purchase" exploded in the French and Indian War one year later.

Realizing that the provincial governments were beset by confusion in their relations to indigenous people, the British crown made an effort to coordinate a unified policy which was mostly military in scope and approach. In 1755 General Edward Braddock arrived from England to muster a combined force of British regulars with Virginia militia under the command of George Washington, now a colonel. Their objective was Fort Duquesne. As his columns advanced at a crawl through the wooded back-country, many among the Native Nations applauded the show of force.

On July 9 an advance guard under Captain Thomas Gage encountered skirmish fire eight miles short of the objective. The redcoats closed ranks and poured a mass volley into the woods, killing the fort's commanding officer in the first volley. The resistance melted away.

Nevertheless Washington suggested reconnoitering the woods. Braddock overruled him; clearly the discipline of the redcoats had intimidated their opponents. The column marched headlong into an ambush. A much smaller force of French and Native warriors, shooting from the cover of trees, mauled the British regulars who were ordered to maintain rank and file. The killing ended when Braddock fell and the surviving troops ran pell-mell through the woods. Fort Duquesne was never seen. Even though the French did not have the force to pursue the beaten column, the redcoats did not stop retreating. They withdrew from Carlisle, abandoning the entire frontier to France and its allies, and holed themselves up in Philadelphia.[83]

For the first time Pennsylvania felt its own peril in the midst of the hostilities between colonial empires. Yet even now the Provincial Assembly and the Governor could not agree on passing a bill for military appropriations. The issue used by the Quaker-dominated assembly to filibuster the measure had to do with taxes. The Assembly took the position that the proprietary lands should be taxed along with the rest to raise the revenue. This stipulation was opposed by the proprietary government on principle. The result was a budget gridlock causing legislative inaction

---

82. Wallace, *Conrad Weiser*, 390–91.
83. Ellis, *His Excellency, George Washington*, 21–24.

and executive paralysis.[84] In a journal entry Weiser states: "Gracious Heaven! What can the English expect will become of them. Will their arms have success amidst so much hypocrisy and dissimulation!"[85]

The bitterness over Livingston Manor in the 1710s had been obviated by the competence of English vision and management in the 1730s and 1740s, leading Weiser to be a firm advocate of the proprietors who employed him. Now government was failing again at its first duty. Here we see Weiser distancing himself from the "English" whose interests he had so faithfully represented. On this issue he shares the palatably bitter frustration of the Ohio Natives and the Six Nations. One wonders if premonitions came to him in the form of memories of French soldiers sacking his home town when he was eleven years old. The balance of powers which is a cherished tradition in American constitutional government, in its precursor form in Pennsylvania, caused the government to deprive its citizens of security. If providing for the common defense is understood as the first duty of a government, a philosophy firmly in keeping with a Lutheran doctrine of the powers of the sword of government, Pennsylvania's government lost legitimacy in its response to Braddock's defeat. Most importantly, it lost legitimacy among the Native Nations on the Ohio. Now convinced of weakness in English resolve, the Native warriors chose to suspend their grievances with the French forts, and turn to violence against the squatters on the Wyoming and those beyond the boundaries of the Albany Purchase.[86]

While the Onondaga Council waited for action from Pennsylvania with mounting disgust, in the fall of 1755 the Delaware and Shawnee of the Ohio Country, along with Seneca warriors of the Iroquois, began to massacre squatters on disputed land. Raiders struck the Moravian mission of Gnadenhütten in the Wyoming Valley, killing eight missionaries in their cabin. Four escaped by jumping from windows and hiding in the woods. The Assembly passed a bill for military spending, taxing proprietary lands. The governor vetoed, having no other orders from the proprietor, Thomas Penn, an absentee landlord in London.[87] Weiser mustered a militia for defense, and marched two hundred men to Paxton as

---

84. Wallace, *Conrad Weiser*, 389–91.
85. Wallace, *Conrad Weiser*, 468.
86. Walton, *Conrad Weiser*, 302.
87. Walton, *Conrad Weiser*, 302.

a show of force. Finding the frontier quiet, they returned to Tulpehocken and disbanded.[88]

The gridlock in Pennsylvania's government was only lifted when Thomas Penn sent a personal gift of several thousand pounds for Pennsylvania to mobilize a defense.[89] While Conrad Weiser was certainly not the only one to have corresponded with the proprietor on the subject, it is likely he was one of the plainest-spoken and least polite about what was required.[90] The assembly, under pressure from the outcries of the public, accepted the compromise and removed provisions for taxing proprietary lands.

Benjamin Franklin designed an organized provincial militia and the assembly passed it into law. Given the relative success of his initial effort, Weiser was chosen to receive a commission as a Lt. Colonel. With around five hundred civilian soldiers he was tasked with defending a front of mountain terrain over one hundred miles wide stretching from the northeast to the southwest through Pennsylvania. His forces were spread out in forts, each with garrisons of around fifty. On Weiser's southern flank, Col. George Washington of the Virginia militia was given a similarly impossible task.[91] Each province's militia was largely ineffective for the style of war the Native Nations were fighting, and Franklin himself admitted as much.[92]

A damaged and unsigned document in English offers instructions on how to muster a militia and maintain some rudiments of discipline. Although included in the Weiser collection of the Pennsylvania Historical Society, it is likely to have been copied or in some way derived from the instructions of Benjamin Franklin. Readiness was paramount, thus when the militia mustered for drill, alcohol was not to be distributed.[93] Evidently this was not a regulation for soldiers deployed to a post. Eight letters from Captain Bussey of Fort Henry were written in German to Conrad Weiser, suggesting the ethnic composition of the militia company stationed at that post. The letters span the year 1756. A ninth letter

---

88. Walton, *Conrad Weiser*, 314.
89. Wallace, *Conrad Weiser*, 415.
90. Wallace, *Conrad Weiser*, 430–31.
91. Ellis, *His Excellency*, 24–33.
92. Wallace, *Conrad Weiser*, 420.
93. "Instructions on Raising a Militia."

from Bussey, addressed to Philadelphia and written in English, implores that the needs of the troops not be neglected, specifically salt and rum.[94]

Another adjutant of Conrad Weiser's, Peter Spycker, encountered reluctance when he tried to raise a militia in Tulpehocken. In Spycker's estimation they had "misunderstood" Weiser's instructions to him, supposing that by agreeing to be deployed at Fort Henry the men might be required to go even further afield from their farms and homes, as far as Shamokin. Spycker was able to compromise and raise up a large number of men who desired to serve as a patrol in their own county.[95]

In Pennsylvania refugees poured into towns and cities south and east of the disputed areas. The disruption to lives and economy was the desired effect of the terror tactics of the Native warriors. By butchering families in isolated homesteads, then displaying the corpses for passers-by, the goal of spreading panic and thus clearing disputed lands was reached. Sometimes the militias left the forts in hot pursuit, sometimes the pursuit was more languid. On both sides there was a notable reluctance to engage armed enemies. As deaths among German, Irish, and English settlers mounted, militias began to contemplate a tactic of their own: reprisal against Native settlements. Some traders at posts on the frontier wanted the government to issue a scalp bounty, a policy Weiser opposed because it would encourage indiscriminate killing of Native American friends as well as foes.[96]

## Heaven Held

Even as a militia commander Weiser remained part of the government efforts to bring peace to the frontier through treaty and reconciliation. As the war lengthened, Quaker politicians and Society leaders in pursuit of these same goals began to act independently of the government. Forming the "Friendly Association to Restore Peace with the Indians through Pacific Means," Quakers led by Israel Pemberton subverted the efforts of the provincial governor and of Conrad Weiser, seeking to pacify the Native Nations with gifts. With a view to embarrassing the proprietary

---

94. Bussey, "Letter to Conrad Weiser."
95. Spycker, "Letter to the Governor of Pennsylvania."
96. Walton, *Conrad Weiser*, 320–21.

establishment, the "Friendly Association" promised to investigate the grievances of the Delaware especially as it concerned disputes over land.[97]

While these independent actions subverted the government's, they did help to soothe the distrust of the Native Nations, not the least of which was the fear that since they had gone on the warpath the white people might be unforgiving.[98] What is perhaps most amazing is the forbearance of many settlers once peace was restored with the Native Nations in 1758. This attitude would not survive the test of the 1760s.

There was also change in the leadership of the French that had an impact on the allegiances of the Native Nations. The Marquis de Montcalm, a French aristocrat accustomed to the manners of Europe's privileged class, took charge of French forces in North America in 1757. A capable military tactician, his strategic vision was inhibited by his contempt for his Native allies. His inability to overcome his prejudice alienated the same bands that had risen up on France's behalf in 1755. In one telling episode Montcalm secured the capture of Fort William Henry in a series of skillful maneuvers. However, he set generous conditions for peace for its British regulars and militia by exempting them from being plundered or dragged away captive, terms deliberately taken at the expense of his Native warriors who had participated in the siege. The Native auxiliaries, having been excluded from the ceasefire negotiations, held that the terms did not bind them. The column leaving Fort William Henry under a light guard of French soldiers was beset by Native warriors, who exacted what plunder they could, in some cases murdering and scalping members of the captive colonial militia.

Although talks between the belligerent Native Nations and the English provinces began as early as the summer of 1756, breakthroughs were not achieved until disenchantment with the French mounted. The late 1750s would mark the last time the indigenous nations of the Great Lakes and Ohio Country would be able to play two imperial opponents against each other to their own benefit.

A receipt from a Philadelphia vendor in February 1756 shows that Weiser had purchased 115 gallons of rum of February 17th.[99] A few days later a small delegation of Iroquois allies were hosted in Philadelphia,

---

97. Wallace, *Conrad Weiser*, 435–38.
98. Wallace, *Conrad Weiser*, 440–44.
99. Weiser, "Receipt of Purchase."

where they stayed most of a week.[100] It is unclear whether Weiser intended to keep an inventory of rum for treaty conferences with allies, or peace talks with enemies, or if this purchase was intended to supply the forts, or for all of these purposes. Nevertheless, in war and in peace rum-sellers did big business in the American colonies.

Easton, near Bethlehem, was chosen as a suitable location for peace talks, and these began in July of 1756. The negotiator for the nations at war with the English was Teedyuscung, by that time notorious as a heavy drinker, and the same chief who had been humiliated in 1742 by the Iroquois Chief Canasatego. Teedyuscung now styled himself as a king speaking on behalf of ten nations. The Onondaga Council objected to these claims and to Teedyuscung's role as a negotiator,[101] but Teedyuscung had the support of Quakers in the Pennsylvania assembly, and he leveraged his clout to every personal advantage, including copious amounts of rum.

That talks were held, however, did not mean that a ceasefire was in place on the frontier. Indeed, warriors in the train of the negotiating chiefs would leave trails of blood behind them on their way to and from treaty negotiations in Easton.[102] Teedyuscung's base was not west on the Ohio, but up north, towards New York, on the Wyoming Valley. The grievances of these Eastern Delaware were the same as those out west: squatters were settling on land that by agreement had been set aside for the Delaware nation.

One of the complicating factors in the negotiations was the jealousy of the Iroquois that a chief from a subject nation would be accorded such authority by the colonial governments. Furthermore, British arms suffered another setback when General Abercrombie's artillery bogged down, and he sent his regulars in a bayonet assault against reinforced positions at Fort Ticonderoga. In pursuing the attack in that vein he was as full of hubris and disregard for his troops as Braddock had been.

For the Native Nations the deaths of British redcoats was of little moment: They were more interested in whether the settlers would keep the promises made by their provincial governments. In Easton in 1758, after a year of Montcalm's high-handed aloofness towards France's allies and in the third year of peace talks, the provinces gave Weiser freer rein while the Quakers' Friendly Association was muzzled and set on the margins.

---

100. Wallace, *Conrad Weiser*, 429–30.
101. Walton, *Conrad Weiser*, 334.
102. Walton, *Conrad Weiser*, 374–75.

In speeches that likely came from Weiser's hand, the colonial governors mollified the Iroquois over the role of the Delaware Chief Teedyuscung.[103] With those hurdles of etiquette overcome, the disputed Albany Purchase boundary was moved eastward, the Connecticut Company's purchases of land in the Wyoming were voided, and the Delaware were guaranteed a reservation.[104] The Native Nations of the Ohio accepted and ratified these terms and returned to neutrality, aiding the French no further.

It had taken all of Conrad Weiser's strength, the wisdom of his 62 years and his thirty years' experience as a negotiator, to conclude a peace that robbed the French of their one advantage—their allied Native Nations. In 1758 he was able to undo the Albany fiasco of 1754 which he had watched from the sideline. Having met their objectives, the Native Nations ended their uprising against the English colonial powers.[105] It is doubtful whether the English, by means of their concessions, felt defeated militarily by the Native Nations. This was of little concern to Weiser and the colonial governments: The overall strategic picture depended on the expulsion of the French, who were invincible with Native Nations support and naked without it.

In the first test of this policy British General Forbes concluded his westward march on Fort Duquesne, arriving in November, 1758, to find it abandoned and burning.[106] The French, stripped of their Native allies, had withdrawn from the Ohio. Then British General Wolfe took the war straight to the fortress at Quebec City, and with its capture the final victory of the British in North America became inevitable.

## Weiser's Legacy

On July 12, 1760 Weiser was about to embark for Carlisle for another treaty conference, but did not get far when he fell ill. He was returned to his home and died the next day. Services were held in Tulpehocken on July 15, with Pastor Kurz presiding, and he was buried at his home. His son-in-law Heinrich Mühlenberg eulogized him to the mission directors in Halle.[107]

103. Wallace, *Conrad Weiser*, 537–41.
104. Walton, *Conrad Weiser*, 372–73.
105. Wallace, *Conrad Weiser*, 551.
106. Walton, *Conrad Weiser*, 368–69.
107. Wallace, *Conrad Weiser*, 573.

Weiser had lived at a fever pitch in his public service and in his religious zeal. While Mühlenberg testified to Weiser's piety in conventional Euro-ethnic terms, the greatest testimony to his ethics-in-action comes from Seneca George, one of the Iroquois partners in treaty negotiations. Holding up a wampum belt in Easton, 1761, he said to Pennsylvania's agents, "We, the seven Nations, and our Cousins are at a great loss, and sit in darkness, as well as you, by the death of Conrad Weiser, as since his death we cannot so well understand one another."[108] The Palatine mediator between English governors and the Native Nations was now gone. In a tumultuous universe that settlers and natives were trying to share in common, Weiser had the same role as Atlas had in the Greek cosmos. The Holder of the Heavens had been removed, and perhaps no one could foresee how quickly the pillars would begin to shake.

Conrad Weiser's daughter and son-in-law, the Mühlenbergs, brought eight of his grandchildren into the world. Two of his granddaughters would marry clergy, solidifying Mühlenberg's Halle-oriented influence over the Pennsylvania Ministerium for a generation after his own death. The three grandsons who lived to adulthood were all in ministry for a time: Heinrich Ernst Mühlenberg, the youngest of the surviving grandsons, remained a career pastor and also became a pioneer in the science of botany. The other two resigned their ordinations for public life: The eldest grandson, John Peter Mühlenberg, became a brigadier general on the staff of George Washington, as will be discussed in chapter 6; the second grandson, Friedrich August Conrad Mühlenberg, rose through legislative politics to become the first Speaker of the House in the Congress of the United States.

His ethnic German posterity remained true to Weiser's own political ethos and commitments in some important ways, and in other ways departed from it. His conviction that loyalty and duty were owed to governments that were effective, coupled equally with the conviction that government must have a function in order to constrain such duty, are woven together into the ethos of those who followed in the second and third generations and to the end of the century.

However, his example as a settler holding genuine affinity for an indigenous people, the Mohawk, and by extension the Iroquois League of which they were a part, vanishes in the tragic events that began shortly subsequent to his own death. Successive French wars were now past, but

---

108. Wallace, *Conrad Weiser*, 573.

successive uprisings of the Native Nations were just beginning, and these spasms of violence would alienate not only settlers but military and legislative leaders. The outcome would be a virulent, racist animosity that would tragically make the Pennsylvania approach up to 1760 an historical anomaly in relations with Native Nations, rather than the standard it might have been.

By 1780, when Weiser's grandsons were rising in stature, attitudes towards indigenous peoples were very different in Pennsylvania from what Weiser had always held close to his own heart as an adopted Mohawk. The treaties of Easton did not prove permanent, for conditions changed as quickly as British administrators in North America. To Weiser's credit and to his own peace of mind, the treaties at least outlived himself.

# 3

# The Pennsylvania Ministerium
## *Heinrich Melchior Mühlenberg*

THE DAYS OF LATE September, 1777, were anxious times for many Mühlenbergs and many patriots. The royalist armies under the command of William Howe occupied Philadelphia on September 26, where two of Mühlenberg's grown offspring lived. One was Heinrich Ernst, the junior German Lutheran pastor. The other was Margaret "Peggy" Kunze, Heinrich Mühlenberg's daughter, and wife of the senior Lutheran pastor Johann Christoph Kunze. The Lutheran Churches in Philadelphia operated two church facilities, St. Michael's, and Zion, as one corporation with one pastoral team and one set of elected lay leadership. The St. Michael's-Zion corporation staffed three pastors, with the elder Heinrich Mühlenberg still officially first in rank even after his relocation to Providence (Trappe) in 1776. Of the three pastors in call to the joint Lutheran churches, only J. C. Kunze remained in Philadelphia by September 28, with his wife, Peggy. September 27 had begun inauspiciously for Heinrich Mühlenberg when his church in Providence had been occupied by the Cumberland County militia and he was forced to cancel the funeral of a child; it ended joyfully with the safe arrival of Heinrich Ernst at his threshold. The young pastor is purported to have disguised himself as a Native American to pass *in cognito* through the royalist lines.[1]

---

1. The elder Heinrich Mühlenberg does not enlarge on his son's adventures in getting to Providence from Philadelphia, except that he is said to have fled the city on Tuesday (September 23) and reached the safety of home "in a very roundabout way" (Mühlenberg, *Journals*, 3:81). The detail of Native American garb is also passed over

The Mühlenberg's family home sat miles to the rear of the patriot lines, yet in the elderly pastor's imagination they were perilously within striking distance of British cavalry. He had not escaped the war as he had hoped; the war had followed him. The British presence in Philadelphia and the rumors of a warrant for his arrest forced Mühlenberg to frame and articulate his own convictions regarding the partisan conflict and what his own role should be.

## Serving the Immigrants

Heinrich Mühlenberg arrived in America in 1742. At that time, during the reign of George II, immigration was a steady stream and the German population was increasing geometrically.[2] The southwestern states of the Holy Roman Empire continued to predominate in the number of German emigrants, who continued to be overwhelmingly Protestant.[3]

Without ecclesial structure or supervision many Germans in America had organized churches on their own initiative, building sturdy log buildings which were, nevertheless, subject to rapid decay. Despite their numbers, the immigrants could not provide pastors with the steady salary, benefits and perks that came with the clerical offices in Germany. Furthermore, the immigrants were disinclined to accord pastors the authority and status that were inherent in the function of Europe's established (state-funded) churches. Instead, the immigrant pastor's job security was contingent on one's popularity among lay people who had little to no theological training. This led to many of these being duped by silver-tongued preachers of suspect background and non-existent credentials. In addition the transportation infrastructure was so primitive and the climate so raw and volatile that every journey to an out-parish was a mortal risk. German pastors for the most part took little interest in forsaking a comfortable career ladder in a German state's parish system in order to serve pioneer settlers in an untamed wilderness.[4]

---

by historiographer Paul A. Wallace (Wallace, *Muhlenbergs of Pennsylvania*, 145). The apocryphal legend, as is true of other myths pertaining to the Mühlenbergs, may have had currency before the recovery of the elder Mühlenberg's Journals. The legend is preserved in Richards, *Pennsylvania-German*, 431.

2. Glatfelter, *Pastors and People*, 4.
3. Fogleman, *Hopeful Journeys*, 36–51.
4. Explaining the conditions for Lutheran clergy in Pennsylvania was a favorite theme of complaint for Heinrich Mühlenberg. On the environment and perils of

Neither a farmer nor native to Germany's southwest, Heinrich Mühlenberg came from a different German socio-cultural sphere from most of the lay people he served. In 1711 he was born into a shoe-maker's family in the Electoral Realm of Hanover-Braunschweig. He attended the new university in Göttingen on a scholarship, where he was brought under the wing of Göttingen scholar Joachim Oporin, who had been trained at Halle University at the time that its faculty was under Pietist hegemony. Under Oporin, Heinrich Mühlenberg experienced the conversion to a heart-religion described in the writings of Lutheran Pietism's founder, Philipp Jakob Spener, and by the founder of the Halle Institutes and Oporin's mentor, August Hermann Francke.[5] In 1738 Heinrich Mühlenberg moved to the city of Halle, in the Kingdom of Prussia, intending to prepare for foreign mission at the Halle Institutes which had by then passed under the direction of Gotthilf August Francke (1696–1769), the founder's son.

While teaching in the institute's orphanage schools a call was issued to Heinrich Mühlenberg to take over an orphanage at Grosshennersdorf in Upper Lusatia in the Kingdom of Saxony. At first inclined to reject it to pursue his mission goals, he was urged to accept it by the director at Halle, Gotthilf Francke himself. This put Mühlenberg in service to the Baroness von Gersdorff, the estranged aunt of Nicholas Ludwig von Zinzendorf.[6] On the merits of this call he was ordained by the consistory of Leipzig.[7] Although he cherished the ministry, the financial model of aristocratic largesse subscribed to by the baroness' mother was proving

travel, see Mühlenberg, *Journals*, 1:230; on economic conditions and challenges for getting the churches on secure footing, see Mühlenberg, *Journals*, 1:84–85; on pastoral imposters and the difficulty of vetting clergy, see Mühlenberg, *Journals*, 1:89–90, 152, 154–55. Spaeth et al., *Documentary History*, traces through its annual meeting minutes the saga of a circuit of churches centered in Manheim that could not keep a stable pastorate for lack of funding it (Spaeth et al., *Documentary History*, 188, 194, 199, 209). Spaeth et al., *Documentary History*, also notes that bequests for the Pennsylvania Ministerium disbursed from Halle helped supplement the clergy income from the settlers they served (Spaeth et al., *Documentary History*, 202–3, 211–12).

5. Mühlenberg, *Journals*, 1:2–4.

6. Henrietta Baroness von Gersdorff is not to be confused with her mother Henrietta, the grandmother of Nicholas Ludwig von Zinzendorf. The grandmother raised Zinzendorf at her palace in Grosshennersdorf after the death of his father and the remarriage of his mother. The younger Henrietta, his aunt, had been attached to the child in his early years, but they fell out as adults, as described in chapter 4. See Spangenberg, *Life of N. L. Zinzendorf*, 156–58.

7. Mühlenberg, *Journals*, 1:5.

unsustainable. After a little more than two years Mühlenberg, knowing the days of the orphanage were numbered, paid a visit to Halle to consult its leadership about his options.

He was invited to dinner on his birthday, September 6, 1741, by Gotthilf Francke. The Halle director asked him to consider the plight of German Lutherans in Pennsylvania, who due to the shortage of clergy were destitute of the means of grace and whose children were unchurched and unbaptized. Furthermore, the Count von Zinzendorf and his Herrnhuters had cast their designs on these lost German sheep, hoping to corral them into their Moravian fold. After consideration, Mühlenberg committed himself to attend to the mission in Pennsylvania for three years.[8] He was then sent to London to be tutored with the Rev. Friedrich Michael Ziegenhagen, a loyal Halle Pietist who served the royal family as their private chaplain in the Chapel of the Court of St. James.[9] From that time on Mühlenberg referred to his pietist directors in London and Halle as the "Reverend Fathers."

Mühlenberg's was not the first effort in which Lutheran Pietists in Germany and London cooperated together for mission in the Americas. In the 1730s they had arranged for transports of Protestant exiles from the Archbishopric of Salzburg to assist in the colonization of the new British colony of Georgia. Under the leadership of Halle-trained clergy this was a famous experiment in the global Lutheran Pietist community which would endure until the pressures of the American Revolution caused its disintegration, as will be discussed in chapter 8.

This is why Mühlenberg's journey to North America brought him to Charleston first, where he was met by Salzburgers who escorted him to their settlement in Ebenezer in Georgia. Here he stayed over a month. Ignoring the advice of the Rev. Michael Boltzius and others to winter with them, he booked passage to Philadelphia by boat, a journey along the coast that was scarcely less perilous than the ocean crossing as the weather worsened and temperatures fell.[10]

Arriving safely in Pennsylvania, Mühlenberg met with the elders of the three churches who had appealed to the Halle Institutes five years earlier. One congregation was in Philadelphia, the other two were north of Philadelphia. When weather cooperated these churches in Providence

---

8. Mühlenberg, *Journals*, 1:6–7.
9. Mühlenberg, *Journals*, 1:18–21.
10. Mühlenberg, *Journals*, 1:64–65.

and New Hanover were one day's travel apart through dense woods and across streams and rivers. Starting with the two outliers, Mühlenberg met with the church's elders who reviewed his testimonials, certificates, and commission from Ziegenhagen. They agreed that he fit the requirements for what they had asked. Now grounded, he returned to Philadelphia to present himself to its Lutherans. This brought him into direct confrontation with the Count von Zinzendorf, who had been sojourning in North America for nearly two years, and whose presence had at last provoked action among the leaders of Halle Pietism.

The two squared off in a meeting at Zinzendorf's Philadelphia home. The verbatim report of their encounter which Mühlenberg produced is meant to cast Zinzendorf in the wrong, however the prickly aspects of Mühlenberg's own personality surface: He insinuates knowledge of Zinzendorf's character based on conversations with the Count's aunt, Henrietta Baroness von Gersdorff.[11] The personal affronts aside, Mühlenberg was vetted as both Halle's and London's response to a call issued by three congregations including the church in Philadelphia. Zinzendorf had staked his claims to pastoral authority on the basis of his own Lutheran ordination by the faculty at Tübingen, but had come on his own initiative without the regular call that the Lutheran confessions required.[12]

By Mühlenberg's arrival Zinzendorf's time in Pennsylvania had run its course: while the mission to the Native Nations had been launched and the Moravian town of Bethlehem was growing, the Count's vision for establishing an ecumenical cooperation under his personal leadership had steadily lost momentum. He departed for England in the first week of January, 1743, leaving the Moravians firmly rooted in the American religious landscape.

Soon dozens of Lutheran congregations in their log huts in outlying towns and on the frontier, upon hearing of a pastor vetted and commissioned by Ziegenhagen, began to appeal to Mühlenberg for help. In his first months Mühlenberg gave priority to three of these additional churches: Raritan in New Jersey, and Lancaster and Tulpehocken in Pennsylvania.

Raritan had been split by a pastor who had no credentials other than being vetted by colonial Lutherans of suspect qualification themselves. Lancaster, in a region of concentrated German settlement, was spiraling

11. Mühlenberg, *Journals*, 1:79.
12. See *Augsburg Confession*, art. 14.

into schism at the hands of a Swedish Lutheran pastor who was acting on behalf of the Moravians. Tulpehocken, due to its Palatine legacy as one of the first important concentrations of German settlers in Pennsylvania, held a place of esteem in Mühlenberg's heart.[13] Tulpehocken, home to Conrad Weiser, had dismissed the ubiquitous Johann Caspar Stöver, an energetic organizer of Lutheran congregations throughout Pennsylvania, but whose theological credentials were incomplete.[14] Justly or not, Mühlenberg was coveted in Tulpehocken for his vetted credentials and regular call. Rightly or not, Stöver was affronted and became a rival to Mühlenberg until his own death in the 1770s. They would experience rapprochement for only a few years in the late 1760s.[15]

But Mühlenberg was unlike the great majority of the Germans he was serving, and so were most of the pastors who followed in the Halle mission over the next twenty-seven years. Tending mostly to be Hanoverians and Prussians from *burgher* backgrounds and guild families, these clergy were accustomed to the status that the German *pfarrer* held in the established state churches. The Palatines and Württembergers and other southwest Germans who had first arrived with the Palatine Transport and continued to stream to America in large numbers, were relishing their freedom from those systems. Some churches had operated for decades without a regular pastor in call and the lay-leaders had accrued those powers to themselves.[16]

Mühlenberg learned his lessons early and well. By the time of his report of events in 1745 he had decided that his call in Pennsylvania was permanent, confirmed in his marriage to Anna Maria Weiser. Between 1744 and 1770 only thirteen pastors were sent from Halle to the Pennsylvania field, mere drops in an ocean of need, and only a few of these were quality pastors at the outset. Most, though flawed, learned from Mühlenberg the best practices of ministry to immigrant, cash-poor, democratically-minded Lutherans. The Halle missionaries that

13. Mühlenberg, *Journals*, 2:467, 473. Even after Conrad Weiser's death in 1760, his widow, Ann Eve, survived into the late 1770s, and Tulpehocken remained a hub for the Weiser family.

14. Glatfelter, *Pastors and People*, 104.

15. Regarding the temporary peace with Stöver: On his acceptance into the Ministerium in 1763, see Spaeth et al., *Documentary History*, 73; on reports of a schism at which he was the center in Lebanon, and decision to remove him from the roles in 1772, see Spaeth et al., *Documentary History*, 133.

16. For an in-depth discussion of these dynamics, see Roeber, *Palatines, Liberty, and Property*, 243–45.

succeeded overcame their own early tendencies toward being autocratic, and molded themselves to their new socio-cultural circumstances.

Other European Lutheran institutions also took a hand in developing the colonial Lutheran Church. The most important of these were the Lutheran Orthodox consistory of Hamburg, the immigrant Lutheran *classis* in Amsterdam, and the University of Tübingen in the Duchy of Württemberg, Conrad Weiser's homeland. The impact of the last is mostly felt in that its faculty agreed to bestow a Lutheran ordination upon Count von Zinzendorf. Somewhat later but still early in Mühlenberg's career, the congregation in Lancaster, having suffered a conflicted ministry with an inexperienced Halle missionary, by-passed the Mühlenberg-Halle nexus and wrote to Tübingen requesting a pastor. Tübingen sent Johann Gerock in 1754. In 1760 Gerock is shown to be an active member of the Pennsylvania Ministerium, but when a conflict emerged in Lancaster in 1763 he protested that if a change were to be made in his call it would need to be ratified by the consistory of Tübingen.[17] Gerock's mixed experience is typical of that of the called and vetted pastors who did not pass through the Halle-London Royal Chapel network.

Mühlenberg's journals of the early years focus on the effort to ground the Halle mission in the congregations that called him, to establish his legitimacy as opposed to various imposters, and to conduct evangelism by personal visitation. In the years of the French and Indian War he journaled little, and in those years the new synod went on hiatus from its annual meetings. These were also the years when the Mühlenbergs were raising five young children in their home in Providence. By the 1760s the synod meetings were resumed and the journals become devoted to the problems of a domesticated church and family, and the evolving concerns and growing clout of the Pennsylvania Germans in colonial politics. Although Heinrich Mühlenberg's ministry was all-absorbing, over time he developed convictions on American public life, starting with the issues his father-in-law had faced.

## The Emerging Sympathies of Heinrich Mühlenberg

Mühlenberg accompanied Conrad Weiser on part of his journey to the Onondaga Council Fire in 1750. He saw firsthand Weiser's diplomatic

---

17. Glatfelter, *Pastors and People*, 190; Spaeth et al., *Documentary History*, 45, 79–80; Mühlenberg, *Journals*, 1:693.

skill in dealing with a variety of characters, from the well-mannered to scoundrels, noting on August 20, "Weiser's name was held in great esteem wherever we went on this whole journey."[18]

Unlike the years covering the American Revolution in which no month is unrepresented, the Journals have only a handful of entries for the years of the French and Indian War, 1754–1760. There is no entry at all for 1755, thus no comment on Braddock's defeat in July and the violence on the frontier that followed in the autumn. The only entry for 1756 focuses on an account of the massacre of the Moravian missionaries at Gnadenhütten on the Wyoming River at the end of March. Mühlenberg reports that this episode established the credentials of the Moravians as sharers in suffering rather than as secret agents of the French.[19] This is followed by a description of homes filled with refugees from that spring's raids.

There are no entries for 1757 or 1758. Tappert and Doberstein note that journals were likely kept during these years but are no longer extant.[20] On the other hand the punctiliousness of daily entries later in his life also suggests that he had more discretionary time in his retirement to reflect both on the day's mundane events and on the sweeping events of history. On October 30, 1759, he held a "solemn service of thanksgiving for the glorious acts of God . . . to the unspeakable consolation of His Protestant Church that was sitting in ashes." He then lists three victories of allied German and British arms against the French, including the capture of Quebec. A fourth item was an incorrect report of a victory by Frederick II of Prussia, which was actually Prussia's worst defeat. Mühlenberg lists the texts he used for his homily and the hymns that were sung, including "Now Thank We All Our God" [*nun danket alle Gott*].[21]

The entry for July 15, 1760, notes only briefly the funeral of Conrad Weiser. Mühlenberg was more expansive in his correspondence to the Halle directors, as found in the second volume of the *Halle Nachrichten*.[22] While there is little to hint at either his approval or disapproval of Weiser's approach to diplomacy, Mühlenberg would become much more pointed on political matters beginning in 1763.

18. Mühlenberg, *Journals*, 1:248.
19. Mühlenberg, *Journals*, 1:386–88.
20. Mühlenberg, *Journals*, 1:xviii.
21. Mühlenberg, *Journals*, 1:419.
22. Wallace, *Conrad Weiser*, 576n6.

When Conrad Weiser died in 1760 Pennsylvania was safe: the Native Nations were at peace, and the French had been vanquished in North America. However, Weiser's death coincided with the promotion of Jeffrey Amherst as the British crown's commander-in-chief of royal military forces in North America. Had the Holder of the Heavens lived just three years more one wonders whether Pontiac of the Ottawa would have found occasion to wreak such havoc on the Atlantic Seaboard. Pontiac's War, coming on the heels of the Treaty of Brussels, signified a sea-change in the way that the Native Nations and white settlers would relate to one another.

Though France had lost the war it was not the perception of Pontiac and other war captains that their own nations were beaten. Detecting long-term threats to their own cultural survival, Pontiac and his allies became disinclined to tolerate the squatters, poachers and rum-traders pouring over the hills. Suspicions of English motives were further aggravated when Amherst set policies that treated the Native Nations as subject peoples rather than as partners in trade. It is inconceivable that, had Weiser been alive after 1760, he would have supported Amherst's new tactics.

In May 1763 the Ohio frontier exploded with coordinated attacks by war parties on forts and settlements in what became known as Pontiac's Conspiracy, or Pontiac's War. The uprising was a race war in which solidarity was measured in the starkest terms: Red Man vs. White Man; Native vs. Settler. What we call today crimes against humanity, ethnic cleansing, and genocide, were the order of the day during Pontiac's War. The Native Nations as French proxies had pursued limited objectives, targeting settlers on disputed lands and squatters on reserved lands; in Pontiac's War the objective was to drive the European settlers into the sea.

Among settlers, frustration with the government of Pennsylvania now reached a fever pitch. Over-extended militia units were not receiving support from the provincial government. Refugees from the frontier groused that neutral Native Americans lived on the public dole while victims of raids were not even offered tax relief.[23]

A loosely-organized militia, the Paxton Boys, began to drive toward Philadelphia with their grievances in December. Lancaster lay in their path. A peaceful Native band, the Conestoga, had long settled on proprietary estates in the area; the sheriff removed them to Lancaster's jail for

---

23. Silver, *Our Savage Neighbors*, 182–83.

their protection. The Paxton Boys descended on Lancaster, swarmed the jail and massacred its inhabitants on December 27, 1763.[24]

One of the stated objectives of the Paxton Boys was to enter Philadelphia and take into their own custody a group of Delaware that had been Christianized by the Moravian missionaries and who were now under the protection of provincial authorities. Benjamin Franklin was asked by the proprietor John Penn to raise a militia and defend the city against the backcountry rioters, and the residents of Philadelphia rallied to prevent a repeat of the atrocity in Lancaster.[25] This militia included some two hundred Quakers who mustered for duty with their firearms.[26] The Governor's proclamation of February 1, 1764, as reported by Mühlenberg, took exception to the under-participation of the city's German citizens in its defense during the crisis, and raised suspicions that "perhaps the Germans might be making common cause with the malcontents or so-called rebels, etc."[27]

Both the mobilization of the city's Quakers and the aspersions cast upon the city's Germans provoked Heinrich Mühlenberg, who journaled on "the opinion and sentiment of various ones of our German citizens." He makes four numbered points which expose a distinctively German-immigrant point-of-view: First, many German residents had been persuaded that so-called friendly or neutral or Christianized natives, including those "who had lived among the so-called Moravian brethren," were also guilty of killing "a number of German" settlers. Second, there was collusion between Herrnhuters, Quakers, and indigenous peoples to advance their own selfish interests, "without considering at all that they had murdered their fellow Christians." Third, in a grievance anticipating what the Paxton Boys would eventually publish themselves, there was resentment that indigenous peoples were allowed to live under protection at public expense, when there was not "the least evidence of human sympathy, etc. when Germans and other settlers on the frontiers were

---

24. Griffin, *American Leviathan*, 65. See also Silver, *Our Savage Neighbors*, 174–85; Anderson, *Crucible of War*, 611–12.

25. As Franklin puts it, "I wrote a pamphlet entitled a *Narrative* [of the Late Massacres] to strengthen the hands of our weak Government, by rendering the proceedings of the rioters unpopular and odious." On forming the association "at the Governor's request . . . we having no Militia" some one thousand signed on (Zall, *Franklin on Franklin*, 228).

26. Brock, *Pacifism in the United States*, 156.

27. Mühlenberg, *Journals*, 2:18–19.

massacred and destroyed in the most inhuman manner." Fourth, the Germans in Philadelphia would muster in defense of the King, but "they would not wage war against their own suffering fellow citizens for the sake of the Quakers and Herrnhuters and their creatures or instruments, the double-dealing Indians [sic]."[28]

Heinrich Mühlenberg distanced himself from these sentiments in his closing thoughts, adding that it is difficult to make a judgment in a conflict when tempers are so high.[29] Yet a glimpse of Mühlenberg's own sympathies is captured in the entry for February 5, a Sunday, which described an alarm in the city that evening. Quakers and Herrnhuters ran to hastily reinforce the ramparts near where the missionized Native Americans were quartered.

> Some remarked concerning all this that it seemed strange that such preparations should be made against one's own fellow citizens and Christians, whereas no one ever took so much trouble to protect from the Indians His Majesty's subjects and citizens on the frontier.[30]

Alarms rang through the city until day-break.

For Mühlenberg, since the sword in the hand of civil government is given by God then it followed that providing for the common defense was government's first and minimum duty.[31] Failure in that responsibility promoted violence and led to anarchy; thus the key issue was that the inaction of the provincial government had fomented the crisis of the Paxton Boys campaign. It was folly that the same men who did nothing to help their citizens in the west were now brandishing their rifles against those very citizens who were now seeking redress for their grievances. It is a stark contrast that although many Palatines in New York fifty years earlier had seized upon friendship with the Mohawk in order to escape the oppressions of Livingston Manor, the Paxton Boys were now acting in irreconcilable alienation against Native Americans. Yet it is the grievance that the Paxton Boys had *in common* with the Palatines which seems to have been of greater ethical moment to Mühlenberg; the Paxton Boys by their demonstrations were unveiling the hypocrisy and dereliction of duty among those in power.

28. Mühlenberg, *Journals*, 2:18–19.
29. Mühlenberg, *Journals*, 2:18–19.
30. Mühlenberg, *Journals*, 2:18–19.
31. Mühlenberg, *Journals*, 2:55; cf. 1:709.

The Paxton Boys reached Germantown on February 7, and appointed leaders among themselves to meet with a delegation of city and provincial dignitaries from Philadelphia. The meeting was convened by Benjamin Franklin, who plainly informed them of the city's defensive measures. The Paxton Boys were invited to share their grievances, but only on the condition that they stand down. The Paxton militia camped for the night around Germantown and sent a handful to scout the breastworks in Philadelphia. After obtaining an agreement to have their grievances published in a pamphlet they dispersed over the next couple of days.[32]

During the Germantown conference Mühlenberg remained in his home, ill with a lower bronchial condition which he had started to suffer a week earlier. The Provost of the Swedish Church, Karl Wrangel, represented the city's Lutherans in the meeting.[33] Mühlenberg's illness coincides with his pattern of sickness and health, overwork and exhaustion. At the same time his reticence and withdrawal from leadership in the Paxton Boys crisis is a reflection of the attitudes held by Philadelphia's Germans, who at the most offered tepid support for the government.[34]

## Swinging the German Vote

When in the 1760s the parliament of Great Britain began to look to their Atlantic seaboard provinces as a means of revenue, the American public was affronted in at least three overlapping ways: First, there was the concern over the economic impact of taxes. Many now agree that this impact was or would have been negligible as the proposed colonial burdens never came close to the tax rates for subjects living in Great Britain itself. Second, was the political philosophy which objected to the usurpation of the authority of each province's representative assemblies as revenue-raising bodies. Third, these taxes were justified as a means of defraying the crown's expenses for protecting the colonies. Royalist advocates, such as the essayist Samuel Johnson, claimed that the redcoats had won America for the colonists and had protected them from French conquest, and now the colonists needed to help pay the costs of that war. This narrative of the late war with the French rang especially hollow to

32. Silver, *Our Savage Neighbors*, 188–90.
33. Mühlenberg, *Journals*, 2:22.
34. Mühlenberg, *Journals*, 2:19.

Pennsylvanians, who had experienced reluctant and sporadic military measures from their government in the late 1750s and then again in 1763. In Pennsylvania the non-Quaker public's chief grievance was that government was not doing enough to provide for the common defense; neither their assembly and proprietor in their mutual distrust, nor the royal military commanders, had the will to produce an effective deterrent to the depredations of war parties on the frontiers.

Indeed, Pennsylvania's government had as much as admitted defeat to the only enemies that most Pennsylvanians had seen—the Natives who had risen against them. Pontiac's subsequent uprising only emphasized the ineffectiveness of military policy in the hands of either Quakers or redcoats. The frontiers bled freely, and gridlock dominated the relationship between assembly and proprietor, as much in 1763 as in 1755. Mühlenberg's disgust with both the Quaker assembly and the proprietors is palpable when he is informed that, just six weeks after the Paxton Boys had dispersed, the proprietary agents had left town and the assembly had gone into recess.[35] Furthermore, the peace that finally sent Pontiac's warriors home was a tacit admission of the defeat of the colonial provinces.

Mühlenberg identified two main parties that emerged to vie for power in Pennsylvania by the 1760s; most English and German voters supported one or the other. The Quaker Party, long dominant in the Assembly, had the force of Pennsylvania's tradition behind it, and its pacific views were appreciated by the tiny number of German Anabaptists and Radical Pietists such as were found in Bethlehem, Ephrata, and in farms and settlements in Lancaster County—at least among those adherents who did not scruple about voting in secular elections. Opposing the Quaker Party was the Church Party, which joined together a coalition of English-speaking Presbyterians and Anglicans with German-speaking Lutheran and Reformed, all of these being mainline churches which enjoyed official establishment in European contexts.

The first suggestive episode as to Mühlenberg's own convictions regarding Britain's parliamentary policies is that he led a liturgy of *te deum*, praise to God, when news reached Philadelphia of the repeal of the Stamp Act in 1765. A second episode was the unsuccessful attempt, pursued by Benjamin Franklin, to swing the German vote in support of his own political philosophy. As the author of the militia law in 1756 he had obtained credibility among those who wanted the government

---

35. Mühlenberg, *Journals*, 2:54–56.

to function rather than submit to paralysis. In 1764 he proposed appealing to the King and Parliament to remove the proprietary Penn family from their inherited governance and establish Pennsylvania as a Crown Colony, and he both hoped and assumed the Germans would follow suit on the strength of their disillusionment with government gridlock.

In one sense Franklin had good reason to be optimistic. The most organized Lutherans, superintended by Mühlenberg through the Pennsylvania Ministerium, were under the patronage of Halle Pietism. The Halle Pietists were mainline, enjoying official and semi-official patronage and recognition in various German and European governments even after the turn toward rationalism in Prussia. Yet on this point Franklin's genius ran afoul of the conviction of Mühlenberg and tens of thousands of German Lutherans, Halle-oriented or otherwise. When delegates of Dr. Franklin visited Mühlenberg hoping to add his signature to the petition to make Pennsylvania a crown colony, Mühlenberg refused to sign. Involvement in political affairs was not a function of his vocation: "Our office rather required us to pray to God the Supreme Ruler for protection and mercy and to admonish our fellow German citizens to fear God, honor the king, and love our neighbor, etc."[36]

This Lutheran conviction was unlike the longstanding American tradition, Calvinist in orientation, in which Congregationalist and Presbyterian pastors freely engaged in political discourse and took partisan, political leadership. This Lutheran theological orientation meant that German Lutherans vigorously participated in the elections, yet carried with them a conservative disposition of respect to sovereign power and to the state as already constituted.

Supporters of the proprietary government dug up an anti-German article Franklin had published in the *Pennsylvania Gazette* in 1751,[37] and which had reappeared in 1755 in *The Gentleman's Magazine*. The ethnic German publisher Christopher Sauer then reprinted the unflattering paragraph, and ostensibly to keep his German-language readership informed, was careful to explain exactly what the term "boor" meant and resorted to the term frequently. Franklin's rejoinders were weak and unconvincing. He was swept out of the assembly, along with several

---

36. Mühlenberg, *Journals*, 2:55.

37. Franklin, *Essays*, 367–374. The expression is found near the article's conclusion, 374.

Quakers, in an election that saw the turnout of voters more than triple.[38] Mühlenberg fairly gloats:

> There was great rejoicing and great bitterness in the political circles of the city, since it was reported that the German church people had gained a victory in the election. . . . Never before in the history of Pennsylvania, they say, have so many people assembled for an election. The English and German Quakers, the Herrnhuters, Mennonites, and Schwenkfelders formed one party, and the English of the High Church and the Presbyterian Church, the German Lutheran, and German Reformed joined the other party and gained the upper hand—a thing heretofore unheard of.[39]

Just weeks after being swept out of the assembly, Franklin was considered for a new assignment to be the Pennsylvania Assembly's official agent in London. German Lutheran laypeople circulated a petition that urged the Assembly not to appoint him.[40] Franklin did receive the commission, however, and began an illustrious diplomatic career.

## Personal Loss and Disappointment

With the war in France concluded and the seas again open for travel, the Mühlenbergs sent their three oldest sons to the Kingdom of Prussia for their education. They embarked together in April, 1763. Friedrich and Gotthilf Heinrich Ernst, ages 13 and 9, were sent to the boarding school of the Halle Institutes. It was hoped that the Reverend Fathers would be able to arrange a suitable apprenticeship, on terms of indenture, for Peter, aged 16.[41] Through the years of the children's sojourn their parents would be unable to visit.

The three Mühlenbergs left for Europe when the fourth and youngest of the Mühlenberg boys, Enoch Samuel, was four years old. Tragedy struck the family at home when in February 1764, Samuel took ill and died in his father's arms at the age of five. Two months later Anna Maria

---

38. Silver, *Our Savage Neighbors*, 219–24; cf. Isaacson, *Benjamin Franklin*, 214–18.

39. Mühlenberg, *Journals*, 2:123.

40. Mühlenberg, *Journals*, 2:140; cf. Isaacson, *Benjamin Franklin*, 214–15. This narrative completely excludes the participation of the German Americans in Franklin's defeat, stating only that John Dickinson had orchestrated the petition against Franklin being sent to England.

41. Mühlenberg, *Journals*, 1:623; cf. Wallace, *Muhlenbergs of Pennsylvania*, 56–58.

gave birth to Catherine Salome, who died at the age of 16 months in August 1765.[42] In that interval, the second pastor of the Philadelphia Church, Johann Friedrich Handschuh, died in October of 1764.[43] Although he had shown less than stellar competence and judgment in his career in Pennsylvania, Handschuh's death made the shortage of pastors even more acute.

Peter was the first to return from Europe, his apprenticeship having gone badly, causing embarrassment to the Halle directors who had arranged it.[44] Peter was sent to apprentice for the ministry with the Provost of the Swedish Church in Philadelphia, Karl Wrangel. Heinrich Mühlenberg's effusive politeness in correspondence with the Reverend Fathers includes the praise with which Peter was being received as a preacher.[45] In 1770 Mühlenberg asked for his other two sons to be returned from Halle. By then they had graduated from the institutes and were attending Halle University. They returned to Pennsylvania in the company of another Halle missionary, J. C. Kunze, who would soon become their brother-in-law. By the end of 1770 all three sons were serving in the pulpits of the Pennsylvania Ministerium, and a supply of pastors vetted by Halle in the late 1760s reflected a boost in competence and character compared to previous missionaries sent to Pennsylvania.[46]

Even so the 1770s did not bring the stability to the Lutheran ministry which Mühlenberg desired, as churches and pastoral egos clashed, causing disappointments to Mühlenberg's own aspirations. Also in 1770 his wife, Anna Maria, began to decline in health, suffering seizures that Mühlenberg described as epilepsy.[47] As the decade advanced he felt the wear and tear of his own years.

## Enthusiasm and Dread

Mühlenberg turned 63 in September of 1774. Although contemplating retirement, he was commissioned by the Reverend Fathers in Europe to take an extended trip to Georgia. As will be described in chapter 8,

42. Mühlenberg, *Journals*, 2:69, 72, 259.
43. Mühlenberg, *Journals*, 2:124.
44. Wallace, *Muhlenbergs of Pennsylvania*, 59–66.
45. Wallace, *Muhlenbergs of Pennsylvania*, 72–73.
46. Mühlenberg, *Journals*, 2:463; Spaeth et al., *Documentary History*, 121–28.
47. Mühlenberg, *Journals*, 2:446.

Mühlenberg's task was to mediate a conflict between Lutheran pastors in the Halle-sponsored ethnic German settlement of Ebenezer. For this extended itineration he took along Anna Maria and Polly, their unmarried nineteen year-old daughter. They placed their youngest daughter Sally, eight years old, in the care of their daughter and son-in-law, the Kunzes. The itineration took the Mühlenbergs away from Pennsylvania for about six months. They returned in early 1775 to find the German Lutherans in Philadelphia in an uproar.

Mühlenberg was accused of being a royalist and of conspiring to have the province come under the Anglican Church.[48] These surmises were at least plausible, considering that he had helped arrange two crossover ordinations to the benefit of both Anglicans and Lutherans.[49] The second of these ordinations concerned his own son Peter in 1774, whom he agreed should be sent to London to be ordained as an Anglican in order to meet the terms of call to an ethnic-German congregation in the Shenandoah Valley of Virginia. Although Lutheran in liturgy, the Shenandoah Germans had chosen to come under Virginia's Anglican establishment. Peter was serving in Virginia by the time his parents had gone to Georgia.[50]

From there the rumors had taken a turn to the ridiculous. It was supposed that instead of Georgia the elder Mühlenberg had gone to London to participate in the rebaptism of George III into Catholicism, and that Mühlenberg was angling to be installed as the Catholic primate over North America.[51] Since no pro-Catholic sympathy can be found in any of Mühlenberg's copious reflections and voluminous discourse, this rumor signals the depth of resentment and fear among Germans following the passage of the Quebec Act.

Then in 1775 blood was spilt in New England, and the colonies were declared by the King to be in a state of open rebellion. Those with patriot sympathies rallied to form Committees of Safety and of Correspondence. The Halle-missionary pastors Heinrich Helmuth and J. C. Kunze wrote letters to their overseas director at the Halle Institutes, Gottlieb Anastasius Freylinghausen. Helmuth's letter is described by A. G. Roeber as an example of the fervency of the patriots, with which Helmuth seems to

---

48. Mühlenberg, *Journals*, 2:693.
49. Mühlenberg, *Journals*, 2:370; Wallace, *Muhlenbergs of Pennsylvania*, 80–82.
50. Wallace, *Muhlenbergs of Pennsylvania*, 80–82.
51. Mühlenberg, *Journals*, 2:693.

have been personally infected.[52] As the war picked up in pace and ferocity the elderly Heinrich Mühlenberg was not a party to the enthusiasm described by Helmuth among the young men. Instead, Mühlenberg discerned that it was time to enter semi-retirement.

Using funds disbursed from Halle as a bequest, Heinrich Mühlenberg converted a stone farm-house in Providence into a modest retirement home for pastors of the Pennsylvania Ministerium, knowing that he and Anna Maria would be the first residents. The bequest and the retirement home were both under the trusteeship of the Reverend Fathers in Halle and London.[53] In his journal entries through the summer of 1776 he alternates between his comments on the national momentum towards independence with reports of the gradual transfer of his belongings from Philadelphia to Providence.[54]

Mühlenberg hoped that his new home in his favorite town was far enough from Philadelphia for the war to pass him by.[55] In 1777, scarcely a year since he moved in, Philadelphia became the center of the war. It was occupied by royalists from the fall of 1777 through the spring of 1778. Providence is just a few miles north of Valley Forge, where the patriot army camped for the winter. This put his home within range of hungry patriot soldiers foraging for food. It also meant that he had a frequent guest that winter: his son, Brigadier General Peter Mühlenberg.

Peter had not remained long in the Anglican ministry. "Contrary" to the father's "will and warning" he had traded the highest of all callings for a worldly office, supposing that the difference he might make as an army officer in temporal matters was greater than the difference he could make as a pastor in eternal matters.[56] This stress on the relationship, however, is little commented on or criticized by Mühlenberg, the quote above coming from a letter he had written to a loyalist friend in New York in the full expectation that Hessian officers in Philadelphia would read it, as discussed below. However in a private correspondence dated March 7, 1776, he wrote, "The young people are right in fighting for their God-given native liberty."[57]

52. Roeber, *Palatines*, 304.
53. Mühlenberg, *Journals*, 2:712–14.
54. Mühlenberg, *Journals*, 2:721–25.
55. Mühlenberg, *Journals*, 2:713.
56. Mühlenberg, *Journals*, 3:125.
57. Wallace, *Muhlenbergs of Pennsylvania*, 123.

## Heinrich Melchior Mühlenberg on Three Sides

The seeming contradictions may be a function of Mühlenberg's own humanity; rarely do we find a person absolutely consistent in all their principles and constant in all their convictions. On reflection the statements do not collide all that much: That young people are right to fight does not necessarily infer that clergy should resign their ordinations in order to take lesser, worldly offices in politics or the military. Furthermore, the fight for God-given native liberty had not yet become a revolution for independence, but rather was the effort to reject parliamentary supremacy over the Atlantic provinces when clearly such a projection of power had done little to promote security and well-being for the colonists.

By September of 1777 Heinrich Mühlenberg was 66, but his hopes for a quiet retirement and safe retreat from the alarms of war were dashed. Militia desecrated his church, continentals raided his cellar, his nephew had been gravely wounded at Brandywine and spent three days being nursed in Providence on his return to Tulpehocken. In addition Anna Maria was ailing and his daughter Polly had taken up with a boisterous Irish settler who carried about him an air, if not of outright scandal, then certainly of riotous irreverence. With the capture of Philadelphia another of his daughters, "Peggy" Kunze, was behind British lines with her husband, the only pastor for St. Michael's-Zion to remain in the city. All the while he feared that his son Peter, who in three years had gone from being an Anglican priest to a general in the Continental Army, was a target for Tory partisans.

Valley Forge was on the west side of the Schuylkill River, and the British force in Philadelphia was on the east side. Providence was further upstream, seven miles to the rear of the patriots, but it was on the same bank as the British army. In November Heinrich Mühlenberg learned from his daughter Peggy in Philadelphia that he was an object of suspicion to the royalists in charge of the city.[58] The threat was reinforced when Caspar Weyberg, the pastor of Philadelphia's German Reformed Church, was jailed for much of the winter for preaching desertion to Hessian soldiers that had come to church.[59] Mühlenberg fretted that the continentals had left a path open for mounted British Hussars to make off with him before the patriots could help.[60] Peter shared his father's fears, and urged

---

58. Mühlenberg, *Journals*, 3:106.
59. Good, *History of the Reformed Church*, 609; cf. Mühlenberg, *Journals*, 3:128.
60. Mühlenberg, *Journals*, 3:115; cf. Wallace, *Muhlenbergs of Pennsylvania*, 154–55.

his brothers to move their parents to Tulpehocken. Heinrich refused to move in deference to Anna Maria, who likely wanted to keep her seizures and condition from burdening others outside her own home.[61] In hindsight they need not have worried about a royalist operation to seize a retiring Lutheran cleric. Still, at the time the anxiety in the Mühlenbergs was real, as was the struggle in the pastor's own conscience.

His personal issues aside, his ethical and theological premises were shaken by the heightened stakes of a civil war. In Heinrich Mühlenberg's case a distinction should be made between his state of *emotions* versus his state of *convictions*. From the Paxton Boys riots in 1764 and all throughout the entire course of the War of Independence, Mühlenberg held consistently to two theological-ethical axioms: First, he held the premise that God saves sinners by grace alone through the sinner's justification by faith alone. This doctrine of divine, unearned mercy holds fast to a pessimistic view of human nature and its innate sinfulness, along with deep faith in the promises of God for mercy on all who believe. Second, he adhered to the Lutheran "Two Kingdoms" principle stated by Martin Luther in his treatise "On Worldly Authority,"[62] which was given further shape by the reformer in the Large Catechism and by his sixteenth-century colleagues in the *Augsburg Confession*, Articles 16 and 28.[63] The Kingdom of the World was the sphere of human action which, were it not for God's redeeming interventions through the Cross of Christ and proclamation of the gospel, would belong wholly to the Devil. The Kingdom of Heaven was that sphere of divine perfection and joy to which the gospel bore witness. There could be no higher calling then to be a called and ordained servant of Christ in the Church; by comparison the ambitions of the world were petty, and temporary rather than eternal.

Mühlenberg trusted Luther's logic that, since a wretched humanity was dependent on the mercies of an all-wise, all-powerful God who governed history, this inferred a Two Kingdoms social and political view.[64] These axioms, as Mühlenberg and his superiors in Halle Pietism understood them, made it both 1) impossible for him to embrace the triumphalist claims of either partisan side and 2) made it quite possible for

61. Wallace, *Muhlenbergs of Pennsylvania*, 155.
62. Luther, "Temporal Authority," 655–703.
63. Kolb and Wengert, *Book of Concord*, 48, 90–103.

64. The view is political in that it carries implications for how one engages one's society and government. It is not, however, a *partisan* view, by which is meant that one is aligned with a particular faction or socio-economic ideology.

him to expect the worst of sinful behaviors from both sides. Mühlenberg consistently abided by the constraints of his office, publicly maintaining a neutral stance between the warring factions. In his reflections he parsed the inherent contradictions in the ethics of the War of Independence in order to help himself live out his faith in a nuanced, complex application of the Lutheran Two Kingdoms doctrine.

In a 1942 article Tappert paid more attention to Mühlenberg's emotional state, which in his *Journals* are frequently self-disclosed as nervous and fretting. Tappert used these self-disclosures of feelings as the lens through which to interpret Mühlenberg's convictions.[65] While Tappert sees Mühlenberg evolving in "imperceptible stages" from loyalist sympathies toward patriotism, nevertheless, "There is no doubt that the anxieties caused by the war helped to make him a broken, old man."[66] Tappert's conclusion that Mühlenberg held to a neutrality that was anxious and indecisive has informed subsequent arguments by scholars.[67]

The Lutheran church officer, Bishop Samuel Zeiser, is an exception. In a published response to an article by Faith Rohrbough, Zeiser affirmed that, "theological considerations, rather than political inclinations, prompted his words."[68] Despite anxiety and self-doubt, Mühlenberg's stance of neutrality was both principled in theology and decisive in practice; it was a stance in which he persevered even when it endangered his personal safety. The American Revolution was a cross to bear, and Mühlenberg bore with it as a chastening from God for his own sins and for the sins in the land.

## Pietist Networks on Three Sides

While his neutrality provoked hostility from elements in the opposed factions, Mühlenberg was also able to retain warm relationships with partisans and sympathizers on each side as well. Among the loyalists a personality that stands out is a taverner in New York City, David Grimm, a Lutheran elder in the "German" Lutheran congregation.

As a royalist stronghold from the time that Washington's Continental Army was expelled in 1776, New York City was a haven for loyalists

65. Tappert, "Henry Melchior Mühlenberg," 284–301.
66. Tappert, "Henry Melchior Mühlenberg," 284–301.
67. Rohrbough, "Political Maturation," 35–52.
68. Zeiser quoted in Rohrbough, "Political Maturation," 53–59.

until after the war's official conclusion in 1783—two years after the patriot victory at Yorktown, when the British and their German auxiliaries sailed away to Europe. Until then, in New York City, ethnic German merchants and tavern-keepers served German auxiliary troops as gladly as Anglophone loyalists served the British troops. This was Grimm's setting and his vocation.

The earliest that David Grimm (also Grim) appears in Mühlenberg's *Journals* is in reference to a letter Mühlenberg intends to send to him in 1773.[69] By then their relationship had been long established, and Grimm is likely to have been influential in securing Friedrich Mühlenberg's call to the "German" Lutheran congregation in New York City in 1774. The church was disappointed to lose their pastor just two years later, when Friedrich joined the exodus of patriots in flight from the city.

The occupation of the coastal city by the largest concentration of royalist forces in North America makes it unsurprising that, within the colony of New York, the ratio of patriot sentiment to population seems to increase in proportion to one's proximity to the frontier. Bernard Hausihl was clearly safe as a loyalist in New York City's older "Dutch" Lutheran congregation, while David Grimm prospered as a loyalist tavern-keeper and retained his role as a Lutheran elder of the "German" congregation. Part of his duty on behalf of the church was to network with German auxiliary chaplains to supply their vacant pulpit.[70] Near Albany, however, Samuel Schwerdtfeger, another associate of the Pennsylvania Ministerium, was arrested by patriots ahead of General Burgoyne's royalist invasion from Canada. Although persecuted and harassed, Schwerdtfeger was never removed from his pulpit.[71] He and other German pastors in the vicinity were targets of partisan hostility as late as April of 1782.[72] Further west in the colony, a large patriot militia was raised in the Mohawk Valley in 1777 under the command of the Palatine-descended Nicholas

---

69. Mühlenberg, *Journals*, 1:573.

70. David Grimm appears by name in the autobiographical account of Chaplain Philipp Waldeck of the Waldeck Battalion, who preached in the German Lutheran congregation in New York on April 12, 1778. See Waldeck, *Eighteenth-Century America*, 62–63.

71. Mühlenberg, *Journals*, 1:50–51. Muhlenberg comments without much sympathy that Schwerdtfeger had "meddled in political affairs which did not belong to his office." cf. Mühlenberg, *Journals*, 1:266. Schwerdtfeger's absence from the annual meeting of the Pennsylvania Ministerium is noted, along with others, meaning that he was eligible and expected to be in attendance.

72. Mühlenberg, *Journals*, 1:482.

Herkimer, a Reformed layman. They fought a bloody battle to a stalemate with a large force of Native Nations warriors in an effort to raise the siege of Fort Stanwyx, further described in chapter 5.

By contrast the occupation of Philadelphia proved to be comparatively short-lived, but no one would have predicted so in the fall of 1777. After his return from Georgia in 1775, when that round of rumors and accusations subsided, it appears that the supporters of Mühlenberg's leadership at St. Michael's-Zion tended to be patriotic in sympathy, while those who opposed him tended to be royalists. Perhaps, even in the early months of the War of Independence, hints of these sympathies did not escape the notice of Halle Institutes Director G. A. Freylinghausen. Two of the Halle-sponsored Pennsylvania Ministerium pastors, Heinrich Helmuth in Lancaster and J. C. Kunze in Philadelphia, sent letters to the Halle Institutes in Germany in August of 1775. Both pastors described patriot fervor among the Germans, which may have provoked Freylinghausen to respond with a letter dated June 1, 1776. It would be the late fall of 1777 before Mühlenberg was apprised of the contents of this epistle from the director in Halle, and of what the Reverend Father expected of the Pennsylvania Ministerium relative to the "civil unrest" in the American colonies.[73]

Some background in Director Freylinghausen's career and the trajectory of the Halle Institutes themselves will help to set the letter in context. G. A. Freylinghausen became Inspector of the Latin School of the Halle Institutes in 1742.[74] This was early in the tenure of the overall leadership of the Institutes by August H. Francke's son, Gotthilf A. Francke. It was also two years into the reign of Frederick II, "King in Prussia." As soon as Frederick II succeeded to the throne he had begun favoring rationalists over pietists for appointments to ecclesial offices.[75]

As patronage from Prussia's royalty dissolved, other long-standing sources of benefaction increased in importance.[76] Since 1710 the Halle

---

73. Heinrich Muhlenberg's struggle to maintain neutrality, together with G. A. Freylinghausen's letter of June 1, 1776 and his responses, are treated in earlier publications, the most thorough examination of which is found in Wilson, "Switching Sides," 139–46. The author also published an article focused on Freylinghausen's letter and Muhlenberg's reaction to it in Wilson, "Civil Unrest." Some portions of these earlier treatments are presented here with only slight emendation.

74. Ernst, *Die Direktoren der Franckeshen Stiftungen*, 21.

75. Roeber, *Palatines, Liberty, and Property*, 256.

76. Brecht, *Geschichte des Pietismus*, 2:319–20.

Institutes' mission sponsors included the London SPCK, an ecumenical funding base under the supervision of the Lutheran chaplain in the Court of St. James.[77] Rebellion in North America had the potential for harming Halle's relationship with the SPCK, endangering funding on which they relied not only for their missions in North America but around the world as well, especially and most famously in India. The patronage network was further shaken by the death of F. M. Ziegenhagen, the long-serving court chaplain and head of the London SPCK, in January, 1776.

With these concerns in the foreground, on June 1, 1776, G. A. Freylinghausen composed his circular letter admonishing the clergy of the Pennsylvania Ministerium to neutrality in the midst of the "civil unrest."[78] I have published treatments of this letter elsewhere; what is essential to this study is that G. A. Freylinghausen praises Kunze and Helmuth based on their epistles from the previous August: "The Reverend Pastors . . . in this civil unrest remain within the evangelical boundaries and preach repentance and faith, without mixing themselves in the war, which is not their office." He then expresses his hope that Mühlenberg will follow suit and maintain his neutrality. For Freylinghausen what was most important was that the preachers keep emphasizing repentance, trust, and prayer, since that would encourage their German Lutheran congregants to stay out of the war and be safe.

According to Wilhelm Pasche (1728–1792), Freylinghausen's agent in London as Ziegenhagen's successor, the letter was not sent across the ocean until April, 1777.[79] It found its way to royalist headquarters in New York City, and arrived in Philadelphia only by means of Howe's occupation of the city in the fall. There it was read aloud to J. C. Kunze among others, but sources do not specify by whom, nor was it given over to Pennsylvania Ministerium pastors. The letter had taken nearly a year-and-a-half to reach the theater, and though it rested in the custody of an

---

77. Vethanayagamony, *It Began in Madras*, 159.

78. Mühlenberg et al., *Die Korrespondenz*, 4:730–32. A copy of this letter was retained by the author and is now preserved in the archives of the Franckesche Stiftungen in Halle, Germany.

79. Pasche, "Brief von Kensington." Specifically, the boat was part of the flotilla bringing more Braunschweig reinforcements along with Lady Frederika zu Riedesel and her three children to join General Riedesel in Quebec ahead of the 1777 Albany campaign described in chapter 5.

unknown German officer in Philadelphia, it was never actually delivered to its intended recipient, Heinrich Mühlenberg.[80]

Yet Freylinghausen's clout as Director of the Halle Institutes is evident in the stir that his letter caused, not only among Lutheran clergy, but also among royalist officers. On November 12, 1777, Heinrich Mühlenberg received a letter from J. C. Kunze stating: "The officers are rather unfavorably informed concerning my father-in-law. It is believed that we have not lived up to Professor Freylinghausen's expectations."[81]

Mühlenberg made two replies which the author has treated in depth elsewhere; a summary is sufficient for this study. His first response is a lengthy journal entry which was intended for Freylinghausen's eyes as part of his narrative reports.[82] His second response, similar to the first although it is not an exact duplicate, is a letter to his friend David Grimm in New York City. For claiming not to have read Freylinghausen's letter for himself, Mühlenberg's second-hand knowledge of its content is detailed and precise. In his journal entry he expresses "filial gratitude" for Freylinghausen's "reiteration of the good rule which was inculcated in us when we were called and sent over. . . . What is not our office we are glad not to meddle with, because we are already obliged to do more than we can take care of."[83] While he aligns himself and Halle's missionary pastors with Freylinghausen's policy of neutrality, and shares with him in the Lutheran language of vocation, this barbed critique of Freylinghausen's admonishment is thinly veiled.

Mühlenberg protests that others were pinning on him a guilt by association with his son Peter, the patriot Brigadier General.[84] There is no reason to doubt the sincerity of his dismay over Peter's decision to abandon the highest calling of all for military commissions.[85] What Mühlenberg omits, however, is that in 1776 he had vetted a testimonial for Christian Streit (1749–1812) so that he could cross into Virginia to serve Peter's new regiment as a chaplain.

80. Mühlenberg, *Journals*, 3:101.
81. Mühlenberg, *Journals*, 3:101.
82. Mühlenberg, *Journals*, 3:101–4.
83. Mühlenberg, *Journals*, 3:126.
84. Mühlenberg, *Journals*, 3:126.
85. As described in chapter 6. Throughout vol. 2 of Mühlenberg, *Journals*, Heinrich traces Peter's journey to and from Germany and into and out of ministry.

His second defense was a lengthy letter to David Grimm, composed January 14, 1778.[86] Both sides of the war honored the delivery of correspondence through enemy lines, provided that it was unsealed. That this system was dependable explains Mühlenberg's barbs at the unknown officer of the German auxiliaries who had failed to see to the proper delivery of Freylinghausen's letter. The occasion for writing was that Mühlenberg had received a letter from Grimm dated November 19 but not delivered until January 13.[87] Grimm's letter from November is unfortunately not reproduced in either the Tappert edition of the *Journals* or in Aland's edition of the *Korrespondenz*. However Aland does print the reply, dated January 14, which also appears in full in Mühlenberg's *Journals* entry for January 22nd, 1777.

The letter to Grimm recapitulates much of what he had journaled as his first response. He makes his defense in terms that he expects Grimm to understand and even approve and, perhaps more importantly, that the German officers in Philadelphia—in charge of reading all open German-language correspondence passing through lines—would understand and approve as well. The self-disclosures in Mühlenberg's narrative to Grimm are framed to awaken the sympathy of German officers while at the same time informing them that actions of neutrality are the only actions appropriate to his calling in the Lutheran clergy.[88] It is his hope that the British and German officers in service to the king would not rush to judgment based on the rumors without at least the due process that was the distinctive feature of English law.[89]

He begins his defense to Grimm by stating:

> I am a Hanoverian. . . . I have had the good fortune to be a subject, both by reason of birth and naturalization, of their Royal Majesties George I and George II of glorious memory and also of George III, and up to this time I have neither broken nor transferred my oath of fealty.[90]

He then traces a narrative of his life in which he was frequently targeted by patriots for being a royalist; even the sermon he had preached in 1766 in thanksgiving for the repeal of the Stamp Act was used against him,

---

86. Mühlenberg, *Journals*, 3:123–27.
87. Mühlenberg, *Journals*, 3:121.
88. Mühlenberg, *Journals*, 3:121.
89. Mühlenberg, *Journals*, 3:121.
90. Mühlenberg, *Journals*, 3:121.

because he had "too much flattered the king."⁹¹ During his trip to Ebenezer in Georgia over the winter of 1774–75 there were voices back in Pennsylvania that spread rumors that he had been ousted from his pulpit, had fled to London, and on returning to Pennsylvania would be tarred and feathered as a Tory.⁹²

Then in July of 1775 he and other clergy refused to have their names added to a joint declaration of Lutheran and Reformed communicants which endorsed the patriot cause. The statement, framed by the ethnic German lawyer Lewis Weiss, made compelling use of Romans 13:1–10, as Mühlenberg writes:

> The slogan was Romans 13:1ff, be subject to *the* government which has *power* over you. The people had the weapons in their hands and it was regarded as criminal if one wished to refuse anything to the government in power. To drive out force by force was not in my power, nor was it my vocation, and the tongue of the stoutest orator is no match to the danger of a bayonet in the hand of an angry man.⁹³

The Lutheran theology of vocation [*beruf*]⁹⁴ is one of the consistent themes used by Mühlenberg to advocate for himself and his neutrality. Being called to a vocation of pastoral office makes certain conduct inappropriate, especially when wedded to the ethics that are shaped by a Two Kingdoms theological perspective. Such conduct included: meeting force with force, or, peddling influence in order to steer political outcomes, as he had stated to the delegation from the Congress in 1775. His assessment of the patriots' use of Romans 13 is therefore ambiguous precisely for the reason that Mühlenberg found it compelling.

At this point it is illuminating for this study to interject his response to American Independence, declared eighteen months earlier, in July, 1776. True to his theological assumptions, he acknowledges that the Declaration of Independence was brought about with God's full knowledge and providence. The greater crisis for Mühlenberg came a year later, on July 1, 1777, when the Pennsylvania Assembly required "all white inhabitants of Pennsylvania, eighteen years of age or over, to swear an oath of allegiance and acknowledge the new government as the lawful

---

91. Mühlenberg, *Journals*, 3:124.
92. Mühlenberg, *Journals*, 3:124.
93. Mühlenberg, *Journals*, 3:124–25.
94. Mühlenberg et al., *Die Korrespondenz*, 6:82.

authority."⁹⁵ This brought Mühlenberg to further reflection on Romans 13, and to the writings of the Anglican pastor Thomas Pyle (d. 1756). Mühlenberg states definitively his ethical position: "Be subject to that power which rules and offers protection, or, as it is put, which has the strongest arm and the longest sword."⁹⁶ By the time of his November, 1777 journal entry his thoughts concerning one's duty to government were more fully developed. His defense to G. A. Freylinghausen returns to Romans 13:

> If it is objected that we ceased to pray publicly for His Britannic Majesty George III ever since the declaration of independence [sic] and accordingly committed sin, it may be said in reply that we were not allowed to engage in politics and had to observe the express command of God's Word in Romans 13: Let every soul be subject unto the higher powers which have authority over you and protect you *pro tempore,* or for the time being.... For even the question of sovereignty has become so complicated that it must be decided by the stronger sword.⁹⁷

The "stronger sword" does not here refer to the tensions between the temporal powers and the heavenly kingdom, but rather to the rivalries among temporal powers. This was the view that Mühlenberg held consistently throughout the War of Independence. Early in the conflict in 1775, when the patriot cause was more certain to be defeated than victorious, then even though the patriots held sway in Pennsylvania and made it the seat of the Continental Congress, Mühlenberg resolutely included prayers for the king in his liturgy. However, when the province declared its independence, this new "law for the land" combined with the power of the patriots in the region to enforce it even if only *pro tempore* meant that a consistent two kingdoms ethics of neutrality required that he desist from praying in public for the king.

In his letter to Grimm, as it concerned those choices of his grown children that were "contrary" to their father's "will and warning,"⁹⁸ he cites Deuteronomy 24:16 and Ezekiel 18:20 to absolve himself.⁹⁹

---

95. Mühlenberg, *Journals*, 3:55.
96. Mühlenberg, *Journals*, 3:55.
97. Mühlenberg, *Journals*, 3:103.
98. Mühlenberg, *Journals*, 3:125.
99. Mühlenberg, *Journals*, 3:125.

Perhaps the letter to Grimm and the journal entry to Freylinghausen persuaded the German auxiliary officers who read unsealed German language correspondence that Mühlenberg was truly nonpartisan or, at any rate, harmless. Perhaps Howe was just too indolent a commander to order a squad of cavalry to skirt the patriot pickets, dash to the Trappe, make an arrest, and drag General Mühlenberg's father back to Philadelphia. Perhaps it never crossed the minds of Howe or his staff that the arrest of a retiring elderly Lutheran cleric carried the least bit strategic value to justify mounting such an operation. Families were split by their opinions on the war: Most famous, perhaps, is that Benjamin Franklin disowned his son, William Franklin, the royalist Governor of New Jersey. There was no reason to presume that an elderly Lutheran pastor shared or approved the military sentiments of his son, especially one who resigned the cloth to join an army. At any rate Heinrich Mühlenberg was never molested by the redcoats or their German auxiliaries, and in 1778, with Howe recalled and Clinton withdrawing from Philadelphia, the battle lines moved off from Pennsylvania permanently.

## Conclusion

Heinrich Mühlenberg's Lutheran theological orientation towards vocation and the ethics of Two Kingdoms begin to surface in 1759, when he hosted a thanksgiving service for the conquest of Quebec. In the 1760s he stayed aloof from the Paxton Boys episode except to report what he considered the general opinions of ethnic Germans in Pennsylvania—which happened to be critical of the provincial government. Shortly afterwards he gloated over Benjamin Franklin's failed effort to swing the Germans, and he cheered that the immigrants had won seats in the Pennsylvania Assembly. In 1765 he publicly celebrated the revocation of the Stamp Act.

The consistency of his Two Kingdoms ethics regarding the duties of government brought him to political views that he shared with his father-in-law, Conrad Weiser. The victory over Quebec was a clear example of the sword in the hands of government performing God's will, while the neglect of settlers during Pontiac's War was a dereliction of that same duty, which Weiser had prophesied all the way back in 1741. It was good and right for Germans to elect representatives from among themselves who would uphold settler interests and otherwise promote justice for the immigrants, as Weiser had sought to do over the course of his career.

The patriot effort to sever overseas bonds, however, did not serve Mühlenberg's interests publicly or privately. The colonial pastor had spent decades massaging relationships with his Prussian, Hanoverian and British patrons. War in the Atlantic World, with its disruptions to communications, made these relationships difficult to sustain. An outright rebellion against the British crown threatened to alienate the very patrons and overseers on whom Mühlenberg depended for bequests, medicines, books, and pastors.

Heinrich Mühlenberg was, by interests and by identity, a royalist, but his sympathies lay with those patriots whose grievances had initially been with the crown's derelictions of duty. Such aid that Mühlenberg did render during the course of the War of Independence was to the patriots, in that he prepared the credential so that Christian Streit could receive a call as regimental chaplain. After royalist withdrawal in 1778 he returned to Philadelphia to perform military funerals. Circumstances until their withdrawal had landed him for a time within the patriot zone of operation, the winter base at Valley Forge being not far away especially on horseback. Even so, one can clearly imagine him performing duties in like manner for royalists had he happened to have been the pastor in New York City in the late 1770s; one doubts that he would have fled a pulpit in that city as his son Friedrich had done. It is also clear that Mühlenberg's patriot sympathies never led him to adopt the moral triumphalism for the cause that many of its leaders espoused. When Col. Dunlap's patriot militia defiled his sanctuary and bullied him as a Hessian sympathizer, he was adamant that their patriotism did not excuse them from God's judgment.

# 4

# Serving God from Three Sides

## *The Moravians in Bethlehem*

THE UPHEAVAL AND UNCERTAINTY in Pennsylvania in September, 1777 extended north to Bethlehem, a religious community of immigrant German-speaking Moravian pietists on the banks of the Lehigh River. Bethlehem's industries were centrally planned and its residents lived in dormitories, all on a scale of architecture that awed early Americans. This made Bethlehem of interest to the Continental Army's commissars, quarter-masters and surgeons general, who found its buildings ideal for warehouses, prisons, and hospitals.

On September 5, 1777, the administrative and spiritual director of Bethehem, Johann Ettwein, appealed the Continental Army's order to house up to 250 prisoners of war, as well as the garrison of guards. He protested on the grounds of the religious constraint to neutrality that belonged to the faith of Bethlehem's townspeople. His appeal was denied, and on September 7 two hundred Scottish Highlanders were quartered in the Family Dormitory.[1] On September 19, 1777, the Single Men's Dormitory was transformed into a hospital. By September 27, 1777, what had been a cloistered, pacifist community designed to support missionary evangelists among the Native Nations, had become a military stronghold for the Continental Army with a garrison, prison, hospital and munitions depot. For Ettwein acquiescence to these demands was by no means an enthusiastic endorsement of the patriot cause. Indeed, for Ettwein, word

---

1. Hamilton, *John Ettwein and the Moravian Church*, 172.

of the defeat of Burgoyne in October was a "fatal blow" with the tragic consequence of lengthening the war.[2]

## The Foundations of Bethlehem

The Renewed Unity of the Brethren, headquartered in Europe, built and populated the town of Bethlehem with German-speaking immigrants. The religious movement it represented had not always been so tightly managed or global in its scope, until it found sanctuary on the estates of Count Nicholas Ludwig von Zinzendorf in the German Kingdom of Saxony. Guided by their patron's grandiose vision, the Renewed Unity wove together many origins and narratives, some national, some theological, some personal and mystical, into a new tapestry of Protestant expression.

One of the dominant threads in the tapestry is the story of German Lutheran pietism and its impact on the Count of Zinzendorf. In 1675 the Lutheran Superintendent in the free Imperial City of Frankfurt, Philip Jakob Spener, published *Pia Desideria* (Pious Wishes). In this short work aimed at laypeople he proposed ways to restore spiritual life to the Church through the personal renewal of its pastors and communicants. After Spener transferred to the Kingdom of Saxony to serve as its royal chaplain, he so impressed one noble courtier, Count Johann von Zinzendorf, that they maintained a friendship even after Spener departed to serve in Berlin in the Kingdom of Prussia. When the Count's son Nicholas Ludwig was born the child was presented to Spener's protégé August Hermann Francke for baptism.

Count Johann died and when his widow remarried, she sent Nicholas to live with his grandmother in her castle at Grosshennersdorf. There Nicholas Ludwig absorbed his grandmother's pietistic faith. When he turned 10 his grandmother sent him to August Francke's "orphan schools" at the Halle Institutes, where he was boarded and trained in a closed society. Despite the school's austere discipline Nicholas Ludwig was inspired by Halle Pietism's overall vision of the regenerate life and of global evangelization. From Halle he was sent to Wittenberg for university; in his letter of farewell to Director Francke he left to him the charge of a student conventicle he had formed under their very noses.[3] In Wittenberg he was required to study law in order to learn the art of

---

2. Hamilton, *John Ettwein and the Moravian Church*, 172.
3. Zinzendorf, *Christian Life and Witness*, xv.

bearing rule as was deemed proper to his caste. Inheriting his estates in Upper Lusatia on his majority and a job in the government of Saxony on his commencement, the young Nicholas Ludwig Count of Zinzendorf nevertheless cherished the dream that had formed in him in Halle, to spearhead global mission.[4]

In 1722 a handful of homeless Moravian Protestants crossed the Bohemian border onto his estates. Their leader, Christian David, explained that they were a remnant of the Unity of the Brethren, a group that traced its origins to the Bohemian priest and martyr Jan Hus (d. 1415).[5] This is the second major thread woven into the tapestry of the Renewed Unity of the Brethren. Following the martyrdom of Hus in 1415, the established Church in Bohemia (modern Czech Republic) eventually gained the right to share the chalice of communion with the laity, and so they, as "Utraquists," remained in union with Rome. Followers of other Hussite priorities left the established Church and formed the Unity of the Brethren, a communitarian, pacifist movement with its own bishops. As were the Lollards of England and the Waldensians of the Alps, the Unity was a disestablished, non-conforming proto-Protestant Church existing in Catholic Europe decades before Martin Luther ignited the Reformation. Being pacifists and communitarians they anticipated later Anabaptists, but they practiced all seven sacraments, baptized infants, and held to the historic episcopacy in their orders.[6] Like the Utraquists and later Protestants, they offered both the bread and cup of communion to the laity.[7]

Although the Thirty Years War began with a riot in Prague 1618, the terms of the Treaty of Westphalia that brought a cessation to hostilities in 1648 nevertheless excluded the Czech Unity of the Brethren from protection. This left them vulnerable to the whims of intolerance in the same way that Anabaptist groups were vulnerable. The Unity was driven underground or otherwise dispersed, many arriving in Poland where they continued their religious practice under a measure of toleration.[8] Two generations following the Treaty of Westphalia, Christian David and his small group appeared on Zinzendorf's estates in Upper Lusatia. The

---

4. Zinzendorf, *Christian Life and Witness*, xv, xviii.
5. Zinzendorf, *Christian Life and Witness*, xviii.
6. Atwood, *Theology of the Czech Brethren*, 177–82.
7. Atwood, *Theology of the Czech Brethren*, 180–81.
8. Atwood, *Theology of the Czech Brethren*, 10.

Count opened part of his land to settle them and in 1723 they broke ground on the town of Herrnhut.

As their noble benefactor and patron the young Count Zinzendorf took the lead in their reconstitution as a religious community. Herrnhut became no ordinary town, but an experiment in holy living.[9] While other Moravians of the Czech Unity of the Brethren joined Herrnhut, it was not long before the community was swallowed up by various German religious seekers and exiles from intolerance. Even as the community Germanized, the appellation "Moravian" stuck when it was applied to Zinzendorf's Herrnhuters. These fugitives and Protestant misfits brought myriads of threads and influences of their own to the tapestry, blending various practices and pieties that would emerge as one distinctive movement under Zinzendorf's leadership.

The third major thread woven into the tapestry is the personality of Nicholas Ludwig von Zinzendorf himself. He was possessed of an aristocrat's ego on the one hand, and proclivities toward passionate mysticism on the other. Exercising his aristocratic offices, Zinzendorf made himself arbiter over Herrnhut's internal disputes, but steered complainants toward reconciliation on Christ's terms of the Beatitudes in Matthew 5 and accountability in Matthew 18.[10]

Raised in the mysticism of his grandmother, Zinzendorf had a fervent religious imagination all his own. At Herrnhut millenarians, Philadelphians, mystics, and ascetics came together and formed a cohesive community on a model designed to replicate itself around the world. In 1727 a revival took hold, captivating the community and its patron with a zeal for mission.[11] This energy was channeled by the force of Zinzendorf's personality. By the 1730s this religious community numbering around three hundred souls began to plant versions of itself in other settlements in Germany, and also to send teams of missionaries across oceans to unreached peoples at the ends of the earth: from Siberia to the American colonies, and from Greenland to the South Seas. However, in replicating the Halle model Zinzendorf engaged many of the same patrons that supported Halle's endeavors, such as the royalty of Denmark, who permitted Moravian missionaries to the Danish possessions of St. Thomas and St. Croix in the Caribbean. This independent streak on Zinzendorf's part

---

9. Spangenberg, *Life of N. L. Zinzendorf*, 77–91.

10. Smaby, *Transformation of Moravian Bethlehem*, 6–7.

11. Zinzendorf, *Christian Life and Witness*, xviii–xix; Smaby, *Transformation of Bethlehem*, 6–9.

aroused the jealousy and enduring hostility of the Lutheran pietists at the Halle Institutes. In a power struggle August Spangenberg, Zinzendorf's disciple and eventual successor, was removed as an inspector at the Halle Institutes in 1733 and became a confirmed "Zinzendorfer."

At around this time Zinzendorf also fell out with his Aunt, the Baroness von Gersdorff, with whom he had grown up in Grosshennersdorf. They grew estranged in adulthood over the issue of sheltering the Moravian exiles, whom the Baroness found insubordinate.[12] By the late 1730s, when the Baroness von Gersdorff extended the call for an orphanage director to the young pastor, Heinrich Mühlenberg, her dispute with her nephew remained bitter.

The British colonies on the Atlantic seaboard presented a unique opportunity to the Moravians. There were unreached indigenous peoples, but there were also growing numbers of Germans settlers who were underserved by pastors and, consequently, were raising an unchurched generation. At just the time that missionary excitement was sweeping through Herrnhut, the British were founding Georgia and settling it with Alpine German Protestants.

Moravians tried to expand into Georgia themselves, but were given a chill reception by the Rev. Johann Martin Boltzius (1703–1765), the pastor in the Halle-sponsored Lutheran settlement of Ebenezer. The Moravians soon withdrew from Georgia for Pennsylvania.

For the Moravians the city of Philadelphia was both a cultural and an eschatological icon. Culturally, more Germans made landfall in Philadelphia than in any other port. Religiously the *Philadelphians* were a pietistic group of prophecy enthusiasts inspired by the seventeenth-century mystic Jakob Boehme. Key to their beliefs was that the letter to the Angel of the Church in Philadelphia in Revelation chapter 3 was a descriptive allegory of a fresh spiritual dispensation that was being inaugurated among themselves. Philadelphianism was a theological influence on Zinzendorf. To him there seemed no better place than the city of Philadelphia in Pennsylvania to give birth to the Philadelphian Era when the Church as a whole would be characterized by love and unity, while confessional distinctions and denominational hierarchies would recede.

In one of his seasons of exile Zinzendorf came to Pennsylvania, where he arrogated to himself the title "Inspector of the Lutheran Churches of Pennsylvania." He cast a vision for the German Lutheran, Reformed

---

12. Spangenberg, *Life of N. L. Zinzendorf*, 156–57.

and peace sects to assemble together and seek a new form of cooperation, a Pan-Protestant Church divorced from the divisive state-funded establishments of Europe. He held a series of seven meetings, which he called synods, but interest dropped off after the second meeting when it became clear to most of the delegates that what Zinzendorf really had in mind was an ecclesial structure with himself at the head. As momentum for the Philadelphia vision fizzled out, he invested his energies toward consolidating Moravian community and mission in Pennsylvania.

## The Mission and Function of Bethlehem

The land where the Moravians had broken ground for their first communities, starting in 1740 with Nazareth, had been included in the Walking Purchase discussed in chapter 2. This disputed treaty became an issue of contention between the Delaware Nation and the proprietary government of Pennsylvania and its Iroquois allies. An early deed-holder of the Nazareth tract was George Whitefield, the Anglican cleric and evangelist, who at first rented his land to the Moravian developers and then sold it to them. Nazareth soon became a rural-outlier, with farming as its key industry, but connected with the main settlement of Bethlehem, for which ground was broken in 1741. These settlements were founded as one *Pilgergemeine*, a pilgrim community designed to be both economically self-sufficient and the base of material support for Moravian missionaries living and evangelizing among indigenous peoples.

In the fall of 1742 Zinzendorf took the first Moravian missionaries on a tour of the Miami and Delaware villages along the North Branch of the Susquehanna River to the Wyoming. They were accompanied by Conrad Weiser as their guide, having already been tutored by Weiser in native languages and customs. This excursion is discussed in detail in chapter 7. After a service of consecration for the missionaries in Pennsylvania's wilderness they returned to Bethlehem. Zinzendorf raised August Spangenberg to director of the *Pilgergemeine*, then returned to Philadelphia and, shortly thereafter, to England.

Spangenberg became the chief architect of the communal economy, replicating the choir system of the Moravian communities of Germany while also introducing innovations unique to Bethlehem. "Choir" was the term used for each segment in the segregated living arrangements designated by life-stage. Since men were needed most at the outset of Bethlehem's operations, in the clearing of land and the construction of buildings, the pattern was set for an imbalance in the numbers of male and female; the perpetual shortage of women extended through the end of the century. In the early years of the community even married couples were strictly segregated. By life stage the divisions were as follows: the children's choir for weaned children served as a pre-school and was supervised by single women; the young boys and the young girls choirs, akin to boarding schools; the single women and the single men's choirs, which paralleled monastic communities and which were in many ways the back-bone of this early communal or "general" economy; married choirs with husbands and wives dwelling apart; and eventually separate choirs for widows.

Efforts by the Moravian leadership to control marriage had mixed results. One tenet of Zinzendorf's that was closely followed was the conviction that pastors and missionaries were called to serve as teams of husband and wife. In the choir system the communities were segregated for life and discipleship according to their sex and life-stage. In this setting men were pastors to men while women pastored women. Thus, pastors were teamed in marriage with only a few exceptions. Until the 1760s women also had a voice in community and regional leadership. While this is an important historical precedent toward vocational equality in the pastoral office, equality was not their concern so much as that they took a realistic view towards boundaries and temptation.

Arranging and assigning compatible unions among the laypeople depended on demographic factors that the community's elders were unable to control, so that by the mid-eighteenth century the Single Men's Choir in Bethlehem was seven times larger than the Single Women's Choir.[13] The presence of so many suitors should have predicted a rapid depletion in the number of single women and growth in the married women's choir, but this did not transpire due to the economic premises that guided the general economy. The town's leadership disqualified low-wage earners from consideration as husbands,[14] yet it was riskier financially for a prospering tradesman to marry and be responsible for a family than to remain at their craft in the singles' choir.[15] This dilemma was not solved by the change in the community's economic model starting in 1762, which transitioned toward the nuclear family forming the

---

13. Gollin, *Moravians in Two Worlds*, 114.
14. Gollin, *Moravians in Two Worlds*, 125.
15. Gollin, *Moravians in Two Worlds*, 118.

base of the community's economy and lifestyle. The choir system hung on persistently and Bethlehem saw no weddings at all between December 1775 and August 1778.[16]

A complicating factor in the matchmaking is that the lot was used to approve every marriage, even after 1762; however, if the lot showed that a match was approved that decision was still not binding on either partner. Each one, both the woman and the man, were to enter into the union freely. Some chose to submit to the marriage because they felt that in doing so they were submitting to the will of Christ who had spoken through the lot. But if the lot indicated the negative, the matter was not pursued.

An integral feature of the holistic theology of Christian life and identity unique to the Renewed Unity of the Brethren is that marriage was considered an exalted estate, and nuptial union itself was imbued with sacramental significance.[17] This reverence for marriage may have served as an additional check on the enthusiasm for marriage in prospective matches: Who, on honest self-examination, could deem themselves worthy of so profoundly holy a vocation as marriage? In Zinzendorf's theology marriage enacted and made visible the divine mystery of Christ's union with the church as of a bridegroom with his bride, which was to be perfectly consummated in the Resurrection. For Zinzendorf this meant that the "Wedding Supper of the Lamb" (Rev 19:6–9) did not describe the ultimate participation of life with God. Rather, Christ and his Bride, the Church, will in some mysterious, mystical manner enter into a nuptial union once the wedding supper is concluded.[18] This eschatological mystery is therefore anticipated in the act of sexual union between wife and husband.

Parallel to this theological development, and creating corollary effects, was a high esteem of the wounds of Christ that developed in the worship life, liturgy, art and music of the Moravians. The side wound opened by the spear of the soldier in John 19, with its flow of blood and water, was seen as a life-giving opening in the body of Christ akin to the womb of a woman.[19] These mystical, enthusiastic views of wounds devotion, sexuality, marriage, worship and identity were not part of the fifteenth-century Unity of the Brethren; they emerged from the

16. Gollin, *Moravians in Two Worlds*, 121.
17. Smaby, *Transformation of Bethlehem*, 159–65; Peucker, *Time of Sifting*, 3–4.
18. Peucker, *Time of Sifting*, 83–84.
19. Atwood, "Union of Masculine and Feminine," 28; cf. Fogleman, *Jesus is Female*, 77–83.

idiosyncrasies of Zinzendorf. In the late 1740s there was a convergence of these doctrines and practices that cut against the grain of traditional Christian disciplines governing sexual behavior, which exploded in a scandal that came to be known to Moravians as the "Sifting Time."

Leading the advance into the esoteric and erotic was the Count's son, Christian Renatus Zinzendorf, who in liturgies conducted in December, 1748, may have encouraged the Single Men in Herrnhaag to new explorations in sexual conduct among themselves. This was a means of entering into and anticipating the promise that, as part of the Bride of Christ, even men become female in the resurrection and will experience nuptial union with Christ, the bridegroom.

While plumbing the details of the controversy does not advance this study, there are three outcomes of the Sifting Time that are germane: First, the clouds of suspicion and scandal clung to the imaginations of the general public, among whom allegations of sexual license in Moravian communities continued to be published by disgruntled former members who styled themselves as informants and whistle-blowers. Second, the suspicions and fears in the general public were exacerbated by the Moravian disciplines which kept the communities closed, religious services private, and contact with outsiders restricted. As will be seen in chapter 5 these suspicions were very much in play for a German Auxiliaries prisoner of war in Bethlehem in 1779.

Third, in the aftermath of the Sifting Time the leadership role of August Spangenberg in the global Moravian movement and in Bethlehem was reconfirmed. Spangenberg had been a critic of the sexualized imaginings that had flowered in the Sifting Time,[20] and by the late 1740s he had been set on the margins of leadership. He was replaced by those of a more enthusiastic, mystical bent, personified in the arrival in Bethlehem of Bishop Johann Friedrich Cammerhof and of Johann Nitschmann. Spangenberg moved to Philadelphia and then returned to Europe in November of 1749.

In his biography of Zinzendorf, Spangenberg does not provide lurid second-head details of the behaviors that were taking place, but focuses instead on the Count's response.[21] Spangenberg's polite circumspection regarding the details is wholly consistent with eighteenth-century discourse, and wholly consistent with the conclusions of modern scholars

---

20. Fogelman, *Jesus is Female*, 144.
21. Spangenberg, *Life of N. L. Zinzendorf*, 358–72.

that the scandalous deviations in doctrine and practice were sexual in nature. Spangenberg is also pointed in his acknowledgment that he had personally disagreed with Zinzendorf's approach to the matter, and their arguments had led to dissension between them.

Zinzendorf's actions in the spring of 1749 were good as far as they went: The Count sent a pointed yet vague letter of rebuke to the congregations, communities and choirs throughout the world, and he recalled Christian Renatus to London, who arrived in May. With these steps Zinzendorf hoped to close the matter, but as months passed into 1750 it became clear that confusions persisted. It was not Zinzendorf's generous approach to discipline and restoration that troubled Spangenberg, but rather the Count's impatience with those who tried to bring the issue to the front of his attention in order to effect a broader and more productive resolution across the whole of the Moravian Church.

It was particularly galling, perhaps, that the crisis unfolded concurrently with Moravian efforts to procure the endorsement of the Moravian Brethren as an "ancient, apostolic church" from the parliament of the United Kingdom. To then have public attention called to practices that were patently at odds with mainstream Christian faith was an embarrassment of high order. Yet the issue could not finally be contained by being ignored. Zinzendorf sent Spangenberg and Johannes de Watteville to conduct investigations, enforce discipline, and mend doctrines and relationships.[22] The effort culminated in the Synod of Barby in the fall of 1750, almost two full years after the inception of the crisis with a liturgy in the Herrnhag Single Men's Choir in December of 1748. The synod facilitated public, liturgical repentance, reconciliation, and affirmation of the doctrines and practice of the church.

Bethlehem was designed to be a self-sustaining community that could support missionaries among the Native Nations and, in its early years, among unchurched Germans.[23] The efficiency of a communal economic base allowed for focused efforts by the missionaries among the people they sought to reach. This model was effective to the point that it incurred the resentment of the Halle Mission rival Heinrich Mühlenberg. He groused that the Moravians with just a few people were able to send and support preachers everywhere, while thousands of resident Lutherans could not find their way to support a handful of pastors in

---

22. Levering, *History of Bethlehem*, 233; Peucker, *Time of Sifting*, 144.

23. Smaby, *Transformation of Bethlehem*, 94.

Pennsylvania.[24] The difference between these two German immigrant communities is that one was based on communitarian principles where resources were shared, while the other was premised on Luther's catechetical descriptions of the self-dependent nuclear family.

The architect of the General Economy was August Spangenberg, who devised the system in his first stint as director. Cammerhof and Nitschmann, however, turned Bethlehem away from the sound principles of industry, their enthusiasm instead leading them to emphasize sensuous lives of worship. Zinzendorf had been chastened by the crisis of the Sifting Time: On Cammerhof's death in 1751, he recalled Nitschmann and urged Spangenberg to return to Bethlehem and restore it to order. In Spangenberg's second tenure Bethlehem was growing surpluses of food again by 1753.[25] This productive capability would become crucial to helping the town through the crises it would face in the middle of the decade.

## A Moravian Family in Bethlehem

In August 1742, still early in its experiment with the General Economy and when Zinzendorf was still in Pennsylvania, Bethlehem received an indentured, unskilled laborer named Samuel Mau, a German immigrant. He had been given a few days to try to find another employer to pick up the balance of his contract. Bethlehem bought out his obligation, but resolved to treat him as a hired wage-earner.[26]

At some point Mau converted to the Moravian faith. What in many respects appears unexceptional is in fact exceptional compared to the overall patterns. Although never attaining to more than a day laborer, which would have made him less than desirable as a candidate for marriage in the eyes of the elders, Samuel Mau was able to marry nevertheless. His wife was Anna Katherine Kremper, who had moved with her family from South Carolina to Bethlehem in 1742.[27] Samuel and Anna Mau were in Bethlehem for Spangenberg's first stint as director, throughout the troubled period of the Sifting Time in Europe and the leadership of Cammerhof and the Nitschmanns, the second administration of

---

24. Mühlenberg, *Journals*, 1:148–49.
25. Smaby, *Transformation of Bethlehem*, 30.
26. *Bethlehem Diary*, 1:69.
27. Levering, *History of Bethlehem*, 492.

Spangenberg, the French and Indian Wars, and the transition from the General Economy to the cooperative starting in 1762.

Samuel and Anna had at least three children: At least one of these children, born in 1761, was conceived prior to the end of the segregation of the marriage choirs, when Samuel and Anna would have been living in separate dormitories and reserving their turns in "the cabinet," a special room in the Married Women's dormitory reserved for conjugal relations. The couple was sharing an apartment reconditioned for the nuclear family by 1779, at which time they were asked to billet a prisoner of war. Years after the Revolutionary War their son Samuel Mau became a licensed evangelist of the Pennsylvania Ministerium in Kentucky,[28] while two daughters married clergy.[29] We will meet the elder Samuel again in chapter 5 when, in 1779, one of these clergy suitors arrives at his door.

## From Pennsylvania to the Native Nations

Throughout the 1740s Bethlehem's relations with indigenous peoples was friendly. Still it would be an anachronism to credit the Moravians with values that were centuries ahead of their social climate. Chauvinism in their attitudes towards persons of unlike culture and custom is inescapable in their discourse. From the perspective of indigenous peoples, the Moravians could not escape representing all the privileges and threats associated with Euro-ethnic colonial power, despite the attempts by missionaries to distance themselves from those associations.

One model for understanding dynamics between cultures, proposed at the turn of the twenty-first century, accurately summarizes key aspects to Moravian engagement with Native Americans. In *Guns, Germs and Steel* author Jared Diamond, looking at the broad sweep of Euro-ethnic colonialism over the last four hundred years, explains the advantages inherent to the European side: their expertise in metallurgy, their advantage in firearms, and their relative immunity from the diseases for which they were themselves often carriers.[30] A brief glimpse of Bethlehem's function hits on each of Diamond's points: First, Bethlehem's metal cookware and tableware were coveted trade goods. Second, clauses in treaties negotiated between Native Nations and Pennsylvania through

---

28. Spaeth et al., *Documentary History*, 276.
29. Levering, *History of Bethlehem*, 492.
30. Diamond, *Guns, Germs, and Steel*, 23.

the likes of Conrad Weiser often included the stipulation that Moravian gunsmiths would repair rifles brought to them by Native Americans. A Moravian became a resident gunsmith in the Native Nations town of Shamokin in exchange for the Moravians being permitted to establish a mission close by.[31] Third, in terms of germs and disease, Moravian hospitality was famous among the indigenous peoples, who frequently camped near Bethlehem; tragically this friendly proximity at times spelled doom for Native American guests, since smallpox epidemics were frequent in the eighteenth century.

Bethlehem constructed Nain in 1758 as a settlement for Native Americans. This was done to meet the needs of friendly Native American refugees when the French-allied war parties began to terrorize the frontier in the mid-1750s, however the segregation of Nain was certainly an ethnic and social matter which served to allay the fears of Bethlehem's own inhabitants.[32] In keeping with their overall priorities the Moravians also constructed two inns, one on each side of the town, so that Euroethnic strangers were prevented from staying within the town' limits.[33] Bethlehem was a closed religious community whose citizens were required to remain focused spiritually and to avoid contamination from outside influence.

The emphasis on the religious exceptionalism and communal aspects of the Moravian lifestyle may act to disguise their inherent complicity with settler interests, and the degree to which they belonged to the milieu of threat to the cultures of indigenous peoples. Moravians, Anabaptists, radical Pietists and Lutheran Pietists were all part of the westward push to clear and farm new land, and that is the very ambition which constituted the greatest single threat to the coherence and survival of indigenous cultures. Bethlehem was built on land that Pennsylvania claimed under the disputed terms of the Walking Purchase of 1737. Compassionate, peace-oriented efforts such as those of the Moravian missionaries notwithstanding, the stories of all Euro-ethnic communities in Pennsylvania, whether radical in their piety and peace orientation or not, are stories of the Euro-ethnic ambition for intensive agriculture. This ambition is the single greatest factor in the evolving contemplation

---

31. Zeisberger, *Moravian Mission Diaries*, 43–44; cf. Gordon and Lienemann, "Gunmaking Trade in Bethlehem," 6, where reference is made to the general reliance of Native American hunters on Moravian gunsmiths.

32. Smaby, *Transformation of Bethlehem*, 100.

33. Smaby, *Transformation of Bethlehem*, 97, 99.

of a solidarity of "White People" in early America. Although the Paxton Boys were an early signal of the dark potentialities of this racialized form of solidarity, even the Moravians (whose protection over their Native American charges had provoked the Paxton Boys to march on Philadelphia) shared in the core ambition of the settlers to farm the land for surplus. This ambition threatened the survival of indigenous cultures no matter how many songs the missionaries sang and no matter the number of beads and iron pots they distributed to their indigenous converts.

## The French and Indian War

Open hostility against the Moravian missionaries and towns flared up in 1755. The actions against the Moravians particularly were rooted in resentments over the "Walking Purchase" of 1737, a treaty of which they had not been a part but from which they had directly benefited. This treaty had alienated the Eastern Delaware, who were consigned to a reservation in the Wyoming Valley. Delaware efforts to redress what they considered to be a swindle were rebuffed by the English governments and the Iroquois, and this pushed them into alliance with the French. After General Braddock's epic failure in the forests west of Fort Duquesne and the flight of the British redcoats from Carlisle all the way to Philadelphia, many Native war captains sided with the French.

Early in the French and Indian War there was suspicion that the Moravians were themselves aiding and abetting the French and their Native Nations allies. The rumor abounded that the Moravians were sympathetic to the French as crypto-Catholics. This rumor was sparked by their otherness as a foreign language population and fanned into flame with the privacy of their religious ceremonies.[34] Their neutrality and pacifism was also misunderstood as leading directly to the aid and succor of the enemy. These rumors were arrested when a French-allied war party murdered eight Moravian missionaries at their settlement of Gnadenhütten in the Wyoming Valley.[35] Bethlehem and Nazareth stood on territory the Eastern Delaware felt had been stolen from under them. Although the missionaries had gone to Gnadenhütten at the invitation of Wyoming Valley leaders, the Delaware Nation had less oversight over dissenting war captains than did the Iroquois League.

34. Mühlenberg, *Journals*, 1:387
35. Levering, *History of Bethlehem Pennsylvania*, 313–18.

Two Moravians escaped and made their way separately to Bethlehem, each not knowing the other had survived, and reported the news. Spangenberg at once pulled in his missionaries from other settlements and appealed for help. In response to the wave of violence, the two branches of government in Philadelphia infamously tied themselves into gridlock. Quakers hid their Pacifist inclinations under a guise of tax justice, while the proprietors insisted on the rights granted them in the charter. Despite Benjamin Franklin's efforts to craft a militia law for the defense of the province, the government remained paralyzed.[36]

Spangenberg saw the crisis for what it was: the war parties had known the missionaries and where they had come from; the score being settled was over the Walking Purchase land, and Bethlehem was next. On the heels of the survivors Bethlehem became awash in a sea of fugitives from the violence as mobs of settlers from north and west fled their farms in the general direction of Philadelphia. With no help from the proprietary governor and the Quaker-dominated assembly, Spangenberg re-interpreted his pacifism to meet the situation.

Spangenberg ordered the construction of a palisade around the town and mobilized a rotation of armed sentries for a round-the-clock patrol.[37] The civil defense plan which he designed stipulated that if attacked the men would mobilize, rifles and ammunition would be distributed, and they would defend the defenseless. Indigenous residents in Bethlehem and those Native Americans passing through saw the preparations and spread the word—all by design. Clearly a raid on Bethlehem would be costly; it was best to leave it alone.[38] By some estimates there were never more than 50 or so working firearms in the entire community, but organized against war party tactics this was more than enough.[39] War parties were small in number, usually between 4 and 10 warriors, who attacked isolated farms with a view of spreading terror in neighboring farms and causing them to flee, thus emptying the land of the unwanted settlers. Quick attacks and murders by night might have occurred in Bethlehem had the town not organized its defense.

Benjamin Franklin was at this time the prime mover in placing Pennsylvania on a military footing against the Native Nations uprising.

---

36. Wallace, *Conrad Weiser*, 411–12.
37. A palisade is a wall of logs standing vertically with the tops carved to a point.
38. Levering, *History of Bethlehem*, 320–29.
39. Levering, *History of Bethlehem*, 320–29.

After learning of the murder of the missionaries, he formed an armed detachment to ride with him to the Wyoming Valley on a fact-finding mission, and passed through Bethlehem along the way. Decades later he reflected on his impressions: "I was surprised to find it in so good a posture of defense. The destruction of Gnadenhut [sic] had made them apprehend danger." The militia that Franklin finally formed built a fort at the abandoned missionary settlement.[40]

Where does a posture of self-defense fit into ethical, Christian pacifism? Considering that the Moravian guards never went on a pursuit march, never organized a punitive expedition, never took the field in an any kind of offensive campaign, and are not recorded to have even fired a shot in anger, it seems to fit rather well. Their vigilance and preparedness preserved the lives of the women and children, refugees, and peaceful Native Americans in their charge. Furthermore, since this duty was being performed by the Moravian men, Spangenberg was able to argue for their exemption from the general militia law and for garrison duties elsewhere once such laws were finally passed.[41]

Christian pacifism is only partially based on the premise of the words of Jesus to turn the other cheek (Matt 5:39). That reaches as far as an individual's response to an insult and assault upon oneself. In the individual aspect of pacifism one endures violence as a testimony to one's faith, but some also hold that there is also a personal responsibility to protect others who have no power to choose for themselves to turn the other cheek.

Also to be considered is pacifism in its social aspect and forms. For some the social commitment to pacifism rests on the premise of a functioning government with office-holders who, faithful to their vocations, provide for wider social order and common defense as stipulated in Romans 13:1–7. Therefore many Christian pacifists extend the Two Kingdoms logic of vocation by holding that no believers have a vocation to the coercive arms of government. This vocational boundary is set as a discipline over their Christian community, even as they fully admit that their logic of pacifism rests on the Two Kingdoms premise that a government is in place and is functioning with the power of the sword. Then there those who seek to impose their pacifism by obstructing the

---

40. Franklin, *American Revolution*, 1445–46.

41. Franklin, *American Revolution*, 337–38.

government from its vocation in the performance of police powers and the conduct of warfare, even in measures that are purely defensive.

The dilemma for the Moravians pacifists in Bethlehem is that after the uprisings began, the Quaker pacifists in the Pennsylvania Assembly were forcing the government to fail at its most basic vocation, its duty to provide for the common defense. If some Moravian pacifists approved of the Quaker stance, Spangenberg opted to interpret the duties of Christian pacifism in other ways. For Bethlehem, pacifism was revisited in light of the town itself being the only functional governing entity in the region with the power to protect the defenseless. He stepped into the vacuum, built the palisade and mustered an armed watch, and the result was that violence was reduced and people dwelt in safety.

As discussed, for Heinrich Mühlenberg and quite possibly for tens of thousands of mainline Lutheran and Reformed Germans in Pennsylvania, their loyalty to the sovereign government would never have been at issue, except, that the Quakers who dominated the Assembly failed to do their part to keep order and defend the frontier. Even more tragically, this theologically-informed trend persisted despite events. The inability to recognize the validity of those vocations that belong to the Kingdom of the World caused the Quakers of Pennsylvania to lose their majority in the assembly in the 1760s, and in the 1770s, to lose their king.

Pacifists also diverge in their political action. Spangenberg showed that pacifism can be more than a mere idealism about turning one's cheek and then forcing societies to do the same; indeed, such ideals are best abandoned if the net result is that it fosters more violence and creates more victims. For Spangenberg, pacifists could also exercise vigilance to reduce overall violence and mitigate the opportunities for violence. For other pacifists the testimony of personal non-participation in any kind of violence is absolute, even to the point of obstructing governments from their exercise of the sword, even when the results of that idealism is that governments are paralyzed and the innocent are terrorized. In the 1770s, even as Bethlehem Director Johann Ettwein was forced to comply with patriot appropriations of Bethlehem's facilities for hospitals and prisons, his personal attitudes tended to diverge from Spangenberg's approach and to line up more with the obstructive attitudes of the Anabaptists and Quakers.

## The Bethlehem Cooperative

It can never be known how long the General Economy experiment might have lasted, although the continuing existence of Old Order Amish and Mennonite fellowships prove that faith-based communitarianism can be sustained for generations and centuries. In Bethlehem the model survived the uprising of the Native Nations, but could not long survive the deaths of Zinzendorf and his wife within two weeks of each other in 1760. An audit then found that the Saxon count had poured everything of his own fortune into the Church, its communities, and its missions. It was also discovered that debts had accumulated against the Renewed Unity corporation, of which its towns and church properties were assets.

In the wake of the Count's passing, Spangenberg and de Watteville led the Moravian Church through major adjustments in doctrine and economy. Theologically the Moravians steered away from the heterodox innovations that had originated with Zinzendorf, but retained the Protestant stamp of two sacraments and other mainstream doctrines and practices.[42] Financially, the global Moravian corporation needed Bethlehem to generate cash to defray its debts and prevent foreclosures on their churches and communities. The towns were to transition away from the communal model where subsistence was distributed, and be set on a footing whereby farmers, craftsmen, and laborers could earn cash and pay in. The commune of Bethlehem's "general economy," in 1762, transitioned to became a cooperative economy of independent leaseholders. In this system a Moravian smith or shopkeeper owned his building but rented the ground on which it stood from the Renewed Unity. As a cooperative, the economy was still tightly controlled. Prices were fixed, competition was prohibited, profiteering and desires for individual prosperity were frowned upon.[43]

While the end of the General Economy was a watershed moment in the evolution of Bethlehem as a town, even so the town remained an exclusive community of Moravian members. The choirs persisted in the cooperative economy. After 1762 many residents simply transferred their dependence from the community elders to their own choirs, where they continued to live without generating cash income and receiving subsistence on their choir's dole to which they directly contributed with their

---

42. Franklin, *American Revolution*, 147–48.

43. Smaby, *Transformation of Bethlehem*, 34–37; Levering, *History of Bethlehem*, 378–85.

labors. Marriage to outsiders was still discouraged, while the effort to plan marriages continued to under-perform against the wishes of the elders. Many worship services and events remained closed to the public, but the town's architecture of residential and industrial buildings was impressive to visitors.

Nathaniel Seidel arrived in 1761 to replace Spangenberg, who returned to Europe to assist de Watteville on the Renewed Unity's central committee. Seidel began to implement the transformation from the General Economy.[44] This process took several years and involved negotiations with the Unity in Europe, who were trying to retire debt. He was also the executive director over all of North America, and in 1766 Seidel received Johann and Johanetta Ettwein to assist him in the leadership of Bethlehem itself. Because of Johann Ettwein's English skills he was made the chief envoy to Anglophonic local officials and royal and provincial dignitaries.

The Ettweins had been heading up the married choir at Herrnhut when the sifting time crisis fanned out like a spreading fire from the Single Men's Choir in Herrnhaag. The Ettweins were put under discipline for their role, whatever that might have been—perhaps fostering or perhaps passively accepting the new practices in sexual embodiment—yet they seem to have been thoroughly rehabilitated by the early 1750s.[45] After arriving in Bethlehem Johann Ettwein held the office of director for over thirty years, and after Seidel's death in 1782, he was raised to bishop himself in 1784.[46]

## Bethlehem in the War of Independence

In the middle of the 1770s Bethlehem's buildings were in good repair, its people had a cheerfully meek demeanor that was unique and identifiable with their faith, and its craftsmen had solid reputations—including its gunsmiths.[47] The town impressed the enemies of the patriots and was coveted for military use by the patriots. Starting in December, 1776, the Continental Army began the importunate habit of appropriating

44. Seidel, "Supplement."
45. Hamilton, *John Ettwein and the Moravian Church*, 23–24.
46. Levering, *History of Bethlehem*, 529.
47. Moravian firearms in the American Revolutionary War is another fascinating dimension to the overall picture of German Pietists' involvement. See Gordon and Lienemann, "Gunmaking Trade in Bethlehem."

buildings in Bethlehem for their own use. Despite these levies on Moravian hospitality, local magistrates and militia recruiters remained suspicious of Bethlehem and demanded that its young men enlist or pay fines that steepened as the war lengthened. Ettwein refused to allow the war to take Bethlehem's men, although his success was mitigated. On the whole, then, while the contributions of the Moravians to the patriot war effort were remarkable, it must be admitted that they were in large part coerced. The Moravians, like their political allies the Quakers, were pacifists, and they suffered for it.

Under Ettwein the town of Bethlehem retained its distinctive "otherness" among Pennsylvanians. This "otherness" was evident in the lifestyle, governed by a daily schedule of prayer and meetings and a year-long liturgical calendar of special services. Furthermore, even into the 1780s the effect of the transition from the General Economy to a cooperative was ameliorated by the choirs themselves, which continued to act as communes for many of their members. There was additionally an otherness in their values. Pacifism was a community discipline among the Moravians, as was true in the Anabaptist groups, among the Dunkers and their rivals in Ephrata, and among the ubiquitous English Quakers. As will be described in chapters 5 and 7, as late as the Revolutionary War the otherness of the Moravians in their lifestyles, pacifism, and secrecy, made Moravians and their dependents the objects of admiration among many, and the targets of suspicion and military reprisal in many others.

In describing the upheaval in Ettwein's town and in his soul in late September of 1777, one need go no further than the situation that confronted him in one wounded Continental officer, who becomes a symbol of the importunity and contradictions besetting Johann Ettwein. After the Battle of Brandywine the need for hospital space had been critical, leading to the appropriation of the Single Men's Choir Dormitory on September 19th. On September 21 a wounded senior officer arrived, and needed to be housed separately from the enlisted men, in the Sun Inn. Concerning this officer Ettwein had received a personal note from George Washington: "Treat him as though he were my son." The officer was a nineteen year-old French émigré, the Marquis de Lafayette, who had been commissioned a Major General by Congress. At Brandywine he had been wounded in the leg. Arriving September 21, he stayed in the Sun Inn for over a month, missing the action at Germantown.

The manners of a French noble combined with the meekness and hospitality of the Moravians surely guaranteed that the conversations between them were polite, perhaps effusively so. Lafayette wrote home of his experience to his young wife, of the attentiveness of the care, although he also expresses the impatience of his youth at the length of his recuperation.[48] Even so the Moravians could not avoid the whiff of scandal and the birth of myth: it is supposed that Lafayette had an affair—of sorts—with one of his Moravian nurses, a woman of the community who never married. The story grew to the point that it was thought that he was sent to convalesce in the home of the young woman's father.[49] Whether such gossip reached Ettwein's ears at the time or was only spawned later, the independent persistence of this story illustrates the kinds of worries in the heart of the town's director: Outsiders posed the threat of contaminating the souls of his charges, those seeking a purer worship and experience of Jesus Christ.

Several famous persons passed through Bethlehem during the course of the war, beginning with Surgeon General John Warren in December 3, 1776, whose mission was to implement George Washington's orders to establish the Continental Army's General Hospital in Bethlehem. Warren and his associate William Shippen, Director of Hospitals, selected the Single Brother's House. Within two weeks General Horatio Gates was also in the town. In the hectic month of September 1777 General de Kalb and three French officers visited on the same day that Bethlehem began to be used as a depot. On their flight from Philadelphia several Continental congressmen including John Adams, John Hancock and Richard Henry Lee visited Bethlehem.[50] Sixteen of these dignitaries, impressed by the character of the townspeople and very likely beseeched by the town's leaders, signed a letter instructing Continental troops to "refrain from disturbing the persons or property of the Moravians in Bethlehem, and particularly that they do not disturb or molest the Houses where the women are assembled."[51] Other war-time visitors included George Washington in July, 1782, who met with Ettwein and attended worship, and John Paul Jones in 1783.[52]

The war, meanwhile, put intense pressure on the Single Men's Choir. The repeated appropriation of their dormitories for hospitals and prisons

---

48. Williamson, "Marquis de Lafayette." Williamson cites the Bethlehem Diary, which firmly locates Lafayette at the Inn.

49. Levering, *History of Bethlehem*, 465.

50. *Bethlehem of Pennsylvania*, 108–9.

51. *Bethlehem of Pennsylvania*, 115.

52. *Bethlehem of Pennsylvania*, 123.

meant that they were turned out and decentralized, causing their community to unravel.[53] Indeed, they never recovered their social and economic vitality. Starting in 1788 what had once been one of Bethlehem's most productive choirs had to be subsidized by the community just to keep going.[54] This was one of the early indicators that Bethlehem was going to experience another major reorientation of church and community life soon after the turn of the century.

It is unsurprising that the Single Men's Choir was the most vulnerable to the pressure of conscription laws and fines on the one hand, and on the other the most susceptible to patriotic suggestion, that is, to the recruiters in their midst. Ettwein had to send warnings of discipline and even expulsion from the communities if any Moravian showed up to drill when the militia were mustered. When seeing one's neighbors take on martial duties, the temptation was real, especially to the young men, for shouldering their arms and joining other men in camaraderie.[55]

## Ettwein and the Militia Laws

This threat to community discipline is the context in which Ettwein exercised his pacifist convictions in contrast to Spangenberg's. Although an election in Pennsylvania had returned a Quaker-Loyalist majority to the assembly in 1776, a patriot coup forced its adjournment and exile and established a revolutionary government. The peace churches that had been so generously accommodated in the province since William Penn received his charter nearly one hundred years earlier—that is the English Quakers, German and Dutch Anabaptists and German radical Pietists—found themselves under new and wholly unfamiliar legal pressures. These pacifists were required, along with the rest of the population, to abjure their oaths of loyalty to the crown of England and swear a new oath to the revolutionary government. This assault on conscience intensified with Pennsylvania's conscription laws for service either in the militia or in the province's Continental line.

The "test oaths" were just as much a conundrum to the Moravians as to the Quakers and Anabaptists. In a letter of May 29th, 1778 Ettwein finds the revolutionary government's attitude a betrayal of the former

---

53. Hamilton, *Johann Ettwein*, 67.

54. Hamilton, *Johann Ettwein*, 70. Cf. Levering, *History of Bethlehem*, 532.

55. Hamilton, *Johann Ettwein*, 68.

tolerance afforded to them by the previous administration as "peaceable strangers."[56] It was already a given that they could not be "perfectly neuter," and Bethlehem had already been "assisting the country in all lawful ways ... we shall never be active against the liberties of America." Thus, in Ettwein's logic, the very religious scruple that makes the oath impossible also makes it unnecessary. If it came to the choice of obeying God rather than government, he considers that the Moravians might abandon Pennsylvania altogether and flee to Canada.[57] This option is prophetic; it is the choice eventually made by the missionary David Zeisberger, discussed in chapter 7.

Concerning the conscription of men for militia or army duty, Ettwein has a strongly-worded letter for Bishop Matthew Hehl, the Pastor of the Moravian settlement of Lititz near Lancaster, dated June 1, 1777.[58] At this relatively early date in the war the general agreement among Moravian men is that they will not join the musters or enlist, and pay their fines instead. The issue is whether a Moravian male could satisfy the law by paying another non-Moravian to be his proxy. This was considered a legitimate alternative under the law, and the practice was common. Hehl pointed to a precedent set by Zinzendorf himself. In 1744 during a conscription in Saxony, Zinzendorf paid others to preserve the men of Herrnhut.

Ettwein does not agree that the action of a lord on behalf of his manor is ethically equivalent to that of an individual paying someone else to exempt himself. Zinzendorf was not ransoming himself, but his residents of Herrnhut. Thus the Count was not acting for himself, but for others, while the residents of Herrnhut, out of duty to their liege, could accept their ransom without compunction. A pacifist individual paying a proxy as a ransom for himself, however, is hiring a mercenary to do that which he knows is evil. The issue is less that the proxy is put in harm's way, and more that the proxy is being paid to do violence to others; this is why the hiring of proxies should be ethically repugnant to Moravians. "But what I fear is the tendency to let self-will, greed, ease, and a desire to escape the cross dictate [our course] [sic]."[59]

---

56. Hamilton, *Johann Ettwein*, 237.
57. Hamilton, *Johann Ettwein*, 236.
58. A translation of the letter appears in Hamilton, *Johann Ettwein*, 238–42.
59. Hamilton, *Johann Ettwein*, 241.

Fines were already steep, at 15 pounds or 25 pounds, and were assessed for each failure to muster.[60] Yet Ettwein insisted that they be paid, and set up a fund to do that to help poorer Moravians avoid military duty. Joseph Levering estimates that the total amount in fines paid by Moravians refusing to turn out for military duty far exceeds the bills for damages and consumables paid by the United States government to Bethlehem for the use of its buildings.[61]

Yet Ettwein's pacifism remains distinct from that of the Quakers, who refused to pay war-time taxes or pay the enlistment fines, since these funds were used to sponsor the war effort. Quakers also refused the use of their wagons for hospital transport, and they refused to provision hungry soldiers, because these supported the ability of armies to wage war. The Moravians, however, submitted meekly to all of these demands, and paid their fines.

Like most Quakers Ettwein leaned to the royalists in sympathy, inasmuch as the blame for any civil war rooted in overthrowing the established social order had to be placed on the rebels. His sympathies reached the point that he considered exiling his community to Canada rather than face the test oath. Even so, they remained in place and Ettwein took no actions to harm the interests of the patriots; the Moravians stood aloof from the active non-violent resistance of the English Quakers and German Anabaptists by their meek acquiescence to patriot demands, including the payment of militia fines. The Moravian conscience drove them to help those in need: they fed the hungry even if they were soldiers; they tended the sick and wounded even if they were soldiers.

## Conclusion

Bethlehem was a living contradiction during the American Revolution: it was a pacifist community storing munitions and garrisoning prisoners of war. Yet for all these favors to the patriot cause, local Pennsylvania recruiters and judges refused to exempt them from the conscription laws. The changes brought by the war had special impact on the Single Brothers Choir, and set in motion the changes in the town's character that were even deeper and more pervasive than the shift from the General Economy in 1762.

60. Hamilton, *Johann Ettwein*, 241.
61. Levering, *History of Bethlehem*, 482n20.

Ettwein met many of the important dignitaries associated with the American Revolution as they passed through Bethlehem, or stayed in its inns, because it was he rather than Seidel who was proficient in English. These celebrity visitors tended to speak highly of Bethlehem. Hundreds more whom history has forgotten passed through as well: the wounded and the prisoners for whom a sojourn in Bethlehem became a chapter of their own lives.

## 5

# Crossing Over

## *A Lutheran Chaplain Discovers America*

### Imagining a Battle

On August 8, 1777, a royalist flank column was detached from General John Burgoyne's main army to secure the crossroads and patriot supply depot at the town of Bennington, in present-day Vermont. By August 14 they encountered a patriot force up to three times their number under the command of New Hampshire's militia general John Stark. The royalist column was comprised of over 200 dismounted dragoons of the Braunschweig (German) Auxiliaries under Lt. Col. Friederich Baum, who also had charge of hundreds more Canadians, loyalists, and Mohawk warriors. They dug in to defensive positions at an unincorporated hamlet ten miles short of their objective. Baum sent for reinforcements. Pitched battle was postponed for a day due to rain, but on August 16, early in the afternoon, the patriots attacked.

Accounts of the Battle of Bennington describe an American Army Chaplain, Thomas Allen (1743–1810) behaving martially and heroically, leading the charge of the Pittsfield Militia with sword drawn. No account describes the behavior of the chaplain on the other side, the German Lutheran Friedrich Valentin Melsheimer. That he was wounded in the arm is the testimony of the field surgeon, Julian Wasmus, who treated him and then became his roommate for over a year of captivity.[1] As to the German chaplain's movements, general historical information reduces speculation to a very few probabilities.

Outside of Prussia, German regiments of the eighteenth century viewed their regimental chaplains as civilian noncombatants; when a regiment was engaged in battle, its chaplain remained behind the baggage with the other civilian camp-followers.[2] In the course of the Battle of Bennington Chaplain Melsheimer most likely stayed where he was supposed to, and was struck there in the arm by a stray bullet as likely by an accident of his own men as that of the rebels.

Melsheimer was small of stature and asthmatic; despite his interest in nature and love for the outdoors, he had discovered by that spring that he had no heart for the military life. Military custom, and his own distaste for violence, very likely places the dragoons chaplain with the baggage once battle erupts. In the midst of the noise and confusion he becomes aware of a sudden searing pain, then sees blood seeping through the hole in the arm of his black clerical coat. Perhaps he faints. He awakens just minutes later, but all is already lost: His regiment of dragoons is throwing down their carbines and broadswords in surrender, and the cries of the men reach his ears that their commanding officer is down.

Perhaps something more heroic occurred to balance, on the royalist side, the actions and courage of the patriot chaplain Thomas Allen. Hunkered down behind the baggage the dragoon chaplain knows little of what is happening until an ensign, Cornet Stutzer, barks at him, "*Prediger, brauch dein Pferd.*" "Preacher, get your horse." The regiment means to break through the encirclement, gain the road and make a dash in the direction of Major Breymann, whose grenadiers are marching to their relief.

Melsheimer mounts his nag but finds her skittish in the cacophony of battle; the reports of field pieces, carbines and rifles, the buzz and whistle of flying projectiles and the shouts and agonies of men. He steers to the cluster of dragoons and artillery at the center of a grassy meadow littered with cartridge paper, where the acrid wisps of gun smoke stubbornly refuse to dissipate in the moist, still air. The field is ringed by log shacks and stone houses, wood-piles, posts and out-buildings. The blue-coated Braunschweig troops, with white shirts and trousers and black

---

1. Wasmus, *Journal*, 75–85.
2. Burgoyne, *Hessian Chaplains*, vii.

boots, are fixing bayonets, modeling discipline under harassing fire. Several of them are lying on the ground, some motionless, others in pain as parts of themselves spill dark and red from within, through their shirts and pants and onto the grass. There is a lump in the chaplain's throat and a sourness in his chest. He fears for his life, but even more he loathes the violence and human catastrophe of war.

From his saddle Melsheimer ascertains that the center is the only position remaining in Baum's line of defense. The white-cloaked patriots have overrun the redoubts but are slow to press now, preferring to shoot into the knot of blue from the superior range of their hunting rifles. The Germans, equipped with the short-range carbines of a mounted infantry but not with horses, had run out of ammunition. Now it was to be broadswords and bayonets to save them, to slash a hole in the circle that was tightening around them. But there are so many rebels, before and behind; even from the vantage of horseback Melsheimer can scarcely comprehend the numbers of the enemy.

Lt. Col. Baum's order is repeated by captains and sergeants and the Braunschweig dragoons charge forward, with a roar of defiance rising out of their chests. The rebels rush forwards themselves now, their answering cry more akin to the high-pitched howls of coyotes, like that heard among Native warriors. They are holding their long rifles with both hands on the muzzle, the butts high up in the air, to swing them like clubs. When the melee is joined it is a dizzying, disorienting, sickening sight. Melsheimer would shut his eyes to it, but he must keep his horse. Then at once Baum cries out, slumps in his saddle, and slides off his horse.

As the rebels swarm the chaplain cries out to his commanding officer, the only man in the outfit for whom he felt loyalty and friendship. Wanting to pull him up and gallop them both out of this nightmare, Melsheimer stretches out his hand towards Baum, and then feels the searing pain, and sees the hole in the upper arm of his coat. When had that happened? No matter. All around him the dragoons, seeing it is hopeless, are throwing down their guns and swords. Men, rebels and dragoons both, are trying to help the fallen colonel, to see where he is wounded, but they push and pull against each other and Baum cries out again in anguish. Melsheimer cannot reach him. Several rebels are now shouting at him, brandishing their rifle butts. "Get down!" His nag rears, wild-eyed at the hostile motions. Chaplain Melsheimer has not learned English, but it is clear what they mean.

## Melsheimer in Germany[3]

Friedrich Valentin Melsheimer was born in Negenborn on September 25, 1749[4] to Joachim Sebastian Melsheimer (1720–1800), and Clara M. Melsheimer, nee Reitemeyer.[5] Joachim Melsheimer was the superintendent of forests in the Duchy of Braunschweig-Wolfenbüttel in northwest Germany. In Friedrich's autobiography he refers gratefully to his parents bringing him into the covenant of baptism as an infant.[6] Friedrich began boarding school in Holzminden at the age of seven.[7]

On October 21, 1768, Melsheimer matriculated at the University of Helmstedt.[8] He studied under a generation of scholars that stood in the shadows of Helmstedt's more celebrated and controversial forebears, the most famous of whom was George Calixtus (1586–1656).[9] By the time of Melsheimer's enrollment Helmstedt had steered toward Lutheran orthodoxy.[10] After rationalist views expressed by a Helmstedt instructor had sparked riots in 1764,[11] leading to that scholar's removal, the Duke commissioned Johann Carpzov IV, "*ein strenger Lutheraner*"[12] (a strict Lutheran) in a lineage of stalwart Lutheran Orthodox scholars, to compose a systematic theology. Carpzov's effort was published in 1767, a year before Melsheimer's studies began.

---

3. This chapter re-presents information first published in the author's dissertation on Melsheimer (Wilson, "Switching Sides"). Some passages are reproduced verbatim. Corrections based on new research and fresh reading of the sources are also noted.

4. Melsheimer, *Selbstbiographie*, is extant only in its final recension, "Autobiography," a type-written redaction dated to 1935 of an original from Melsheimer's hand. On source discrepancies see Wilson, "Switching Sides," 41n57.

5. Clara Melsheimer's dates are not known.

6. Melsheimer, "Autobiography," 1.

7. Melsheimer, "Autobiography," 1.

8. *Wolfenbütteler Digitale Bibliothek*, 3:265. The "Autobiography" lists the year as 1769. Most likely the error in the year is Melsheimer's, since he spent only a fraction of 1768 at Helmstedt (Melsheimer, "Autobiography," 1).

9. Melsheimer, "Autobiography," 1. Scholar Sabine Ahrens writes that Calixtus's irenic inter-confessional approach remained influential in *Niedersachsen* (Lower Saxony), the modern political designation of the region.

10. Wilson, "Switching Sides," 44–46.

11. Ahrens, *Die Lehrkräfte*, 45.

12. Siegfried, "Carpzov, Johann Benedict."

Melsheimer completed his studies at Helmstedt in 1772.[13] The only information for the time between his graduation and his appointment to the dragoons regiment in 1776 is his own statement that he served as a tutor for two families.[14]

## Lutheran Chaplains of the German Armies

Melsheimer's appointment to the regiment was made in the weeks between the conclusion of Braunschweig-Wolfenbüttel's treaty with Great Britain and before the corps mobilized.[15] Melsheimer was 26 years of age at his call. In these ways he was fitting into a standard career trajectory for Lutheran clergy throughout Germany's kingdoms, electorates, and principalities. In Prussia a generation earlier a minimum age for chaplains had been set at 25 in the belief that younger soldiers would have more respect for a seasoned adult.[16] With the candidate for ministry often graduating between the ages of 21 and 23 this meant a wait of several years before qualifying for the chaplaincy. In the interval few parishes in Germany were eager to be chew-toys where inexperienced pastors cut their teeth. The waiting was often filled by tutoring the children of privileged benefactors. This was a common track for pastors throughout Germany, including the German auxiliary chaplains Johannes Braunsdorf (1752–1826) of Anhalt-Zerbst,[17] and Philipp Waldeck (1749–1884) of the Waldeck Battalion.[18] Few pastors took calls to regiments as a lifetime vocation and typically served for three or four years.[19] The service in North America which stretched for seven years in a losing cause was more than most chaplains would have expected or desired. On their return to Germany the chaplains of Hesse-Kassel (Reformed) were discharged and given pensions until they secured pulpits.[20] Chaplain Braunsdorf of Anhalt-Zerbst (Lutheran) married the daughter of a courtier,

---

13. Melsheimer, "Autobiography," 1.

14. Melsheimer, "Autobiography," 1.

15. Riedesel, *Memoirs, Letters, and Journals,* 2:265–73. On the confusion between "surgeons" (*chiurgeon*) and "chaplains" in the lists of staff in William Leete Stone's translation of Eelking, see Wilson, "Switching Sides," 48n88.

16. Marschke, *Absolutely Pietist,* 35.

17. Burgoyne, *Hessian Chaplains,* 112.

18. Waldeck, *Eighteenth-Century America,* 11.

19. Marschke, *Absolutely Pietist,* 35.

20. Burgoyne, *Hessian Chaplains,* ix.

then resigned from the chaplaincy and founded a parish which he served until well beyond the Napoleonic era.[21] Of the seven Braunschweig chaplains, all left the military and four of them including Melsheimer served churches until their deaths.[22]

Most armies in the eighteenth century did not confer military rank on their chaplains: Prussia was the exception in Germany, and the Continental Army may have intentionally borrowed from the Prussian example. For each of the six German states that sent auxiliaries to North America the military chaplains were civilians. In the eighteenth century it was normative to defer the decision to retain chaplains to each regiment's commanding officer.[23] Six of the eight Braunschweig regiments were served by chaplains.[24] Outside Prussia, Lutheran Chaplains in Germany were thus accountable both to the civilian consistory that ordained them, and to the commanding officer who issued the call. As commander of the dragoons,[25] Lt. Col. Friedrich Baum (c. 1727–1777) looked to the local consistory in Wolfenbüttel to recruit a chaplain for his regiment. Melsheimer was examined by the Wolfenbüttel Consistory on February 6, 1776, ordained on February 7, and preached his first sermon to the regiment on February 10.[26]

The authority of a civilian chaplain was defined by status rather than rank. The standard is that chaplains were paid as junior officers and entitled to a like share of the plunder,[27] however in the command structure they were equal to a major, and answered only to the regiment's commanding officer.[28] Chaplains, like officers, went on horseback, and

---

21. Burgoyne, *Hessian Chaplains*, 112–14.

22. Riedesel, *Memoirs, Letters, and Journals*, 2:268 (Chaplain Schrader), 269 (Chaplain Togel), 271 (Chaplain Milius). That Melsheimer prospered in a career in the United States was either not known to Eelking or omitted as irrelevant to the greater dishonor to the corps for his having "deserted." See Riedesel, *Memoirs, Letters, and Journals*, 2:266.

23. See Marschke, *Absolutely Pietist*; cf. Thompson, *From its European Antecedents*, 110.

24. Riedesel, *Memoirs, Letters, and Journals*, 2:265–73, when subtracting Stone's translations of surgeon (*Chiurgeon*, abbreviated "ch") as "chaplain" from the list.

25. Dragoons were mounted infantry armed with carbines and broadswords (Ketchum, *Saratoga*, 137).

26. Melsheimer, "Autobiography," 1.

27. Burgoyne, *Hessian Chaplains*, vii; cf. Marschke, *Absolutely Pietist*, 20–22.

28. Marschke, *Absolutely Pietist*, 22.

were assigned a personal servant.[29] To the end of his life this distinction in status was important to Melsheimer, and he referred to his "brother officers" in his "Autobiography."[30]

While infantry regiments numbered around six hundred soldiers and officers, cavalry regiments were smaller.[31] There were fewer than three hundred Braunschweig dragoons, yet they were the only mounted regiment of all the German auxiliaries sent to North America. The decision to include them might have been a function of the vanity of the Commanding Officer of the Braunschweig Corps, Major General Friedrich Zu Riedesel, who on the eve of the campaign had been promoted from the rank of Colonel by Braunschweig's Duke Karl I in an effort to put him on par with the British generals.

Portraits of Riedesel suggest that he was small of stature, and that he preferred the dragoon's accoutrements for himself, while it is reported that dragoons formed his personal bodyguard.[32] Shipping a mounted regiment presented a practical difficulty. When Col. Sir William Faucitt (1727–1804), England's ambassador for recruiting auxiliaries, concluded the treaty with Karl I, Duke of Braunschweig-Wolfenbüttel (1713–1780), neither party wanted to pay for shipping all those hundreds of horses on a months-long ocean voyage. It was conveniently assumed that horses could be procured for the dragoons in Canada, a strategy founded on the premise that hundreds of battle-trained horses were to be found among Canada's few thousand residents. Early in the century something of the same single-minded obliviousness to facts and sound reason had deluded the investors in the Navy Stores Project at Livingston Manor, who invested their fortunes on the assumption that Sweden's fir trees would be found foresting New York. Riedesel's extravagant optimism did not end there; he also insisted that his wife and young children join him on deployment. They would not arrive in Canada until a year later, in 1777, to join their dear Pappy in defeat, capture, parole and prison.

29. Burgoyne, *Hessian Chaplains*, vii. This is confirmed by Braunsdorf (Burgoyne, *Hessian Chaplains*, 97). Melsheimer never mentions a servant.

30. Melsheimer, "Autobiography," 2.

31. Stephenson, *Patriot Battles*, 46.

32. Wasmus, *Journal*, 2. The coats for all German auxiliaries were royal blue with the exception of each corps' Jaegers, the sharp-shooting rifle companies that wore green coats in an early anticipation of camouflage gear. Illustrations of the Battle of Bennington depict Braunschweig Dragoons wearing plumed tri-corner caps. Regimental chaplains were distinguished by their black clothes and white tabs at the collar (Waldeck, *Eighteenth Century America*, iv).

Melsheimer's commission as a chaplain to a regiment embarked to North America was an opportunity for self-publicity. He arranged to keep a *Tagebuch* (daily diary) of his observations and experiences for publication with a press in Minden, a city under Prussian control.[33] His first volume appeared in the late fall of 1776, having been rushed to press almost as soon as it had been received. He is not alone in writing travelogues for publication. Another to write with self-promotion and an eventual audience in view is Chaplain Philipp Waldeck of the Waldeck battalion. Some of the differences between the two authors point to differences in their overall character and spiritual priorities, as will be seen below. Waldeck's journal remained unpublished.

### Discovering Canada

Melsheimer's *Tagebuch* begins with the first division of the Braunschweig Corps marching out of Wolfenbüttel on February 22, 1776, heading north for the seafaring port of Stade.[34] Melsheimer provides no autobiography and no pious reflection, in contrast to the traveler of a generation earlier, Heinrich Mühlenberg, whose reflections on his departure from Europe are peppered with scripture and leavened with pious lament and prophecy.[35] The regiment was embarked on March 13 and sailed on March 19. Melsheimer was aboard the *Minerva* with most of the dragoons and Lt. Col. Baum.[36]

Crossing an ocean was perilous. For John Wesley (1703–1791) a storm at sea was life-changing when he compared his own terror to the serene faith in the Moravian passengers.[37] For Heinrich Mühlenberg life onboard was an opportunity to be light in darkness out of concern for the spiritual welfare of the passengers and crew.[38] A few months after the Braunschweig flotilla took sail, Chaplain Philipp Waldeck's Waldeck Battalion set out for New York. While embarked but waiting on the coast of England, Waldeck held communion not only on his own vessel but

33. Minden was a non-contiguous possession of Prussia, a situation not unusual in the Holy Roman Empire of the eighteenth century and earlier.
34. Waldeck, *Eighteenth Century America*, 2.
35. Mühlenberg, *Journals*, 1:25–57.
36. Melsheimer, *Journal of the Voyage*, 2.
37. Hamilton, *History of the Moravian Church*, 79; cf. Anderson, *Lord of the Ring*, 145–48.
38. Mühlenberg, *Journals*, 1:26–28.

was taken by skiff to other ships as well.[39] Yet one can only guess that Melsheimer held worship amidships; he would rather describe his own sea-legs. Rather than Heinrich Mühlenberg's graphic descriptions of illness, Melsheimer boasts of his resistance to sea-sickness.[40] In contrast to Wesley his trust was firm, not in God, but in the design of the ship to ride over the waves even in a gale.[41] The first hint that Melsheimer serves a Higher Power of some sort comes on page 8 of the *Journal*, "The wind being nearly always good we were able, by the help of the weather and the grace of God, to promise ourselves a prosperous voyage."[42] Ironically the next day's entry notes the first death on the ship due to illness.

The Braunschweig flotilla skirted the coasts of the Maritime Islands and reached the St. Lawrence by May 20, arriving beneath the fortress city of Quebec on June 1. While the ships were scattered and arrived over the course of a week, none were lost. Melsheimer's final comment on the voyage: "So often in danger, so often rescued by the hand of Providence."[43] Part I of Melsheimer's *Tagebuch* ends with the note on June 3 that Canada's Governor General, Guy Carleton, departed with General Riedesel for Montreal at the head of the majority of British and German forces, "and left the command to that excellent man, Lt. Col. Baum."[44] The dragoons were held in reserve to guard the fortress, a sensible mission for a mounted infantry that had no mounts.

Part II of the *Tagebuch* begins with orders to disembark on June 6.[45] Setting foot on land Melsheimer is unimpressed with the architecture of the fortress city and the overall meanness of Quebec's economy. He and other enterprising dragoons tried to brew a potable German-style

---

39. Waldeck, *Eighteenth-Century America*, 6.
40. Mühlenberg, *Journals*, 1:26.
41. Melsheimer, *Journal of the Voyage*, 5.
42. Melsheimer, *Journal of the Voyage*, 8.
43. Melsheimer, *Journal of the Voyage*, 18.
44. Melsheimer, *Journal of the Voyage*, 19.

45. The second volume was published in Leipzig with the title, *Geographische Beschreibung von Canada besonders der Hauptstadt Quebeck; nebst den Handlungen, Sitten, Gebräuchen und Lebensart der Einwohner* überhaupt sowohl Christen als Wilden, einer Nachricht von den dasigen deutschen Truppen, und einer von einem Wilden Könige gehaltenen Rede. A second edition was then published in Leipzig, combining the two Melsheimer journals into one volume. William Wood and William L. Stone each translated one part and published them together in one volume as *Journal of the Voyage*.

beer to make up for the disappointing local beverages.[46] In his opinion the French Canadians were poor farmers and peasants from Braunschweig could teach them better methods.[47] He does offer high praise to the colony's justice system. "There is no country in which the points at issue are decided more justly and in accordance with natural right than in Canada."[48]

The chaplain also describes a village of 120 families of the Huron Nation in vivid detail. "As regards their morals, they are surely just as good, if not better, than the best Christians."[49] Melsheimer writes this after observing a ceremony in which the Hurons declared alliance to the royalists and war against the American patriots. Melsheimer's comparison of Huron warriors to Christians is made before he witnessed frontier war in North America and before his experience of Puritans in Massachusetts and Moravians in Pennsylvania. In this early assessment of the Native Nations he does not share in the typical attitudes of Pennsylvania Germans and their pastors. However, between his *Tagebuch* and his internment in a Moravian town, Melsheimer went on campaign with Native warriors attached to the British force. As is discussed below, the harsh imperatives of military duty caused a crisis of conscience; it is not a coincidence that this crisis ensued as he became witness to the conduct of war on the frontier.

Montreal was re-occupied by royalists in June of 1776. Melsheimer's *Tagebuch* concludes on the eve of Carleton's counter-offensive in September. It does not appear that Melsheimer published more *Tagebuch* volumes after September 1776. With scant mention of chaplain duties in Melsheimer's own account, and nothing extant from his own hand between September 1776 and April 1779, other sources fill in some of the gaps. Dragoons company surgeon Julian Wasmus notes that on June 30, 1776, there was a "great procession and communion was held by all the German regiments." This occurred again one week later.[50] On October 6, a *Te Deum* celebrated the recovery of Braunschweig's Duke Karl from an illness.

---

46. Melsheimer, *Journal of the Voyage*, 19.
47. Melsheimer, *Journal of the Voyage*, 24–25.
48. Melsheimer, *Journal of the Voyage*, 26.
49. Melsheimer, *Journal of the Voyage*, 31.
50. Wasmus, *Journal*, 25.

Carleton's counter-offensive against the Americans retreating headlong from Montreal is a minor episode in the course of the War of Independence. During the preparations of the summer Riedesel drilled his men in forest skirmishing, and they acquitted themselves well in August maneuvers observed by the English generals. The dragoon regiment, however, did not participate, as they remained in garrison in the city until September. The dragoons were then mustered to take part in the campaign.

The late start was due to the slow pace with which conscripted French Canadian workers built a fleet for sailing troops down Lake Champlain. Carleton's campaign was successful but limited, the only notable action being the Battle of Lake Champlain from October 11–13. Here Carleton's lake fleet smashed the one constructed hastily by Benedict Arnold. Although a tactical victory for the loyalists, Arnold's objective of covering the retreat was successful: the patriots proved elusive to the advancing royalists. The dragoons, and Melsheimer with them, had advanced south of St. John where they were held in reserve. Rather than pursue further, Carleton chose to withdraw to fortify the St. Lawrence and take winter quarters.[51]

News then reached the royalists that the wife of General John Burgoyne, Carleton's second-in-command, had died. Burgoyne returned promptly to England to settle his wife's affairs and to present to Colonial Secretary George Germaine (1716–1785) a plan to win the war. It was a plan of Burgoyne's own devising; he did not consult either Carleton or Howe, both of whom were his superiors. He had also expressed his displeasure with Carleton for retiring to winter quarters without pressing the offensive. This impolitic approach to his chain of command would doom him in the field, even though from hindsight his plan appears to have been the only one viable to produce a British victory by conquest.

Meanwhile winter on the St. Lawrence in 1776–1777 had its share of cold days but Melsheimer makes no remarks about the suffering of the soldiers as such. The Braunschweig Corps bivouacked in Trois-Riviéres, a village south of the fortress of Quebec, and does not seem to have suffered inordinately in the climate, aside from the routine miseries of the eighteenth century when little was known about hygiene, germ theory and the body's circulatory system. Sledding was taken up as a sport

---

51. Riedesel, *Memoirs, Letters, and Journals*, 2:66–75.

among the men, while officers took turns hosting balls and *fetes*.[52] It is unknown whether Melsheimer attended these socials.

Burgoyne returned with his orders on May 15 and the army ramped up its preparations for a campaign.[53] By the end of June Melsheimer's attitude toward army life had changed.

## On Campaign

The clue to Melsheimer's state of mind in June, 1777, is found in a letter from 1779. By then a prisoner of war, he was being billeted in the home of Samuel Mau in Bethlehem. The letter he wrote is to Johann Ettwein, and he has several goals, both formal and informal, including that he is asking permission from the town's leadership to marry Samuel's daughter Marie Agnes.

How he came to Bethlehem is related below, but in describing his state of mind in June, 1777, Melsheimer writes: "For already two years hence, and before we became prisoners at Bennington, I wished for nothing more than this, that God wanted to show me my way to where I could serve in peace."[54] Daily experience has strongly convinced him that the military life and the peace-loving life described in the "Scriptures of Salvation" were as far different as Heaven is different from Earth.[55] The scriptures "preach love, kindness, meekness, conciliation, purity, and piety"—virtues encouraged by godliness—"and to flee from sloth, bloodthirstiness, ill-gotten gain, and vice"—which are the values encouraged and practiced in the military life by the very nature of war.[56]

The term Melsheimer uses for ill-gotten gain is *Raub*, plunder, a critique of the eighteenth-century chaplain's personal stake in the loot of a

---

52. Wasmus, *Journal*, 44.

53. Riedesel, *Memoirs, Letters, and Journals*, 1:98.

54. Melsheimer, "Letters to Johann Ettwein," 400. This corrects my reading of "nach" (page 1, line 16) as "noch" (Wilson, "Switching Sides," 102). Ergo, from the end of line 15: "Seid schon 2 Jarhen, und noch ehe wir zu Benington gefangen würden [sic]." The thrust of my argument has not changed from "Switching Sides," it has been strengthened.

55. Melsheimer, "Letters to Johann Ettwein," 400. This reads *weit* in line 23 rather than *weil*, which would otherwise render the sense that "because" Heaven is so different from Earth, the military life is so different from the love of peace described in the Scriptures.

56. Melsheimer, "Letters to Johann Ettwein," 400.

campaigning army. Since the root of the godly life is peace, to benefit from plunder gotten by force and violence was not a contradiction Melsheimer could reconcile. The two year time-frame he relates for this conviction dates it to the spring of 1777, approximately the beginning of Burgoyne's campaign. Perhaps he had already seen enough of the violence of war during Carleton's campaign the previous fall, but the lack of action for the dragoons makes that unlikely. It may be that the relative inactivity of the army's winter quarters in Quebec soured him on the military life. Even though he dates his awakened conviction to the spring of 1777, he had also written no further installment of his journal of travels in the intervening months.

If these earlier experiences under the affable leadership of Governor General Carleton had been enough to plant seeds of doubt in Melsheimer's conscience, conviction came to harvest in the more earnest warfare conducted by the ambitious General Burgoyne beginning in June of 1777. On June 23, at the outset of the campaign, General Burgoyne published a proclamation throughout New York which provides an independent textual framework for those military requirements that Melsheimer had raised as objections to conscience. In Burgoyne's own words:

> I trust I shall stand acquitted in the Eyes of God and Men, in denouncing and executing the Vengeance of the State against the willful outcast. The Messengers of Justice and Wrath await them in the Field, and Devastation, Famine, and every concomitant Horror that a reluctant but indispensable Prosecution of Military Duty must occasion, will bar the Way to their Return.[57]

Writing in April 1779, the "two years hence" to which he referred could very well mean that Melsheimer's new convictions were provoked by Burgoyne's published philosophy of war.

## Early Success

Montreal, in present-day Quebec, is three hundred miles directly north of New York City. In the eighteenth century these two cities were linked by a waterway of rivers and lakes and a few overland portages. The southern terminus was the mouth of the Hudson River, while the northern key to control of the route was Lake Champlain, pointing south-to north like a finger. At the same time that Carleton was chasing the patriots down

---

57. Burgoyne, "Proclamation," 303–4.

Champlain from Canada's frontier, in the Fall of 1776, British General William Howe sailed an enormous army down the Atlantic coast from Halifax and seized New York City, decisively routing the Continental Army in a series of engagements. This gave the British control of the headwaters of the Hudson and thus both ends of the waterway.

Burgoyne's strategy for the campaign of 1777 was to take most of the forces under Carleton's command in Canada and advance on Albany, New York, in two columns.[58] The main column would follow the Champlain waterway and secure the chain of forts on its way to Albany. On their right (to their west on a southward march) a brigade of loyalists, Canadians, and Native Americans, under Col. Barry St. Leger, would capture Fort Stanwyx and advance on Albany from the northwest. Meanwhile Howe's army would proceed north from New York City along the Hudson River, securing West Point on its way to linking up with Burgoyne. This would put Boston within marching distance of the combined armies and isolate New England from the rest of the colonies.

It likely would have worked had Howe followed it, but Burgoyne was his subordinate, and the orders for the campaign season sent to him from Colonial Secretary Germaine in London were vague enough to be loosely interpreted.[59] In the months-long lag in communications between generals in America and their civilian overseers in London it was too late to clarify orders once the campaign began. Howe took his army on a languid, round-about course to Philadelphia, Washington refused to trap his own army in a futile defense of that city, Congress fled to York and continued to govern, and as Howe sat in Philadelphia Burgoyne's entire army was lost. But these outcomes were far from inevitable in June, 1777.

Burgoyne's army mounted its invasion on June 20, 1777. While his force included the navy built by Carleton the year before to sail Lake Champlain, there was a shortage of draught animals for the prodigious supply train. Warriors from allied Native Nations served the army as scouts, in tracking down deserters, and in quick, harassing strikes. Thus the Native Nations auxiliaries filled the role of a cavalry, and had the advantage of knowing the terrain. This made the Braunschweig dragoons redundant and they remained on foot; horses had not been supplied, despite promises, since landing in Quebec over a year earlier.[60]

58. A comprehensive treatment of the Albany Campaign is offered by Ketchum, *Saratoga*.

59. Ferling, *Almost a Miracle*, 189–92.

60. Ketchum, *Saratoga*, 137.

The advance to Crown Point was uncontested. Much of the progress took place on the water which allowed for rapid movement.[61] They covered 229 miles in ten days and reached Crown Point on June 30. On July 2 the royalists found a trail cutting through the dense woods to the ridge at the top of Mount Hope overlooking Ticonderoga.[62] On July 5 the patriots inside Fort Ticonderoga awoke to find royalist cannon above them, and the commanders chose to abandon the post despite an impassioned sermon by militia Chaplain Thomas Allen, a Congregationalist pastor who had marched with his regiment from Pittsfield, Massachusetts.[63]

In the midst of a heat wave in early July a series of actions took place in which royalist forces defeated patriot rearguards and secured several posts along the waterway. The patriots continued their flight from royalist arms that had begun at the gates of Montreal 18 months earlier. On July 7 the dragoons commander, Lt. Col. Baum, unsure of where the other regiments were encamped and whether the support of his regiment was needed, ordered his regiment forward without having been given that order from above. Before the end of the day he was reprimanded by Burgoyne.[64] The dragoons regrouped and proceeded further down the lake, in the rear of the army, rowing themselves in boats.

The entire army held a feast of thanksgiving on July 13, at which a *Te Deum* was sung.[65] We can only speculate on Melsheimer's frame of mind as he led the service for his regiment. He would have experienced that summer's heat and mosquitoes,[66] but in military terms the campaign could not have gone better. The morale of everyone else involved with the royalist column would have been at its peak. Yet his testimony two years later is that, even when the campaign was proceeding so well, he had already rejected military life and its aspirations.

## Bogging Down

The events over the rest of July and into early August doomed the campaign. The seed of the first disaster was planted in Burgoyne's proclamation

---

61. Wasmus, *Journal*, 56, 58.
62. Ketchum, *Saratoga*, 171.
63. Thompson, *From its European Antecedents*, 282.
64. Ketchum, *Saratoga*, 171.
65. Wasmus, *Journal*, 60.
66. Wasmus, *Journal*, 57.

of June 23, which included his threat to punish patriot settlers with Native Nations warriors.[67] On July 17 Burgoyne triggered the next round of frontier warfare.[68] For the first time Mohawk warriors from towns in New York joined the war against Euro-ethnic settlers. Instead of intimidating New York's settlers, this threat and tactic alienated them: Many neutrals were radicalized into patriots and many embarrassed loyalists became neutral. By the end of July the redcoat officers had learned to their horror and chagrin that distinctions between a loyalist settler and a patriot settler meant little to warriors paid by plunder and scalp bounties. In late July a war party murdered Jane McCrae, a loyalist whose distinctive red hair made her scalp a coveted prize. The frontier was electrified.[69] Burgoyne revisited his policy, trying to limit the butchery to men while sparing women and children, and ending the scalp bounty. At this rebuke the bulk of his Native auxiliaries abandoned the campaign. By early August he had lost the eyes and ears of his army.[70]

The second disaster was Burgoyne's decision to march overland toward Fort Edward, rather than continue down the waterway. His pursuit of the patriots had meant that returning to the water would have been tantamount to a retreat, which, he supposed, would harm the morale of his troops and the country's loyalists.[71] Thus Burgoyne gave up the advantage of the water for his transportation, and played into the patriots' strengths in guerilla warfare. Patriot woodsmen felled trees, blocking the advance and forcing detachments to clear their paths of the logs. The army's progress ground down to less than a mile a day, while the patriots rallied their militias with propaganda about the depredations of the royalist forces and their Native Nations allies. The army reached Fort Edward in early August, emerging from the dense woods into open country;

67. "I have but to give Stretch to the Indian Forces under my Direction, and they amount to Thousands, to overtake the hardened Enemies of Great Britain" (Burgoyne, "Proclamation," 304).

68. Ketchum, *Saratoga*, 265–73.

69. Ketchum, *Saratoga*, 274. These sentiments are shared by William Digby, a British officer, in his memoirs: "The melancholy catastrophe of the unfortunate Miss McCrea . . . affected the general and the whole army" (Digby, "Journal," 306). In his entry for August 1, Julius Wasmus notes McCrea's murder, by name, and states: "This misfortune caused quite an uproar in the army; everyone mourned the fate of this fine young woman. She was not even nineteen years old. What cruelty!" (Wasmus, *Journal*, 66).

70. Ketchum, *Saratoga*, 275, 282.

71. Ketchum, *Saratoga*, 240–51.

but their crawl through the July heat had consumed much of their provisions, and illness ravaged the army. Then on August 3 Burgoyne received the third piece of disastrous news: Howe was not going to march up the Hudson after all; Burgoyne was on his own. Howe concluded his letter: "Success be ever with you."[72]

By then St. Leger was laying siege to Fort Stanwyx as planned. The patriot militia of Tryon County in New York's Mohawk Valley, under Colonel Nicholas Herkimer, a second-generation Palatine, set out in relief. St. Leger set an ambush with a few loyalists and regulars and several hundred Native Nations warriors in the woods near Oriskany on August 5. After six hours of battle some 465 patriot militia were killed or wounded, over half the force. By the time Benedict Arnold's column of Continental reinforcements linked up with Herkimer the battle was over and the militia was limping home again.[73] Herkimer himself would die ten days later, bleeding to death after the amputation of his wounded leg.

Although the battle itself was a stalemate, Oriskany was the fourth disaster for Burgoyne; for as St. Leger was engaged the besieged patriots at Fort Stanwyx sallied forth to raid the camps of the Native Nation warriors. Those warriors, bruised by the fight against Herkimer's men, came back to find their own lodges pillaged and destroyed.[74] Arnold then sent a spy forward to spread the rumor that his own relief force was much larger than what he truly had.[75] The Native Nations melted away from the theater, forcing St. Leger to lift his siege and withdraw to Canada. This, in turn, allowed Arnold and 950 Continentals to wheel about and rejoin the patriots that were rallying north of Albany.[76]

In order to reach his campaign objective Burgoyne needed to secure his left flank against the rising swell of hostile New Englanders marching his way, he needed more provisions and draught animals for his supply train, he needed to compensate for the loss of Native Nations warriors by recruiting more loyalist companies, and he needed a mounted, mobile strike-and-scout force which meant he needed his Braunschweig dragoons to find themselves some horses. To meet these needs required

---

72. Ketchum, *Saratoga*, 283.
73. Ferling, *Almost a Miracle*, 230–31.
74. Stephenson, *Patriot Battles*, 295.
75. Stephenson, *Patriot Battles*, 295–96.
76. Stephenson, *Patriot Battles*, 296.

pulling the dragoons regiment up from the rear and appointing them to a new mission.

## The Bennington Expedition

Whereas General Riedesel contemplated quick strikes into Connecticut to harass the patriots and provision the army, Burgoyne imagined a major campaign on his left flank with numerous contradictory objectives: Mount the dragoons, obtain draught animals, recruit loyalists, and reconnoiter the Connecticut River, all under the command of an officer who spoke no English.[77] Riedesel's objections were originally over-ruled and Baum was briefed, but on August 8 Burgoyne received word that the town of Bennington, now in Vermont, was a major crossroads and depot for corn and livestock. The new plan that took shape based on this intelligence was a compromise of the two strategic visions. Riedesel states, perhaps with a memory colored by hindsight, that he had made further objections "with fear and astonishment" concerning the distance to Bennington and the number of patriots gathering east of their position. Burgoyne briefed Baum on the new, much more limited objective: the dragoons, with loyalist, Canadian, and Nation Nations support, were to raid Bennington.[78] The backbone of the force of 750 was to the dragoons, augmented by small artillery pieces worked by soldiers from Hesse Hanau who had been attached to the Braunschweig Corps.[79]

On August 9 Baum's force left the main army at Fort Edward, bivouacked for a day at Fort Miller as they awaited Native Nations warriors to join them, and forayed south by southeast into hostile territory beginning on August 11.[80] By evening they had captured their first heads of cattle.[81] On August 12 they were still in reach of Burgoyne, who rode out to them for a personal conference with Baum in the afternoon.[82] On

---

77. Ketchum, *Saratoga*, 293–96.
78. Riedesel, *Memoirs, Letters, and Journals*, 1:127–28.
79. On discrepancies in the numerical estimates, see Wilson, "Switching Sides," 76n79.
80. Stephenson, *Patriot Battles*, 296.
81. Wasmus, *Journal*, 69.
82. They spoke in French, as neither knew the other's language (Allen, *Tories*, 229).

August 13 they had contact with the enemy, capturing six rebels, fifteen horses, and enlarging their herd of cattle.[83]

On the afternoon of August 14 the column camped along the Waloomsac River in a hamlet composed of a cluster of houses and a bridge. The dragoons camped on one side of the river, the loyalists and Native Nations auxiliaries on the other. The Battle of Bennington took place at this hamlet ten miles northwest of the actual town, and began as a series of skirmishes on August 14.

Between 1,800 and 2,000 militia had rushed to Bennington's defense, coming under the overall command of General John Stark (1728–1822), who had been commissioned by the New Hampshire legislature.[84] The patriots were gathering behind a large hill a mile distant from Baum's camp. When a Mohawk war captain was killed by a patriot sniper, a burial with military honors was conducted at which sixteen dragoons fired a three-volley live-ball salute.[85] The patriots heard this salute and thought that Baum was attacking.[86] As the patriots began to push out their flanks, Baum rushed to take defensive positions. Patriot skirmishers advanced as far as a house on the outskirts of the hamlet and were driven back. An English [Canadian?] officer thought this was an opportunity to press pursuit, but Baum dug in instead. By evening Baum knew that the patriot force in front of him outnumbered him nearly three-to-one and sent word to Burgoyne. Stark, however, saw that the royalists had dug in and was content to harass the flanks with skirmish fire. These snipers ignored the dragoons and targeted Native warriors and loyalists, killing one and wounding two others.[87]

Rain on August 15 postponed the battle. Baum learned that the Braunschweig grenadiers were marching to reinforce him, under the command of Lt. Col. Heinrich Breymann (d. 1777). Baum erected redoubts and breastworks under fire from patriot snipers. The entry from Surgeon Wasmus for August 15 shows the bitterness in the patriot snipers occasioned by the cycles of frontier violence: "The Savages are all lying behind the baggage, dispirited; they do not want to go forward. . . . Also

---

83. Wasmus, *Journal*, 69.

84. Wasmus, *Journal*, 301, 303.

85. Ketchum, *Saratoga*, 299. It was not a Christian burial and no mention is made of Melsheimer taking part in the ceremony (Wasmus, *Journal*, 70).

86. Ketchum, *Saratoga*, 299.

87. Wasmus, *Journal*, 71; Ketchum, *Saratoga*, 300.

today, we have neither dead nor wounded; the Tories and Canadians, however, have had losses both yesterday and today."[88]

On the morning of August 16, aware now of the approaching grenadiers, Stark moved to encircle Baum. The Native Nations warriors "lay down behind trees and refused to go forward against the enemy."[89] The patriots pressed the attack at about 1 P.M. Patriot chaplain Thomas Allen was with them, having returned with his militia from Pittsfield, Massachusetts. According to a contemporary newspaper account, on August 16 Allen approached the breastworks, urging the dragoons to surrender since their position was untenable. The Germans responded by shooting at him. Allen returned to his line and the battle commenced in earnest.[90]

The Hesse-Hanau artillery on Baum's left blazed away until the gunners were all killed or wounded.[91] From the breastworks the dragoons kept up a rapid fire with their carbines, but patriot snipers picked them off with long-distant, accurate rifles. Then the patriots rushed from all sides, with Chaplain Allen, sword drawn, leading the charge of the Pittsfield Militia.[92] Combat was hand-to-hand. As positions were overrun on the flanks the dragoons withdrew to the center, where Baum stood with the last remaining field piece.

As Baum made his last stand his field piece ran out of balls and canister; the gunners loaded rocks from the ground until the powder gave out.[93] The dragoons held the patriots at bay with disciplined volleys from their carbines until they ran out of cartridges. Then they charged with broadsword and bayonet, their design to break through to the road and make for Breymann's line. The attempt failed against overwhelming numbers. When Baum fell, shot through the stomach, the surrounded dragoons threw down their weapons.[94]

Breymann's grenadiers had been much too slow in their relief march. Miles short of the beleaguered dragoons, they encountered Seth Warner and the Green Mountain Boys bearing down with superior numbers. In

---

88. Wasmus, *Journal*, 71. The "we" refers to the German dragoons.
89. Wasmus, *Journal*, 71.
90. Thompson, *From its European Antecedents*, 162.
91. Ketchum, *Saratoga*, 313.
92. Thompson, *From its European Antecedents*, 162.
93. Wasmus, *Journal*, 73.
94. Ketchum, *Saratoga*, 313.

a hot firefight the grenadiers sustained heavy losses and barely escaped the field.[95]

At some point in the battle Melsheimer was shot in the arm. Perhaps he was behind the baggage, perhaps he was attending the mortally wounded, perhaps he was trailing the attempt to break through and escape the encirclement. Neither can it be known whether, in the last long night of Baum's life, Melsheimer was permitted or capable of ministering to him in any way. Baum died early in the morning, his own regiment's medical personnel forbidden from attending to him.[96] The death of his commanding officer meant Melsheimer lost his most supportive patron, the one who had issued him the call.

The defeated soldiers were marched toward Bennington under heavy guard and quartered in farms the night of August 16. On August 17 the prisoners entered Bennington. Officers were quartered in a tavern and soldiers were put in the church.[97] Here the surgeon Julius Wasmus encountered the "barbaric" Chaplain Allen slapping a captured soldier with the flat of his sword, perhaps thinking to quell a riot among the prisoners. Wasmus credits a patriot major for calming the chaplain and saving the prisoner's life, stating, "I have never seen a man so enraged as this noble pastor."[98]

## Prisoner and Guest

On August 19 the prisoners signed their parole and began marching toward Massachusetts. Parole was an honor system in which a captured soldier was released on his own cognizance after signing a promise neither to be involved in the war anymore nor to discuss the war with civilians.[99] Away from the front the prisoners moved about freely and unguarded and received their pay from their own armies, the wages passing through lines under truce, so that they could pay for room and board. Parole was a practical measure allowing prisoners to be billeted in private homes, as the Bennington prisoners were for various lengths of time as they made their way eastward.

95. Stephenson, *Patriot Battles*, 299; Ketchum, *Saratoga*, 314–19.
96. Wasmus, *Journal*, 73.
97. Bennington's sole church was Presbyterian (Wasmus, *Journal*, 76).
98. Wasmus, *Journal*, 75–76.
99. Wasmus, *Journal*, 77.

On August 29 Melsheimer and two other wounded, Cornet Stutzer, and Lt. Gebhard of the Grenadiers, were grouped together with Wasmus. They called themselves "The Committee."[100] They stayed in Springfield before being sent to Brimfield, Massachusetts, 83 miles west of Boston, arriving the night of September 22 in the home of Joseph Hitchcock, father of fifteen children. The five year-old daughter greeted the new guests with screams, for she had been told that the German auxiliaries "were cannibals, Savages from Germany, etc."[101] The pastor and surgeon won her over. Gebhard and Stutzer were boarded at a neighboring farm.[102]

On September 27, 1777, Congress convened in Lancaster, Pastor Mühlenberg was scolding militia in his church in Providence, and Lafayette was convalescing at a Moravian inn on the outskirts of Bethlehem. That day is not given an entry in the journal of Surgeon Wasmus. Melsheimer had expressed to Wasmus how much he missed coffee, and Wasmus notes how deep his disappointment had been at their first breakfast with the Hitchcocks on September 23. According to Wasmus the same food was offered each morning and evening: milk, bread, and a baked apple. On Thursday the 25th the four prisoners attended the funeral of a child, a friend of the Hitchcock family. There they met the town's pastor, Nehemiah Williams (1749–1796), the same age as Melsheimer, and found him to be very friendly. The next entry is for the 28th when they attended worship at Williams's Congregational Church. One presumes, for lack of an entry, that nothing happened of note for the Brimfield Committee on September 27, 1777: They were getting accustomed to their hosts and their breakfasts.[103]

On October 13 Wasmus stated that Melsheimer had "recovered" from his wound.[104] While in Brimfield Wasmus provided medical care[105] and Melsheimer preached occasionally in the Congregationalist

100. Wasmus, *Journal*, 109.
101. Wasmus, *Journal*, 84.
102. Wasmus, *Journal*, 84.
103. Wasmus, *Journal*, 86.
104. Wasmus, *Journal*, 88.
105. Wasmus, *Journal*, 108.

Church.[106] Meanwhile as paroled prisoners they received the news of the war just like the citizens around them.[107]

## The Battles of Saratoga

After the defeats at Bennington and Fort Stanwyx Burgoyne pushed on stubbornly but blindly, deprived of Native Nations warriors to scout the patriot positions.[108] In the weeks that followed Bennington, American forces circled behind him and retook Ticonderoga[109] and the other forts that Burgoyne had captured with such flair, sealing off his retreat to Canada. Battle was joined on September 19 at Freeman's Farm near the hamlet of Saratoga. Major General Horatio Gates, in command of the patriots, kept his numbers and the depth of his lines concealed as Burgoyne's British troops ground into them. The result was a stalemate.

The lines did not move for three weeks. On October 7, with supplies running out and the weather turning, Burgoyne engaged Gates's left at Bemis Heights. As the royalists were turned back Gates's subordinate Benedict Arnold called several units forward to pursue the retreating redcoats all the way to the redoubts on Burgoyne's right flank. The redoubt of the Braunschweig Grenadiers fell after furious hand-to-hand combat in which Lt. Col. Breymann was killed.

Burgoyne retreated north but found his army surrounded by a tightening ring. On October 14, under patriot shelling, Burgoyne drafted terms and asked for a parley. Gates accepted his terms, called the Convention of Saratoga. The royalist army was to march to Boston, board ships and return to Europe, its soldiers never again to participate in the war in North America.[110] On these conditions Burgoyne's troops grounded their arms.[111]

---

106. Julius Wasmus notes on this occasion that Melsheimer wore "a white vest and trousers underneath his black coat when he climbed into the pulpit to preach" (Wasmus, *Journal*, 112).

107. Wasmus, *Journal*, 89.

108. For a detailed study of the Battles of Saratoga, see Ketchum, *Saratoga*, 350–407; Ferling, *Almost a Miracle*, 204–41; Stephenson, *Patriot Battles*, 288–310. From the perspective of the Braunschweig command, see Riedesel, *Memoirs, Letters, and Journals*, 1:145–90.

109. Ketchum, *Saratoga*, 377–78.

110. Pettengill, *Letters from America*, 109–10.

111. Riedesel, *Memoirs, Letters, and Journals*, 1:185–90.

## The Breach of the Convention of Saratoga

All combatants expected the Convention of Saratoga to be ratified and the defeated army, now called the Convention Army, to be embarked for Europe in the spring.[112] On November 2 Surgeon Julius Wasmus held a personal conversation with Braunschweig's corps commander, Riedesel, at the general's quarters in Brookfield. Riedesel reassured Wasmus and the Brimfield Committee he represented that the dragoons captured at Bennington were under the Convention. Riedesel also warned them that they were now prisoners and that conditions were subject to change.[113] Riedesel's caveats presaged the future.[114]

Melsheimer represented the Committee to headquarters in January, 1778, and returned with news that the ships to take them home would arrive in February, and that the guineas had arrived for the captured army's payroll.[115] However, in March Congress refused to allow the Convention Army to board the ships that were waiting under truce in Boston Harbor. The promise the royalist prisoners would go home was being reneged.

Wasmus represented the Brimfield Committee on a disastrous visit to Riedesel in April. Headquarters had received the payroll guineas and taken charge of distributing them, and on April 24 Wasmus received money for everyone in the Committee except Melsheimer, because, "he had not written to the general asking for money as the other gentlemen had done and therefore he did not get anything." Headquarters had also lost the mail for the Brimfield Committee.

In all, Wasmus and Melsheimer roomed together at the Hitchcocks of Brimfield for one year and five days. In late September of 1778 several of the officers captured at Bennington were ordered to Newport, Rhode Island to await a possible exchange. Wasmus was not included; he was ordered to Westminster with select officers charged with keeping the dragoons a militarily cohesive unit.[116] Melsheimer and Wasmus made an affectionate, tearful departure from the Hitchcocks, and then

---

112. Wasmus, *Journal*, 91.
113. Wasmus, *Journal*, 90.
114. Wasmus, *Journal*, 90–92.
115. Wasmus, *Journal*, 106.
116. Wasmus, *Journal*, 106; cf. Riedesel, *Memoirs, Letters, and Journals*, 2:46. Wasmus is not named, but the cluster of officers ordered to stay with the army matches his own record. In William Leete Stone's translation the exchange appears to have been already effected, but it was only anticipated.

the two friends parted ten miles later at Westminster, with Melsheimer riding on. After November of 1778 Wasmus makes no further mention of Melsheimer.

## Melsheimer's Pilgrim Journey

Prisoners sent to their own army's lines on parole could take no active role in the military exercises until the actual "exchange" of prisoners was in effect. The Germans auxiliaries on duty in Rhode Island hailed from Ansbach-Bayreuth. Just a couple of months earlier they had joined the British units in repelling an invasion by the Continental Army.[117] Such royalist victories improved the prospects for a prisoner exchange. As late as November, 1778, hopes ran high among the dragoon officers that their exchange was imminent.[118]

That same fall General Sir Henry Clinton (1730–1795), now supreme royalist commander in North America after Howe's recall, wrote to his counterpart George Washington that since Congress treated Burgoyne's men as captives rather than parolees, the provisions for the Convention Army would no longer be supplied by the British side; the army that held prisoners in custody was responsible for their well-being.[119] As a result, in October the main body of the Convention Army was ordered to march to a prison garrison in Virginia.[120] Clinton then encouraged the captured soldiers to attempt escape. No longer paroled prisoners but captive, if they escaped to their own lines they could fight again. Washington knew this as well and shadowed the Convention Army's march with a few companies. Hundreds of British troops did make their escape and joined other royalist units.[121] Because of the exchange agreement, Melsheimer and the dragoons officers billeting in Newport with the German Auxiliaries of Ansbach-Bayreuth were bound by honor to their parole; they could not "escape."

As yet another exchange agreement collapsed, the Newport parolees came under Clinton's policy. They were returned to patriot custody,

---

117. Ferling, *Almost a Miracle*, 311–13.
118. Riedesel, *Memoirs, Letters, and Journals*, 2:50.
119. Riedesel, *Memoirs, Letters, and Journals*, 2:44.
120. Riedesel, *Memoirs, Letters, and Journals*, 2:45.
121. Riedesel, *Memoirs, Letters, and Journals*, 2:53–54.

and were marched to Pennsylvania.¹²² The English-language recension of Melsheimer's autobiography states:

> I was on the 29th Sept. 1778 paroled and sent to New York [sic]. In the following year all paroled prisoners of war were recalled, and so it happened, that on the 3d of March 1779 I, with the officers of the regiment, were again prisoners and we were sent to Bethlehem in the province of Pennsylvania.¹²³

Other sources in his own hand along with independent witnesses state that Melsheimer and the dragoons officers were paroled to Newport, not New York.¹²⁴ The error most likely surfaced when his autobiography and other eighteenth-century German script sources were transcribed into English, because *Neuyork* and *Neuport* look very similar in long-hand writing, and both cities were occupied by royalist forces in 1778.¹²⁵ Another issue is the "3d of March" date. The Bethlehem diary lists the arrival of the Braunschweig officers, including Major Meibom and Melsheimer, on January 26, who were to be "accommodated in and around Bethlehem, with their servants."¹²⁶

Melsheimer's actual status even by January 26 is unclear. *The Dictionary of American Biography* states that he was "exchanged for W. Cardelle," chaplain of the 11th Virginia Regiment, and given "freedom to travel" in order to cross lines to the royalists; the article cites a document dated January 19, 1779 in the Library of Congress.¹²⁷ In what remains extant Melsheimer never indicates knowledge of his exchange. By January 19, 1779 most of Riedesel's command was in Virginia. Communication in the eighteenth century was difficult enough and warfare only compounded the problems. If word of the agreement was slow in reaching Newport, and he was already enroute to Bethlehem, perhaps the exchange order

---

122. Melsheimer, "Autobiography," 1.

123. Melsheimer, "Autobiography," 1–2. Wilson, "Switching Sides" accepted the transcription's March 3rd date. This transcription is in doubt, however, and is perhaps the result of the difficulty of reading German long-hand script.

124. Melsheimer, "Letters to Johann Ettwein," 400; *Journal of the Voyage*.

125. Ferling, *Almost a Miracle*, 309. For a history of German auxiliary operations on Rhode Island, see Schroder, *Hessian Occupation*.

126. *Bethlehem Diary*, 127.

127. American Council, *Dictionary of American Biography*, 12:519. Parker Thompson gives the patriot chaplain as John Cordell, of the same regiment; his source is a documentary history published in Baltimore by a private citizen in 1894. Thompson indicates that by May 1779 Cordell was serving again as a military chaplain in Virginia.

never caught up to Melsheimer, or when it did, he had already deserted.[128] As Melsheimer tells the story, long before seeing Bethlehem he had made up his mind to give up the chaplaincy.

In his letter to Ettwein dated April 26, 1779, Melsheimer writes: "As soon as we arrived in Newport I wrote to our spiritual, consistorial Chief Knittel in Wolfenbüttel, and pleaded for a change in my call."[129] This means that at some point before he arrived in Rhode Island he had made up his mind. In his letter to Ettwein he declares that his letters to the Wolfenbüttel Consistory constitute his resignation (*dimihssion*) from his chaplaincy.

In his autobiography he states that he resigned because of differences with his brother officers. But his letters to Ettwein suggest that it was his decision to resign that caused the falling out. Likely both are true. The Brimfield Committee seemed to have gotten on very well with each other, yet that year saw the embarrassment of Wasmus coming back from Riedesel with money for everyone but Melsheimer. As far as the Continental Army knew, Melsheimer was exchanged as of late January, 1779, yet in April the Bethlehem Diary refers to him collectively with the other Braunschweigers as prisoners.[130] He writes to Ettwein on April 26 that he felt he had resigned his chaplaincy already, but on April 4 the Bethlehem Diary notes that he and the dragoons officers held a worship service on Easter Sunday in the Single Men's Chapel.[131]

In the letter of April 26 he asks, "Am I a deserter?" Then where was the regiment he was supposed to serve? It was scattered across North America.[132] Riedesel had maintained the military cohesion of the whole corps, but Melsheimer was not called to the corps as such. His patron, the regiment's commanding officer, was dead, and the regiment did not exist in such a way as to allow him to fulfill his *civilian office*. His question is legitimate: Had he deserted?

---

128. Mühlenberg, *Journals*, 3:301. In a synopsis of Melsheimer's life in his journal entry for March 1, 1780, Heinrich Mühlenberg notes that Melsheimer had been "exchanged."

129. "So bald wir in Neuport angekommen waren: so schreib ich, an unseren geistlichen Consistorial=Rath Knittel in Wolfenbüttel, und bath um meine zurückberufung" (Melsheimer, "Letters to Johann Ettwein," 400).

130. *Bethlehem Diary*, 136.

131. The sermon topic: "The blessed fruits of the resurrection of our Lord Jesus Christ" (*Bethlehem Diary*, 136).

132. Melsheimer, "Letters to Johann Ettwein," 400.

## Army Desertion in the Eighteenth Century

Desertion was an endemic problem for all European armies in the eighteenth century,[133] but it also plagued the patriots in the rebelling colonies of North America.[134] Militia units requiring enlistments of as few as thirty days did not suffer as much from desertion as such: they simply disbanded when their time expired regardless of the strategic situation.[135] The Continental Army suffered mutinies and desertions as the war lengthened, the economy worsened, and paper currency lost value.[136]

Beginning as early as 1776 the patriot strategy was to entice enemy combatants from Europe to desert,[137] with promises of liberty and land.[138] By an act of Congress in May, 1778, British and Germans who deserted their units would be settled instantly and exempted from militia service. Invitations to desert were posted on walls and trees especially wherever prisoners of war were barracked or billeted.[139] One episode of enticement to desert was recounted second-hand to Melsheimer and the Brimfield Committee and recorded by Wasmus in his journal. It involved the Rev. Johann Hartwick, the Halle Pietist who had come to America of his own accord to serve the Lutheran congregation in Rhinebeck, New York, and whom Mühlenberg had visited in New York in 1750.

In 1777 Hartwick boarded a prison ship holding British and Braunschweig troops in Boston Harbor under the pretext of delivering a sermon. When he made his theme American liberty versus German slavery, he was expelled by a British officer on behalf of his fellow prisoners. Hartwick returned to shore and complained, at which time the imprisoned officers were removed from the ship and quartered in Westminster. The next day Hartwick returned to cajole the German enlisted men to join him in building a new community in Pennsylvania. This notion was "rejected with contempt."[140] That nothing came of his appeal to German

---

133. Atwood, *Hessians*, 192.

134. Stephenson, *Patriot Battles*, 81.

135. Stephenson, *Patriot Battles*, 32.

136. Stephenson, *Patriot Battles*, 98.

137. Rodney Atwood devotes a chapter to desertion as it pertains to the Hessen-Kassel army; the patriot enticements were uniform for all German auxiliaries (Atwood, *Hessians*, 184–87).

138. Atwood, *Hessians*, 187.

139. Riedesel, *Memoirs, Letters, and Journals*, 2:22.

140. Wasmus, *Journal*, 96–97.

prisoners of war is seen in Heinrich Mühlenberg's entry describing the annual convention the following October (1778). Hartwick "took leave on Tuesday, October 6, intending to go to Virginia."[141] Still, this entry shows that Melsheimer and the Brimfield Committee had become aware, at least through this secondhand account of Hartwick's "sermon" if not earlier, that ethnic Germans were a flourishing community in Pennsylvania.

Only one other Lutheran chaplain chose to stay in North America at the end of the war. This was Johann Christoph Wagner (dates unavailable) of Ansbach-Bayreuth. The garrison chaplain in Germany who received Wagner's regimental records, G. M. Stroelein (dates unavailable), states: "[He] remained behind in North America, because he was promised great benefits." Ansbach soldier Johann Conrad Döhla (1750–1820) noted in his memoir that Wagner had remained in Frederick, Maryland, where they had been garrisoned as prisoners after their capture at Yorktown. "He had been promised a position in Maryland and planned to marry."[142]

An entry by Heinrich Mühlenberg during the royalist occupation of Philadelphia suggests that Pennsylvania pastors were enticing Wagner to desert. Wagner had been billeted with Mühlenberg's daughter Peggy and son-in-law J. C. Kunze. Writes Mühlenberg:

> The Lutheran chaplain of the Ansbach troops, who all this time has been lodging and boarding with Pastor Kunze in the parsonage, sent his greetings and said that he hoped to see and speak with me soon. . . . I suspect that he wants to remain here when the troops depart. . . . I do not understand the mystery.[143]

It is unclear whether Wagner and Heinrich Mühlenberg ever met. Furthermore it appears that Wagner, enticed or not, did not desert, but was honorably discharged by the Ansbach regiment. He moved with his family to Nova Scotia,[144] where he joined other royalist troops and loyalist colonists who had accepted George III's invitation to settle in the maritime colonies. Therefore, as a deserter to the United States Friedrich

---

141. Mühlenberg, *Journals*, 3:189.

142. Döhla, *Hessian Diary*, 234n6. The memoir by Karl Bauer inflates the promise to three thousand acres for officers to settle in Nova Scotia or Canada (Bauer, *Journal*, 176).

143. Mühlenberg, *Journals*, 3:153.

144. Döhla, *Hessian Diary*, 230.

Melsheimer is an exception among the German military clergy, perhaps the only one.

## Ethical Awakening

In Melsheimer we find a different man writing to Ettwein in 1779, one who is far more spiritually and piously oriented than the man of the world who had written his *Tagebuch* in 1776. Sometime around June, 1777, Melsheimer experienced a conversion of the kind that Pietists of both the Halle Lutheran and Zinzendorfer stripes could appreciate. One author esteemed in common by these Pietists is Johann Arndt, who in the seventeenth century wrote:

> True Christianity consists, namely, in the exhibition of a true, living faith, active in genuine godliness and the fruits of righteousness. . . . We bear the name of Christ, not only because we ought to believe in Christ, but also because we are to live in Christ and he in us. . . . The heart, mind, and affections must be changed, so that we might be conformed to Christ and his holy Gospel.[145]

In this vein Melsheimer could not reconcile the vicious habits of "the heart, mind and affections" required of military life with the virtues taught in Christ's "holy Gospel." This crisis brought him to an ethical awakening, to Arndt's reckoning of "true Christianity."

His conversion did not require of his conscience that he also switch sides. Indeed, it is not at all clear that he embraced much of the patriot ideology, and he was certainly no advocate for the "rights of Englishmen." What is certain is that in Pennsylvania he found an extensive German immigrant culture where he was encouraged—by his hosts and by patriot policy—to make himself at home.

## Pennsylvania's Germans

In his April 26 letter Melsheimer states that he had a firm desire to "work with another congregation in this land."[146] "This land" where Melsheimer

---

145. Arndt, *True Christianity*, 21.

146. Melsheimer, "Letters to Johann Ettwein," 400. Wilson, "Switching Sides," extends the discussion of "in this land" to other possibilities that existed, at least theoretically, for auxiliary chaplains to choose to serve loyalist congregations from New York

hoped to find a parish, is Pennsylvania. He may never have met Johann Hartwick but it is possible that even at second-hand the vision that the aging Hallenser had cast for the German auxiliaries had sunk deep in Melsheimer's heart. Not only was he resigning his call to the regiment, he was switching sides, abandoning the royalist cause altogether.

Ten years later Melsheimer wrote again to Ettwein, offering a reflection on the months he spent among the Moravians. In this essay, "A Candid and Unbiased Account," he states that soon after visiting the town, "I was determined to stay in Bethlehem."[147] Melsheimer is not alone in his positive impression; descriptions of German Americans, Pennsylvania, and Bethlehem, are found in several writings from German auxiliaries. One notes the ethnic pride in General Riedesel's description of Pennsylvania:

> The province of Jersey is . . . populous and . . . well cultivated. . . . A great many Irishmen have settled there, whose natural abilities are pretty fair, though they do not equal the Germans in economy and in the cultivation of the soil. Nor do they by any means come up to the Herrnhuters, who, forty years since, settled a few places, among which is Bethlehem. . . . The state of Pennsylvania may be said to be as well cultivated and populated as the best German province. Besides her chief city Philadelphia, it has many large and beautiful cities, and is the corn magazine for the middle provinces of North America. Inasmuch also as it has been made rich by industry, its prosperity is an honor to the German nation.[148]

Chaplain Waldeck of the Waldeck Regiment never saw Bethlehem himself, but he described it second-hand based on a report from a German officer who had been there as a prisoner:

> He told of the wonderful organization of the Herrnhuters at Bethlehem. . . . For rearing their children, especially those with only limited means, they set up the most beautiful establishment. They built the most beautiful building, at a common cost, which is dedicated to the education of their children. As soon as

---

to Nova Scotia in the Fall of 1778, which may account for his motives in writing his letter of resignation while in Newport before he ever saw Pennsylvania. This logic can be inferred from his flow of thought in his letter to Ettwein, but is not necessary to its interpretation: a firm desire to remain "in this land" may not have emerged until he had been in Pennsylvania for several weeks.

147. Melsheimer, "Candid and Unbiased Account."
148. Riedesel, *Memoirs, Letters, and Journals*, 2:60.

a child has attained an age to profit from instruction ... if a boy, he is placed in the wing of the building where the males will be raised.... His parents have no need to spend the least amount on him. But he must work to earn his support.... [The girls] occupy the other wing of the building.... All is activity, all is work, each one instructs and encourages the others to do their best. ... God bless you, you hard-working Herrnhuters, also you, you peace-loving, quiet Quakers. You are useful members of society. Through you, Pennsylvania is beginning to bloom, and you will be the ones, who will bring it to ultimate maturity, by industry, by truth in dealing with others, by thrift and tolerance, and with the protection of God, whom you also love. God will not permit these peaceful, affable citizens to be disturbed in their homes by this war.[149]

Waldeck wrote this months after the royalists retreated from Philadelphia. In military terms Waldeck's prophecy was correct about Pennsylvania and curiously corresponds to G. A. Freylinghausen's promise: The war shifted southward.

On first arriving in Pennsylvania the Dragoons officers were quartered in the apartments for single men in Christiansbrunn, a farm connected to Bethlehem. Melsheimer chose to billet separately, paying "one dear guinea a month" for a bare room on a farmstead "2.5 miles from Easton."[150] On hearing, to his surprise and chagrin, of Bethlehem's high moral reputation, he requested permission to visit the town. After two weeks he was given permission and paid a visit to Ettwein, who showed him the whole community, including Bethlehem's manufacturing centers and dormitories.[151] "The cleanliness, order, and good arrangement was very evident.... I was determined to remain in Bethlehem."[152]

This may shed light on the discrepancy with the autobiography's date of "March 3d." From Melsheimer's testimony the officers were quartered in the Single Men's dormitory of Christiansbrunn in Nazareth, which means it is not necessary for any of them to have entered Bethlehem at all on January 26. The list of names in the diary may have been provided to Ettwein by Col. Hooper, the American commissioner in charge of the

149. Waldeck, *Eighteenth-Century America*, 77–78.
150. Melsheimer, "Candid and Unbiased Account." This reading corrects an error in my dissertation, "Switching Sides," in which I had understood that all the officers had been quartered in a non-Moravian home.
151. Melsheimer, "Candid and Unbiased Account."
152. Melsheimer, "Candid and Unbiased Account."

prisoners. This fits the description "in and around Bethlehem" in the diary and demonstrates the manner in which Ettwein followed his orders. With the German form of his autobiography unavailable, it is possible that a complex sentence construction was misinterpreted and that March 3 was the date that Melsheimer was, himself, received in Bethlehem after his petitions, and billeted in the family apartment of Samuel and Anna Catherine Mau. The Bethlehem Diary does not find the event of the chaplain's move into town noteworthy enough for an entry. However by Palm Sunday, March 28, it is noted that the Braunschweig officers participated in the Renewed Unity's Palm Sunday service, and one week later held an Easter service of their own.[153]

After the cold shock of life in a German military garrison in Newport, Melsheimer found himself among true kindred spirits at last: These were Germans who loved peace and whose piety rivaled or exceeded that found among the Puritan-descended English in Brimfield. This community also featured a dormitory for single women of unassailable reputation.

## Maria Agnes Mau

Women played a large role in the choices made by German auxiliaries to desert. Having praised Pennsylvania's industry and wealth as an honor to the German nation, Riedesel stated further: "Our troops were received in some of their houses far too well, as we knew to our sorrow."[154] Wherever German auxiliaries were stationed for an extended period of time, pairings occurred with local women. In Quebec, Chaplain Johann Braunsdorf kept a record of marriages of Anhalt-Zerbst soldiers to Canadian women. In New York City a daughter of the loyalist taverner David Grimm married Ansbach officer Johann Andreas Carl von Stein zu Altenstein. It appears Stein was honorably discharged at the end of the war and remained in the United States.[155] After eight months under occupation in Philadelphia some five hundred German American women, of whom one hundred had married soldiers, followed the royalist army on its retreat to New York.[156]

153. *Bethlehem Diary*, 135–36.
154. Riedesel, *Memoirs, Letters, and Journals*, 2:60–61.
155. Burgoyne, *Hessian Chaplains*, 144.
156. Roeber, *Palatines, Liberty, and Property*, 306.

Whether loyalist, neutral, or patriot, many German-American families took an interest in the German auxiliaries: political considerations were secondary to the need of farms for workers and women for husbands.[157] "Bundling" was employed on German auxiliaries, whether as active duty soldiers pairing with loyalists, or as billeted prisoners of war residing among patriots.[158] Bundling was not practiced in Bethlehem, where for a time the boundaries around sexual relations were so strict even married couples lived in separate dormitories and scheduled their conjugal visits in a reserved room.[159] As we have seen, Melsheimer was curious to visit Bethlehem which had such a reputation for morality, a reputation that challenged the lurid rumors which he confesses to have heard while growing up.[160]

For his personal laundry needs he was introduced to the Mau family's eighteen-year-old daughter, Maria Agnes, already a resident of the Single Women's Choir and a laundress.[161] Interest flowered quickly, and with it an absolute determination to begin a new life. Depending on the veracity and meaning of his autobiography's March 3 date, Melsheimer was writing to Ettwein to request permission to marry Agnes Mau within about seven weeks of meeting her.

From early in the eighteenth century the Moravian protocol had been that "no marriage may be contracted without the prior knowledge of the elders," and Bethlehem adopted a similar policy.[162] In 1752 Zinzendorf prohibited inter-marriage with non-Moravians. As with Samuel Mau, a person could become Moravian[163] by converting and accepting the rules of the community. After Zinzendorf's death the strictures surrounding marriage were gradually loosened. "After 1770 the number of non-Moravians brought into the community through marriage increased rapidly."[164] A critical study states, "But even for the unmarried the choirs had by the seventeen-seventies degenerated into respectable boarding houses for lodgers who paid rent."[165] The key is that it was "respectable"

157. Roeber, *Palatines, Liberty, and Property*, 196.
158. Roeber, *Palatines, Liberty, and Property*, 197, 197n66.
159. Atwood, "Union of Masculine and Feminine," 24.
160. Melsheimer, "Candid and Unbiased Account."
161. *Bethlehem Diary*, s.v. "May 10, 1779."
162. Gollin, *Study of Changing Communities*, 111.
163. More accurately, part of the *Unitas Fratrum*, or Unity of the Brethren Church.
164. Gollin, *Moravians in Two Worlds*, 120.
165. Gollin, *Moravians in Two Worlds*, 97.

in terms of the morality of the boarders. The town's communitarian arrangements, although in transition, were still impressive to outside observers in the 1770s.

Nothing extant describes the courtship between Melsheimer and Mau. The Bethlehem Diary states that Maria was given in marriage at the permission of her *Eltern*,[166] implying perhaps both her own parents and the elders of the community. By virtue of this "inter-marriage" Maria Agnes Mau left the community, in that sense fulfilling the rule from 1752. Melsheimer's friendly tone toward Bethlehem in 1789, however, shows that there was no ill will on the community's part toward their former sister.

On May 10, 1779, the Bethlehem Diary notes the arrangement for "Agnes" to marry Melsheimer.[167] In Melsheimer's letter to Ettwein dated May 11, 1779, he processes the personal humiliation he had endured on May 6 when the whole company of officers shamed him with threats, cursing, and name-calling.[168] The appendix to Riedesel's memoir notes that on May 11, 1779, Chaplain Melsheimer "deserted."[169] Melsheimer's third letter to Ettwein reports the slander that he was a bigamist, with one wife in Germany, another in Massachusetts, and his intention to marry a third.[170] His alienation from the Braunschweig dragoons was complete. When the officers left Bethlehem for quarters in Lancaster in the middle of the month, Melsheimer did not accompany them. His life as a German American was about to begin.

## The Deserter and the Pennsylvania Ministerium

In his third letter to Ettwein, still in the spring of 1779, Melsheimer notes that he had sent to "*Prediger Herr* Helmuth" in Lancaster a copy of the letter he had written to Wolfenbüttel in November 1778. He considered this letter his resignation from his chaplaincy.[171] Helmuth was a Halle

---

166. *Bethlehem Diary*, s.v. "May 10, 1779."
167. *Bethlehem Diary*, s.v. "May 10, 1779."
168. Melsheimer, "Letters to Johann Ettwein," 401.
169. Riedesel, *Memoirs, Letters, and Journals*, 2:266.
170. Melsheimer, "Letters to Johann Ettwein," 402.
171. Melsheimer, "Letters to Johann Ettwein," 402.

missionary who arrived in 1769[172] and took the pulpit in Lancaster.[173] He had been praised by Halle Director G. A. Freylinghausen for remaining neutral during the civil unrest, in a comparison that reflected unfavorably on Heinrich Mühlenberg. That Melsheimer reached out to the Pennsylvania Ministerium makes it clear that he had never wished to convert to the Moravians; he wanted a call in a Pennsylvania Lutheran parish. Due to the war and the Pennsylvania Ministerium's public posture of neutrality, his pathway into acceptance was by no means straightforward.

In his autogiobraphy, Melsheimer notes that he preached his first sermon to a Lutheran congregation on May 13. This was at *Berg Kirche* (Hill Church) in Lebanon, Pennsylvania, a congregation founded by Johann Caspar Stöver Jr. (1707–1779) and served by him until his sudden death. Details quickly get murky. May 13 was a Thursday, the Day of Christ's Ascension. It is reported that *on that day* Stöver died, in the parsonage, while preparing for a Confirmation service.[174] By then Hill Church had been split into a pro-Pennsylvania Ministerium faction and a pro-Stöver faction. Clearly, if Melsheimer's first sermon was in fact May 13, it was to the group that had left Stöver already. The founder's death created, in theory, an opportunity for the church to reconcile their schism.

Subsequent events suggest that Melsheimer did not preach on Ascension Day, but on Ascension Sunday, May 16, stepping in after Stöver's death. This is probable considering that, according to information Heinrich Mühlenberg was receiving second-hand, Melsheimer was the favorite of the Stöver party and was almost immediately opposed by the Ministerium faction, which was being occasionally served by Emmanuel Schultze from his call in Tulpehocken.[175]

His autobiography further notes that Melsheimer and Mau were married on June 3, 1779, in Bethlehem. Lebanon was their first home, and *Berg Kirche* with its outlying parishes was Melsheimer's first call in the fledgling United States. Finally quit of the regiment, newly wed and in a pulpit, Melsheimer may have supposed that his frustrations had finally come to an end. The ongoing schism in the congregation, however,

---

172. Mühlenberg, *Journals*, 3:382
173. Mühlenberg, *Journals*, 2:395–403.
174. Mühlenberg, *Journals*, 3:242.
175. Mühlenberg, *Journals*, 3:377.

foreshadowed what would occur that October at the annual meeting of the synod.

Several churches were experiencing tensions and pastoral transition, so that the annual meeting in Tulpehocken was poorly attended.[176] It surely would have helped Melsheimer's application had Heinrich Helmuth, to whom he had written, been present. But after ten years at Trinity Church in Lancaster, Helmuth was being sought for the joint Philadelphia parish of St. Michael's-Zion. Philadelphia had a troubled history of pastoral relations compounded by the placement of the youthful Heinrich Ernst Mühlenberg, often called the "young Heinrich," followed shortly thereafter by the semi-retirement of the elderly Heinrich Mühlenberg, who had long been feeling the wear and tear of his years.[177] When Philadelphia was occupied by the royalists only the Kunzes remained in the city; Heinrich Ernst had fled for the family home in Providence. He then returned to Philadelphia after the royalists withdrew.

In March of 1779 acrimony tainted the elder Heinrich Mühlenberg's final parting with St. Michael's-Zion. This was due in part to his son-in-law Kunze, who wanted to see the senior role of rector actually performed rather than held by an absentee. However it was the son, Heinrich Ernst, who stirred the pot on behalf of his father's honor. The father had to protest to the son on May 2, "God and nature have placed me in a position where I can no longer fill the office."[178] This was in reference to his hearing loss when, at a militia funeral, an honor guard fired their volley to close to his ear. One outcome of the conflict was that the younger Mühlenberg finally sought his own exit from Philadelphia's pulpits.[179] This pastoral conflict in the Philadelphia churches was taking place at the same time that Melsheimer was staying in Bethlehem and writing letters to Ettwein.

The Pennsylvania Ministerium's pulpits would eventually be sorted out with the younger Mühlenberg and Helmuth trading calls, and a few years later Kunze leaving Philadelphia for New York. These parishes would all enjoy long and settled tenures with these pastors, and Melsheimer would himself eventually enjoy a lengthy tenure in Hanover near the Maryland border beginning in 1789. In 1779, however, the synod was fraught with turmoil.

176. Spaeth et al., *Documentary History*, 156–57; Mühlenberg, *Journals*, 3:265–66.

177. In January 1775 he reported chest pains and drafted a will. He would live almost thirteen more years (Mühlenberg, *Journals*, 2:672).

178. Mühlenberg, *Journals*, 2:235.

179. Mühlenberg, *Journals*, 3:227–41.

Only nine pastors appeared at the convention beside Melsheimer, one-third of the synod.[180] Those present included Johann Nicholas Kurz (1720–1794), the Halle missionary who was president that year, and his son Johann Daniel (1764–1856); the two brothers Friedrich and Heinrich Ernst Mühlenberg, and Emmanuel Schultze, the host pastor at Tulpehocken who occasionally visited Lebanon's larger, pro-synod faction. The protocol for the meeting comes from the elder Heinrich Mühlenberg's hand, although he was not present;[181] he reproduced the minutes of the meeting deposited with him by Johann Daniel Schröter,[182] one of the participants.

The unanimous decision of the synod on October 4, 1779, was to offer friendship to Melsheimer, but not to admit him into the synod until 1) they knew him better, and 2) he obtained his discharge from his regiment.[183] The taint of desertion clung to him.

Melsheimer's application was rejected as the second order of business. The third item concerned Schultze, who would not accept a call to Lancaster because "his congregations strongly protested against it." This shining approbation for Schultze, the synod's host who happened to be the favorite of the synod party at Hill Church in opposition to Melsheimer, follows immediately on Melsheimer's rejection. The fourth item resolved "that in the future no preacher shall leave his congregations unless he has well-founded reasons, and can also present them to the Ministerium when it has met; on the other hand, no one shall be permitted to accept a call from new important congregations without first having the consent of the President and at least four ordained preachers."

While the precipitating events for this policy were most likely those in Philadelphia and Heinrich Ernst Mühlenberg's desire to leave that parish by any possible means,[184] the order of discussion implies a criticism of both sides of Melsheimer's call to Lebanon: First, that he could not provide satisfactory reasons for leaving his chaplaincy without a discharge, and second, that he offered himself to Lebanon without pursuing the proper channels of the synod. Again, Helmuth was not present at the meeting to speak for him.

180. Spaeth et al., *Documentary History*, 156.

181. The description of the meeting can be found in Spaeth et al., *Documentary History*, 156–57; Mühlenberg, *Journals*, 3:265–66.

182. Dates for Schröter are unknown.

183. Spaeth et al., *Documentary History*, 157; Mühlenberg, *Journals*, 3:266.

184. Mühlenberg, *Journals*, 3:235.

Aside from the manner in which Melsheimer began in Lebanon, there are four additional factors at play in the Ministerium which may account for its strictness towards Melsheimer. First, the synod needed to protect its interest with the larger of the two parties in Lebanon's schism. Second, the synod needed to vouchsafe that a military chaplaincy was a valid Lutheran call regardless of the politics of war. If they set a precedent of simply receiving Melsheimer they risked alienating, in addition to the Lutheran consistory of Braunschweig-Wolfenbüttel, other German sources of Lutheran ministers that were neutral in the war, such as Halle, Hamburg and Württemberg. Third, there may have been suspicion that Melsheimer was crypto-Moravian, representing a fresh Moravian effort to insinuate one of its own into a divided and vulnerable Lutheran congregation. Elderly members such as Kurtz remembered these tactics from prior decades.[185] As late as 1772 Heinrich Mühlenberg had suspected that the Moravians were waiting to exploit the developing schism in Lebanon.[186] Fourth, the Halle Institutes were a vital support to the Pennsylvania pastors, and they in turn depended on the benefactions of British members of the SPCK. To receive a deserter from the royalists would both violate the neutrality of the Ministerium and offend its benefactors.

Despite the strict official rulings the friendship that was offered and entered into the minutes seems to have been sincere. The extent of the synod clergy's sympathy for Melsheimer, however, had to remain a private and unofficial matter for the time being, just as their collective sympathy for the patriot cause had to be collectively unspoken.

## Acceptance

The impasse lasted for the duration of the war. Melsheimer served in Lebanon and faithfully cultivated relationships with the Pennsylvania Ministerium. On March 1, 1780, Melsheimer along with two men from his congregation visited the elder Heinrich Mühlenberg in Providence. They were enroute to Philadelphia in hopes of seeing Friedrich Mühlenberg, who had by then resigned his ordination and been elected to the assembly.[187] With this meeting Melsheimer became acquainted with all three

---

185. On Moravian designs on the Lutheran parish in Lancaster in the 1740s, see Mühlenberg, *Journals*, 1:109–15.

186. "Zinzendorfers" were "watching closely" (Mühlenberg, *Journals*, 2:512).

187. Mühlenberg, *Journals*, 3:301.

Mühlenberg sons and their venerable father. General Peter Mühlenberg gave Melsheimer an English letter addressed to "Colonel William Grayson, Member of the Hon. Board of War," making Melsheimer a courier for Continental Army correspondence. On March 10 Melsheimer returned through Providence with a letter for Heinrich Mühlenberg from his son Friedrich. Eight days lodging for the three men and horses in Philadelphia had run to £512 in paper currency, a sign of hyperinflation.[188]

In December of 1780 Heinrich Mühlenberg received a visitor from Lebanon, named Fischer, "who told of conditions in the congregations of that vicinity."[189] Schultze refused to visit the synod party any more.[190] Mühlenberg speculated that his son-in-law had found the schism too difficult when he had his own call at Tulpehocken. Just as likely, Schultze approved of Melsheimer and felt that all parties in Lebanon were in good hands. In 1781 the synod ruled on a request by the church in Reading to call Melsheimer:

> Resolved, to inform the congregation that Mr. Melsheimer was not yet received as a member of the Ministerium, and therefore nothing could be decided concerning him; but as we regard him as a friend, whose merits we appreciate, we will not consider it a rupture of the union between the Reading congregation and us, if they call him to be their pastor.[191]

The call to Reading did not materialize, yet the incident shows that the Ministerium indeed was sincere in its "friendship" with Melsheimer, who after two years in Lebanon had become a preacher to be sought after.

The royalist forces left New York City, their last stronghold in the new United States, on November 25, 1783. Melsheimer did not attend the annual convention that followed, in June 1784, when his second child was six weeks old, even though the convention's location in Lancaster was fairly close. Perhaps the synod party's insistence that he receive a discharge, rather than becoming moot, had now become irreconcilable. Finally he left Hill Church and in November, 1784, took the call to

---

188. Mühlenberg, *Journals*, 3:303.
189. Mühlenberg, *Journals*, 3:377.
190. Mühlenberg, *Journals*, 3:377.
191. Spaeth et al., *Documentary History*, 178. Neither this event nor the actions concerning the constitution appear in Mühlenberg's account of the meeting (Mühlenberg, *Journals*, 3:426–27).

Manheim.[192] The minutes for the synod held in Philadelphia in May, 1785 show Melsheimer present for the first time since 1779 and, for that year only, lists Manheim as his call.[193]

Among the fourteen voting pastors present in 1785 were Schulze from Tulpehocken, the synod's president that year; Schmidt, another Halle missionary who served as secretary; Helmuth, now settled in Philadelphia; Heinrich Ernst Mühlenberg now in Lancaster and the only one of the synod founder's sons still in the pastorate; and Christian Streit, a veteran Continental Army chaplain.[194] Melsheimer's appeal for acceptance was received as the fifteenth of sixteen items of business for the agenda, but was taken up first. It was "unanimously resolved, that Mr. Melzheimer [sic] be received into the United Ministerium."[195] The end of the war seems to have been the decisive factor. On the evening of his reception he preached on Romans 1:16, "I am not ashamed of the gospel. It is God's power to save all who believe, Jews first, and also Greeks" (NIV). The sermon outline is included in the minutes of the convention. "The Gospel a power of God unto salvation. 1. How is it called a power; 2. For whom?"[196]

---

192. Melsheimer, "Autobiography," 2.

193. Spaeth et al., *Documentary History*, 199.

194. Spaeth et al., *Documentary History*, 198.

195. Spaeth et al., *Documentary History*, 199.

196. Spaeth et al., *Documentary History*, 201.

6

# The Time to Fight

## *The Career of Peter Mühlenberg*

ON SEPTEMBER 27, 1777, as Heinrich Mühlenberg was excoriating the spiritual qualities of the Cumberland County Militia, his 30 year-old son, Brigadier General J. Peter Mühlenberg, was beset by a host of problems confronting the Continental Army. The royalists under General William Howe had only occupied Philadelphia one day earlier, and on the 27th their disposition and intentions were unknown. The Continental Congress had fled westward in plenty of time, meeting on September 27 in Lancaster, the very heart of Pennsylvania German country. Pennsylvania's Patriot Assembly would soon make its headquarters there while Congress crossed the Susquehanna to York, near the Maryland frontier. The news that British General John Burgyone was trapped by superior numbers of patriots near the hamlet of Saratoga, New York, would take on much larger significance weeks later, when Burgoyne's surrender of his army on October 17 would make Howe's victory in Philadelphia a pyrrhic royalist illusion. On September 27th, however, George Washington's staff was in crisis mode.

The patriots had been soundly beaten at Brandywine Creek on September 11. The engagement had cost them nearly one thousand killed, wounded, captured and missing, almost 10 percent of their force. A series of maneuvers and counter-marches followed, at times extending the lines of the two armies nearly to Providence. Eventually the patriots found themselves on the wrong bank of the Schuylkill, leaving open the way to

Philadelphia for the royalist forces, who entered the city unopposed on September 26.

Peter Mühlenberg was involved in the meetings that took place when intelligence reports, troop deployments and battle plans were discussed. The regiments in his brigade belonged to the Virginia line, and they had acquitted themselves well at Brandywine. On Sunday, September 28, Washington called his generals to a council of war to discuss the possibility of attacking the British positions in Germantown, the flank of Howe's position.[1] The biographers Edward W. Hocker and Paul A. Wallace, publishing critical secondary histories in the middle of the twentieth century, are silent about this meeting.[2] The general's great-nephew Henry A. Muhlenberg, who uncritically reported numerous dubious accounts in his heroic narrative biography in 1849, notes that General Mühlenberg advised waiting to attack until more reinforcements arrived. H. A. Muhlenberg then asserts, through the glorious vision of hindsight, that had his relative's wisdom been followed the outcome of the Battle of Germantown might have turned out a patriot victory.[3]

Peter Mühlenberg's military career had begun, as is true for many in the revolution, in the accidental happenstances of militia recruitment and election. His prior experience in the British army had been arranged only as a means of securing his passage back to North America; the skills he had learned as an indentured store clerk for a Halle patron had been put to use when he acted as a secretary to the redcoat officers aboard the ship. As will become clear, Peter did not obtain the martial background in Europe that legend attached to him in the nineteenth century.[4]

1. Ferling, *Almost a Miracle*, 253.
2. Hocker, *Fighting Parson*; Wallace, *Muhlenbergs of Pennsylvania*.
3. Edward W. Hocker describes the decision to attack Germantown as Washington's and does not describe the council of war (Hocker, *Fighting Parson*, 85–91). Wallace similarly skips over the council (Wallace, *Muhlenbergs of Pennsylvania*, 151). Military historian John Ferling describes the September 28 council of war as "balky," and that Washington did not summon a second one before planning and ordering the attack to commence with a forced march on the night of October 3 into the morning of October 4 (Ferling, *Almost a Miracle*, 253–56). The most detail is provided by Henry A. Muhlenberg, who lists the opinion of each general (Muhlenberg, *Life*, 104–5).
4. H. A. Muhlenberg, arguing for the credibility of many myths of Peter Mühlenberg from his time in Europe through the Battle of Yorktown, did not make use of and perhaps was not aware of much archived materials for either Peter or his father Heinrich. In 1913 the mythical flourish of Peter's story in Europe was exposed and a critical biography constructed by William Germann. See Germann, "Crisis," 283–329, 450–70.

## Upbringing

A native of Pennsylvania, John Peter Gabriel Mühlenberg was born at the Providence home on October 1, 1746, to Heinrich Mühlenberg, who in two years would form the synod of Halle Lutherans, the Pennsylvania Ministerium. Through his mother Anna Maria's side he was a grandson of Conrad Weiser, the leading German public citizen of the middle colonies until his death in 1760. This pedigree was certainly no hindrance to Peter's success at achieving rank and status as an adult; neither was it a guarantee. The ethnic Germans were an "other" people in Pennsylvania, large in population, sometimes feared, and kept on the margins of power.

Peter became the eldest of seven who survived into adulthood. His father arranged for the three brothers Peter, Friedrich and Heinrich Ernst to travel to Europe. The goal for Friedrich and Heinrich Ernst was school at the Halle Institutes in Prussia. The plan for Peter was an indentured apprenticeship to be finalized once he arrived at Halle and the Reverend Fathers could assess him.[5] Any intention for Peter to have been schooled in Halle may have been interrupted by the Seven Years War, which did not end in Europe until 1763. Although hostilities had abated earlier in North America, the seas were still a dangerous place crawling with hostile battleships. Peter was sixteen years old, Friedrich was thirteen, and Heinrich Ernst was nine years old when they sailed from Philadelphia at the end of April, 1763.[6]

Hoping to enter business, Peter had been recommended by his father for an indentured apprenticeship where he might learn the skills for shop-keeping and accounting. He was apprenticed to Leonhard Niemeyer, a cousin to a family that had married in to the leadership at the Halle Institutes. Peter moved to Niemeyer's village in northern Germany. The arrangement had been made based on Niemeyer's promises and did not include a site-visit by any Halle Institutes dignitary. It turned out that what Niemeyer ran was more akin to a liquor store, and he pressed Peter to serve extended hours in serving customers but did not show him other skills, such as book-keeping, requisite to running a business. The

---

5. Germann, "Crisis," 300–301.

6. Mühlenberg, *Journals*, 1:623. The three boys embarked on April 27, after prayers and benedictions by their father and his peer, the Dean of the Swedish Lutheran Churches, Karl Wrangel.

exploitation worsened as Niemeyer sought to cut corners in other ways, so that Peter was not even given the clothes he had been promised.[7]

H. A. Muhlenberg published the story that Peter fled the Halle Institutes and joined a regiment, his first in a series of enlistments in a mercenary life which took him across Central Europe and taught him the arts of war. One tall tale "still preserved as a family tradition" in 1849 has Peter Mühlenberg serving with German dragoons; he was then recognized 11 years later as *"teufel Pete"* (Devil Pete) by that same dragoons regiment which fought dismounted at the Battle of *Brandywine*.[8] This is clearly a fable, as the only German regiment of dismounted dragoons in North America in September, 1777 had already been captured at the Battle of *Bennington* the preceding month. Such myths are born by conflating facts with like-sounding syllables.

The facts presented by the discursive and documentary evidence are that after enduring his situation with Leonhard Niemeyer for about two years, Peter's complaints in writing became more pointed in early 1766. In reply the Halle Pietists became more defensive and procedural.[9] An agreement to shorten the indenture did not satisfy him. In the fall he encountered a British recruiting officer who was embarking with the British 60th Regiment of Foot for service in North America. On interviewing Peter, the officer offered him an enlistment in which he would be returned to North America, his passage paid for, and while enlisted he would act for the officers aboard the ship as a secretary. Peter leveraged this offer to force Niemeyer to release him and send him on his way.[10]

Leonhard Niemeyer, already put on the defensive by Heinrich Mühlenberg's polite inquiries into Peter's welfare, complained to the Halle directors and demanded the value of the balance of the indentured service in cash. This occasioned embarrassment for Halle's Reverend Fathers. Gotthilf Francke wrote to the Pennsylvania Superintendent of his disappointment in Peter and of the young man's inveterate, unregenerate flaws.

7. Hocker, *Fighting Parson*, 24–25.

8. Muhlenberg, *Life*, 29.

9. William Germann reproduces much of the correspondence in English translation involving Peter, his master, and the Halle Institutes. See Germann, "Crisis," 306–29.

10. Germann, "Crisis," 324–25. This corrects a previous understanding I held based on the reading of Henry A. Muhlenberg and other uncritical historiography, which I then misattributed to the narrative arch of vol. 2 of Mühlenberg, *Journals*. See Wilson, "Switching Sides," 144n91.

Heinrich Mühlenberg, meanwhile, sent Niemeyer the balance in cash for the unused years of indenture.[11]

That this estranged the Halle Institutes to its American missionaries is perhaps a given. On the other hand this was also the period in which the quality of pastoral candidates sent from Halle to Pennsylvania, in the likes of Helmuth, Schultz, and Kunze, markedly improved. After G. A. Francke died in 1769 the bonds between the Halle Institutes and their missionaries to Pennsylvania seemed to strengthen through the early 1770's. The Halle directors acquiesced to Heinrich Mühlenberg's request to be the trustees for a retirement home in Providence, and soon after the elderly colonial pastor obeyed the request from the Halle directors to investigate the discord among the Lutherans they sponsored in Ebenezer, Georgia in 1774.

## Trained and Ordained

Not long after his return Peter was apprenticed for ministry in North America. Karl Wrangel, his father's close friend and the Dean of the Swedish Lutheran Churches in Philadelphia and the Delaware Valley, became his tutor. Heinrich Mühlenberg then extended his pulpit at St. Michael's in Philadelphia to Peter on Good Friday, 1768. Although the superintendent stayed at home, fretting, he was later able to write to the Reverend Fathers of how highly the congregation spoke of Peter as a preacher.[12]

Peter was soon raised to the office of catechist, which entailed preaching duties in an extended circuit of outlying parishes of the Pennsylvania Ministerium, mainly in New Jersey. In this capacity Peter befriended another catechist, like him an ethnic German *creole*, Christian Streit.[13] These two set a pattern for the way in which the Ministerium would train its next generation of pastors: by direct, personal mentoring in the vocation rather than by formal education in European institutions.

Peter's brothers Friedrich and Heinrich Ernst had been sent to the boarding school at the Halle Institutes, and then to Halle University. For each of the younger brothers the sojourn in Halle was a mixed experience. Heinrich Ernst was recognized by Halle Institutes instructors as

11. Wallace, *Muhlenbergs of Pennsylvania*, 59–69.
12. Germann, *Crisis*, 451–54.
13. Mühlenberg, *Journals*, 2:360–61.

the better student of the two, but precocious. For his own part the elder Heinrich Mühlenberg had gotten wind of the rationalism at the University of Halle, and preferred that his sons stay under the tutelage of the pietistic Halle Institutes rather than be graduated and sent to the University.[14] By that time the vestiges of pietism at the University were fading. That request reached Halle too late, as both Friedrich and Heinrich Ernst enrolled in university courses. Years later their father still blamed the theological rationalist Johann Semler for being a corrupt influence on the faith of Heinrich Ernst.[15] After the two youths had spent six years in Halle, their father requested that they be returned to him. They were put on board ship with another missionary to the Ministerium, J. C. Kunze, the last to be sent from Halle until 1785 and one of the most effective of the missionary leaders among the ethnic German American Lutherans. They arrived in Philadelphia in 1770.[16]

While at that time Heinrich Ernst was not of the same maturity and effectiveness of either of his brothers or of the other newcomers to Pennsylvania, he was nevertheless the only Mühlenberg son to stay in the ministry through the course of the Revolutionary War and beyond. Heinrich Ernst Mühlenberg, along with Emmanuel Schultz, Heinrich Helmuth and J. C. Kunze, became the *de facto* leaders in the Halle-allied Pennsylvania Ministerium through most of the War of Independence.

One critical, quantitative study explores the impact of the Halle missionaries on American Lutherans in the eighteenth century. Of concern is the shift from the handful of pastors sent by Halle, into a mentoring system for raising ordinands, which, it is argued, meant that Heinrich Mühlenberg applied a double-standard.[17] As discussed in chapter 3, Heinrich Mühlenberg established himself by presenting his credentials and qualifications, distinguishing himself from those whose ordinations or callings were irregular in the traditional Lutheran sense. Several of these irregular clergy had actually done the work of planting the congregations into which Heinrich Mühlenberg insinuated himself.

Yet recruiting the needed clergy from Germany's divinity graduates proved too difficult. The prospects of chronic indigence that awaited service to a disestablished immigrant church in North America was not

14. German, *Crisis*, 454.
15. German, *Crisis*, 467; cf. Wallace, *Muhlenbergs of Pennsylvania*, 75.
16. Mühlenberg, *Journals*, 2:433, 459.
17. Splitter, "Divide et Impera," 47.

appealing, especially when compounded by the risks that came with crossing the ocean. The ethnic German community barely paid its pastors enough to live, and it was also unable to successfully establish a seminary in North America during Mühlenberg's lifetime. The synod was forced to rely on its two generations of vetted pastors trained in universities to raise up protégés on American soil and tutor them personally for ordination. This was not a double-standard so much as an evolving need. As late as 1770 Heinrich Mühlenberg held to his standard of his preference for formal education when he raised his teen-aged son for ordination over his eldest son, based on the younger Heinrich's schooling in European classrooms.

The impact of the mentoring system meant that the second and third generations of pastors were cut from the Pietist cloth of their mentors, the missionaries from the Halle Institutes. This carried forward the Pietist culture and may have slowed the influence of rationalism among immigrant German Lutherans after 1770.[18]

## "Hanna," Anna Barbara Meyer

Peter was the oldest of the Mühlenberg children, but his sister Elizabeth "Betsy" was the first to marry. After a gap of four years Peter was the second. During these years the family was centered in Philadelphia. Although Peter's work took him across a wide circuit, it was in the Philadelphia congregation that he found his match. Anna "Hanna" Meyer was the daughter of Matthias and Esther Meyer. Matthias was a successful potter. Anna was 19 and Peter was 24 when they married on Tuesday, November 6, 1770.[19] The consent of the parents on both sides had been published, however, Peter's father was absent from the wedding, having betoken himself on an itinerary of several parishes in Lancaster County. Pastor Schmidt from Germantown performed the ceremony.[20]

Hanna and Peter stayed married until Hanna's death in 1801. They had six children together. All of them survived infancy and four of them lived into adulthood, but only two, Peter and Hester, lived past the age of 36. The parents grieved the loss of their third child, Charles Frederick, in

---

18. Splitter, "Divide et Impera," 45–91.
19. Wallace, *Muhlenbergs of Pennsylvania*, 83.
20. Mühlenberg, *Journals*, 2:473.

a boating accident at the age of seventeen in 1795. Their last child born to them, Mary Ann in 1793, died in 1805.

The birth of Charles Frederick in 1778 was the occasion for a vocational crisis in Peter as he struggled between duty and family, as will be described below. Indeed the references to Hanna Meyer in *The Journals of Henry Melchior Muhlenberg,* Volume Three, show a partnership between husband and wife that both conformed to the marital roles of the eighteenth century's upwardly-mobile class, and yet transcended those roles through a mutual affection and self-sacrificing concern each for the other.

At his death in 1775, Hanna's father Matthias Meyer left an estate of 1152 pounds to be divided between his wife and two daughters.[21] Considering that a live-in maid might get paid three pounds a year, this is no mean sum. In eighteenth-century terms, despite his own past as a runaway indentured shop-clerk, Peter married well. Certainly his pedigree as grandson to Conrad Weiser and son to the German Lutheran superintendent did no harm. The match also proved to be mutually beneficial for the couple's trajectory in society. First in the Pennsylvania Ministerium, then in the established Anglican clergy of Virginia, then as a commissioned officer in the Continental Army, Peter Mühlenberg became acquainted with and then moved among elite social circles by the age of thirty. This elevation in status brought with it the airs of polite society. When after the war Peter and Hanna moved to Providence, and Peter served as the Vice President of Pennsylvania under Benjamin Franklin, Hanna began to host afternoon tea parties for society's leading women. This custom provoked a growl of disapproval from her pietistic father-in-law.[22]

At the same time the married couple was conventional enough in their social milieu that they kept slaves.[23] German Pietist views on slavery were not uniform. Heinrich Mühlenberg condemned at least certain aspects of the custom, but accommodated the reality of his world in order to minister in it. Similar attitudes were seen in the German Pietist leadership in Georgia, which had begun as a colony with a proprietor

---

21. Mühlenberg, *Journals,* 3:576–77.

22. "Today Mrs. Hanna had a first visit at her table from several neighboring women according to the prevailing fashion. They drink a glass of wine or a cup of tea and some cakes in the afternoon and evening and entertain one another with vain conversations. This fashion is not according to the counsel and command of our Lord and Saviour, Luke 14:12–14" (Mühlenberg, *Journals,* 3:746).

23. Mühlenberg, *Journals,* 3:39.

who forbade slavery. The experience of raising cash crops in the other southern colonies, however, had Georgia relenting on slave ownership after just twenty years. The first of the Halle Lutheran pastors to lead the communitarian experiment in Ebenezer, Michael Boltzius, approved of Georgia's early prohibition on slavery but found himself powerless to prevent the eventual introduction of the custom by the later transports of German colonists. This will be discussed further in chapter 8, in the story of the Halle missionary and staunch loyalist Christoph Triebner. Of interest to Peter Mühlenberg's story, is that slaves came to be associated with pastoral *glebe* land.[24] Peter's first call as an ordained pastor was to a congregation in Woodstock, Virginia, which offered, as part of the parsonage, two hundred acres.

One hint as to how Peter and Hanna thought of themselves as the "betters" in relationship to servants and slaves and extended treatment accordingly, is that, during a war-time visit to Providence, Hanna had a quarrel with her in-laws' maid, Suzy Klein. This provoked Klein to leave Heinrich Mühlenberg's service even though another of the guests, Peter's sister Polly, was ill at the time and in need of Suzy's help. What the quarrel had been about is not divulged. Hanna, however, seems to be vindicated in that episode in the eyes of her father-in-law when it is learned just weeks later that by the time of that falling out, Suzy had been expecting a child out of wedlock. Some years later Suzy Klein reconciled with her former employers.[25]

Peter behaved as several others in that generation of the revolution: Surviving his wife by a year, he retained the services of Kitty, his domestic slave, until his death, and made her emancipation a condition in his will.[26]

Peter and Hanna were also solicitous of each other's families, with extended visits to the elderly Mühlenbergs in Providence, and, after 1775, to Hanna's mother, "the widow Meyer," in Philadelphia. When Pennsylvania was under threat, Peter and Hanna had the idea that the elderly Mühlenbergs should remove to Woodstock, over two hundred miles away. The parents did not take them up on the offer.[27] From 1783–1802, when Peter's post-war career turned to politics, he and his family lived in

---

24. Glebe land was to be cultivated for the direct support of the clergy.
25. Mühlenberg, *Journals*, 3:295, 310, 581.
26. Hocker, *Fighting Parson*, 174.
27. Mühlenberg, *Journals*, 3:20.

Providence. By 1787 they had taken responsibility for the care of Peter's parents, creating a sub-lease situation where Hanna functioned for them as a land-lady, supervising their laundry, cooking, and cleaning needs.[28] Heinrich died in 1787, and Anna Maria eventually transferred herself to her daughter Polly Swaine until her death in 1802.[29]

## The Establishment Path

Returning to the chronology of Peter Mühlenberg's career, his service as catechist spread his reputation as a preacher. By 1771 a German congregation had gathered in Woodstock in the Shenandoah Valley in Virginia and offered him a call, with a condition: These Germans wanted to be Lutheran in liturgy but part of the Anglican establishment in Virginia, whereby their pastors would be supported by taxation.[30]

Virginia's Lutherans were not alone in seeing affinities between themselves and the Anglican tradition; the view was shared by Peter Mühlenberg's father.[31] Heinrich Muhlenberg, on hearing that Presbyterians, German Reformed and Dutch Reformed were contemplating stronger ties, had speculated that the German Lutherans would have to become united with the "English Lutherans," that is, the Anglicans, in order to maintain the "balance."[32] The model for this kind of accommodation were the Hanoverian kings of England, who were publicly the heads of the Anglican Communion, yet privately retained their German Lutheran practice through the ministry of the Royal Chapel of St. James, which had been staffed by agents of Halle Pietism since the time of Queen Anne, the precursor to their own dynasty.

Another point of view is that Peter Mühlenberg and the congregation he served were authentically Anglican in their theological dispositions.[33] It is certainly the case that, contrary to myth and misunderstanding, Mühlenberg was never ordained a Lutheran.[34] However,

---

28. Mühlenberg, *Journals*, 3:751.
29. Wallace, *Muhlenbergs of Pennsylvania*, 304.
30. Wallace, *Muhlenbergs of Pennsylvania*, 80.
31. Wallace, *Muhlenbergs of Pennsylvania*, 81.
32. Mühlenberg, *Journals*, 2:412.
33. Rightmyer, "Holy Orders of Peter Muhlenberg," 192–93.
34. Germann, "Crisis" 469. I published in error that Peter Mühlenberg resigned "his Lutheran ordination." As discussed above, it would have been more accurate to say that he had resigned "his Lutheran congregation." See Wilson, "Keeping the Synod

militating against this view that the Anglican tradition was Peter's true orientation, are the following considerations: First, on his resignation of ordination to enter military and public life, Peter returned to the Lutheran fold; at his death he was a member of the St. Michael's-Zion Lutheran churches in Philadelphia. Second, as a Colonel in the Virginia line he retained his friend from his days as a catechist, Christian Streit, a Lutheran in the Pennsylvania Ministerium, as a regimental chaplain. Third, like the Hanoverian Kings of England and his own father, if Peter agreed concerning Lutheran and Anglican affinities, he would have no compunction about agreeing to Anglican orders any more than the German Lutherans of his Virginia parish would have compunctions about aligning themselves with the establishment. He was neither an Anglican at heart nor a hypocrite for accepting Anglican ordination.

The confusion of the status of Peter Mühlenberg and the church in Woodstock is ongoing in recent publication, due in large part to reliance on assumptions made by historiographers of the nineteenth century who were without ready access to dispersed archival materials. Nevertheless, as of 2018 two churches in Woodstock, Virginia, claim to have descended from the church served by the Rev. Peter Mühlenberg. These claims are mutual and not exclusive of each other. These are Emanuel Lutheran Church [sic], the other is Emmanuel Episcopal Church. Both websites have "history" pages that feature articles from the Shenandoah County Library. Both history pages acknowledge that the complexion of the congregation in the early 1770s was German and that it performed the Lutheran liturgy when its services were in German, and that once the War of Independence began it was the German Lutheran community that maintained historical continuity. The Episcopalian website acknowledges that their tradition became dormant in the area until its revival in 1876.[35]

This is not to say that the Shenandoah Germans or Peter were casual in this matter; it is true that because he could not take orders and perform ministry as an establishment Anglican priest without testimonials, that it was therefore appropriate for him to take Anglican orders. Furthermore, without an Anglican see in America, Anglican candidates had to risk the Atlantic crossing to travel to England. Peter Mühlenberg made this trip alone, leaving Hanna behind, and was gone for four months from April

German," 115.

35. Emanuel Lutheran Church, "Our History." Emmanuel Episcopal Church links directly to the library website. See Shenandoah County Library, "Emmanuel Episcopal Church."

through late July, 1772. All but three weeks of that time were spent at sea. It was his second round-trip, amounting to three more ocean-crossings than most of even the heartiest immigrants to the New World wanted to dare. He did not cross the Atlantic again: Public life did not bring him into the world of international diplomacy.

His three weeks in London were productive. He was ordained first as a deacon, and four days later as a priest by the Bishop of London. He kept an appointment with Pennsylvania's proprietors, Thomas and John Penn. He also met with Friedrich Michael Ziegenhagen, of whom his father spoke highly, the aging Lutheran chaplain to the King and patron in the Halle network of Lutheran pietist missionaries throughout the British empire. Although their time together was pleasant, Ziegenhagen did not agree that a Lutheran could take Anglican orders and remain a Lutheran.[36] Peter preached at the German Church, St. Mary's on the Savoy, whose liturgy had, at Heinrich Mühlenberg's behest, become the model for the Pennsylvania Ministerium.[37] Returning home, he and Hanna, still childless at that time, prepared to move. The new Anglican priest set out for Woodstock, Virginia, a distance of some two hundred miles from Philadelphia, on September 6, 1772.

Since Peter Mühlenberg's path into the military began during his call in Woodstock, it is important to note the vows he took, and how they might have constrained other Anglican clergy from choosing the patriot faction. He was required to sign his name to three paragraphs, the language of which is generous rather than strict or legalistic as it concerns theological boundaries. The third paragraph, concerning the Thirty-Nine Articles, is that they are "agreeable to the Word of God"; the second paragraph, concerning the Book of Common Prayer, contains "nothing contrary to the word of God" and "may lawfully so be used . . . in public prayer, and administration of the sacraments, and none other." The unwritten caveat here, or a tolerated understanding, is that this applied when leading services in English. The first paragraph is anti-papist in its context and thrust, but for clergy who took the vow its opening statement may have presented difficulties relative to the patriot cause: "That the king's majesty, under God, is the only supreme governor of this realm."[38]

---

36. Wallace, *Muhlenbergs of Pennsylvania*, 81.
37. Wallace, *Muhlenbergs of Pennsylvania*, 81.
38. Rightmyer, "Holy Orders of Peter Muhlenberg," 192–93.

The Boston Tea Party of 1773 provoked Britain's parliament to close Boston harbor beginning in March, 1774. Committees of safety and of correspondence were formed in counties and townships throughout the colonies. Peter Mühlenberg was elected to chair a committee for drafting resolutions of support for Boston on June 16, 1774. In the meantime Virginia's House of Burgesses declared a day of fasting and prayer for Boston on June 1, and in response to this show of support, Virginia's governor, John Murray Lord Dunmore, dissolved the House. The elected Burgesses formed the patriot Virginia Convention, to which the Rev. Mühlenberg was elected in August, 1774. In this role he witnessed the speeches of Patrick Henry and met George Washington, most likely for the first time.

Concurrent with these events, it may have been in part to unify his province against a common enemy and to address the acute concerns of its western settlers that Virginia's Governor Dunmore conducted a war against the Shawnee Nation starting in 1774.[39] This resulted in a treaty in October which pushed the Native Nations beyond the Ohio River. Yet it was during these months that he dissolved the House of Burgesses, and that patriots elected the Virginia Convention. The Boston Tea Party and Parliament's response had catalyzed a crisis that outpaced Dunmore's vision. After the insurrection in New England just six months later his tactics in support of royalist rule alienated much of the colony including its ethnic Germans.

Just one day after the battles at Lexington and Concord, before news of the violence reached Virginia, Dunmore confiscated the gunpowder from the provincial magazine. On June 8 he retreated to a British warship off Norfolk and commanded his troops to fortify the town. In October, he sent a squadron of gun-boats to shell patriot positions in Hampton from the river. Militia fire raked the decks, killing several sailors and gunners, and the squadron withdrew. On November 7, 1775, Dunmore offered emancipation to slaves who fled their masters and joined loyalist ranks. Militia units, fearing that Dunmore would make Norfolk into an enclave where he could equip and train escaped slaves, occupied the village of Great Bridge to cut off the city's communication with the province, and to prevent fugitive slaves from passing through to Dunmore. On December 9, Dunmore's forces attacked the patriot positions at Great Bridge. In a smaller-scale version of the Battle of Bunker Hill, the redcoats were decimated, only on this occasion the patriots had the ammunition and

---

39. Hinderaker and Mancall, *At the Edge of Empire*, 159.

powder they needed to remain in the field. The British withdrew from Norfolk, and the Patriots occupied the city on December 14.[40] Peter Mühlenberg did not participate in these military actions.[41]

## From Enlistment to Valley Forge

Peter's unfolding partisan alignment starting in 1774 does not follow an intuitive path, nor can extant diaries of self-disclosure be turned to for explanation. The redcoats had rescued him from his indentured service in Germany so that his passage home was paid for by a short-term enlistment. He then agreed to serve Shenandoah's Lutherans under the auspices of Virginia's Anglican establishment. While Virginians took the lead on disestablishment and the separation of church and state, it was not Virginia's Anglicans such as George Washington in the vanguard but its non-conformists, such as the Deist Thomas Jefferson.

The call to the Shenandoah Valley put Peter Mühlenberg much closer to the frontier than he had lived before, and the sympathies of the ethnic Germans he served were much the same as in Pennsylvania's backcountry. As settlers aspired to push westward into the territory that had been won from French control, it was the royal government's duty to pacify and defend that territory. Dunmore's punitive expedition against the Shawnee in 1774 was, in its way, politically astute, but it was his minimal duty; dissolving the assembly concurrently with the campaign did much to annul what otherwise might have been the unifying effects of the war. It was unjust of parliament to tax the colonies as a means of paying for its past failures to contain indigenous uprisings; it was an outright betrayal for royalist government to foment social disorder by encouraging slaves to revolt against their masters.

Into the 1770s the ethnic Germans of Shenandoah had been prepared to play by English rules, even to the point of conforming to the Anglican establishment. However, if in Pennsylvania the frontier's ethnic Germans had become restive about the derelictions of duty by an assembly dominated by Quakers, in Virginia the Shenandoah's ethnic Germans were aroused against the tyrannies of a martial governor. Nevertheless, at the urging of his father and of his brother Friedrich, Peter Mühlenberg

---

40. Wilson, *Southern Strategy*, 5–15.

41. Wallace, *Muhlenbergs of Pennsylvania*, 110–14; cf. Hocker, *Fighting Parson*, 50–58.

tried to withdraw from his political offices.[42] His crisis of conscience did not last beyond the closing months of 1774.[43] By January 1775, while his parents were doing what they could to resolve matters amicably among Lutherans in Georgia, Peter was taking the minutes of a committee in Woodstock that had been elected "agreeable to the resolves of the General Congress." Their first order of business was to take an inventory and requisition available stores of gunpowder.[44]

Through most of 1775 Peter Mühlenberg served as both an Anglican priest and a patriot politician. It was possible to hold these commitments together because, even after the pitched battles fought in Massachusetts that spring and then in Virginia in the late months of the year, patriotism had not yet entrenched itself at the pole of republican independence.[45] In July, 1775, the Second Continental Congress sent an "olive branch petition" to the King by two dignitaries who arrived in London in September. This petition offered loyalty on the basis of the relationship that had been practiced before Parliament began over-reaching in the 1760s. This petition was supported in Parliament by Edmund Burke, who proposed motions for conciliation on March 22, 1775, and later had his speech printed.[46] All such efforts were rejected by Parliament and the crown in preference for a harder line. First in an edict on August 23, and then in a speech to Parliament on October 27, George III proclaimed that the colonies were in open rebellion.[47]

After October 1775 the choice to be a patriot no longer meant one opposed an over-reaching faction that controlled parliament, it meant one was guilty of high treason as a traitor to the King. Confronted with this edict, some who had been patriot sympathizers retreated to loyalism, such as the Pennsylvanian statesman Joseph Galloway. The edict radicalized many others, perhaps Peter Mühlenberg at that moment. Even so, the Second Continental Congress issued a response on December 6, 1775, insisting that the grievances of the colonies were with Parliament, not with the King, and that in the consequent violence they were only

---

42. Baglyos, *Muhlenbergs Become Americans*, 54; Wallace, *Muhlenbergs of Pennsylvania*, 120–21.

43. Wallace, *Muhlenbergs of Pennsylvania*, 112.

44. Muhlenberg, "Minutes of the Meeting."

45. Griffin, *America's Revolution*, 118–20; cf. Middlekauf, *Glorious Cause*, 50–52.

46. Burke, "Speech on Moving His Resolutions."

47. Middlekauf, *Glorious Cause*, 320–22. See Frederick, "His Majesty's Most Gracious Speech."

defending their rights. Peter Mühlenberg continued to serve his congregation under Anglican orders.

By the end of 1775 he was being offered a colonel's commission to take command of a regiment that he would recruit personally from the Shenandoah Valley.[48] His dual affinities to the Lutheran and Anglican traditions made it impossible for him to accept the military post and remain in the ministry: It was a confessional standard in the Lutheran tradition that clergy were not to mix their office with the offices of government,[49] and as an ordained Anglican priest he had signed a vow that he acknowledged the King as the supreme governor of the realm. Conscience would not allow him to serve as a patriot militarily unless he resigned his pulpit and his ordination, and turned his back on ministry as a vocation.

Then on January 1, 1776, Governor Dunmore ordered the warships to shell the town of Norfolk, setting it ablaze.[50] Virginians were horrified, but rather than being intimidated, they were radicalized.[51] The extent to which this action helped confirm Peter in his choice must be argued from silence, but he preached his farewell sermon in Woodstock, Virginia on January 21, 1776. It is said that immediately following the service some three hundred men signed up for his regiment, and that spontaneous singing of Luther's Reformation hymn "A Mighty Fortress is Our God" broke out after his benediction.

The moment is related by the biographer H. A. Muhlenberg and told in the art of Pennsylvania Lutheran churches and institutions. Peter, preaching on "A Time for Every Purpose" from Ecclesiastes 3, said that there was a time to pray, but also a time to fight. Then he pulled off his clerical robe to show his colonel's uniform underneath.[52] A mural of this scene adorns the wall of the foyer in Abdel Ross Wentz library in Gettysburg, Pennsylvania, with Peter Mühlenberg at the pulpit, his chest thrust forward as he pulls off his gown, baring a blue officer's coat with gold epaulets and trim. Across the floor on the opposite wall, looking upon the scene with a smile of approval, is a portrait of the Lutheran historian for whom the library is named. As of June, 2014, a table-top porcelain

---

48. Wallace, *Muhlenbergs of Pennsylvania*.
49. *Augsburg Confession*, art. 28.
50. Wilson, *Southern Strategy*, 15–16.
51. Middlekauf, *Glorious Cause*, 322.
52. Muhlenberg, *Life*, 53.

statue of Mühlenberg pulling off his robe to show his military colors was resting to the side of the altar and platform in the basement chapel of Augusta Lutheran Church in Trappe, Pennsylvania. There is clearly a stake in the historicity of this event for Pennsylvania's German-heritage Lutheran churches.

An alternative story by an early chronicler is, on balance, more liturgically appropriate but hardly less dramatic.[53] After preaching his stirring farewell sermon, Peter Mühlenberg went into the sacristy to divest of his clerical garb, and emerged in his military regalia; this would also have made an impression, and perhaps have even inspired singing and an immediate response in enlistments. There is no doubt that he was an effective recruiter for the Virginia line.

His new duties came with immediate head-aches, as egos and personalities crossed in the sensitive politics of recruiting a regiment. He received a letter dated January 23, 1776, from Benjamin Wilson, a captain in the militia, informing him that he would not accept a commission as a Lieutenant in Peter's regiment or "in any of those Regular Companys Now to be Raised for I Will Not Serve, in any station lower than what I am already appointed." The occasion for writing was that Wilson had brought twenty-five men with him to enlist in the regiment, but Peter's adjutant and brother-in-law, Francis Swaine, had stirred resentments by informing Wilson that they would be combined into Captain Langdon's company, and Wilson would receive the subordinate rank to Langdon.[54] Similar clashes over status took place through the war's duration, even in the highest echelons of the Continental Army.

Yet from early on Colonel Mühlenberg proved himself to be effective in command. The regiment he formed was the 8th Virginia. It was heavily but not exclusively German, as is seen by the above letter from "Wilson" and by Peter's choice of his Irish brother-in-law as an aide. The 8th Virginia marched to South Carolina to reinforce patriot general Charles Lee in defense of the city in the First Battle of Charleston. For the patriots this was a victory against British General Henry Clinton's abortive attack.[55]

Lee then sent the regiment to Georgia where it wintered in 1776–1777. Here the climate caused far more suffering than had enemy fire in Charleston. The Virginians from the Shenandoah Valley were not

---

53. Wallace, *Muhlenbergs of Pennsylvania*, 119.
54. Wilson, "Letter to Peter Muhlinburg."
55. Wallace, *Muhlenbergs of Pennsylvania*, 129.

acclimated to the Georgia coast and suffered their worst casualties due to sickness. Colonel Mühlenberg caught a disease that damaged his liver; a condition that cut short his life.[56]

Based on his record in battle and his garrison discipline, Congress conferred upon him the rank of brigadier general and summoned him to join Washington's staff. Peter Mühlenberg's first mission as a brigadier general was to recruit more Virginians that he would bring with him to Washington's headquarters. To that purpose Mühlenberg recommended his adjutant and brother-in-law Captain Francis Swaine, a gregarious and charming immigrant from Cork.[57] Swaine was promoted to brigade-major.[58]

Francis Swaine had entered the family by eloping with Maria Catherine (Polly) Mühlenberg, who as a nineteen year-old had accompanied her parents to Georgia ostensibly as a care-giver for her mother, but chiefly out of their concern about leaving her unsupervised.[59] Polly's brothers had exchanged a flurry of worried epistles at the time of her taking up with Swaine.[60] The nepotism by which Swaine subsequently clung to Peter's coat-tails for his own upward mobility was standard practice at the time, however the responsibilities of a brigade major seem to have exceeded his competence. After doing him the favor Peter Mühlenberg appears to have let him succeed or fail on his own. Swaine was court-martialed for dereliction of duty, in particular as it concerned the care of the brigade's sick during the torpid summer of 1777. He was reprimanded in General Orders on August 22 and resigned on August 23.[61] Although he understood the public nature of his shaming, he was also irrepressible. During the war he became a courier and chauffer for his German in-laws as he pursued a succession of business failures. Yet later in life he would take a commission in the militia and eventually retire as a brigadier general and distinguished citizen.[62]

Before Peter Mühlenberg received his command Washington's Continental Army had sunk to the nadir of its reputation as a fighting force.

56. Wallace, *Muhlenbergs of Pennsylvania*, 129.
57. Wallace, *Muhlenbergs of Pennsylvania*, 90.
58. Wallace, *Muhlenbergs of Pennsylvania*, 133–34.
59. Mühlenberg, *Journals*, 2:560.
60. Wallace, *Muhlenbergs of Pennsylvania*, 89.
61. Wallace, *Muhlenbergs of Pennsylvania*, 138.
62. The details of Swaine's life are given treatment throughout the narrative in Wallace, *Mühlenbergs of Pennsylvania*, esp. 89–90, 133–34, 290, 303.

The army had been chased out of New York in a disastrous campaign that featured whole-sale routes and narrow escapes. Washington had then salvaged the morale of his force and the confidence of Congress in a small but successful campaign in New Jersey in the week following Christmas, 1776. The campaign featured the capture of the entire Hessian garrison at Trenton followed up by a series of forced marches and maneuvers that outwitted the British and scored another victory in Princeton. Peter Mühlenberg had then received his promotion and transfer orders in February, 1777.

In losing Philadelphia the following September the taste of defeat, although new to Peter Mühlenberg, was not as bitter as it might have been. At Brandywine his brigade of Virginians had been at the center of the line, where they were expecting to engage General Knyphausen's Hessians at Chad's Ford in what the patriots supposed was the vanguard of the main attack. Washington realized that his lines were about to be outflanked and surrounded by the main force under General Cornwallis, and urgently re-deployed the Virginians. It was likely clear to the patriots that the battle as such was lost, and that their mission had become surviving to fight another day by extricating themselves from the field.

The two Virginia brigades, one commanded by Mühlenberg and the other by George Weedon, covered four miles in forty minutes. This required jogging through the country with their weapons in hand: an amazing feat over such a distance. On reaching Cornwallis's line they covered the withdrawal of the patriots in good order, at one point checking the redcoats' advance at close-quarters, bayonet to bayonet. What might have been a disaster for the patriots was merely a campaign setback. The last to retire the field, Mühlenberg's and Weedon's Virginians earned a commendation from their corps commander Major General Nathanial Greene.[63]

The First Family of German Americans did not escape Brandywine unscathed. Peter Mühlenberg's cousin Peter Weiser was badly wounded, shot through the chest. A lieutenant in the First Pennsylvania Rifles under Colonel Chambers, whose regiment was attached to General Maxwell's command, Peter Weiser had been sent forward with skirmishers early in the battle to oppose a company of Hessian Jaegers—the marksmen and snipers of the German Auxiliaries, also armed with rifles. The patriots withdrew, leaving the wounded Weiser to be captured. The Jaegers took

---

63. Hocker, *Fighting Parson*, 78–81; cf. Wallace, *Muhlenbergs of Pennsylvania*, 140.

him prisoner and he was treated by army surgeons in Philadelphia. With germ theory and antibiotics unknown to armies in the 1770s his wound remained unhealed. He was paroled in order to convalesce at his home in Tulpehocken. On his journey he spent three days at his Uncle Heinrich Mühlenberg's in Providence. In Tulpehocken on the two year anniversary of the battle, September 11, 1779, Peter Weiser died of his wounds.[64]

More than two weeks after giving battle at the Brandywine the royalists under William Howe marched unopposed into Philadelphia. Washington's staff, meeting on September 28, evinced a lack of enthusiasm for pressing an attack on Germantown, so in the days that followed he held conferences one-to-one with his generals.[65] Receiving intelligence that part of the British force had been withdrawn from Germantown to Philadelphia, Washington chose to strike.

On October 4 the Continental Army attempted to encircle the British forces in Germantown by attacking in four columns. This turned into another debacle of confusion, miscommunication and retreat, due in part to a thick fog that settled over the area in the early morning. Even then, Peter Mühlenberg's brigade obtained its objectives, the soldiers leaping backyard fences to engage the enemy at close quarters, before the confusion in their rear forced Washington to order a general withdrawal.[66]

Court-martials were then conducted later in October to determine the failings in the Philadelphia campaign. Peter Mühlenberg, facing no charges personally, sat in at least three of the tribunals. In one proceeding General Anthony Wayne was acquitted for the midnight attack on his camp that resulted in a massacre of his troops by bayonet. The tribunals then cashiered both General Stephens for being drunk at the Battle of Germantown, and General Maxwell, whose brigade included Peter Weiser, for being drunk at the battle of Brandywine.[67]

Despite such unpleasant duties General Mühlenberg found time to visit his parents in Providence on October 18. It is possible that the

---

64. Wallace, *Muhlenbergs of Pennsylvania*, 184. This specific engagement might be the one described by the Jaeger captain Johann Ewald, in which he describes that after just a half-hour's march that began in the early morning hours, his regiment "ran into a warning post of the enemy, five to six hundred men strong, who withdrew from one favorable position to another under constant skirmishing until around noon-time," as one would expect in an encounter between enemies equipped with rifles but not bayonets (Ewald, *Diary of the American War*, 83).

65. Ferling, *Almost a Miracle*, 253.

66. Hocker, *Fighting Parson*, 90–91.

67. Muhlenberg, *Life*, 116.

brigadier general brought to them a copy of the official announcement from Albany of the capture of General Burgoyne's royalist force on the banks of the Hudson (described in chapter 5). Heinrich Mühlenberg copied and included verbatim the announcement, sent from Albany, in his journal entry for October 18.[68]

During the weeks of campaign the army bivouacked at various locations near Philadelphia before settling at length in Whitemarsh. Washington solicited suggestions from his staff on how to compose the army for winter quarters. In 1849 Henry A. Muhlenberg reproduced Peter Mühlenberg's letter of reply to Washington, December 1, 1777, which proposed that the force be withdrawn and dispersed through several towns and settlements north and west of Philadelphia on a line running from Reading northeast to Easton, or from Reading southwest to Lancaster. Dispersing the troops would mitigate the effects of epidemic diseases which were always worse in the crowded conditions of a camp, and it would expand their options for supply while shortening distances to provisions and forage. Although they would be at some distance from Philadelphia, the distances were not so great to prevent their ability from rapidly mustering and deploying to meet any projection of British force into Pennsylvania's interior.[69]

Washington chose instead to keep the troops contained in large cantonments. One of his strategic concerns was that the dispersion of the army across such a wide line would encourage desertion and the break-down of discipline, hamper communication, and foster rumors about the army's inherent, internal weaknesses.[70] Had Washington taken Mühlenberg's advice and chosen Easton as his left flank, the Moravians at Bethlehem would likely have been put to even greater inconvenience by the Continental Army.

## In Defense of His Honor and Family

In some ways the defeats at Brandywine and Germantown were Peter Mühlenberg's finest season in the war, as it was the performance of the Virginia brigades that kept both of those battles from becoming

68. Mühlenberg, *Journals*, 3:87; cf. Hocker, *Fighting Parson*, 90; Wallace, *Muhlenbergs of Pennsylvania*, 154.

69. Muhlenberg, *Life*, 118–21; cf. Ferling, *Almost a Miracle*, 275n4.

70. Ferling, *Almost a Miracle*, 275; cf. Washington, "General Orders," 281.

catastrophic to the patriot cause. Yet he was denied the promotions that were his due, in status if not in rank. In March 1778, during cantonment at Valley Forge, Brigadier General Woolford, who had first resigned as a colonel and then re-enlisted later, was given preference by Congress as the "senior" brigadier general from Virginia. It took the urging of Washington himself and a resolution of Congress to keep General Mühlenberg from resigning.[71] George Weedon, however, whose brigade had performed just as admirably alongside Mühlenberg's in traversing four miles at Brandywine, tendered his resignation. An act of Congress followed, after an interval of 21 months, to mollify Peter's personal honor.[72]

Peter Mühlenberg was present at the Battle of Monmouth, the action engaged by the patriots to put the exclamation point on the royalist army's withdrawal from Philadelphia. Yet the disappointment to his honor in the matter concerning Woolford was compounded by the needs of his immediate family in the summer of 1778 that followed. Patrick Henry, the Governor of Virginia at that time, replied to Mühlenberg's inquiry regarding compensation with the legislature's plan to reward Virginia's officers with land in the Ohio Country. The letter, dated September 6 and copied verbatim by Peter's father into his *Journals*, draws toward its close with the statement, "Let me take the Liberty just to hint, that I think a Resignation now, might defeat a Claim, which otherwise I trust will be approved by everyone."[73]

The occasion for sending on Governor Henry's letter to his father, was that Peter needed advice. He enclosed a second letter, from George Washington, which denied him his request for leave. This also was copied into his father's journals. But Hanna was expecting their second child, other officers had either been granted leaves or resigned their service, and unsettled acres in Ohio represented a potential for returns that were too far into the future to meet his family's immediate needs. Which of his duties should take priority? The letter, dated November 1, did not reach his father until November 22.[74]

Heinrich Mühlenberg's response is a reflection on the ethics of duty in the vocations of family and career, and how conflict between the pressing demands of each may be resolved. Theologically it is a straightforward

---

71. Hocker, *Fighting Parson*, 96–99.

72. Wallace, *Muhlenbergs of Pennsylvania*, 171.

73. Mühlenberg, *Journals*, 3:195. Heinrich Muhlenberg made the copy part of his entry for November 22, 1778.

74. Mühlenberg, *Journals*, 3:194–95.

application of the principles of Luther's *Large Catechism*. Spiritually it is a letter filled with empathy and encouragement; Heinrich Mühlenberg is at his best as both a pastor and a parent in his letter, including that he begins by reassuring Peter, "I have kept your affairs in my poor prayers, which are able to accomplish something when they are said in earnest." He does not prevaricate; he has been personally persuaded by Washington's letter and advises, "The circumstances make it clear that neither resignation nor furlough could occur without great risk and harm." In terms of concrete suggestions, he then offers his own home to Hanna and the young children, proposing that Francis Swayne, Peter's cashiered aide, might be dispatched to fetch them.[75] The letter was written already after the birth of Charles Frederick Muhlenberg. Its effect on the brigadier general seems to have been fortifying, as Peter served through even more trying and frustrating circumstance to the end of the war and the decommissioning of the Continental Army.

## For Virginia

The capture of Burgoyne's royalist force had robbed the occupation of Philadelphia of any inherent strategic and moral purpose for the royalist cause. William Howe was recalled. Henry Clinton, already in place, took command of the royalist forces in North America. British offers of peace now accepted the Olive Branch petition of 1775, but these were now rejected by a Congress that had declared independence for the United States in 1776. Clinton withdrew from Philadelphia, and after a savage artillery duel near Monmouth, New Jersey, returned to New York City. The royalist strategy shifted southward, where, it was supposed, loyalist sympathies were more fervent, and where they might be aided by emancipating and then recruiting from the much larger and more concentrated slave population.

The ongoing British military presence, along with the economic stresses of war, nearly unraveled the patriot cause. Enlistments fell off. Beginning in February 1780 Peter Mühlenberg was relieved from his field command and dispatched with the mission of raising recruits for the Virginia line. By then the inflation of Continental currency was spiraling out of control: the price he paid for a horse in February of 1780

---

75. Mühlenberg, *Journals*, 3:195–96.

was $6,000, already outrageous. Within a couple of months horses were costing $20,000 in Continental currency.[76]

In May, at the Second Battle of Charleston, General Benjamin Lincoln surrendered the garrison and 6000 patriot troops, including thousands of Virginian continentals, in the single worst defeat for the patriots in the entire war.[77] Mühlenberg's recruits, meanwhile, were being mustered and marched to field camps without weapons, uniforms, or provisions. None of those things were being supplied whether by Virginia, Congress, or the Continental Army, despite Mühlenberg's repeated appeals to his superiors, to Congress, and to Virginia's governor Thomas Jefferson.[78]

When Woolford was captured at Charleston, Mühlenberg became the senior Virginia Brigadier General on active duty. While the rank might have come as a vindication of sorts, his position was by no means enviable. Horatio Gates, who had been given credit for the victory over Burgoyne in New York, was now put in charge of the Continental Army's Southern Department. In September the Continentals were routed at the Battle of Camden, South Carolina, and the flight of Gates ahead of his army eventually put him over sixty miles to their rear.[79]

The royalists unleashed 3000 redcoats, under the command of General Leslie, to raid the Virginia countryside. Mühlenberg assembled 5000 militia on short enlistment to thwart Leslie's brigade as it burned and plundered up and down the James River. Leslie's army withdrew by ship to New York, and the force Mühlenberg had raised returned to their homes.

The British attention on the south forced the Continental Army to restructure its Southern Department. Gates was relieved and Nathaniel Greene took command. In December Baron Friedrich von Steuben arrived to assume overall command in Virginia while Peter Mühlenberg finally took leave to his home in Woodstock. But the redcoats returned in January, 1781, now under the command of the turn-coat Benedict Arnold, formerly a patriot who had been heroic at Saratoga. As Steuben's

76. Wallace, *Muhlenbergs of Pennsylvania*, 192; Hocker, *Fighting Parson*, 108.

77. Lincoln's surrender was a windfall for captured royalist soldiers and officers who had been awaiting exchange, especially for the Convention Army. The Riedesels and other Braunschweig forces, including Surgeon Julian Wasmus, were given safe passage to Quebec.

78. Hocker, *Fighting Parson*, 107–9.

79. Ferling, *Almost a Miracle*, 442.

subordinate Peter Mühlenberg, returning from Woodstock, took command of 800 militia with the mission of countering Arnold's operations.[80]

At Governor Jefferson's behest Mühlenberg crafted a plan to draw Arnold out of his post at Portsmouth and take him prisoner. In a letter to General Mühlenberg Jefferson seems to have conceived of the plan as a work of espionage which, if the would-be abductors were caught, would have them subject to execution according to the conventions of war. As those conventions had been enforced on the patriot side against Arnold's co-conspirator, Major Andre, despite pleas for clemency, no clemency could be expected in return. That may be the reason Jefferson offered a bounty of five thousand guineas to be divided by the operatives on the successful completion of Arnold's capture.[81] General Mühlenberg did not conduct espionage, however, but a tactical military operation instead, in which a detachment of patriot cavalry hoped to lure General Arnold into an ambush. The mission failed in its objective when Arnold refused to sally forth and give chase, but the mission succeeded in harassing the British pickets and taking several prisoners.[82]

British operations in Virginia were a diversion as they concentrated their war effort further south. This included capturing Savannah, Georgia and subduing that entire colony. This would have a direct impact on a Halle Lutheran experiment in communitarian living in Ebenezer, Georgia, as will be discussed in chapter 8. The main concentration of royalists under British General Cornwallis, however, was intent upon the destruction of patriot forces and resistance in the Carolinas. A cat-and-mouse game began with Cornwallis giving chase to patriot Continentals and militia under the command of Nathaniel Greene.[83] Unlike Gates and Lincoln, Greene followed in the philosophy of their commander-in-chief, Washington, for keeping the army intact and ready to fight another day. Steuben together with Peter Mühlenberg were hard-pressed to provide

---

80. Hocker, *Fighting Parson*, 111.

81. Jefferson, *Writings*, 773–74.

82. Wallace, *Muhlenbergs of Pennsylvania*, 208–11, in which the letter from Jefferson noted above is reproduced verbatim (209–10). Hocker adds the tall tale that George Rogers Clark was involved in the raid, and that it resulted in the capture of an American, who told Arnold to his face of the plan to "cut off that shortened leg wounded at Quebec and Saratoga and bury it with the honors of war, and then hang the rest of you" (Hocker, *Fighting Parson*, 112).

83. Washington, *Writings*, 400–401.

Virginians to Greene's command; appeals to Governor Thomas Jefferson were met with polite embarrassment and apologies.[84]

Continental efforts were buoyed, however, when the Marquis de Lafayette was sent to take command in Virginia with a reinforcement of 1200 continentals, departing from New Jersey in March of 1781. They were at first diverted to Chesapeake Bay, however, leaving Mühlenberg and Steuben with an unstable militia force opposing a much larger British raiding army. The Virginians suffered a tactical defeat when 1000 militia took the field under Mühlenberg with Steuben assuming command. 70 men were killed in two hours. Their object had been to check Arnold's advance on Richmond, and though the Patriots left the field and inflicted only slight losses on the British, the redcoats never entered the town. Then Lafayette arrived toward the end of April with his force, while Anthony Wayne further reinforced Virginia with 900 Pennsylvanians.[85]

In the summer of 1781 the tide turned for the patriots in the southern department. A patriot victory over a large detachment of loyalists at King's Mountain was followed by Daniel Morgan's patriot victory over British Col. Brandon Tarleton at Cowpens. Greene's tactical defeat by British General Cornwallis at Guilford Courthouse was in fact a strategic and moral victory: Cornwallis's force was exhausted from chasing Greene and Morgan through the southern climes and Cornwallis was discouraged that loyalist companies had not turned out in greater numbers to support him. Cornwallis withdrew his royalist army to the Yorktown Peninsula on Virginia's coast, near Williamsburg, thinking this the best position to be able to withdraw from the southern colonies by sea and return to New York.

In August Washington identified Cornwallis's position as an opportunity for a decisive blow.[86] Lafayette was commanded to link up his forces to Washington's large army of Continentals and French allies who were marching to Yorktown to cut Cornwallis off from land. General Mühlenberg was once again put in field command of a Continental brigade.

---

84. "Mild laws, a People not used to prompt obedience, a want of provisions of War and means of procuring them render our orders often ineffectual" (Jefferson, *Writings*, 774–75).

85. Hocker, *Fighting Parson*, 115–16.

86. Washington, *Writings*, 451.

## Yorktown and Afterwards

In one of the war's most important turning points, the French fleet under Count De Grasse behaved with surprising boldness and a British fleet with surprising timidity; after an engagement the Royal Navy retreated from Virginia's coast, leaving the French in control of the waters beyond the harbor. This caused the royalist General Clinton, in New York, to rescind his promise of sending a task force with transport ships to rescue Cornwallis, who was now hemmed in at Yorktown. The strategic assumptions on which Cornwallis had based his decisions collapsed beneath him; the Royal Navy had proven to be less than invincible, and what had been the route of escape by sea had been slammed shut. Cornwallis constructed a string of redoubts to project the range of his royalist artillery and disrupt siege efforts as patriots and French allies closed in to invest the city.

As Major General Lafayette's subordinate, Brigadier General Mühlenberg commanded a brigade of about 1000 "effectives" (men fit for duty) at the Siege of Yorktown.[87] This was less than the combined strength of two standard regiments, and shows that the enlistment crisis was pervasive in the Continental Army in 1781. However, for the first time French troops were cooperating with the patriots on the ground.[88]

Mühlenberg was positioned next to a brigade under the command of Brigadier General Hazen. By October 14, 1781, the Continentals and French were in a position to deal with Redoubts 9 and 10, which stood opposed to the center and right of the patriot line. The strategy called for a bayonet assault just after nightfall, to be effected by surprise and with unloaded arms.[89] Count Rochambeau, commander of the French army, was responsible for Redoubt 9 in the center of the line, and Washington planned the assault on Redoubt 10 on the Patriot right.

---

87. Hocker, *Fighting Parson*, 118–19.

88. Earlier attempts at coordination had not featured effective cooperation between the allies in the chain of command and had ended in debacles in Rhode Island and in Georgia.

89. The time of the attack is not consistently reported. Wallace had it as early as the late-afternoon, perhaps on the assumption that after-dark operations were practically impossible in the eighteenth century. George Washington's terse statement concerning the redoubts is that "at half after Six both were carried" (Washington, *Writings*, 459). John Ferling sets 6:30 P.M. as the time of a diversionary attack at another location, and 7 P.M. as the time the battalions moved forward against redoubts 9 and 10 (Ferling, *Almost a Miracle*, 533). It was certainly in the early evening in mid-October.

Major General Lafayette was himself subordinate to Major General Lincoln, but Redoubt 10 was under Lafayette's operational horizon when Washington ordered the attack. Washington himself assigned the brigade and the deployment of three of its battalions designated each by their colonel. The assigned brigade was Mühlenberg's, and three colonels each led a column. The mission of protecting the flank from a counter-attack was given to Colonel Vose. The mission of supporting the assault vanguard was given to Colonel Barber. The mission of storming the redoubt itself had been assigned to Colonel Barber at first, or possibly Lt. Col. Gimat, a personal friend of Lafayette's, but after Lt. Col. Alexander Hamilton sought the mission for himself on a personal appeal to Washington it was re-assigned to him.[90]

Within nine minutes of deploying their companies the patriots, led by Hamilton, took Redoubt 10 and several prisoners. The French operation under Col. Deux-Ponts had a bloodier business at Redoubt 9, where German Saarlanders under French command grappled with Hessians in an all-German hand-to-hand combat. But patriot and allied flags were soon flying from both redoubts and new artillery platforms were already being dug in that same night.

Alexander Hamilton then wrote a report of the battle to Lafayette which has been accepted in military history and among Hamilton biographers, but which stirs controversy in German American ethno-historiographers, because Mühlenberg is not named in the report either as a participant in the action or as the intervening commander between Hamilton and Lafayette.[91] Lafayette, making his own report, added to Hamilton's account some additional details of the dispositions of the forces and their commanders, naming Mühlenberg. But as accounts reached newspapers for publication, many preferred to print Hamilton's version without Lafayette's clarifications.[92]

Hamilton had arrived in New York from England as a child. As a teenager he had fervently embraced patriotism, and entered the privileged inner-circle of the Continental Army's high command as a personal aide and confidential secretary to Washington. Even so, he itched

---

90. Wallace, *Muhlenbergs of Pennsylvania*, 239–40; cf. Wood, *Battles of the Revolutionary War*, 288; McDonnel, *Alexander Hamilton*, 25; Middlekauf, *Glorious Cause*, 589–90; Ferling, *Almost a Miracle*, 533–34; Stephenson, *Patriot Battles*, 351.

91. Images of Hamilton's report immediately following the action can be found online through the Library of Congress. See Hamilton, "Hamilton to La Fayette."

92. Wallace, *Muhlenbergs of Pennsylvania*, 236.

for battlefield experience and reputation. He was Lafayette's own age and a close friend. It is certain that when Hamilton gained the palisades of Redoubt 10 in the vanguard of the patriots he behaved with the sort of alacrity and courage for which he also gave credit to everyone involved.

One of General Mühlenberg's aides, Major Heydt, was an eyewitness of the events at Redoubt 10. He lived until 1840. Heydt's account of the battle was circulated independently in the early nineteenth century, then became part of Peter Mühlenberg's obituary in 1808,[93] and was proffered by H. A. Muhlenberg in 1849. The great-nephew finds historical support for Heydt's account in Lafayette's independent report that Mühlenberg was in command of the operation.

According to Heydt, heavy fire from Redoubt 10 was causing the attacking vanguard to waver. General Peter Mühlenberg called forward Colonel Barber's supporting column to strengthen the attack, and as Hamilton led the charge of the vanguard, Mühlenberg simultaneously and personally led Barber's battalion into the redoubt. The battle was brisk and decisive and General Mühlenberg was wounded before the defenders capitulated.[94]

A number of circumstances converge to keep the details of Peter Mühlenberg's involvement at Redoubt 10 under the darkness of that October evening. Mühlenberg's personal participation at Redoubt 10 is not documented, nor is there record of his supposed injuries. Secondary narratives are bound to give Hamilton's version preference over an oral account surfacing decades later by Mühlenberg's family relative, particularly when nothing from Lafayette's account or from Washington's letter to Congress offers a contradiction to Hamilton.[95] As the action was relatively minor, subsequent military historians have focused on Redoubt 10 at the battalion level and thus assign the credit of its capture to the commander of the battalion in the vanguard of the attack, Alexander Hamilton, based largely on his own account.[96]

Among Peter Mühlenberg's twentieth-century biographers, Edward Hocker's retelling of the action in the redoubt includes the further heroic detail that he intervened to keep his troops from massacring the surrendering royalists. Hocker himself is non-committal as to the overall

93. Hocker, *Fighting Parson*, 120.
94. Muhlenberg, *Life*, 242; cf. Hocker, *Fighting Parson*, 119–20.
95. Wood, *Battles of the Revolutionary War*, 288; Stephenson, *Patriot Battles*, 351; Ferling, *Almost a Miracle*, 532–34; McDonald, 25.
96. Stephenson, *Patriot Battles*, 351; Ferling, *Almost a Miracle*, 532–34.

veracity of the narrative that places Mühlenberg in the redoubt. That the surrendering royalists were not massacred is a detail that seems rather to depend on Hamilton's own account, which states that the patriot troops showed the poise, despite the heat and desperation of the fight, to accept the surrenders of the enemy as they lay down their arms.

Paul A. Wallace, however, views Mühlenberg's personal participation in the action as probable and suggests that its loss to historical memory was facilitated by Hamilton's grab at the credit.[97] Even then, Wallace acknowledges that the story that Peter Mühlenberg was wounded in the fight must be treated skeptically.[98]

Militating against his being wounded is Washington's "Journal of the Yorktown Campaign," in which the commander-in-chief meticulously lists the losses of the campaign in killed and wounded, by rank but not by name, in a manifest outlined by the discrete stages of the campaign. Seven officers total are listed as having been wounded at the storming of Redoubt 10, none of them above the rank of Lieutenant Colonel.[99] In correspondence to Congress in which he gives details of battles, such as after Brandywine, he lists by name those generals that were killed, wounded or captured.[100] No such announcement pertaining to wounded generals appears in his letter to Congress of October 19, 1781.[101]

By the morning of October 16 patriot guns dominated Cornwallis's positions and put British vessels in the harbor within range. After a couple of days of incessant bombardment Cornwallis offered terms, and the English, Scots, Hessians and Ansbach-Bayreuthers of the royalist army grounded their arms in an elaborate ceremony on October 19. Receiving the surrender from Cornwallis's subordinate was Benjamin Lincoln, who had been defeated at Charleston. When news reached Philadelphia of the victory, Congress asked to use Zion Lutheran Church, built by the Halle missionary Heinrich Mühlenberg, for its service of thanksgiving, since it was the largest in the city.[102]

---

97. Hocker, *Fighting Parson*, 119–20; Wallace, *Muhlenbergs of Pennsylvania*, 235–41.

98. The evidence of his being wounded "is not strong." See Wallace, *Muhlenbergs of Pennsylvania*, 241.

99. Washington, *Writings*, 460.

100. Washington, *Writings*, 274.

101. Washington, *Writings*, 464.

102. Mühlenberg, *Journals*, 3:454. This entry is dated October 25, 1781.

After Yorktown Mühlenberg took a leave of several months, and stayed in Woodstock to convalesce from a fever.[103] With his leave already approved by his immediate superior Lafayette, Peter Mühlenberg made his request to the commander-in-chief in a letter to General Washington dated October 23: "A constant and violent fever I have had for Ten days past, has . . . reduced me very much."[104] It is here stated that Peter Mühlenberg was already ill at the time of the storming of the redoubt.

That Peter Mühlenberg confessed to a violent illness beginning by October 13 may allow one to surmise the following: First, that the general in command of the brigade might have been too ill to throw himself into the hand-to-hand combat of Redoubt 10. Being ill he may have nevertheless been engaged as most generals were in the eighteenth century, in observing the action and issuing orders from the rear; he may have urged reinforcements forward, as Heydt contends, but that General Mühlenberg mounted the redoubt alongside Lt. Colonel Hamilton becomes less likely by a large degree.

Second, it may be the case that taking a sick leave became conflated, in the imagination of some, with an assumption that his health problems resulted from being wounded at Yorktown. Leaping the logic along, since his brigade stormed Redoubt 10, that must have been where he was wounded too. But as word of his being wounded is not found in Washington's report to Congress of October 19, and as no protestation of being wounded surfaces in his letter to Washington of October 23, and what is instead described is a serious and "violent" illness, it is conclusive that Mühlenberg's wounds in Redoubt 10 are the stuff of myth rather than of history.

Third, by his death in 1807 Peter Muhlenberg had maintained his reputation in political and civil life, as treated below. Alexander Hamilton, however, had fallen in grace, becoming a divisive and scandalous figure before his murder in 1804 in a duel by fire-arms against Thomas Jefferson's vice-president, Aaron Burr. It is more likely that the diminishment of Hamilton's reputation late in Peter Mühlenberg's life encouraged a revision of the events in Redoubt 10 among ethnic Germans in a way that would reflect more glory on one of their own.

Fourth, Paul A. Wallace argues that Peter Mühlenberg's silence on the matter is gentlemanly and quietist. However, considerations of

---

103. Wallace, *Muhlenbergs of Pennsylvania*, 241.
104. Wallace, *Muhlenbergs of Pennsylvania*, 242.

distinction and status had nearly caused Peter Mühlenberg to resign during cantonment at Valley Forge; it is not likely that if Hamilton was deliberately overshadowing or excluding Mühlenberg, that he would have borne it, if for no other concern than that the truth of events be known.

Fifth, that Peter Mühlenberg did not make the report of his brigade for Lafayette, but had Hamilton write it, fits both scenarios: that he was ill and in the rear of the action so he gave the honor of reporting to Hamilton who had been in the thick of the fighting; or, wounded in the thick of the fighting himself, he asked Hamilton to write the report. If Mühlenberg had been wounded in the redoubt, however, it is doubtful that he would have endorsed his subordinate's version which excluded him completely from the narrative. Even if that point is arguable, the silence on the matter of being wounded in Mühlenberg's letter to Washington and in Washington's report to Congress renders the verdict decisive.

Sixth, the eye-witness versions that put Mühlenberg in the redoubt come after his ability to deny them, that is, after his death. Hamilton's document, which presented facts that were falsifiable by hundreds of participants including officers of similar and superior rank, has stood up to the scrutiny of time. Hamilton himself wrote: "I do but justice to the several corps when I assure you, there was not an officer or soldier whose behavior, if it could be particularized, would not have a claim on the warmest approbation."[105]

## Post War Life and Legacy

The Treaty of Paris to end the Revolutionary War was signed in April, 1783 and in November, 1783 the last royalist forces sailed away from New York City. In December, 1783, Peter Mühlenberg was present for the resignation and retirement of George Washington as commander-in-chief of the army. At his own retirement Mühlenberg was promoted to major general. He became a founding member of the Society of Cincinnati, an association of former patriot officers that would devolve membership on their progeny. Despite many of them being broke financially and with the army itself dissolved, the exclusive nature of the group was derided in newspapers as an attempt to impose an aristocratic class on the new nation. The argument in the press subsided, and the society quietly persisted.

---

105. Hamilton, "Hamilton to La Fayette."

Peter Mühlenberg was one of the many officers who could scarcely make ends meet after the war. Among his many ventures, he led a survey expedition of the Ohio Country to stake claims promised by the Virginia legislature and Congress. He began the trek from Fort Pitt in February of 1784, and did not return home until June 26.[106] Among the parties for which he acted as agent was Friedrich von Steuben, the Prussian hireling with whom he had become acquainted at Valley Forge. It became clear to Peter Mühlenberg however that these lands, wooded and remote and still disputed by indigenous peoples, would not return a profit in his lifetime.[107]

Not long after his return from this expedition he parlayed his record in the Revolution into public service. His career in elected office began with running for and winning election into the Pennsylvania Legislature. He rose to Vice President of the Supreme Executive Council for the term 1786–1789, during the administration of Council President Benjamin Franklin.[108]

The constitution that governed Pennsylvania had been put in place in 1776 by supporters of the American Revolution. It had widened the franchise to all "tax-paying" adult males, upwards of 87.5 percent of Euro-ethnic males in Pennsylvania.[109] Additional laws were passed during this period to remove barriers from the colonial era that had kept many Germans out of serving in local and county offices.[110] However by its design Pennsylvania was served by a unicameral legislature and an executive committee, and it was these and other elements that were soon regarded as in need of replacement. Peter Mühlenberg had a hand in the formation of the new state constitution, which went into effect in 1790, after his term on the Supreme Executive and his election to the federal House of Representatives.[111]

After 1776 the politics in Pennsylvania were realigned; gone were the pre-Revolution sympathies divided between Quakers, Proprietary

---

106. Peter Mühlenberg kept an unpublished journal of this survey expedition. It is now available in electronic form through the Gilder Lehman Institute of American History. See Mühlenberg, "Diary."

107. Wallace, *Muhlenbergs of Pennsylvania*, 258–59; Hocker, *Fighting Parson*, 129–32.

108. Hocker, *Fighting Parson*, 140.

109. Ratcliffe, "Right to Vote," 223.

110. Splitter, "Germans in Pennsylvania Politics," 39–76.

111. Hocker, *Fighting Parson*, 145.

sympathizers, and Crown colony activists. After 1776 the "Constitutionalists" advocated for the revolutionary constitution passed in 1776. The Democratic Republicans were those who were inspired by the philosophy of Thomas Jefferson. The ratification of the federal constitution in 1788 forced another realignment, and in place of the Constitutionalists the Federalists emerged. Those distinctions are discussed below. During his term as a legislator and as Pennsylvania's vice-president, Peter Mühlenberg represented Pennsylvania's ethnic Germans as a whole but also, in particular, the Democratic Republican Party that held to the philosophies of Thomas Jefferson.

Scholar Wolfgang Splitter, writing in 1998, quantifies the impact of the 1776 state constitution on ethnic German political involvement, that is, on party affiliation, service in the assembly, and service in offices at the county level through to its replacement in 1790. Splitter asserts that while religious affiliation had an impact on the distribution of elected offices and appointments, *religion did not predict actual partisan alignment*. This revised an earlier assumption made by many that Pennsylvania's Reformed tended to line up with the "Constitutionalists," whereas the Lutherans tended towards Jeffersonian philosophy.[112] Splitter found that the division by religious affiliation is too close to validate the generalization: 8/14 elected Lutherans identified as Republicans, and 6/11 Reformed identified as Constitutionalists. Most telling is that another 10 Lutherans and 8 Reformed in the Pennsylvania assembly have an undetermined political affiliation. Only one third of assemblymen from each denomination named declared for the supposedly preferred party affiliation; a plurality from each denomination remained unaligned, one might say "independent" (or even "neutral"). This confirms the conclusion from an earlier article by Frederick C. Luebke, encompassing several waves of German immigration and ethnographic impact on politics, that "German-American voters were frequently spread across the socioeconomic spectrum and hence rarely held uniform views on the political issues of the day."[113] The opportunities or challenges that are associated with one's status in society and one's participation in the economy, when they are combined with one's aspirations as the head of a household, are much more predictive of political alignment than is the faith espoused at one's church.

---

112. Splitter, "Germans in Pennsylvania Politics," 63–64.
113. Luebke, "German Immigrants and American Politics," 57–74.

Owen S. Ireland points out, however, that during the years of the revolutionary constitution a low turn-out of German Anabaptists and "Sectaries" (Christian communities outside mainstream denominations and doctrine), Lutherans and Quakers contributed early on to power being retained by the Constitutionalist party. "The re-emergence of these groups as a political force after 1786 accounts for ultimate Republican control."[114] Yet as Splitter's subsequent quantified study shows, the aggregation of these groups at times expressed a greater sympathy for the Republican party, but these religious affiliations do not uniformly predict Jeffersonian sympathies. The volatility of the voting public is seen in Peter Mühlenberg's own career in the Congress of the United States starting in 1789.

What these demographic studies of political patterns do not include, is the effect which a particular candidate might have on galvanizing the support of an ethnographic and/or a religious base. The degree of stature and reputation in an ethnic German candidate, such as that of Peter Mühlenberg, might have galvanized more votes from a base that had stayed home for several prior elections. Such passion among Germans to vote had been seen in an election during the colonial era, in 1764, which sent the Lutheran Heinrich Kappelle to the legislature and ousted Benjamin Franklin.

If Peter Mühlenberg won elections as an ethnic German, he lost them as a Democratic Republican. His Lutheran membership and lay-leadership did not enter consideration in any meaningful way that has yet been documented or determined quantifiably.

## A Leading Lutheran

As a private—albeit leading—citizen Peter Mühlenberg served a term as president of the Philadelphia German Society, a civic and benevolence organization begun by his father in the 1760s to help with Germans as they arrived at the Port of Philadelphia for the first time. He was also involved as a lay-person in the interests of his church locally, and in the Pennsylvania Ministerium's efforts to strengthen faith and education. In 1786, while serving on the Supreme Executive Council of Pennsylvania, he signed his name to the petition for the establishment of a German College and Charity School in Lancaster, a joint venture of the Pennsylvania

---

114. Ireland, *Religion, Ethnicity, and Politics*, 240.

Ministerium and the German Reformed Coetus. The school took the name Franklin College in honor of Pennsylvania's President and most renowned citizen, who had donated a modest amount to the school's establishment.[115] Twenty years after German voters had mobilized for Franklin's ouster from the assembly, all seems to have been forgiven.

Mühlenberg was one of the school's founding trustees, and sent his own sons to be educated at Franklin College. He had them billeted in the home of the former German Auxiliaries chaplain turned instructor of Biblical and Oriental Languages, Friedrich Melsheimer.[116] Students in the Charity School were enrolled from the beginning of primary school, while the College functioned as a high school. The project of higher education was still too soon for the ethnic German base which was still too cash-strapped to send sons off to boarding school, especially if they were needed at home for chores. As subscribers failed to meet their commitments the school's teachers ran up debts on the credit of their back-salaries until they were forced to quit, first Heinrich Ernst Mühlenberg and then Melsheimer a year later. The school closed but the corporation continued to exist until, two generations later, its resources were combined with Marshall College to become Franklin Marshall, a thriving university deep into the twenty-first century.

When Peter Mühlenberg's political career took him to Philadelphia he became a member in the church that had been long-served by his father, St. Michael's-Zion Lutheran. As a layman Peter Mühlenberg signed his name, with four others, to a letter addressed to the annual meeting of the Pennsylvania Ministerium which met in June of 1805. The letter represented a faction within St. Michael's-Zion that desired accommodation for English language services.

With this letter Peter Mühlenberg's shared interest with his ethnic German counterparts takes on a perspective that is peculiarly nativist. Concerns are expressed about the quality of German immigrants now arriving in Pennsylvania; it is rumored German and Dutch states are emptying their prisons to ship their undesirables to America. The investment of Zion Church in Philadelphia, and of the Pennsylvania Ministerium as a whole, in German immigrants was misplaced. It was rather to the second

---

115. Glatfelter, *Pastors and People*, 501–2.
116. Glatfelter, *Pastors and People*, 501–2; cf. Mühlenberg, *Journals*, 3:751.

and third generations, the bi-cultural, bi-lingual English-speakers, that the Ministerium should be reaching out.[117]

The letter caused a stir and was no small embarrassment to the senior pastor in Philadelphia, Heinrich Helmuth, of whom it was sharply critical and who was himself a landed immigrant from 1768. It may have also embarrassed Heinrich Ernst Mühlenberg, Peter's brother. Friedrich Melsheimer, who had boarded Peter's children in Lancaster, chaired a taskforce to craft an answer to the letter.[118] The process that Melsheimer steered basically urged those who wanted English to form separate congregations, ostensibly with the blessing of their parent church, and to affirm that German was the language of synod business. This answer was approved unanimously, including Heinrich Ernst Mühlenberg's vote. The answer was then unanimously appended to the synod's constitution. This action kept the Pennsylvania Ministerium German in language into the 1820s.

That the retired brigadier general signed his name to the petition is troubling for the aspersions cast on incoming immigrants and on current pastors. However, on the issue of English language accommodation Peter Mühlenberg was in step with his father, who cast such a vision in the 1750s.[119] Both his father Heinrich Mühlenberg and his grandfather Conrad Weiser had obtained fluency in English. It is not impossible that Heinrich Ernst, by then a member of the American Philosophical Society, shared these sympathies. If the letter had omitted personal attacks and derogatory remarks, and emphasized the positive benefits of accommodation to English, support for such an initiative might have been engendered.

## The Congress of the United States

The first experiment in national government, guided by the Articles of Confederation, had given rise to two distinct factions among the victorious patriots of the American Revolution, the Federalists and the Democratic Republicans. Both factions were rooted in radical Whiggery.[120] Peter Mühlenberg became part of the emerging Democratic Republican

117. Spaeth et al., *Documentary History*, 352.
118. See Wilson, "Keeping the Synod German."
119. Mühlenberg, *Journals*, 1:294.
120. Middlekauf, *Glorious Cause*, 50–51; Griffin, *American Revolution*, 242–48.

faction that was given philosophical leadership by Thomas Jefferson, and which emphasized the egalitarian nature of the enfranchised, not only of individual voters with one another, but also of each state in the union. This philosophy stood opposed to the evolving platforms of interstate and international trade, capitalized industry, and centralized monetary policy which made the national interest supreme and became the Federalism of John Adams and Alexander Hamilton.[121] After the ratification of the Constitution of the United States the nation's first president, George Washington, famously kept both factions represented in his cabinet and administration.[122]

Elected to the first Congress, Peter Mühlenberg leaned against the Federalists and for the Jeffersonians. Such a view resonated with enfranchised ethnic Germans who were living their American dream as freeholders. Pennsylvania was, however, divided between the two factions, and Peter Mühlenberg's repeated terms in Congress were frequently interrupted by election defeats.[123] The first Congress met in New York City in 1789. His brother Friedrich Mühlenberg was elected the Speaker of the House. Peter Mühlenberg voted against honorary titles of address for the President; his view carried. He also voted against the plan for the "District of Colombia" as the seat of the nation's capital, preferring a site that had been proposed in the Susquehanna Valley; his view was defeated. Meanwhile, although he held commission and rank, Mühlenberg did not serve in any of the military actions of Washington's Presidency: The Fallen Timbers campaign, the Whiskey Rebellion, and a campaign to punish the Iroquois.

## Retirement and Legacy

In June 1801 President Thomas Jefferson commissioned Peter Mühlenberg to become the Supervisor of Customs for Pennsylvania, which included the lucrative Port of Philadelphia. On taking the post he resigned

---

121. "A steady choice of tried and approved republicans, to fill the departments of government, must effectually frustrate the scheme of your enemies, and invigorate the confidence of your friends" (Muhlenberg et al., "Address of the State Committee," 16).

122. Ellis, *His Excellency, George Washington*, 216–20.

123. Wallace, *Muhlenbergs of Pennsylvania*, 281.

his commission as a brigadier general in the Pennsylvania militia, which left an opening for his illustrious brother-in-law, Francis Swayne.[124]

Hanna suffered an illness for two months before her death in late October, 1806. Peter survived her for a little less than a year before his own passing, on his sixty-first birthday, on October 1, 1807. Throughout the second half of his life he had suffered from the liver disease he had contracted in garrison in Georgia. Services were held at the Zion Church. He was then interred next to his parents and his wife Hanna, in the yard directly behind Augustus Lutheran Church in Providence, now Trappe.[125]

General Mühlenberg's stature as a war hero faded from public memory, along with the stories of a host of other patriot colonels and brigadiers whose letters, diaries, and orders of the day are filed in archives up and down the Atlantic coast. Rich as these stories are in detail and controversy, they must be bypassed in the telling of the broader narratives, which focus on Washington as commander-in-chief and those who, for one reason or another, achieved celebrity and notoriety in the public memory: Greene, Gates, Lafayette, von Steuben, Arnold, Hamilton. General Mühlenberg is unique on the general staff, however, in representing the non-Anglophonic immigrant community of ethnic Germans.

While Peter Mühlenberg had imbibed much of the patriot platform and partook of the emerging national consciousness, in some important ways he lived out the German pietist values that were his inheritance from both sides of his family. Cut from the cloth of the clergy on the one hand, he was also cut from the cloth of the public and military service of his grandfather, Conrad Weiser. In eventually choosing his grandfather's footsteps over his father's, Peter Mühlenberg nevertheless did live out the values inculcated by his father Heinrich: He resigned the pulpit in the knowledge that he could never return, yet to the end of his life the Lutheran Churches of the Halle-sponsored Pennsylvania Ministerium retained his allegiance as a committed layman.

---

124. Wallace, *Muhlenbergs of Pennsylvania*, 303.
125. Wallace, *Muhlenbergs of Pennsylvania*, 305–6.

# 7

# Loving the Enemy

## *The Moravian Missionary David Zeisberger*

WHAT COLONISTS IMAGINED TO be the wild, unsettled country of the Ohio Valley was in fact a homeland to several complex indigenous cultures. One Pietistic group did not see the Native Nations of the Ohio as impediments to the advance of civilization, but as human beings in need of the once dead but now living Savior. These were the Moravians, headquartered and supplied in Bethlehem, Pennsylvania. The Moravians spread their gospel that the Spirit of the Savior was transmitted through the sharing of his story and through participation at his feast, which celebrated the blood the Savior shed from his own body.

Isaac, converted by Moravian missionaries as a youth, belonged to both the Delaware Nation and to one of its subsets, the Moravian community of converted Native Americans.[1] Converts like Isaac numbered several hundred by the mid-1770s. With the agreement of the Delaware Council Fire, believers from the Delaware and other nations were clustered in three towns under the supervision of the German-speaking Moravian missionaries. Isaac was the representative of the Christian towns to the Delaware Council Fire at Goschachgünk.[2]

On Friday, September 26, 1777, Isaac returned from the Council Fire and reported to the German Moravian in charge of the overall mission, David Zeisberger, in the settlement of Lichtenau. Isaac informed

---

1. Zeisberger, *Moravian Mission Diaries*.
2. Zeisberger, *Moravian Mission Diaries*, 413.

him that he had rescued the two patriot messengers from Fort Pitt that had presented their greetings to the Council Fire; he had saved them from being taken hostage at least, and possibly murdered, by heading off a war party of Shawnee that had sat in at the Council Fire. The Shawnee were angry, and this party had set out in pursuit of the patriot messengers in defiance of the orders of the elders in Goschachgünk.[3]

Not only the Shawnee but the Wyandot (Western Huron) were agitating for the war path by 1777, and it seemed that the Delaware Nation itself was on the point of unraveling over the issue. White Eye, the presiding head chief, had stepped in after the death of Netawatwees in 1776. Netawatwees had governed with diplomatic skill as a firm Moravian sympathizer. His grandson, Gelemind, also called John Killbuck, who was presumed to be his eventual successor, was also pro-patriot and pro-Moravian. As Gelemind was deemed too young to take the role immediately, White Eye was called upon to step in on what Eurocentric cultures of today might consider an interim basis. The elders with White Eye were increasingly unable to keep their War Captains in check, and those Captains, in turn, were derisive of the Moravian missionaries and the converted proselytes in their charge, godly braves like Isaac, whom they blamed for causing the Delaware to be a weak people.

Isaac's report caused Saturday, September 27, 1777, to be a busy day for David Zeisberger. He spent it on a round-trip from Lichtenau to Goschachgünk to meet with the Council's elders. Each trip he made to Goschachgünk, with its increasingly restive war captains, put him in more peril than the last. His diary notes that some Delaware villages were openly declaring their alliance with the royalists and going on the war path. Zeisberger writes of the Goschachgünk leadership: "White Eye and the chiefs are being worn down and do not have any real power anymore."[4]

Yet the meeting went well. The entries for September 28, 29, and 30, 1777, are more hopeful in tone. After worship in the Moravian town of Lichtenau on Sunday, Zeisberger hosted the delegation of Shawnee, the warriors Isaac had turned back from their murderous errand, along with Goschachgünk's elder White Eye. Messages encouraging peace were prepared for the Shawnee guests to take back to their council at Beaver River. On September 30, the diary noted that day's devotional Watchword for

---

3. Zeisberger, *Moravian Mission Diaries*, 411–13.
4. Zeisberger, *Moravian Mission Diaries*, 413.

all Moravians around the world, Matthew 28:20, the promise that Jesus Christ was present always with his followers until the end of the age.[5]

For all that the indigenous peoples appreciated dealing with the royalists as traders and agents, they knew from experience in the French and Indian War that serving as their military auxiliaries was a mixed bag. Indeed, the Native Nations divided on all three sides of the War of Independence. Those firmly in the sphere of British power, near Detroit to the northwest and Montreal to the northeast, roughly corresponding to the frontiers of Canada, were ready to join the royalists sooner than were the Nations that lived closer to the patriot forts. Other native groups, whether whole nations or towns within them, allied themselves to the patriots. Burgoyne's Albany Campaign had featured Native Nations auxiliaries fighting on both sides, albeit in greater numbers for the royalists. The Delaware Nation, with many of their towns situated between the patriots at Fort Pitt and the royalists at Fort Detroit, were caught in the middle. The Moravians among them, by advocating neutrality, were speaking a wisdom consonant with what the Delaware chiefs perceived to be in their own nation's best interest. Nevertheless, Wyandot war parties passed through Delaware territory on their way to and from attacks on settler farms. First Shawnee, and then Delaware towns, picked up the hatchet as well; their right to act independently of Council directives was a function of Delaware culture and philosophy.

The chiefs and the missionaries used their influence to keep neutral those whom they could despite two pressures constantly working against them: the positive pressure of repeated overtures, gifts and promises from the British officers and agents in Detroit, and, the negative pressure of the poverty of the Continentals at Fort Pitt which made patriot promises ring hollow.

The gains for peace and neutrality in the last week of September, 1777 were not sustained over the duration of the lengthy war. By 1781 patience was wearing thin at both partisan poles against those in the middle, the Moravian-converted Native Americans living in closed church communities with German names: Gnadenhütten, Schönbrunn, and Lichtenau. In 1782, after the Battle of Yorktown, royalist efforts to intimidate the pacifist communities into allegiance led to a forced internment, while patriot efforts to exact a punitive reprisal against indigenous peoples led to war crimes.

---

5. Zeisberger, *Moravian Mission Diaries*, 414.

## Moravians in the Middle: The Missionary Effort Among the Native Nations

Cross-cultural religious evangelism can itself exert pressure on the integrity of a society, yet it has been pursued relentlessly for thousands of years as the Church has obeyed the command of Jesus Christ found in Matthew 28:16–20. The premise of cross-cultural efforts among Pietist missionaries is that all humankind shares two traits alike: a common dignity which is rendered by the image of God in each person, and, a common curse of sin which alienates each person from God. The remedy for this curse requires that each person repent of their sin and accept salvation and new life in Jesus Christ: The opportunity to receive this remedy is occasioned by the proclamation of this gospel of salvation (Roms 10:9), hence the onus on followers of Christ for preaching, evangelism, and mission.[6]

However western Europeans in the Enlightenment were observing the steepening curve of a technology gap compared to indigenous peoples in Africa, the Americas, southeast Asia and Oceana. For many the command to proselytize among "savages," those living in harmony rather than domination over their environment, was less clear. As discussed in chapter 1, racial assumptions posed by some Enlightenment rationalists competed with stadial assumptions posed by others, and eventually, tragically, the race model gained the upper hand.

The mission impetus for Count Nicholas Ludwig von Zinzendorf was clearly stadial in its anthropology. When Moravians arrived in Pennsylvania they found two fields of work that were under-served by either pastors or missionaries. The one field was the geometrically increasing population of mainline Germans who were greatly outpacing trained clergy in their emigration. This field was considered ripe for a harvest. The second field was among the indigenous peoples, many of whom had been exposed to Christian religion, including Catholicism in their French allies, but few of whom had been baptized or were receiving any kind of Christian care. This field, Zinzendorf shrewdly discerned, needed careful and patient cultivation. By 1741, in the early phases of Bethlehem's construction, missionary candidates were being coached in Native Nations customs, etiquette, and language. One of their key tutors was Conrad Weiser.

---

6. These presuppositions concerning humankind's need for the gospel are taken for granted by the author, who is ordained in a mission-oriented evangelical denomination with roots in Moravian spirituality.

Zinzendorf instructed his cross-cultural missionaries to work in teams, to learn the languages and customs of the people to whom they were sent, to discern where God's Spirit had been at work ahead of them rather than waste their efforts on those whose hearts were closed to the gospel, and to settle any uncertainty through divine guidance by drawing lots. All of these were based on Biblical injunctions and precedents. The use of the lot, while Biblical and performed among the Apostles in Acts 1, was recovered by Zinzendorf as a distinctive practice for the Renewed Unity and was highly controversial.

In the spring of 1742 Zinzendorf hosted an Onondaga chief at his residence in Philadelphia. On August 3 the Count dropped in at Weiser's home in Tulpehocken, where that same chief and others were visiting after a treaty conference. Here the informal request was raised: Might the Count and others of the Brethren be permitted to travel among the towns to speak to them of the Great Spirit? With a string of wampum he was assured that he would be welcome among them.[7] The Iroquois dignitaries Canasatego and Shickillimy took part in extending the invitation.

It took over a month to prepare the expedition. Weiser and Zinzendorf limited the itineration to the Delaware and Shawnee towns at Shamokin and then along the North Branch of the Susquehanna to the Wyoming Valley. The advantage of Shamokin was that it was also where Shickillimy lived as an Iroquois agent among the Delaware, acting, in Euro-ethnic state-building terms, as something between an ambassador and an imperial prefect. In September, 1742, Zinzendorf and Weiser set out with five missionaries and two Native American guides.

On arriving in Shamokin they spent only a day, but left the Macks, a missionary couple, to remain there as the rest journeyed east by northeast along the North Branch. At the town of Ostonwakin they met a refugee French Canadian woman named Montour and her son Andrew, whose father was Native American. They happily spoke French with the Count. After meeting Weiser, Andrew Montour himself grew into an important agent and negotiator. Weiser's own attention was divided by that fall's election, and no doubt supposing that Zinzendorf had found helpful friends in the Montours he returned to Tulpehocken to attend to matters.

However, the auspicious beginning with Madame Montour quickly soured when Zinzendorf declined her request to baptize her children. Leaving that town, and in Weiser's continued absence, they journeyed

---

7. Wallace, *Conrad Weiser*, 133–34.

on to the Wyoming. Their Zinzendorf's saddle broke loose and he fell into the river. Then he pitched his tent without consulting local native leaders, and it was too near one of their burial grounds. Efforts to appease them with gifts, including the buttons of his coat and the buckles of his shoes, were to no avail, and after subsequent embarrassments his Native American guides abandoned him.

Weiser, meanwhile, would have returned much faster, if he had not been waylaid by three more Moravians arriving in Tulpehocken. They had come from Bethlehem under orders, they said, to accompany him to a mission conference that Zinzendorf was assembling in the Wyoming Valley. On his return to Zinzendorf's camp Weiser had to cool the tempers of the Shawnee, and then had a lengthy and heated argument with Zinzendorf in his tent. What finally penetrated the Count's sense of wounded aristocratic dignity was Weiser's plain warning that all of their lives were in danger.[8]

While Zinzendorf's vision impelled Moravian missions forward, his own personality was putting that mission in peril. Repelled by several customs and manners of different indigenous groups, Zinzendorf had held himself aloof from their hospitality, yet he also expected that his own demands for personal attendance be met. This was a significant blind-spot from his aristocratic background.[9]

He had hoped to consecrate several missionary teams in a service of worship in a Native American village that had opened their hearts to them. But God had not opened those hearts, and it was by no means clear where the missionaries might be able to begin their work. Zinzendorf had heard that there was a village of Mohicans further upstream, and he associated the Mohicans with greater friendship towards the Euro-ethnic colonists than he had hitherto been shown by the Shawnee. However, Weiser received definite word that the village they spoke of was no longer inhabited. Zinzendorf insisted that God had spoken to him that it was that place where the missions conference and consecration service was to be held. This led to a second argument, but on this Weiser consented, if for no other reason than to put some distance between themselves and the Shawnee.[10]

---

8. Wallace, *Conrad Weiser*, 140–41.
9. Wallace, *Conrad Weiser*, 141.
10. Wallace, *Conrad Weiser*, 141–42.

Zinzendorf pitched his tent outside the abandoned Native American village and submitted the missionaries to a series of commissioning oaths, prayer, and the singing of a hymn. This was the beginning and the end of their missions conference. What followed was an argument as to the path to be taken to return to Bethlehem. Zinzendorf proposed drawing lots on the question of whether to return by Shamokin or to take another route. The lot indicated the other route. This occasioned the third argument. Weiser insisted that Shickillimy was waiting for the party back at Shamokin and that Zinzendorf had promised to return that way. After all the embarrassments hitherto, breaking this promise would be sure to alienate the friends they had remaining, and lead to obstacles being set against the missionaries. Weiser refused to have his own reputation smeared by that association; he would return to Bethlehem via Shamokin and make a full report of everything to August Spangenberg. If Zinzendorf and the missionaries pursued this other course, Weiser would not guide them.

In response Zinzendorf decided to submit the question to the lot again, and had Weiser hold the slips. The question was phrased, should the party return by way of Shamokin, and Weiser handed him the "Yes" slip, having, without thinking, seen which hand held which. Although this allowed Zinzendorf to save his face, the argument chilled relations between them. Even so, in August Spangenberg's biography of Zinzendorf the entire episode of the tour to the Wyoming glosses over these conflicts. Acknowledging that Zinzendorf's life was indeed in peril among the Shawnee, Spangenberg presents his deliverance as a miracle: Weiser, who had left him for a time, was filled with a mysterious apprehension for the Count's safety and rode to the camp just in time to foil the plot.[11]

The missionaries returned to Bethlehem, and Zinzendorf went on to Philadelphia and then, after a tense encounter with Weiser's future-son-in-law Heinrich Mühlenberg, he sailed for London in January, 1743.

While Zinzendorf never set foot again in North America, he did leave in Bethlehem an earnest zeal for mission among the Native Nations and important lessons as to how one goes about it. The Moravians who served the indigenous peoples followed in the vision and zeal of Zinzendorf, while steeping themselves in the hardheaded practicality and openhearted flexibility of Weiser as it concerned crossing cultures in the wilderness. By keeping the best of what they learned from these

11. Spangenberg, *Life of N. L. Zinzendorf*, 310–11.

two examples, the Moravians established a lasting presence among the indigenous peoples of North America.

## David Zeisberger and the Delaware

During his tour to the Wyoming River Zinzendorf had been rebuffed by an elderly Shawnee chief who described his world-view in terms of the two creations anthropology. This chief did admit to being a subject of the Iroquois, and would say nothing against the Iroquois if they chose to learn to pray like the Europeans.[12] The Shawnee were left alone, and due to the connection through Weiser's friend Shickillimy the first Moravian work was undertaken among the Iroquois.

The Iroquois Confederacy had tolerated Christian work in its long association and friendship with English colonists, with the occasional chief or captain submitting to baptism. Some Canadian Iroquois were Catholicized along with their Huron neighbors. However, while the Iroquois permitted Moravians among them, the small harvest of souls after more than twenty years may indicate that this permission was extended more out of their deference to Weiser than by a particular hunger for the gospel.

The Moravians opened a mission at the Mahican town of Checomeco in New York in 1744. They came immediately under the suspicion of the colony. Unlike the affirmation with which they were accepted in Pennsylvania, New York required that oaths of loyalty be taken, which the Moravians refused to do. 1744 was also the outset of King George's War, and the beginning of hostilities with the French and their indigenous allies in Canada. The Moravian missionaries, under interrogation, refused to answer questions about their loyalties and whether they were crypto-Catholics. As a result New York passed laws against their ability to work, and they were forced to leave in 1746. When the missionaries left, their charges, largely Mahican, followed. The Moravians were permitted to build a missionary town in the Wyoming in Pennsylvania for these refugees, which they called Gnadenhütten. This work had upwards of ten missionaries among over a hundred Native Americans.[13]

Shickillimy drove a hard bargain with the Moravians for a mission station in Shamokin. Among his terms were that the Moravians establish

12. Wallace, *Conrad Weiser*, 144.
13. Zeisberger, *Moravian Mission Diaries*, 43–44.

and staff a smithy in Shamokin, so that warriors could have their weapons repaired for free on their way to and from their campaigns against the Catawbas in Virginia. This unsettled the consciences of the Moravians but by 1746 Bishop Cammerhof, at that time the director in Bethlehem, broached a compromise. Since the firearms and hatchets were used for hunting game, the smithy could serve them, but he ought to be paid from what the braves earned from their hunts. Shickillimy played along with the ethical gymnastics that allowed pacifist Moravian smiths to fix rifles used by warriors in battle, and missionaries were sent to Shamokin, among them David Zeisberger (1721–1808).[14]

Zeisberger was born in Europe, in a village in the western Carpathians. The region of his home had passed under a succession of rulers through the centuries, including that during the Middle Ages it had once formed part of the medieval kingdom of Moravia. While Zeisberger was in his infancy his family fled across the Bohemian border to Count Zinzendorf's estates in Upper Lusatia, joining the town of Herrnhut as refugees from persecution. In 1736 his parents migrated to Georgia; David caught up with them somewhat later. In 1740 the whole family took part in the removal of the Moravian colony from Georgia to Pennsylvania.[15] The Zeisberger family models the Moravian narrative, linking the "hidden seed" of the Unity of the Brethren's deep past in Czech lands and Hussite roots to the Renewed Unity under Zinzendorf and its bold projects of community and mission in North America.

In April 1749, Zeisberger reported the death of Shickillimy to Conrad Weiser. This may have led Weiser to assume on his own that Shickillimy had also been baptized by the Moravians, which is otherwise unsubstantiated.[16] The Moravians had been made aware of the Onondaga chief's Catholic baptism in Canada by a priest.[17] Aside from the friendship of Shickillimy the work among the Iroquois had not borne the fruit that Count Zinzendorf had indicated should be present in open hearts, so shortly after the chief's death the Moravians shifted their focus to the Delaware Nation.

Shickillimy's death also ended the era of a uniform policy of friendship towards English colonial governments by the Iroquois Confederacy

---

14. Zeisberger, *Moravian Mission Diaries*, 45–46.
15. Zeisberger, *Moravian Mission Diaries*, 72.
16. Zeisberger, *Moravian Mission Diaries*, 46; cf. **46n157**.
17. Wallace, *Conrad Weiser*, 274.

and their tribute nations. France had learned its lessons from their recent defeat in King George's War; now its agents began to do their utmost to bribe and cajole the Native Nations of the Great Lakes and Ohio Country into hostility towards the English. As years passed the English provincial governments failed to show the Native Nations a unified policy of their own.

The stunning, decisive route of Braddock's army in July of 1755 tilted many Native Nations to the French. Iroquois Suzerainty tottered as the Eastern Delaware, with Teedyuschung as a spokesperson, joined the uprising. Eight Moravian missionaries at Gnadenhütten on the Wyoming River in Pennsylvania were murdered on November 24, 1755. Peaceable Native Americans fled for Bethlehem, joining hundreds of refugee settlers and overwhelming the town. How Spangenberg effectively addressed the crisis of the town's defense has been described in chapter 4. The community built Nain, beyond Bethlehem's palisade but still nearby, to house the indigenous refugees.

In 1760 another settlement, later called Friedenshütten, was built further west to settle around two hundred indigenous inhabitants. This town was served for a time by Friedrich Post, the Moravian missionary who had brought the news of the Treaty of Easton to the Ohio nations. This treaty, organized by Conrad Weiser, had returned to neutrality the nations that had been French allies. The frontier was pacified and the French were soon defeated. In 1763 Zeisberger organized Friedenshütten as a missions town, as Checomeco and Gnadenhütten had been.[18]

In the twenty years between the start of the mission in Shamokin and the reorganization of Friedenshütten the Moravian missionaries had learned many lessons. Close proximity to neighboring settlers tended to corrupt the morals of the Native Americans, especially as it concerned alcohol. Proximity also made indigenous peoples vulnerable to the violence of settlers who were increasingly viewing frontier conflict on the terms of an irreconcilable racial alienation. What was needed was a mission far enough away from Euro-ethnic settlers for the indigenous believers to be 1) safe from rum dealers, 2) protected from the animosity of settlers, and yet 3) still hold themselves as a community apart from unbelieving Native American towns.[19]

18. Zeisberger, *Moravian Mission Diaries*, 50.
19. Zeisberger, *Moravian Mission Diaries*, 50.

The Delaware Nation, which had once claimed territory far to the east along the river that bore its name, was now concentrated in Ohio. Their most important town, the center of its Council Fire, had become Gekelemukpechünk, and Moravian missionaries were invited to live among them in the late 1760s. Then the Treaty of Stanwix, negotiated by William Johnson, set new western boundaries for the colonies in 1768, and settlers began to cross the mountains near Gekelemukpechünk. The Delaware Council held a conference in 1771 with Bishop Nathaniel Seidel along with David Zeisberger. The Delaware invited the Moravians to situate themselves on the Muskingum River—on the condition that they close Friedenshütten. Moravian teams with Delaware guides set out to find suitable sites, and in 1772 two Moravian towns were planted on the Muskingum: Schönbrunn, which was largely Delaware, and Gnadenhütten, where many Mahican settled, having followed the mission from location to location since Checomeko. Gnadenhütten in Ohio was named in honor of the Moravian mission town in Pennsylvania where the missionaries had been murdered in 1755.[20]

## Rules for Residents and Missionaries

The general principles governing the Moravian missionaries and the settlements they established had been set by Zinzendorf decades earlier. Believing that God alone saves, the first rule was for the missionary evangelist to live among the natives in silent observation to discern where and with whom the grace of God might be preparing a heart to receive the good news. The evangelist was to share the gospel only with such a person, otherwise where God has not prepared hearts such labors would be in vain. Furthermore, they were to share only with the unbaptized and unchurched. The missionaries were "not to build on a foundation laid by others nor to disturb their work, but to seek the outcast and forsaken."[21]

Zeisberger held himself as an exception to one of the cornerstones of Zinzendorf's ministry philosophies; he served as an unmarried man until he was 60 years old. He was always assisted by Moravian husband-and-wife teams, but that no suitable wife was found in the first forty years of his career is a sign of the challenges that were inherent in the Moravian approach to marriage. Perhaps he had been disappointed in love. Perhaps

20. Zeisberger, *Moravian Mission Diaries*, 50–51.
21. Olmstead, *Black Coats Among the Delaware*, 5.

the lot had denied matches proposed by the elders. At all events, when he made a trip from the Muskingum to Bethlehem in 1781 to report and take a brief furlough, it was at that time that the elders insisted that he not return to the field without a bride.

Native Americans who wanted to reside in Moravian towns had to abide by lifestyle expectations and restrictions as well, by means of which the proselyte was thought to exhibit the visible fruits of conversion. Conversion meant an ethical transformation of one's life, which in turn meant at minimum the cheerful willingness to adopt the community's strictures and rules. Moravian members all over the world were forbidden to serve in secular government in offices that held the power of the sword, such as in the military or in the court system. The Moravians applied this principle to the Native Nations Council Fires that held the power of the hatchet. Zeisberger speaks with regret of Gelemind (John Killbuck), the converted believer and grandson of the Delaware chief Netawatwees. Before and after being raised to chief himself, Gelemind was very supportive of the Moravians and of peace. On becoming chief he requested permission to live in the Moravian towns, but he was refused because he could not see his way clear of his Council Fire responsibilities.[22]

The Moravian ethics of vocation brought changes to converted Native American males in terms of their roles in indigenous society. Missionary males set examples for proselytes by their farm labor, even though tending the gardens was traditionally the task of Native American women. No longer was a converted male of the Delaware, Mahican, Huron or Shawnee to consider the traditional ladder for advancement and status in their culture, by which men of reputation might advance from warrior to War Captain, or be appointed to the Council Fire, or be elected Sachem (chief).[23] Furthermore the farming vocation as taught by the missionaries reflected Euro-ethnic approaches to nature; horticulture to aid in subsistence was overtaken by intensive agriculture and animal husbandry for the production of surpluses.[24]

Converted Native American men still hunted, however the various rituals and dances to petition spirits to grant them success were discontinued. Monogamous marriage was enforced; men with more than one wife could not live within a Moravian mission town. Although wine was

---

22. Zeisberger, *Moravian Mission Diaries*, 548–49.
23. Turdo, "Different Kind of Indian Conversion," 149.
24. Zeisberger, *Moravian Mission Diaries*, 65–69.

served at communion, which was held every six weeks,[25] drunkenness was a sin and rum and other strong liquors were banned from the mission towns. These rules emerged through trial and error and the consequences of infractions were modified over time, but they were set in place as indications of how a regenerate life was to be lived.[26]

The Moravians had no coercive power at hand to foist these changes on the larger Delaware or Mahican cultures. These strictures were only in place for the converted who desired to live in a mission town. Given the extent of the repudiation of cultural norms concerning gender roles, hunting customs, violence, and attire, it is small wonder that the number of converted Delaware remained just a tiny remnant of the whole nation. Furthermore, as of the 1770s the Six Nations as a whole remained unconverted, as did the Shawnee.

Closed communities are self-limiting and the Moravian Native Americans never represented the mainstream of any indigenous society. Yet they were not expelled or excluded from the Delaware Nation who hosted them on their land, despite the distrust of War Captains. In Isaac, a Moravian Delaware, the Moravian towns had an ambassador to the Council Fire at Goschachgünk, and in Gelemind they had a sympathetic supporter at the highest level.[27]

## Peace and Mistrust in the War of Independence

The tensions at the Council Fire were real nevertheless. One of the leading opponents to both reconciliation with the settlers and to the Moravian mission was the war leader Captain Pipe, who had friends among the Wyandot on the Sandusky River and with the British at Fort Detroit. The move to the Muskingum suited the Moravian vision for, first, isolating converts from their own cultural environment as well as from pernicious settler influence, and second, to appease the growing nativism that Captain Pipe represented. Delaware nativists at Gekelemukpechünk, along with their Seneca neighbors of the Iroquois Confederacy, welcomed the closure of Friedenshütten and the departure of the Moravians from their vicinity to the Muskingum.[28]

25. Zeisberger, *Moravian Mission Diaries*, 561
26. Zeisberger, *Moravian Mission Diaries*, 563–64.
27. Olmstead, *Blackcoats Among the Delaware*, 16–17.
28. Olmstead, *Blackcoats Among the Delaware*, 16–17.

The nativist movement among the Delaware revolved around a constellation of resentments: against white settlers, against the threats to indigenous cultures posed by rum and trade goods, and against the Christian faith. The movement sparked a revival of religious and national pride espoused by several indigenous prophets, many of whom taught the doctrine of Two Creations. Adherents to Nativism became increasingly radicalized and violent. War parties of the Shawnee, living southeast of the Delaware in what is Kentucky today, engaged in a guerilla war against Virginia's westward expansion throughout the early 1770s. Finally Virginia's governor, John Murray, Fourth Earl of Dunmore, organized an expedition to punish the Shawnee and bring them to terms in 1774, in what became known as Lord Dunmore's War.[29] The Shawnee did not agree to the terms forced on them which marked the Ohio River as their eastern boundary, so when the War of Independence erupted just a couple of years later many Shawnee allied themselves with the royalists, including Dunmore himself.[30]

Although Dunmore had authorized a punitive campaign, he did not follow in Amherst's philosophy. Dunmore seemed to be more in line with Gage, Johnson, and Weiser, that the Native Nations were both impressed by, and reassured by, displays of force. When Dunmore marched on the Shawnee, the other Native Nations remained neutral and did not flock to the uprising as had happened ten years earlier with Pontiac. A passage from Dunmore's correspondence seems to confirm the stadial anthropology held by himself and other royalist elites, and which stood opposed to the racial alienation flowering among frontier settlers. Dunmore found that the settlers felt entitled to expand into land that they considered empty, except

> as a shelter to a few Scattered Tribes of Indians. Nor can they be easily brought to entertain any belief of the permanent obligation of Treaties made with those People, whom they consider, as but little removed from brute Creation.[31]

With the onset of the Revolutionary War the Delaware Nation transferred its seat of government westward, to Goschachgünk, nearer

---

29. Murray, "Indian Expedition."

30. Events outpaced his effort to unify Virginia around a war with the Shawnee in 1774, concurrent with which he dissolved the Virginia Assembly. By the fall of 1775 he was conducting military operations against Virginia's patriots.

31. Zeisberger, *Moravian Mission Diaries*, 28.

to the Muskingum and the Moravians. The chiefs were concerned that in war Schönbrunn was too remote from their protection and vulnerable to the anger and misunderstanding of British-allied war parties of the Shawnee and Wyandot. The Moravians complied by building Lichtenau closer to Goshachgünk and the protection of its warriors.[32] At what was considered the height of the danger, the residents of Gnadenhütten abandoned that town and stayed in Lichtenau.[33]

Netawatwees had presided for decades over the Delaware council until his death in 1776. Gelemind (John Killbuck), a grandson, stood in line to succeed him, but the council was slow to approve him.[34] Although he was the preferred candidate among the Moravian congregations and the patriots holding Fort Pitt, the nation was divided, with many wanting to follow Captain Pipe's British-friendly nativism. In the meantime Gelemind's uncle, White Eye, continued to foster the position of patriot-friendly neutrality to which Netawatwees subscribed and which Gelemind, fond of the Moravians, was committed to follow.

For the first three years of the American Revolution, the Continental Congress secured peace with the Delawares through treaties and gifts. In the spring of 1778, however, the British and their close allies, the Wyandot, gained the friendship of the Delaware war leaders Captain Pipe and Captain James, each with their villages, and they added their war parties to those of the Shawnee, Seneca and Wyandot preying on the settlers on the Ohio. David Zeisberger maintained contact with the patriot headquarters at Fort Pitt, often passing intelligence to its commander of the movements of royalist war parties. It was noted by settlers in the area, however, that Gnadenhütten frequently showed hospitality to those same hostile warriors. Suspicions were heightened on both sides against the Moravians in the middle.[35]

The settlers were correct, royalist war parties did pass frequently through Gnadenhütten and the other towns, making demands on their hospitality, all as part of a strategy to intimidate their fellow braves into joining the war. This strategy was ineffective. Native Moravian braves lived by their faith, just as the German Moravians did. Captain Pipe,

---

32. Zeisberger, *Moravian Mission Diaries*, 59–60.
33. Zeisberger, *Moravian Mission Diaries*, 59–60.
34. Zeisberger, *Moravian Mission Diaries*, 312n765.
35. Griffin, *American Leviathan*, 167.

meanwhile, was certain that the white missionaries in Gnadenhütten were sympathetic to the patriots.

In the Fall of 1778 the Council Fire at Goschachgünk censured the independent actions of its two war captains. As noted, already in September of 1777 David Zeisberger was reporting that Captain Pipe was on the warpath: the independent action of villages and war leaders was characteristic of the Delaware and Shawnee nations, however it caused much confusion to the patriots. To counter the treaty between Captains Pipe and James with the British in Detroit, the Delaware Council concluded a treaty of friendship with the patriots at Fort Pitt in September, 1778. In return for trade goods, patriot forces were allowed to move through Delaware ground.

Captain Pipe, now isolated, protested, but the embarrassments were soon heaped on the Delaware Council: White Eye was murdered by patriot militia in October, 1778 while returning from Fort Pitt.[36] In the wake of the murder Gelemind was raised to leadership. In its complete lack of distinction between friend and foe the murder of White Eye is utterly senseless; it is only understandable within the frameworks of racial prejudice where differentiation over-rules all other considerations. Early in the eighteenth century an experiment in co-existence had been conducted in the Mohawk Valley; it had started with the offer by the Iroquois to settle Palatine refugees. The demographics had shifted with increasing population pressure so that, by mid-century, Euro-ethnic settlers and colonial interests clearly held the advantage. Yet it was not the demographic shift, but rather the attitudes of racial alienation, that now made impossible a relationship of mutuality between the indigenous and the immigrant.

In 1779 the royalist armies scarcely stirred from New York City. Washington took that opportunity to show force on the frontier. The Iroquois Confederacy had been divided, with the Mohawk and Seneca joining the royalists and the Oneida siding with the patriots. Reprisals against settlers escalated on a frontier arch from Ohio in the southwest to upper New York on the northeast. John Sullivan commanded four thousand Continentals, moving in three columns, who invaded the heart of the Iroquois League with the express purpose of demolishing Mohawk and Seneca towns and destroying their winter stores.[37] The warriors and their loyalist allies could not stand against the force and withdrew; one

---

36. Zeisberger, *Moravian Mission Diaries*, 481.
37. Calloway, *Indian World of George Washington*, 251–57.

estimate is that Sullivan's campaign destroyed forty mostly abandoned towns and 160,000 bushels of corn.[38]

Washington wrote to Continental Congressman Benjamin Harrison (1726–1791) in late October of 1779, fairly gloating in his puzzlement over British inertia and stating that their inaction allowed a small force of continentals to "be employed in the total destruction of all the country inhabited by the hostile tribes of the Six Nations, their good and faithful allies!"[39] Scholars, however, are divided on the military value of this campaign, since the warriors and loyalists returned in 1780 for more depredations.[40] In terms of engaging and destroying enemy forces, the campaign is argued to have been a failure that only served to harden the resolve of the Iroquois braves.[41]

However the show of force was designed more for its political consequences, in order to destroy the infrastructure of the Iroquois nation and with it the ability to govern itself and others, and to create a refugee crisis for the British in Canada, on whom five thousand displaced Iroquois descended, many of them women and children seeking sustenance. Many perished during the harsh winter that immediately followed in 1779–1780; the population as a whole did not return in force to New York. Meanwhile Washington had the foresight to have the columns accompanied by surveyors to create tracts for settlers after the war. The Six Nations, which had once dominated the Ohio Country and had vied for imperial supremacy on equal terms with France and Great Britain, never recovered.[42] Sullivan's campaign helped to dissolve whatever had remained of Iroquois suzerainty over the large and increasingly restive nations of the Ohio. A conference at Fort Pitt in September, 1779, in the midst of Sullivan's campaign, showed that the Native Nations in the Ohio Country were duly impressed and inclined to either remain neutral or to return to neutrality.

---

38. Ferling, *Almost a Miracle*, 352–54.

39. Washington, *Writings*, 366–69.

40. For example, John Ferling calls it a "nearly useless operation," although he acknowledges the presence of surveyors (Ferling, *Almost a Miracle*, 354; cf. Ellis, *His Excellency, George Washington*, 123–24).

41. Calloway, *Indian World of George Washington*, 257.

42. Ellis, *His Excellency, George Washington*, 124.

## A False Dawn

Thinking the crisis of the Native Nations uprisings to be now past, the Moravians distanced themselves once more from the Council Fire. They reopened Gnadenhütten and Schönbrunn, and in 1780 they closed Lichtenau and opened a new town, Salem, six miles from Gnadenhütten.[43] These were the locations of the three Moravian towns in 1781, and the Native American Moravians seemed to be entering a flourishing and stable time. Zeisberger, now pushing 60, returned to Bethlehem for several months, where new surprises awaited him.

At the direction of the elders he was married to Susan LeCron, 37 years old, on July 4 (Independence Day!) 1781. She had been born in Lancaster to German immigrants who had been brought in to the Moravian fold through the ministry of the Swedish pastor Laurentius Nyberg, and who moved to Bethlehem in 1764.[44] Nyberg's Moravian sympathies and the schism of the Lancaster Lutherans occupies much of Mühlenberg's journal for the mid-1740s, in which the Halle Pietist takes a hostile view of Nyberg's ministry.[45]

Gelemind continued the patriot-friendly policies of Netawatwees and White Eye. Even so, the season of peace that the Moravians supposed had come, was short-lived. Although Cornwallis surrendered at Yorktown in October, 1781, the British did not withdraw support from their allied Native Nations in the west. Leaving Lichtenau and re-opening Schönbrunn was supposed to be a means by which the Moravians reasserted their neutrality. Instead it made them highly vulnerable to hostilities from both sides. As the poverty of the patriots at Fort Pitt became evident in the leanness with which they met their treaty obligation for trade goods and provisions, many Delaware admired the relative wealth of the British, and their long record of keeping promises.

Captain Pipe brought formal charges against the Moravian missionaries and their Christian towns to the British military governor Arent De Peyster (1736–1822) in Detroit. In the fall of 1781 the British permitted Captain Pipe to lead a large war party of Delaware and Wyandot into Gnadenhütten and Schönbrunn and remove all of the inhabitants by force. They were taken as prisoners to Wyandot territory on the Sandusky,

---

43. Zeisberger, *Moravian Mission Diaries*, 50.
44. Zeisberger, *Moravian Mission Diaries*, 73–74.
45. Mühlenberg, *Journals*, 1:109–10.

until their loyalties could be determined or their crimes investigated and punished.

## The Exile

Having just been married in July and having returned to Gnadenhütten after a furlough of six months, this development came as a cold shock to David Zeisberger. At first he refused Captain Pipe's demand despite the warrant, since corn had not yet been harvested and their captors had made no other provisions for the winter. Since the ears were not yet ripe, Captain Pipe considered that protest a stalling device, and refused the request to wait. Finally the missionaries had to comply with De Peyster's order, and the Moravian Delaware settlements were disbanded with the corn still standing. The residents were marched under Native American guard west to the Sandusky.

Once the Christian Native American prisoners were settled under Wynadot supervision, the white missionaries were taken to the governor's at Detroit in Captain Pipe's custody. There they were interrogated. The next day De Peyster held court and summoned Captain Pipe to testify against the missionaries. Pipe stalled, and then under De Peyster's no doubt mortified questioning, Pipe admitted that he had no evidence. However, the evidence does exist, in correspondence between Zeisberger and the patriot headquarters at Fort Pitt; Captain Pipe's suspicions were valid.[46] The governor promised the missionaries safe conduct back to their exiled charges at the Sandusky, and apologized privately, excusing himself on the basis of needing to follow up on the accusations given the state of war. Although De Peyster exonerated them preliminarily, he could not allow them to return to their towns without alienating his Wyandot allies. The missionaries returned to the Sandusky.[47] The year 1781 ended with the Moravian mission in exile and captivity.[48]

At Fort Pitt and in Washington County, meanwhile, plans were set in motion by patriot militia. One called for a reprisal campaign against Delaware and Wyandot war parties on the Sandusky, but this was cancelled by General Irvine at Fort Pitt for lack of manpower in the Continental Army. The Washington County militia mustered around 100 men

---

46. Olmstead, *Black Coats Among the Delaware*, 28.
47. Gnadenhuetten Monument Society, *True History of the Massacre*, 4–5.
48. Zeisberger, *Moravian Mission Diaries*, 35–37.

under Lt. Col. David Williamson, to do essentially what Captain Pipe had done and for the same reasons—only from the patriot side out of settler suspicions that the Moravians were aiding the British.[49]

Washington County, Pennsylvania, officially formed on March 28, 1781, and named itself in honor of George Washington, at that time the commander-in-chief. Formed by sub-dividing Westmoreland County, Washington County's lines began west of Fort Pitt and extended to the border of the Ohio Territory. Settlers had moved in after the Treaty of Stanwyx in 1768, and Westmoreland County had been organized in 1773.

All of Westmoreland County, and then of Washington County carved out of it, lay on the west of the Alleghenies, and its settlers had been in a constant war with Native bands since the Shawnee and Seneca had gone on the war-path in 1777. There had never been an effective remedy against the terror tactic in which small war parties attacked isolated farms. The only military tactic available was reprisal against the native villages that were home to the warriors or that aided them on their way, as Sullivan had accomplished on a large scale in Iroquois territory. Although after Yorktown the British and their German auxiliaries suspended offensive operations, the Indian raids never let up. In November 1781 the Washington County militia set out to arrest the Moravian Native Americans and force them to Fort Pitt, but they must have felt like they had chased wild geese. When they arrived at Gnadenhütten they found it mostly deserted, with only a handful present there to pick corn. These they marched to Fort Pitt, but General Irvine released them.[50]

## God in 96 Graves

By January, 1782 conditions for the Moravian exiles on the Sandusky had become desperate. On appealing to Captain Pipe as their "protector," they were permitted to send a portion of their people back to the abandoned settlements on the Muskingum to harvest the corn. One hundred men, women and children, about a third of the group, were allowed to return to Gnadenhütten and Schönbrunn.

Mild weather encouraged an early return to the war-path, and the Wyandot and Shawnee began attacks on settlers on February 8.[51] On

---

49. Crumrine et al., *History of Washington County*, 102.
50. Crumrine et al., *History of Washington County*, 102.
51. Crumrine et al., *History of Washington County*, 103; cf. Silver, *Our Savage*

February 10 a party of Shawnee raided a home on Raccoon Creek belonging to Robert Wallace, who was not home at the time. They took the family captive, and then murdered the mother and an infant. The posse organized by Robert Wallace was forced to turn back when snowfall erased the trail. One might begin to comprehend the pain and frustration of Wallace and those with him, and perhaps the deep-seated desire to see reprisal where justice is impossible.

Had Wallace pursued the Shawnee to Gnadenhütten they might have caught up with the war party. According to the account given in Crumrine's *The History of Washington County*, the Shawnee traded to the "unsuspecting" Gnadenhütten residents some of the plunder from the Wallace home, and then departed.

Another settler, John Carpenter, added his own story, which was oil to the fire of settler resentments. Carpenter claimed to have been taken captive with two of his horses. Among his captors were two "Dutch-speaking" Native American Moravians, who treated him worse than the others did. He escaped because the war party had hobbled the captive horses and then let them loose at nightfall to graze. The next morning they sent Carpenter to fetch them from wherever they had roamed. Seeing his opportunity, he rescued his horses and made for Fort Pitt, where he shared his story.

Whatever may motivate such a tale is a matter of pure speculation. No settler was a witness to Carpenter's alleged ordeal; they only ever saw him together with both his horses. Nevertheless his tale inflamed the countryside. Now settlers and their militia were certain that the Moravian Indians were just as guilty as all the others. When Williamson mustered the militia on March 3, 1782, one hundred sixty mounted troops turned out to ride to the Muskingum.[52]

As March unfolded De Peyster once again put the white missionaries under arrest and summoned them to Detroit, this time in response to the complaints of a Loyalist officer. Once again David Zeisberger and his missionaries were acquitted. They were finally returned to the settlements at Schünnbrunn and Gnadenhütten in April. By that time the worst had happened. It is important to note that when Williamson rode into Gnadenhütten with his *patriot* militia on March 8, Zeisberger and the other missionaries were in the custody of *royalists* in Detroit.

---

*Neighbors*, 165–68.

52. Crumrine et al., *History of Washington County*, 103–4.

On coming upon some harvesters in the corn, the soldiers promised friendship. The militia entered Gnadenhütten by this subterfuge, and then asked that all the workers be summoned from the field. They soon had 98 people under their power. Not that these Native American villagers offered resistance anyway: These Moravian Delaware and Mahican had been instructed in pacifism and in the Christian hope.

Only when the men voluntarily surrendered their hunting weapons did the true designs of the militia become clear to them. All the men, women and children were put under arrest, and then in the interests of due process, Williamson presided over their court-martial.[53] They were accused of aiding and abetting the royalist war parties, and of benefitting from the plunder of the dead settlers. The patriots brought as evidence against them the European-style clothes and implements for cooking which, in one narrative, had been planted among them by the Shawnee war party to incriminate them.[54] This narrative spin seems to be an effort to ameliorate the actions of the Washington County militia: With this planted evidence the ensuing massacre becomes a gross miscarriage of criminal and military justice in a war zone where such mistakes are regrettable, with the ultimate blame to be placed on the shoulders of the indigenous peoples, that is, the Shawnee braves who had framed them. But what took place was in fact a racially-motivated act of genocide; it was a patriot war crime. Moravian historiographers insist that the militia presumed that such trappings of Euro-ethnic lifestyles had to have come from the plunder and murder of white setters, when in fact these implements and clothes were part of the lifestyle of the Moravian mission community, where European tastes for modesty were part of the discipline of their common life under the missionary's supervision.[55]

They were found guilty en masse, including the women and children.

Williamson then chose to defer sentencing to the will of his men. In one sense this is in keeping with the deep democratic traditions of militia units. But the mission that had been given to the militia was to complete what they had not been allowed to do in November, which is, the removal of all the Moravian Native Americans they found to Fort Pitt. Williamson abrogated his military responsibility by making their next move a matter

---

53. Gnadenhuetten Monument Society, *True History of the Massacre*, 8; Crumrine et al., *History of Washington County*, 106.

54. Crumrine et al., *History of Washington County*, 106.

55. Gnadenhuetten Monument Society, *True History of the Massacre*, 8.

of popular vote. He set forward two alternatives: March the captives to Fort Pitt, or, Execution.

Sixteen or so voted for resettlement to Fort Pitt, as the mission had been mandated. The rest, around 90 percent of these patriots, voted for the execution of 98 unresisting Christian pacifists. What remained to settle was the manner of execution. Ammunition was expensive. Hanging all those people was inefficient. The method chosen was to use clubs to bludgeon the skulls of their captives and then, of course, use knives to take the scalps. The sentence was declared to the captives, to be carried out early the following morning. That night, as the patriots reveled in what would come, the Native American Christians comforted each other by singing psalms.[56]

The next morning, March 9, the 98 Delaware and Mahican Christians were led in pairs to the cabin of their execution. Some were tearful. None resisted. Ninety-six were killed, including 34 children. Some prayed until the club silenced them.

Two youths were able to exploit moments of darkness or confusion to escape with their lives. One climbed through a window. The other, stunned and scalped, was able to lie still beneath the bodies of the dead. These two survivors bring the testimonies on which the accounts of the massacre rely, but the story is not theirs alone.[57] Members of the Washington County Militia bragged of their deeds. On finding Schönbrunn empty and a campaign to Sandusky arduous, they rode to Fort Pitt to boast of their accomplishment and display the plunder of Gnadenhütten. Considering the gloating of the patriot militia, there is little reason to dispute the testimony of the two indigenous Christian youths.[58]

## Racism, Alienation, and the West

Writing on July 7, 1782, Benjamin Franklin expressed pain and vexation for "the poor Moravian Indians." From what he had heard third-hand and months after the fact, he was able to judge that the "excuses or palliations . . . [were] extremely weak and insufficient." Nevertheless he lays

---

56. Silver, *Our Savage Neighbors*, 270–71; Griffin, *Leviathan*, 167; Crumrine et al., *History of Washington County*, 106; Gnadenhuetten Monument Society, *True History of the Massacre*, 9.

57. Gnadenhuetten Monument Society, *True History of the Massacre*, 10–11.

58. Crumrine et al., *History of Washington County*, 107.

the blame ultimately at the feet of George III, whose policy-makers had created an environment of hostility, escalation, and reprisal.[59] In other words, for Franklin, it was not patriotism itself that was to blame. Yet it was patriotism that encompassed settler interests for westward expansion at the expense of Native Nations lifestyles, cultures, and claims, and it was for that very reason that patriotism was resisted by many Native Nations and war captains.

A secondary lesson, but important for this study, is that those who took a neutral, nonviolent posture still shared in all the risks and horrors of the civil war in their land. The most important historical lesson from this grievous event is what it signifies in the patriot consciousness. This war crime cannot be laid at the feet of a Shawnee war party that "framed" the innocent in the Christian Moravian villages, as the historiographers of Washington County wished to surmise one century later. Rather, the genocide at Gnadenhütten is best understood in the context of frontier warfare, which over the course of 30 years had intensified animosities and hardened attitudes towards permanent, irreconcilable, racial alienation.

This massacre was perpetrated *against patriot sympathizers*. Although neutral (and nonviolent) by virtue of their pacifism these Native American Moravians and their missionaries routinely passed information to the patriot headquarters at Fort Pitt.[60] The patriot militia of Washington County could scarcely have been ignorant of Gnadenhütten's importance to the Continental Army's western command. This mass murder was aimed at that particular community, it was ratified by a vote so that no one in the Washington County militia can even hide behind the excuse "we were following orders," and it was rationalized by the outward mechanisms of due process. This was a war crime, and like many war crimes since, it was motivated by theories of racial differentiation and feelings of visceral alienation.

The stadial model predicted that if indigenous societies were leavened by the gospel of Jesus Christ that they would voluntarily assimilate into the more refined manners and lifestyles approved by ethnic Europeans. By the sensibilities of the twenty-first century this stadial approach is wrong-headed and chauvinistic, but setting aside contemporary anachronisms, the Moravian missionary towns ought to be viewed as a laboratory of the stadial model: *And the experiment was working.* That

---

59. Franklin, *Writings*, 1051–52.
60. Olmstead, *Blackcoats Among the Delaware*, 27–28.

is the key to the horror of Gnadenhütten which peels back every other rationalization and excuse. From that time to the present, racists have never admitted and will continue never to admit any amount of data, any stories of success, any working experiments in integration, or assimilation, or education, or even the testimonies of a shared faith, to overthrow their visceral, bigoted premises of alienation and racial entitlement.

A Pennsylvania justice of the peace, Hugh Henry Brackenridge (1748–1816), who would later found the University of Pittsburgh, spoke of the indigenous Christian victims as "animals, vulgarly called Indians." For Brackenridge the very nature of the Native American was unredeemable, so that their nature could "justify extinction."[61] Brackenridge expressed the sentiment that won out over both the gradualism of the stadial view and the generosity inherent in Christian notions of shared humanity. The genocide of an entire village of unresisting Christian pacifists in Ohio in 1782 by American patriots, for the mere reason that they were indigenous people, set the pattern for the future of westward expansion for the United States and its dealings with Native Nations for all of the nineteenth century.

It is unknown whether Zeisberger himself or the other Moravian missionaries on his team would have been murdered along with their charges. The nature of the crime makes it unlikely. It is important to remember, however, that though the royalists did not commit murder, nevertheless they are not innocent of wrongs towards the pacifist Moravian Native Americans. Royalists took into captivity most of the mission town's residents, despite a lack of preparation and provision for an extended winter internment. The need for food forced the royalists to return a remnant of the captives to their towns, and it was this event that created the opportunity for the Washington County militia.

Into his old age David Zeisberger sought to find a space between, where Native American proselytes could grow spiritually according to what he considered the necessary conditions of discipleship, without fear of alienated white settlers or suspicious Native warriors. This sojourn eventually brought himself and Native American followers into Ontario, Canada, where they built and operated the mission town of Fairfield from 1792 to 1798.

Zeisberger was not alone in his vision of how a proselytized indigenous mission community could function and how it might dwell safely

---

61. Griffin, *American Leviathan*, 176–77.

in the dangerous world of the frontier; his vision had continuing appeal for several hundreds of baptized Native Americans throughout his lifetime. In 1798, in his upper 70s, he was brought back by canoe to the Muskingum, escorted personally by Gelemind, now baptized. There they established Goshen, Zeisberger's last mission settlement which he served nearly ten years until his death in January, 1808.[62]

---

62. Olmstead, *Blackcoats Among the Delaware*, 14, 107–24.

# 8

# The Halle Hessian

## Introduction

A PASSAGE OF WAGON-RUTTED trails and river fords near the South Carolina border linked Savannah, Georgia to Augusta, Georgia one hundred miles northwest. The town of Ebenezer had risen up along that road, twenty-five miles from Savannah, where Brier Creek flowed into the Savannah River. Ebenezer was the most important settlement on the trail to Augusta, and control of the Augusta trail, the life-line to loyalists in Georgia's back-country, was one of the key objectives when a royalist force of the 71st Regiment (Fraser's Highlanders), Hessians, and Loyalists, all under Lt. Col. Archibald Campbell, landed on Georgia's coast.

Campbell commanded a force of a size usually led by a brigadier general, but in assigning him the mission Henry Clinton had demurred on promoting him due to sensitive egos in the British command structure. He was by design only temporarily in command anyway, as the plan was that the force he would deliver to Georgia would rendezvous with Major General Augustine Prevost's force marching north from St. Augustine in British East Florida. So Campbell received the pay but not the rank of a brigadier general. Although he chafed as would have most officers and gentlemen of the eighteenth century, he devoted his singular skills to the mission.

On December 29, 1778 Campbell chose a surprising landing spot which was left lightly-defended, and then, sending a diversionary column straight towards the patriot formation on the high ground, he marched his main force on a trail with a local slave for a guide. Emerging from the woods to envelop the patriots' flank and rear, the royalists routed them, capturing hundreds as they fled through the streets of Savannah.[1]

As the royalist force consolidated control of the provincial capital, a Lutheran pastor appeared in Savannah to pay his respects.[2] Perhaps he first made his explanation to a Scottish corporal at a check-point, who called over a Hessian sergeant for a more fluent understanding, who then deemed it appropriate to escort the visitor himself to make an introduction to a Hessian officer, who supposed it of enough importance to call attention about the visitor to Lt. Col. Campbell's adjutant. Or perhaps the clergyman already had the proficiency in English that he would demonstrate later in his life in London.

At all events, the Rev. Christoph F. Triebner, who might have styled himself as the "rightful but displaced" pastor of Zion Lutheran Church in Ebenezer, welcomed Campbell as a conquering hero and the savior of Georgia. The pastor offered information as to what awaited the royalists up the Augusta trail, and offered to serve them as a guide as far as Ebenezer. All he asked is that they would re-instate him in the pulpit of Zion Lutheran Church, from which he had been ousted by a schismatic faction led by the rebel John A. Treutlen, the enemy of the King who had been elected Georgia's first patriot governor.

By January 2 the bulk of Campbell's army, 3,500 highlanders in red coats with green plaid pants, seasoned Tory companies in green coats, and Hessians in blue coats, snaked their way up from Savannah on a Christmastide mission to establish Ebenezer as their base of operations on the Augusta trail. Campell's actual expedition to the town of Augusta would not begin for another three weeks, but Ebenezer was to be the staging area. On January 2 the column was guided by Triebner, the black-garbed Lutheran minister who had been sent to Georgia as a missionary of Halle Pietism.[3] He rode on horseback like an officer, but he rode aloof and alone, not speaking unless called upon, his manner deferential in that awesome company that represented the might of Great Britain and

---

1. Wilson, *Southern Strategy*, 72–77.
2. Melton, *Religion, Community, and Slavery*, 288.
3. Melton, *Religion, Community, and Slavery*, 288.

his own vindication.[4] Once reinstated, Triebner became a frequent dinner guest of the royalist officers.[5]

Christoph Friedrich Triebner had been sent to Ebenezer from the Halle Institutes ten years earlier, in 1768, to fill a pastoral vacancy and continue the vision of the Ebenezer farming cooperative, a hallmark endeavor of the Halle Institutes founded in the earliest days of Georgia's charter. As a missionary pastor Triebner was salaried by the Society for the Propagation of Christian Knowledge (SPCK) headquartered in London. He had been recommended by the same persons in Halle and vetted by the same persons in London as had been his predecessors Michael Boltzius and Wilhelm Lemke in Georgia, and also Heinrich Mühlenberg and more than a dozen other pastors in Pennsylvania. Yet in the ten years that had elapsed between Triebner's arrival and this royalist campaign, his ministry had dissolved in bitter conflict. The opposing church factions had eventually hardened their antipathies along the partisan lines of the War of Independence.

Although an obscure figure today, Christoph Triebner was by no means an insignificant person to the Governors of Georgia, to the European directors of missional Pietism, or to the German congregations in London he would eventually serve. It is difficult to rehabilitate his image from Heinrich Mühlenberg's vitriolic portrait; yet hindsight may be as charitable as critical, and history's verdict must take into account that Christoph Triebner was not alone in being an immigrant Lutheran pietist pastor facing a steep learning curve in his first years in colonial North America.

After his pre-war fits and starts as a young, inexperienced, and overly-ambitious pastor, the war years forged Triebner's theological, ethical and pastoral maturity. That his convictions led him to partisan support of the King and the royalists cannot be construed as proof of faults in his character. Lutheran Pietists, acting under the conscious influence of the Spirit of Christ in their hearts and wills, found themselves opposing one another at mutually-exclusive political poles. In Christoph Triebner we are reminded that, through the hearts of German Pietists, God was truly on all three sides of the American Revolution.

---

4. Campbell, *Journal of an Expedition*, 32; cf. Jones, *Salzburger Saga*, 126.
5. Campbell, *Journal of an Expedition*, 35.

## The Origins of Ebenezer

The story of German Lutheran settlement in Georgia begins with the formation of the colony of Georgia on the drawing boards of British think-tanks. Georgia was conceived as an experiment in colonial administration which took into account climates, frontiers, military objectives, and compassion for Europe's Protestant minorities. As a royal colony governed by Trustees, Georgia was conducting several simultaneous socio-political experiments, and the combination of successes, partial successes and failures led to several reinventions of the colony's constitutional and social premises during the eighteenth century.

Georgia was established in 1732 as a province of small farms owned by freeholders for whom militia service was compulsory and the owning of slaves was illegal. The farms were to produce commodities such as tobacco for import into Great Britain.[6] During these early, idealistic years the first transports of German-speaking Protestants embarked for the young colony. These were exiles from Catholic Salzburg, an independent archbishopric in the Alps that was later absorbed into Austria. Under the guidance of the Halle-trained missionary and native Hanoverian, Michael Boltzius, and his Prussian associate Israel Christian Gronau, the first transports of "Salzburgers" arrived in Savannah in 1736.

The rapidity of the changes in Georgia is disguised by the meticulous nature of records kept by Georgia's founders on the one hand, and on the other the community diaries and correspondence by which Boltzius and his colleagues kept in touch with their European directors on behalf of the Salzburger enterprises, the cooperative settlements, farms, and industries of Ebenezer. The amount of written material produced by Ebenezer's pastors, especially Boltzius, foster an impression that Georgia's original vision of itself was durable in the way that Puritanism endured in New England's constitutions for nearly two hundred years. Historiographers from the late nineteenth century drew such parallels themselves, in reproducing but misunderstanding a quote from Boltzius in the 1730s in which he refers to the New Ebenezer as a City on the Hill, to be a shining testimony of Christian virtue in government.[7] Since Puritanism was still thriving after its first hundred years in New England and stood on the cusp of revival in the 1730s, scholars assumed that Boltzius was making parallels between New Ebenezer and New England. But Boltzius

---

6. Melton, *Religion, Community, and Slavery*, 105–13.
7. Strobel, *Salzburgers and Their Descendants*, xviii, 50, 230.

was relating the City on the Hill image to the Halle Institutes, which New Ebenezer was intended to replicate. By 1730 the Halle Institutes had constructed a massive campus that was an architectural marvel throughout Europe.[8]

The original vision for Georgia as a whole was that it was to be a military buffer between British and Spanish interests. Spanish claims extended north and west of present-day Florida to encompass not only the whole of the Gulf Coast but also much of the southern seaboard. Georgia would act as a base for asserting British claims into southern Appalachia while protecting the Carolinas.[9]

Georgia was originally governed by a Trusteeship, with political principles unique to itself. The early philosophy of the Trusteeship blended the martial purpose of the colony with progressive social ethics including the bans on keeping slaves or trafficking in them. Georgia was to be cleared and settled by small freeholders staked on fifty-acre claims which would be given them for free in return for militia service. Similar to a Roman imperial model, these soldier-farmers would act as a first line of defense against Spanish invasions. They would also bring the land under intensive cultivation so that Georgia could prosper from trade in its surpluses and provide the British empire with commodities.[10]

By design the freeholders would pass their farms down through male-only primogeniture; they would not be allowed to alienate their claims or consolidate them into large plantations.[11] At fifty acres the farms would be small enough for the freeholders to work themselves with the help of indentured servants and wage labor to meet subsistence needs, plus modest profits on surpluses. Small farms meant more gun-toting farmers for the militia. Large plantations, on the other hand, reduced the number of eligible militia by reducing the number of freeholders, while the slaves required to make large plantations profitable would by necessity be ineligible for military service, foolish as it is to arm one's captives.

Another essential component to the vision of the Georgia Trustees was alliance with the Native Nations; they did not want them provoked by squatters, rum-sellers and profiteering traders. At Georgia's origins it was the Spanish, not the Native Americans, who were viewed as rivals

---

8. Wilson, "Halle and Ebenezer," 74.

9. Melton, *Religion, Community, and Slavery*, 106–9

10. Wilson, "Halle and Ebenezer," 37–38.

11. Melton, *Religion, Community, and Slavery*, 201.

and potential enemies.[12] Friendship with the Native Nations was seen as an additional protection against European colonial rivals; this is parallel to the policies of Conrad Weiser on behalf of Pennsylvania in competition with the French during this same period in time. However, no pacifistic culture was rooting itself in Georgia as the Quakers had done in Pennsylvania; its Trustees were military-minded.

Any conclusion that the Trustees were altruistic in their opposition to slavery and in their friendship to Native Nations must be mitigated by the strategic importance of Georgia militarily. The Trustees held that large plantations were against the interests of the colony as they envisioned it, but it would not take twenty years before the ambitions of the settlers themselves would erode the vision; chattel slavery became legal in 1751.[13] The same can be said for the alliances with Native Nations that foreshadowed the strategy of the Proclamation Line thirty years later. This philosophy toward the Native Nations established a bond between them and the royal government throughout the Revolutionary War. Even so friendship was contingent on strategic realities and not forged on ethical or religious ideals.

The creation of a militia class of freeholders tied to their land is a carryover of feudalistic notions still very much alive in Europe in the 1730s. In Great Britain a fondness for the hierarchies of feudalism characterized the Tories, the party with which Georgia's governing Trustee James Oglethorpe identified. It was obvious, then, that the promises and obligations would appeal to some classes of European emigrant and not others. Originally Georgia's trustees had in mind that they would seek out settlers who would welcome the deeds to fifty acres and the attendant prospects of prosperity beyond subsistence, along with the martial duties, as a large step up from their current economic and social prospects. The Trustees did not desire to recruit those whose ambition was to own large slave-farmed plantations.

The natural fit for the vision of the Georgia Trustees was the disaffected European Protestant refugee. This was further delimited: Members of Peace Churches, be they Anabaptist, radical Pietist, or otherwise sectarian, *need not apply*. In the 1730s such groups were finding welcome in Pennsylvania among like-minded Quakers. Georgia was being created as a tactical move in a militarized global race against Spanish and French

---

12. Melton, *Religion, Community, and Slavery*, 39–40.
13. Melton, *Religion, Community, and Slavery*, 252.

competitors, so its Protestant settlers were to have no such scruples about bearing arms.

As the Georgia Trust was forming in London, all Europe was scandalized by reports of Protestant minorities being persecuted in the Catholic Archdiocese of Salzburg. For the rising kingdom of Prussia these fugitives, who numbered over twenty thousand, were an opportunity to extend benevolence while simultaneously advancing its own interests. The great majority of Salzburgers who chose to leave their Alpine homeland rather than convert to Catholicism were invited by Friedrich Wilhelm I to settle Prussia's Lithuanian possessions. He offered generous terms: farm equipment to aid the immigrants in their transition from cattle to cereals, and tax relief for the first several years.[14] His own absolutist proclivities were displayed in that in some instances he forced Mennonite settlers off their stakes to make room for the newcomers, and among those he resettled he had little toleration for any breach of faith. Yet the overland migration through Europe took its toll; of twenty-one thousand, some four thousand were diverted from these purposes by unscrupulous human traffickers, or died enroute.

The alternative, altruistic vision of the Georgia Trust captivated the missionary arm of the Royal Chapel of St. James in London. Since the reign of Queen Anne this chaplaincy had been staffed by Germans trained in Halle and loyal to its Pietist network. These Halle Lutherans provided leadership to the Society for the Propagation of Christian Knowledge (SPCK), a more ecumenical mission organization than its Anglican counterpart, the Society for the Propagation of the Gospel (SPG) directed out of Canterbury. Of particular appeal to the Chaplains of St. James, the SPCK, and their mutual allies at the Halle Institutes in Prussia, was the opportunity that a *carte blanche* settlement in America provided for the redemptive vision of Halle Pietism.

Meanwhile the plight of the Salzburgers caught the attention of August Urlsperger, a Pietist protégé and senior Lutheran Pastor in Augsburg in southern Germany. Aware of the Georgia Trust's desire to recruit settlers from central Europe, he found in the Salzburg dispersion a natural fit. The Georgia Trust agreed, as did Halle's leaders, who were taking a hand in the Lithuanian resettlement. By 1732 the founder of Halle Pietism, August Hermann Francke, had been dead five years. Nevertheless Halle Pietism was still ascendant, consolidating privileges within

---

14. Walker, "Salzburger Migration to Prussia," 74.

the realm relative to the vetting of all Lutheran pastors, the control of the Prussian military chaplaincy, the deanships of the academies, royal boarding schools and orphanages, and public funding of the Institutes in Halle.

Halle Pietists did not see themselves as radical or sectarian, but as mainstream Lutherans who agreed explicitly with the reformer Martin Luther about the rightness of partnership between Church and State.[15] It was hoped that the kind of relationship cultivated with the King in Prussia by the Halle network through the 1730s might be replicated in a relationship between the leaders of the Salzburg community and Georgia's executive powers.

For the right kind of replication to occur, the Halle Pietists wanted leaders over the Salzburg exiles that adhered to their theology. Such leaders were not to be found among the Salzburgers themselves, who were of dubious confessional allegiance. Having long been isolated in a Catholic realm by their mountainous surroundings, catechesis and even sacramental ministry had languished; their Protestant identity was defined more by anti-Catholicism than by the doctrines of any one Protestant confession.[16] This suited the Halle Institutes well, for it meant that the leaders could be proffered upon the Salzburger sheep in the form of well-trained and vetted Halle Lutheran shepherds.

The means of Halle reproducing itself in Georgia was to be facilitated by allowing the pastors to take charge of civil government in the Salzburger settlement. The plan called for the Georgia Trustees to appoint the pastors as magistrates, and assign tracts to the Salzburger immigrants in such a way that it created a contiguous community around a population center with the church as its focal point. The Trustee's risk was hedged by the promise of the SPCK to lend financial assistance to the colonists until they developed a self-sustaining, self-sufficient community. Urlsperger in Augsburg became the chief recruiter for sponsors and emigrants, putting him in the center of a European web of communication and patronage for fostering a new life for Salzburgers in Georgia.

The Halle Institutes saw in Georgia an opportunity to project their values into a new mission. They had little control over the thousands of German emigrants mobbing America's middle colonies, but in the Salzburg refugees they had a self-contained population out of which, by

---

15. Marschke, *Absolutely Pietist*, 93–103.
16. Walker, "Salzburger Migration to Prussia," 72.

means of patronage arrangements with the Georgia trustees, Halle could create a properly-ordered parish community. They would provide this community with pastors in requisite number, that is, with two or three clergy for a few hundred communicants. This was a far more sustainable ratio for a Lutheran ministry than what was found in Pennsylvania until deep into the nineteenth century.

## Soil and Settlement

Six years before Mühlenberg arrived in North America, and scarcely twenty years after Palatines landed in New York, the Halle-Salzburg community began to take shape in Georgia. Sociologically, the chief story of the Salzburg Diaspora is the relocation of tens of thousands in Lithuania by the King of Prussia; a little over four hundred sailed to Georgia, which is a mere side-light featuring only 2 percent of the dispersed population. However, historically, the remnant of Salzburgers that appeared in Georgia played crucial roles in the early evolution of the province, in Georgia's history of the Revolutionary War, and in Georgia's emergence as a state in the young nation.

The Chairman of the Trustees, James Oglethorpe, acting as governor and commander-in-chief of Georgia, first allotted a tract of surveyed territory for the Salzburgers close to the disputed frontier with Spanish claims. The Salzburgers settled and began to build a town which their senior pastor and magistrate, Michael Boltzius, consecrated Ebenezer. However the location reflected the martial aims of the Trust rather than the needs of family and community. The soil at this settlement was too sandy for farming. In addition, the ravages of the Atlantic crossing and the first year of Georgia's climate claimed nearly half of the population of the first transport.

Throughout the eighteenth century nearly 50 percent mortality in the first year could be expected among new migrants to the Atlantic seaboard's southern provinces.[17] This compares to just over 6 percent for new migrants landing in Philadelphia.[18] After the first year the death rates dropped precipitously. Still, as had been true in Jamestown and at Plymouth Rock over a hundred years earlier, this pilgrim settlement in the new world barely survived its first year. The community depended on

---

17. Roeber, *Palatines, Liberty, and Property*, 98.
18. Fogleman, *Hopeful Journeys*, 160.

fresh immigrants to be sustained, yet the death rates held true for every transport to Georgia through the eighteenth century.

Unlike the Palatine community in Livingston Manor, however, the Salzburgers were not governed by narrow-minded taskmasters nor were the farmers indentured to the governor. Recognizing that the land on which the Trust had placed them was unsuitable, Pastor Boltzius stepped into his civic leadership role to salvage the situation. He appointed surveyors from the community and joined them in scouting a more suitable terrain. He then petitioned the governor for permission to move the settlement, and for additional provisions. Oglethorpe proved imaginative enough to grant these requests. New Ebenezer was established several miles to the east of their first location, near the South Carolina border.

The Halle Lutheran experiment in community in Georgia is unique in history. The beginning of the settlement was an effort at a self-replication of Halle Pietism's values and institutions, so that it was a colony of Halle Pietists within the royal colony of Georgia.[19] This is seen in the early construction of an orphanage, in the efforts to create cooperative industries under centralized corporate control with a view toward self-sufficiency, and in the self-described dependency of Ebenezer's pastors on the "Reverend Fathers" in Europe. Distinct from the Halle Institutions, however, are first, that Ebenezer was a rural enclave in a sparsely populated frontier, and second, that its stakeholders were yeomen farmers.

These two mitigating factors meant that in Georgia there was no surplus population of unskilled wage labor, as in Halle; indeed the issue in Ebenezer was the chronic shortage of labor.[20] In addition, the Halle Institutes enjoyed connections both formal and informal to a university within walking distance, and housed indigent divinity students who were willing to trade the instruction of the young for room and board. There was little prospect of any of that occurring in Ebenezer at anything like the speed with which those things had developed in Halle, for there was none of the economic infrastructure on which the Halle Institutes thrived as an urban center of enterprise, education and benevolence. The early development of an orphanage in Ebenezer might be considered not as an intentional self-replication, but as an adjustment to need given the death rates of immigrants with each arriving transport. Ebenezer's pastors brought Halle Pietism's values into a frontier, rural context and

---

19. Wilson, "Halle and Ebenezer," 269.
20. Wilson, "Halle and Ebenezer," 177.

governed accordingly, but the cooperative farming community of necessity functioned much differently from the urban corporation which was the Halle Institutes.

In replicating Halle's values, Ebenezer was not radically oriented to communitarian living as were Ephrata and Bethlehem. These Hallenser, Moravian, and Seventh Day Baptist settlements are each similar to each other in that they were religiously-centered towns which came into existence in America at roughly the same time, each founded by groups that are associated together by scholars in Religious, Church and Social History as "German Pietists." For Boltzius, the theological turns and mystical excesses and pacifism of both Conrad Beissel and Nicholas von Zinzendorf were enough to make each of them and their adherents anathema to a Halle-allied Lutheran like himself. Halle Pietists considered themselves mainstream Lutherans and shared the conviction that state-sponsorship and privilege for the Church was both good and necessary for the strength and blessing of society.

The Ebenezer community was not communal. The fifty-acre lots were owned privately and separately, and the yeomen farmers were expected each to work and to prosper according to their own skill, investment, and grace from God. There was nothing of the Moravian efforts to separate the sexes into communal dormitories. Yet in Ebenezer no farming family was left to itself. The farmers lived in town, held personal garden plots of two acres that ringed the town, and walked to their fifty-acre farms. Ebenezer structured a work-cooperative which obligated the freeholders to one another in the clearing of land, the construction of public buildings and industrial facilities, the cultivation of mulberry bushes on common land, and the creation of a cooperative cattle ranch.[21]

Until his death in 1765, Boltzius proved himself capable as a leader possessing vision, practicality, empathy, and flexibility.[22] Under his guidance the Salzburgers joined the rest of Georgia's first settlers in the learning-curve of what best suited the climate and terrain for cultivation. Much of Boltzius's leadership in the community vis. reporting to European benefactors was related to the native as well as the experimental agriculture of Georgia, which he carefully elucidated in explaining both the reasons for abandoning one project for another, and the reasons for his requests for particular equipment or provisions. For the first ten years

---

21. Wilson, "Halle and Ebenezer," 271–72.
22. Wilson, "Halle and Ebenezer," 177–79.

the 50-acre farms were tilled by hand until Ziegenhagen and other sponsors raised a donation of plows, along with cash so that the settlers could purchase draught teams.[23]

Consequently animal husbandry became more common, as did travel by horseback. Corn was native but had its draw-backs relative to the condition it left the soil; after several years of experimentation the farmers found that a mix of European cereal grains, rice, corn, pumpkins and beans gave them the best returns on their efforts, allowing for year-round crops and hedging against the failures of one or two.[24] Flax, indigo and cotton were included in early experiments, and found their niches in subsequent years when the first small-farm model was modified and larger plantations were permitted.[25] Early hopes that Georgia would produce wine were dashed, but peach brandy was discovered and Boltzius requested, and received, eight sets of brass distillery equipment in 1750.[26]

Thus by 1750 the veteran Salzburger farmers of Ebenezer were selling surplus crops and, under Boltzius's direction, were branching into new experiments in cooperative industries. The chronic problem was Georgia's need for people. The economic infrastructure of tradesmen with concomitant developments of guilds and apprenticeships was slow in forming, and there was never a sufficient supply of farm labor. The model of indenture was in full use at the time and was the lifeblood of the labor force in more populous colonies such as Pennsylvania. The typical indentured servant would sail to the colonies without paying up-front; and then be auctioned off by the ship's captain for terms of room-and-board labor that averaged about six years.

Boltzius appealed to Europe to recruit more labor-class emigrants. Transports arrived in 1749 and 1750 ostensibly satisfying this request. However, many Salzburger settlers were out-bid for indentured workers by Savannah residents. Of those taken to New Ebenezer, several ran away to South Carolina, and the climate claimed its usual grim harvest. Those surviving and remaining became the source of complaints about work-ethic and attitude.[27]

23. Wilson, "Halle and Ebenezer," 180–87.
24. Wilson, "Halle and Ebenezer," 188–89.
25. Wilson, "Halle and Ebenezer," 202.
26. Wilson, "Halle and Ebenezer," 215.
27. Wilson, "Halle and Ebenezer," 146–47.

In these and many other respects Boltzius was reminded of the limits to his own control. He held magisterial power as well as clerical authority, but headstrong settlers insisted on their rights as freeholders. In the first years, after the relocation, Boltzius and his surveyors had chosen land that was not yet cleared. Oglethorpe refused to assign the lots until all the land was cleared, hoping this would motivate a cooperative effort. Boltzius had a less idealistic view of human nature.[28] For the Salzburgers, frustrated at the delay in receiving their farms, Oglethorpe's demand sounded like the feudal obligation of *Frondienste*, service to the lord, a system they had supposed they were leaving behind. The agitations did not become as violent as among the Palatines at Livingston Manor, and with the assignment of the tracts this tension was soon forgotten.[29] Nevertheless Boltzius had learned that any cooperative effort had to be shown to be in the interests of each participant.

While the theocratic dimension in Ebenezer was not as totalitarian in its control over lives as in Ephrata and Bethlehem, Boltzius did foster a much closer-knit religious community among the Salzburgers than they had known in the Alps, or that was known among Lutherans anywhere else in North America. Most important to his leadership was that he fostered trust as an advocate for New Ebenezer and its settlers. In his letters to patrons and superiors he did not shy away from categorically presenting the needs of the community.[30]

In the meantime other changes shaped Boltzius's ministry and leadership for the second half of his career in Ebenezer. His associate, Christian Gronau, died of malaria in 1745.[31] Halle sent a replacement, Hermann Lemke, who arrived in 1746. Arriving with him was the Treutlen family including John, aged 13, who impressed Boltzius at first, but who chafed at his own indenture.[32] With the endemic shortage in labor and high death-rates. Ebenezer depended on immigrant transports for growth. Several transports made landfall from 1749–1752, when the community began to sustain itself by birth-rates.

---

28. Melton, *Religion, Community, and Slavery*, 163–64.
29. Wilson, "Halle and Ebenezer," 177.
30. Wilson, "Halle and Ebenezer," 189, 211, 215.
31. Wilson, "Halle and Ebenezer," 122–24.
32. Morgan, *John Adam Treutlen*, 3.

## Slavery and the End of the Trust

The need for tradesmen and farm labor, chronic in Ebenezer, was felt throughout Georgia, which had only 10,000 people by 1765.[33] The incessant pressure from various constituents finally caused Georgia to relent and permit the introduction of African slaves in 1751. Enlightenment Whigs on both sides of the ocean debated the morality of slavery; some argued against it on the grounds of humanity, and some argued for it on the grounds of the capitalization of land and the production of affordable commodities. Slavery was justified in Georgia, as elsewhere in the south, due to the supply of both wage labor and indentured labor being insufficient to put the desired number of acres under intensive cultivation for commodities such as tobacco, indigo, and cotton. Since labor was in demand, workers commanded high wages, pinching the margins of profitability. There was also the extraordinary death rate of Euro-ethnic colonists in the southern third of the Atlantic watershed. It was assumed that those native to sub-tropical and tropical regions, such as West Africans, would fare better in the climes of the southern colonies. The provincial government bowed to the economic and social pressure. The slave-free vision for Georgia lasted fewer than twenty years.

Slavery was more slowly adopted in Ebenezer than in the rest of Georgia. Boltzius's acquiescence was reluctant. As with the eventual closing of the orphanage, the adoption of slave-labor by New Ebenezer's freeholders was not a development widely published by the missionary sponsors in Europe.

It was also at that time that the Trusteeship was ended and Georgia was converted to a crown colony. New transports of Germans from Ulm arrived in 1752, accompanied by a third pastor sent by the Halle Institutes for the settlement, Christian Rabenhorst. These immigrants had been recruited on the basis of these changes in the posture and vision of Georgia. Most of these Germans were not interested in being indentured to anyone; many came with the ambition to be planters with all that came with it, including owning slaves. For the first time Boltzius, who had taken no hand in this recruitment effort or in the selection of Pastor Rabenhorst, refused to meet the immigrants as they disembarked in Savannah.[34]

---

33. Wilson, "Halle and Ebenezer," 100–101.
34. Wilson, "Land, Population, and Labor," 241.

Christian Rabenhorst, arriving in November, 1752, was quick to embrace the new social and legal realities. He established himself in the rural pulpit of Goshen, closer to the larger plantations and the more recent immigrants.[35] Whereas Lemke married a daughter of Boltzius, Rabenhorst broke a taboo by taking a propertied widow from outside the Ebenezer community. She held five hundred acres adjoining Rabenhorst's glebe land held by Ebenezer, land on which sat the second of Ebenezer's mills. The Rabenhorsts, with Boltzius's permission, consolidated the holdings into a single possession, and Rabenhorst became one of the largest slaveholders in Georgia.

Boltzius later expressed regret for allowing a partial alienation of Ebenezer's communal property, the pastoral glebe land, to private holders who were consolidating the very type of plantation that was anathema to the original vision.[36] This regret was likely shared by a core of Salzburger freeholders from the earliest transports, and it would become a powerful sentiment to divide the community after the death of Boltzius's successor, Lemke, in 1768, just a year after he had superintended the transfer of the deed to the mill.[37] Beneath Boltzius's regret was his disappointment in Rabenhorst's conduct as a slaveholder. His pastoral colleague was reputed to be so severe that his slaves chose to avoid having children, falsifying the hope that Pietists would treat their slaves with greater humanity and kindness than others.[38] For his own part Boltzius never owned slaves, and he never developed the five hundred acres of glebe land he held in trust.[39]

The merger put the status of the mill in question, which was not resolved until 1767, after Boltzius's death in 1765. During the brief tenure of Lemke's seniority, Ebenezer's trustees chose to wash their hands of the saw-mills, a commercial enterprise that was still falling short of profitability under their cooperative model. Ebenezer thus deeded over the mills to Rabenhorst, who in turn leased them to an independent operator in return for an annual fee.[40]

---

35. Jones, *Salzburger Saga*, 113–14.
36. Melton, *Religion, Community, and Slavery*, 277.
37. Mühlenberg, *Journals*, 2:646–49.
38. Mühlenberg, *Journals*, 2:263–64.
39. Mühlenberg, *Journals*, 2:262.
40. Melton, *Religion, Community, and Slavery*, 277; Jones, *Salzburger Saga*, 122.

## Big Shoes to Fill

When Boltzius died in 1765 the ministry was carried on by Lemke and Rabenhorst. Lemke's death in 1768, however, warranted the placement of a pastor to fill the vacancy in the Jerusalem Church in Ebenezer, the flagship congregation of the German settlement. Rabenhorst now had seniority, but he chose to continue to base himself in the church in Goshen. Many in the Jerusalem Church were survivors from the first transports who continued to live in the original vision as independent small farmers. Shortly after arriving in Ebenezer in 1769, Christoph Triebner rallied the loyalties of many in the Jerusalem congregation by marrying Frederica Maria Gronau, daughter of the beloved Pastor Gronau and a niece to Pastor Boltzius of cherished memory. This match also made him a brother-in-law to a church trustee who was the husband of Frederica Maria's sister.[41]

Leveraging that position Triebner went on to make a series of decisions that attach his name to infamy in the history of Jerusalem Church, of the wider Ebenezer settlement, and of the published journals and correspondence of the Pennsylvania Senior, Heinrich Melchior Mühlenberg. The primary sources of the eighteenth century and subsequent secondary historiographers are uniformly unsympathetic, finding in Triebner a foil on which to blame the disintegration of the community. One historiographer, writing in the mid-twentieth century, called Triebner "a grasping, plotting, hypocritical rogue ... with enough stupid cunning to serve his purposes."[42]

The consensus verdict is that Triebner fulfilled the potential of his negative attributes, his character traits that had given pause to Halle Institutes Director G. A. Francke. Due to the dearth of suitable candidates willing to risk the ocean and the climate and other hazards of eighteenth-century emigration, Triebner was extended the call.[43] Yet a critique of the sources is warranted: Pointed reservations concerning negative attributes are features of the correspondence in the Halle-North America nexus. One telling example is that in London decades earlier F. M. Ziegenhagen had reservations about a young pastor being commissioned for the colonies, one Heinrich Mühlenberg. Decades later both G. A. Francke and J. C. Knapp were considerably negative in their assessments of

---

41. Melton, *Religion, Community, and Slavery*, 274.
42. Wallace, *Muhlenbergs of Pennsylvania*, 101.
43. Melton, *Religion, Community, and Slavery*, 273.

all three of Mühlenberg's sons.[44] Suffice to say, German Pietists of the eighteenth century believed very much in the inherently flawed humanity and sinfulness of each other and took pains to hedge their personal recommendations.

This is in no way intended to minimize Triebner's downsides but rather to place his human failings in perspective; the historiography of Ebenezer loses its sense of proportion relative to Triebner's perceived villainy and role in the collapse of the community. By comparing Triebner to others of his ilk, that is, of Pietist German clergy vetted for service in North America, we find that the late 1760s to 1770 saw a cluster of Halle-trained missionary pastors rise up to aid the Pennsylvania Ministerium, and from among them came the stable leadership of the synod in its second generation. This crop, so highly effective in securing the legacy of the Pennsylvania Ministerium, stood in contrast to earlier missionaries that Halle had sent to aid Heinrich Mühlenberg, many of whom presented negatives that grieved and distracted their senior.[45] Several had calls that were cut short because they alienated practically everyone.[46]

It is certain that Triebner did not rise to the same standard as Helmuth, Kunze, Schultz, and Heinrich Ernst Mühlenberg, all of whom began their careers in Pennsylvania around the same time that Triebner was sent to Georgia. Perhaps with the death of Boltzius there was an acknowledgment in the Halle Directors that the days were numbered for the Ebenezer cooperative and for the interests of European Pietists in sustaining it, especially now that its pastors had transitioned from serving orphans to owning slaves. Pennsylvania, its Lutheran population expanding geometrically since the 1730s, was now the place to invest with the cream of the missionary crop, while the mediocre candidate was sent to Georgia. A second possibility is that Triebner was actually on par with his peers, and that his endorsements were hedged as a matter of course among Halle Pietists just in case things went badly. In this scenario Triebner brought a conviction and energy that G. A. Francke had hoped might revive the community and remold it in Boltzius's image. This possibility helps to explain the otherwise puzzling choice of the Halle directors to be vague about Rabenhorst's seniority over Triebner.

44. Wallace, *Muhlenbergs of Pennsylvania*, 68–70, 75–76.
45. Mühlenberg, *Journals*, 1:266–71.
46. For an excursus on the headaches to Mühlenberg's ministry caused by the Halle missionary colleague Johann Friedrich Handschuh, see Mühlenberg, *Journals*, 1:238–40, 452–64.

On arriving in Georgia, Triebner established himself as the one in line with the original vision of the community and the legacy of Boltzius as opposed to Rabenhorst. Much of the conflict around Triebner's ministry can be understood in that, on his arrival, he became the champion for certain aspects of the original vision still cherished by the first settlers after more than thirty years. In their minds it was Triebner, and not their incumbent, Christian Rabenhorst, who was the true successor to Michael Boltzius's spirit and thus the better prospect for preserving more of the values and culture of the settlement as it was originally envisioned. That Triebner was both loyal to Boltzius's legacy and competent to at least some degree helps to explain why Boltzius's former flock was loyal to the young pastor for several years.

Usually a certain level of competence is required in order to inspire loyalty in a faction. Triebner's story may be best understood when it is remembered that Ebenezer was his first regular call. Many Halle Lutheran pastors in North America had to scale difficult learning curves and left churches divided and hurting in their wakes. Not least among these was Heinrich Ernst Mühlenberg, brought home from Halle at the age of 16 and hastily ordained. Thinking himself an advocate for his father, he created enormous problems for his colleague and brother-in-law, J. C. Kunze. The series of episodes finally prompted the elderly Heinrich Mühlenberg to retire more completely from his role. The son found his way to Lancaster where he matured and served productively the duration of his career.[47] Similarly, Christoph Triebner served out a career in Lutheran ministry, in the German churches of London, an arrangement which falsifies the assertion that the British had tried to wash their hands of him.[48]

In materials dated to the 1770s, especially pre-war, Triebner is a major figure in Heinrich Mühlenberg's *Journals*[49] and in Kurt Aland's compilation *Die Korrespondenz Heinrich Melchior* Mühlenbergs.[50] Mühlenberg took a dim view of Triebner early on, and his views have colored secondary constructions of the Ebenezer narrative. Heinrich Mühlenberg's account of Christoph Triebner paints a picture of an ego-driven, inexperienced, ethically confused pastor entering his first call with unrealistic notions of his authority and unrealistic expectations of those

---

47. Wallace, *Muhlenbergs of Pennsylvania*, 308–12.
48. Wallace, *Muhlenbergs of Pennsylvania*, 101.
49. Mühlenberg, *Journals*, 2:596–677.
50. Mühlenberg et al., *Die Korrespondenz*, 4:193, 625–85; 5:16–78, 237–41.

around him. This should be taken as a trustworthy assessment indeed, with similar dynamics experienced in hundreds of Christian congregations every year who receive a pastor fresh out of seminary, even in the twenty-first century.

When Christoph Triebner arrived in 1769 the transfer of the deed to the mill had occurred fewer than two years earlier. It was still a fresh issue in people's minds, and Triebner used it to assert his position over and against Rabenhorst. The suspicions which he raised galvanized a core at Jerusalem Church who saw in him a champion of their opposition to the changes enveloping the community.[51] The community's own trustees had confirmed the agreement with Rabenhorst during Lemke's leadership; at the root of the controversy may have been Triebner's own poor understanding of the arrangement. He charged Rabenhorst with manipulating the former pastors and trustees and of swindling the community out of the mill that stood on Rabenhorst's glebe land.[52]

The alienation between the pastors soon split the community. Others in the settlements rallied around Rabenhorst, insisting that the charges were baseless and that the arrangement had been approved and were above-board. Counter-charges began to be made against Triebner, especially of insubordination and factionalism. Both sides wrote their complaints to the European directors, whose efforts to confirm Rabenhorst's title and seniority did little to appease Triebner's camp.[53]

The schism became official when the pastors refused to serve each other communion. As this alienation threatened to rend Ebenezer apart many of the old Boltzius supporters reconsidered their position on the conflict and the threat it posed. In 1773 a church election put a majority of Trustees in place in Jerusalem Church who supported Rabenhorst. Triebner's supporters refused to accept the results and installed their own slate.[54]

One of these Jerusalem trustees who supported Rabenhorst was the redemptioner John Adam Treutlen (d. 1782), who had arrived in the 1749 transport full of ambition for his future and impatience with his terms of indenture. In scenes reminiscent of Lutheran congregations in Pennsylvania early in Heinrich Mühlenberg's tenure, the battle over

---

51. Melton, *Religion, Community, and Slavery*, 277.
52. Jones, *Salzburger Saga*, 122.
53. Melton, *Religion, Community, and Slavery*, 277.
54. Jones, *Salzburger Saga*, 122.

Jerusalem's pulpit became an "occupy" movement. Under Treutlen's leadership Triebner's party was locked out. Triebner met in the storefront of one of his supporters, while Rabenhorst held service at Jerusalem Church, at precisely the same hour.[55]

The story takes a macabre turn. Late in the summer of 1774 Rabenhorst and his wife were given rat poison in their coffee; they were sickened and nearly died.[56] Slaves in the Rabenhorst home testified that one of their own, an elderly black woman, boasted of the deed. She was burned at the stake in what scholar G. F. Jones calls a lynching, although the circumstances more closely mirror the execution of suspected witches in Puritan and Presbyterian communities into the eighteenth century.[57] In 1750 a domestic servant in her teens was convicted of witchcraft and burned at the stake in the Salzburg village of Mühldorf.[58] As Mühlenberg relates the third-hand account he had received of the incident, he expresses no suspicion that due process had been violated.[59]

Meanwhile, communication had to cross the ocean. In peacetime a letter might take three months to be written, sent by courier with a bundle to a ship, make the ocean crossing, then wait for other personal couriers or post riders to complete the delivery. With the process repeated for a reply, it could be six months between the asking of a question and its answer. In war, when hostile navies threatened interdiction, the process could double again. In 1773 the European directors of Halle Pietism's global mission enterprise appealed to Heinrich Mühlenberg to make a journey from Philadelphia to Ebenezer. Before the arrangements were concluded it was the fall of 1774.[60] He would learn of the attempted murder of the Rabenhorsts in October while ashore in Charleston, waiting to sail the final leg to Savannah.[61]

Heinrich Mühlenberg was in his sixties and feeling his years after three decades filled with arduous overland journeys through wilderness

---

55. Melton, *Religion, Community, and Slavery*, 279.
56. Jones, *Salzburger Saga*, 124; cf. Melton, *Religion, Community, and Slavery*, 265.
57. Jones, *Salzburger Saga*, 125.
58. Archbishop Dr. Alois Kathgasser issued a "Statement of Regret" in 2009.
59. Mühlenberg, *Journals*, 2:585.

60 Mühlenberg, *Journals*, 2:556. The commissions from Ziegenhagen and Urlsperger are reproduced at length, and most of the journal for 1774 is devoted to preparing for and then taking the trip to Georgia. The saga is brought to an end with his return to Philadelphia in March, 1775. See Mühlenberg, *Journals*, 2:688.

61. Mühlenberg, *Journals*, 2:585.

terrain to minister in one church after another, frequently mediating disputes and authoring constitutions. A previous extended itineration in 1751–52 had him in New York City for several months at a time, which left Anna Maria with three young children at home.[62] By 1774, Anna Maria had been suffering from adult-onset epileptic seizures, but insisted on accompanying Heinrich on the trip. This would have left two daughters home alone, Maria Catharina (Polly), 19, and Sally, 9 years old. Propriety forced them to bring Polly along while Sally was boarded with her sister and brother-n-law, the Kunzes. The trip was very difficult on the two elderly adults, although it was enjoyably broken up by a stay of several days in Charleston among German Lutherans while the captain waited for weather to change. In their frequent illnesses aboard ship the two relied on Polly's care.[63]

On arriving in Georgia Mühlenberg met with the pastors jointly to present his commission from Ziegenhagen and Urlsperger, whom they recognized as their superiors. He then met with each pastor separately, held private meetings with supporters of each side, and held several joint conferences, all with a view toward reconciliation.[64] In the process he found Rabenhorst to be more endearing and deferential, and Triebner to be combative and arrogant. He also found the magistrate John Treutlen to be a trustworthy and competent co-worker.

Perhaps one factor in making up Mühlenberg's mind concerning the merits of each faction's point-of-view, was the show of competence versus incompetence in the business affairs of the church. Triebner and his trustees had bungled the incorporation of Jerusalem Church with the Georgia legislature, creating a loophole that might have legally turned Jerusalem Church into an established Anglican congregation in Georgia's St. Matthew Parish. This Mühlenberg saw at once to be the more imminent disaster than the personality conflict, and pulled what strings he could all the way to the governor's office to redress the situation. He was successful in re-incorporating Jerusalem Church as an Evangelical Lutheran church.[65]

As the weeks of winter passed the conviction was formed in Mühlenberg that Rabenhorst had done no wrong. Triebner had erred

---

62. Mühlenberg, *Journals*, 1:276–93.
63. Mühlenberg, *Journals*, 1:560.
64. Jones, *Salzburger Saga*, 124.
65. Melton, *Religion, Community, and Slavery*, 279.

in accusing him and had provoked schism for spurious reasons.⁶⁶ The path to reconciliation lay in Triebner first of all recanting his charges, and second in formally submitting to Rabenhorst as the senior pastor in Ebenezer.⁶⁷ After Mühlenberg played more and more cards from his Halle-Augsburg-London commission to resolve the dispute, including leveraging the possibility of Europe's directors voiding various arrangements Triebner had struck concerning personal loans against his own glebe land, Triebner finally relented.⁶⁸ Mühlenberg also took the opportunity to do one of the things he did best: impose a new and binding constitution on all parties.⁶⁹

Triebner submitted to the rapprochement. Part of his submission was to a clear division of duties; he would serve Jerusalem Church and its allied parish, Zion, while Rabenhorst would serve in Goshen and its outlying circuit. The division then, in a sense, was institutionalized, even if the churches were once again in full communion and cooperation.

While Mühlenberg presented Rabenhorst and Treutlen sympathetically compared to Triebner, circumstantial evidence points to Triebner being more akin to the dour Halle-style pietism so valued by Mühlenberg. Rabenhorst, by contrast, was skilled in worldly affairs and business and enjoyed a freer lifestyle as it concerned certain amenities, such as alcohol. An estimation of character that may have escaped Mühlenberg's knowledge, is that Boltzius had hoped that Rabenhorst as a Pietist slave master would have sought to elicit the Christian affection of his charges, and journaled his disappointment.⁷⁰

## Triebner's Fall

After the Mühlenbergs returned to Philadelphia the peace in Ebenezer was short-lived. Triebner travelled to South Carolina for two weeks in the company of two young adults, the son and daughter of the deceased Pastor Lemke. When they returned, Johanna Lemke was found to have delivered a baby. Accusations surfaced at once. Johanna Lemke insisted that the father was not Triebner, but another man who had assaulted her

66. Melton, *Religion, Community, and Slavery*, 280.
67. Jones, *Salzburger Saga*, 125.
68. Jones, *Salzburger Saga*, 124.
69. Jones, *Salzburger Saga*, 124; cf. Melton, *Religion, Community, and Slavery*, 280.
70. Melton, *Religion, Community, and Slavery*, 265.

and had died shortly afterwards. The magistrate John Treutlen reported the seeming impropriety and his own suspicions to Augsburg, Halle, London, and Mühlenberg. Triebner, insisting on his innocence, refused to resign.

That Triebner was most probably innocent and wrongly accused may be assessed by the following: That Johanna Lemke herself never accused him and always insisted on the pastor's innocence; that her brother Timotheus Lemke did the same; *and so did the widow of the man whom Johanna did accuse.* Witnesses stated, however, that they had seen Pastor Triebner visit this man's home in the company of Johanna Lemke, and why should they have done that if that man had assaulted her? On these matters Triebner refused to answer, and he refused to answer summons for a congregational inquiry.[71]

At issue seems to be Triebner's constraint to silence in this matter: While by the twenty-first century much has changed in society's attitudes towards sexual violence and the pastor's duty to report, what has not changed is that if the pastor is asked to hold something in confidence, that trust is sacrosanct. If it is supposed that Triebner went in company with a young woman to face a man who wronged her in such an ugly way, and then remained silent on the matter in deference to the woman's own privacy, such a supposition leads to a fresh assessment of Triebner's own pastoral fiber and personal courage. Triebner appears to have violated neither Johanna Lemke nor pastoral confidence related to their visits with her abuser. For this, he was wrongly removed from his duties in an action that demonstrates that only the shallowest of reconciliations had been effected in the community. This I hazard on what I discern to be strongly supportable grounds: That the perpetrator's own widow stood with the pastor and vetted the young victim's story speaks volumes.

One of the central issues in the dynamics of pastoral sexual abuse is the manner in which victims have been deprived of their voice. The early twenty-first century has seen various movements and strategies to address that imbalance, including that now many pastoral associations, school districts and so forth mandate a sympathetic presumption that the accuser, being a victim, is telling the truth. Scandals of sexual abuse and misconduct by pastors, teachers, and coaches have reached such a frequency and mass in the public consciousness that one might presume that Triebner's guilt ought to be taken for granted. Applied to

---

71. Melton, *Religion, Community, and Slavery*, 281–82.

the situation facing Triebner, we find instead that *his accuser is not the woman involved*, but an officer of the law. Further, we find that the actual victim's *voice is ignored* by that same officer of the law in order to establish Triebner's guilt. Finally, another woman's voice is silenced: the widow of the man *that the victim identified*. Here then are two women whose stories of pain, violence and betrayal are ignored in pursuit of another, agenda-driven theory of guilt manipulated by an officer of the law, the magistrate John Treutlen, Pastor Triebner's avowed opponent.

The leadership in Europe, and Mühlenberg himself, received Treutlen's version of events. The European Directors removed Triebner, a decision which Mühlenberg approved. Triebner withdrew in disgrace to his private plantation.

One consequence for the community is that when Christian Rabenhorst died in late 1776, having never fully rebounded from his poisoning, there was no trained clergy left in call in Ebenezer. Services were handled by a senior vestryman. The Jerusalem Church Book shows that Triebner presented his son for baptism on January 1, 1778, with sponsors from among his supporters. Yet he remained in exile from call, dividing time between his plantation and Savannah and waiting for an opportunity to return to the pulpit.[72]

## Revolution in Ebenezer

The Magistrate John Treutlen had lent his power to the Rabenhorst faction, at the core of which were the slave-holding planters who worshiped at Goshen. This same core also backed the patriot cause as it took shape in the summer of 1775 following the battles in Massachusetts. Until Lexington and Concord the German immigrants of Georgia and the Carolinas could best be described as loyalists. After the Intolerable Acts closed Boston's harbor in the wake of the Tea Party, several Ebenezer men had signed petitions that defended the crown and objected to the patriot protests.[73] Germans had emigrated for land and had found the royal government generous in its apportionment; they did not want to commit treason and have the land alienated from them and their posterity.

When the bloodshed commenced in 1775, however, German settlers began to re-evaluate their interests. Treutlen attended the convention

---

72. Jones, *Salzburger Saga*, 124.
73. Melton, *Religion, Community, and Slavery*, 282–83.

that sent delegates to the Second Continental Congress, and his political star continued to rise. In 1777 Treutlen was elected the first patriot Governor of Georgia for a one-year term. Triebner took the opposite course. Although his own glebe lands made him a significant planter and slaveholder, his own interests had been tied to SPCK funding and his call had depended on the Royal Chapel of St. James. That he had been suspended due to the suspicions of impropriety makes his loyalism that much more interesting. Perhaps he was holding out hope that his superiors in London would reverse the judgment and vindicate him, especially in light of the death of Christian Rabenhorst in 1776. Triebner was arrested, and with a sword at his throat he was forced to abjure his loyalty to the King and declare allegiance to the patriots.[74]

Treutlen was governing from Savannah when Campbell landed on Christmas, 1778. On December 29, by means of a local slave who served them as a scout, Campbell sent part of his force through what otherwise appeared to be an impassable swamp, and they flanked the patriots on the high ground. Resistance broke. Treutlen fled into exile ahead of the street battle that was fought by retreating patriots against the Scots Highlanders in pursuit.[75] The exiled Pastor hailed the Highlanders and Hessians as the liberators of Georgia. Within days Christoph Triebner was attached to the army and was on the march with them as a civilian guide. They entered Ebenezer at 5 P.M., January 2, 1779, having met little by way of opposition.[76]

Campbell reinstalled Triebner in Jerusalem Church with a proclamation on January 3.[77] Triebner's triumphal re-entry signaled other loyalists to emerge from their hiding places. These included Jacob Buehler and 21 other men who had been hiding in the swamps. Buehler was rewarded by the British with a captain's commission in a loyalist militia.[78]

Campbell reached Augusta with a column at the end of January, but their presence failed to stir the back-country's loyalists. The proximity of the Augusta Road to patriot forces amassing in South Carolina put them at too much distance from Savannah, so Campbell withdrew from Augusta in the middle of February. During their return march, a regiment

---

74. Jones, *Salzburger Saga*, 126.
75. Campbell, *Journal of an Expedition*, 26–28; cf. 28n64, 110.
76. Campbell, *Journal of an Expedition*, 34.
77. Campbell, *Journal of an Expedition*, 35.
78. Melton, *Religion, Community, and Slavery*, 288.

of Scottish loyalists from North Carolina who had set out in support of Campbell were routed at Kettle Creek when their camp was surprised by a smaller patriot force.[79] Once in Ebenezer, Campbell turned command over to Lt. Col. Mark Prevost, the son of Major General Augustine Prevost, and appointed the younger Prevost the Lt. Governor of Georgia. Campbell then boarded a ship for England. The American War of Independence was over for him, but he would receive a knighthood in 1785 and eventually become the governor of Jamaica.[80]

A patriot force entered Georgia from South Carolina and occupied Briar Creek to sever communication between the royalists and any back-country loyalists that might provision them from their farms. Mark Prevost marched two columns out of Ebenezer, a diversionary force that departed with drums and fanfare, and a second, larger force that circled behind the patriot flank on a forced march. As this larger detachment bore down from the north, this maneuver threw the Patriots into confusion. As they fled they abandoned clothes and weapons in order to swim the river.[81]

In terms of immediate consequence Briar Creek was a more decisive victory for the royalists than Kettle Creek had been for the patriots. Under the leadership of Campbell and then Prevost, Georgia became the only rebelling colony where martial law was lifted and the province was returned to its pre-patriot status as a crown colony. However, the expected turn-out of Georgia loyalists did not take place.[82]

After most of 1779 passed, the patriots returned in force to Georgia to lay siege to Savannah. The French landed an army by water from the south and east, while patriot general Benjamin Lincoln invaded from his bases in South Carolina by means of the Augusta Road. With the appearance of French ships offshore, Major General Prevost ordered all troops to return from the outposts. On September 14 the patriots took possession of Ebenezer, which they held for a month.

The patriot siege of the royalist stronghold of Savannah was the second major coordination of French and patriot forces. The first took place a year earlier with the attack on Newport, Rhode Island. Both attempts combined land and sea operations, and both attempts failed. However,

---

79. Wilson, *Southern Strategy*, 87–88.
80. Campbell, *Journal of an Expedition*, x.
81. Campbell, *Journal of an Expedition*, 91–96.
82. Campbell, *Journal of an Expedition*, 90, 97–98.

Savannah represents an evolution towards the success on land and sea of French and patriot cooperation at Yorktown in 1781. At Savannah, for the first time, French ground troops took part in battle. Rain and fog slowed the ability to land their forces, and in that time royalist reinforcements strengthened Prevost's positions and transformed Savannah into a fortified stronghold bristling with towers, trenches, abatis, and artillery. The walls withstood weeks of patriot bombardment. On October 9 the patriots attempted to breach the fortifications at the Spring Hill redoubt, built where the road to Augusta began. Delay and confusion in positioning the troops caused the attack to occur piece-meal rather than as a coordinated assault along a broad front. This allowed the royalists to concentrate their fire at attacking units in turn. Advancing under harrowing volleys of grapeshot, the patriots penetrated the redoubt several times and the fight became bayonet-to-bayonet. Yet those who gained the ramparts were only a handful, and time and again, unsupported, they were forced to withdraw. After an hour the French and patriots withdrew from the field. Estimates vary, but upwards of 800 French and patriot soldiers were killed and wounded in less than an hour; royalist losses were fewer than 100. Among the patriot dead are honored heroes, including William Jasper, a sergeant, whose statue stands in Savannah, and Casmir Pulaski, buried in Savannah, a Polish aristocrat commissioned by Congress as a brigadier general.[83]

The French lifted the siege. The debacle cost the commander-in-chief of French forces, Count D'Estaing, his commission.[84] He returned to France and was replaced by Count Rochambeau, who would prove his competence in his cooperation with Washington at Yorktown. By October 20th Benjamin Lincoln's depleted force was on its way to Charleston, South Carolina, and Ebenezer was once again a royalist stronghold.

## The Royalists in Ebenezer

For the three years 1779–1781 Triebner and the loyalists would enjoy stability. In 1780 Benjamin Lincoln surrendered Charleston and six thousand patriot troops to the British, and Triebner was a frequent guest of the royalist officers. For much of this time one might surmise that the Halle pastor felt the hand of a righteous God vindicating himself and

---

83. Wilson, *Southern Strategy*, 160–73.
84. Wilson, *Southern Strategy*, 174–75.

those who had stuck with him. But no communication came from Halle reversing its decision and restoring him under their supervision.

Meanwhile the royalist occupation burdened the community. About a year after installing Triebner at his pulpit the royalists finally appropriated Jerusalem Church as a hospital—the climate doing far worse to the troops than hostile fire. This was characteristic of British occupations in Philadelphia and New York, but by the time of their withdrawal in 1782 Jerusalem Church was in such poor condition that rumors arose it had been used as a stable. In addition, the British destroyed the mills on the river to widen the passage for their own ships and boats, in one stroke bringing a final end to the dream of a self-sustaining community of co-operative industry.[85]

As Ebenezer "stagnated under British occupation,"[86] Triebner continued keeping the records of Jerusalem's Church Book, which shows that he served a busy pastorate of baptisms and funerals. No marriages are recorded, however, after 1778.[87] He noted that Rabenhorst's widow Anna Barbara was buried on July 1, 1779, and that Ulrich Neidlinger, the vestryman who had conducted worship before Triebner's return, was buried on November 21, 1779. The Church Book reveals that after he took over with royalist assistance he had a core of friends on whom he drew for various ecclesial and sacramental actions: An entry for 1781 shows that the loyalist Captain Buehler had his son baptized by Triebner; Joanna Lemke, the woman who had a child out of wedlock that was rumored to be Triebner's, was a sponsor.[88]

Christoph Triebner also acted as an advocate for the community, acting in that role as his predecessor Michael Boltzius had acted towards the royal government of Georgia. In a letter from 1781 he expresses concern to Governor James Wright about encroachments from South Carolina settlers on an island that was rightfully a part of the Ebenezer settlement and therefore a part of Georgia. The response is written on the back of the letter, instructing that the Reverend be informed that this was not an actionable concern for the time being.[89] While this seems to be dismissive and may provide discursive evidence that Triebner was out

85. Melton, *Religious, Community, and Slavery*, 294.

86. Jones, *Salzburger Saga*, 128.

87. Jones and Exley, *Ebenezer Church Record Book*, 77–83 (on births and baptisms), 104 (on marriages), 140–41 (on burials).

88. Jones and Exley, *Ebenezer Church Record Book*, 82.

89. Triebner, "Letter to the Governor of Georgia."

of royal favor, one should not underestimate the weight of concerns on Georgia's royalist government that might have occasioned the abrupt reply.

For all his efforts in ministry, sacrament, and governance, Triebner was serving unsupported in a vacant mission post, and unaccountable to a ministry structure, having been installed by a military officer. The absence of Halle's endorsement made Triebner's ministry "irregular" by Lutheran definitions.

John Treutlen, meanwhile, had fled to South Carolina where he also held property, and was elected to that state's assembly. For a period of time he held assembly seats simultaneously for both states. Meanwhile, Treutlen was twice-widowed; his wives were victim to the climate and its insect-borne diseases. In the spring of 1781 Treutlen was accosted outside his South Carolina home and murdered. It is unknown whether this was an act of revenge from a romantic rival for his third wife, or an act of partisan violence by loyalists, or if there other motives in play whether personal, political, or economic; as a magistrate he had plenty of opportunities to make enemies, simply by rendering judgments from the bench.[90] The murder of John Treutlen remains unsolved.

Christoph Triebner filled the pastoral vacancy in Ebenezer for over three years, until 1782. The Battle of Yorktown in Virginia was concluded with the surrender of the royalist armies of General Cornwallis in October, 1781. This event convinced the British that the war was too expensive and bloody to be worth the cost of victory. Triebner's ministry in Ebenezer was not viable without the buttress of royalist power. Even with Treutlen dead, the patriots who had opposed him before would never suffer him to remain.

## The Hessian Chaplain

The former Halle missionary transitioned seamlessly into his next commission, a call from the Hessian Colonel von Porbeck, executive officer of the Knoblauch Garrison regiment. Christoph Triebner served von Porbeck as a Lutheran chaplain while the royalist troops waited out the war, first in Savannah, and then in St. Augustine in Florida. Triebner had few options apart from a Hessian commission: Alienated from Ebenezer in Georgia and estranged from Mühlenberg in Pennsylvania, the

90. Jones, *Salzburger Saga*, 128–29.

non-affiliated Lutherans of Virginia and the Carolinas were one prospect, but victorious patriots in those congregations could hardly be expected to receive him. Canada might have been an option, but thirteen hostile United States stood between him and that frontier. Meanwhile he had befriended the Hessian officers and there was an evident need for his ministry.

The list of Hesse-Cassel's regiments with chaplains reproduced by Bruce E. Burgoyne shows that the Knoblauch Garrison regiment was served by the Reformed chaplain Johann Conrad Grimmel (1753-1789).[91] Although most of the Hesse-Cassel auxiliaries were Reformed, the Corps included thousands of Lutherans in the ranks. The diaries of other German auxiliary chaplains show that, while in New York, Lutheran and Reformed chaplains frequently exchanged themselves to each other's regiments to perform communion and liturgies for the other's minority religious constituents.[92] Porbeck would have called Triebner in the hope that his service would aid the overall morale of his regiment.

The call to the chaplaincy was likely on the terms of the other chaplains of Hesse-Cassel, which included an expense allowance in addition to the salary and the assignment of an enlisted man as a personal servant or assistant.[93] For regiments on garrison duty the churches of the city were used for worship services. Attendance at Sunday service was required for the Hesse-Cassel troops,[94] thus Triebner had a dependable congregation filling a church building every Sunday, and ministered to their needs during the week.

A diary kept by a Lutheran colleague, Gottlieb Johannes Braunsdorf, stationed thousands of miles north in Quebec, shows that for a garrisoned regiment there was a steady rate of civilian pregnancies, marriages to soldiers, and baptisms of infants, often in that order.[95] Deaths by natural causes diminished after acclimation in Canada, however in Georgia and Florida the diseases endemic to the warm climates had von Porbeck himself comment that life-expectancy was only forty years.[96] Chaplain Waldeck, while stationed in Pensacola, Florida, noted in his diary, "I fear

91. Burgoyne, *Hessian Chaplains*, xiv.
92. Waldeck, *Eighteenth-Century America*, 56–59.
93. Burgoyne, *Hessian Chaplains*, vii.
94. Burgoyne, *Hessian Chaplains*, ix.
95. Burgoyne, *Hessian Chaplains*, 115–31.
96. Atwood, *Hessians*, 168–69.

we will lose many men. Every regiment that comes here dies out in a few years and we will not be an exception. We have already experienced it."[97] Meanwhile in Canada the incidents of desertion and suicide increased with the length of deployment, spiking after the Battle of Yorktown.[98]

Even with the cessation of combat operations it is quite likely that Triebner for the Lutheran soldiers, and Grimmel for the Reformed majority, had their hands full with funerals. Despair at the length and futility of the deployment finally overtook Waldeck himself, several months before the Battle of Yorktown, in his journal entry of Dec. 31, 1780, "Another year is at an end and if it will be the last one in Florida, we need not know. It is all immaterial. All is in vain." If this was typical of the morale of the German auxiliary chaplains in the southern theater it provides us fresh insight into Triebner's usefulness to von Porbeck as a fresh face and attitude to present to the troops.

## Maturity and Ministry

At the war's conclusion Triebner wrote to Ebenezer asking if he might return to them. Their reply was that he was welcome to return if it was his desire to be hanged.[99] Chaplain Wagner of Ansbach-Bayreuth took a parish in Nova Scotia at war's end,[100] but Triebner sailed for England instead, and succeeded in London as a long-serving pastor to German-language churches in London, including St. Mary's on the Savoy.

Christoph Triebner's journey through the partisan options of the American Revolution took him in the opposite direction as Friedrich Melsheimer's journey. While Melsheimer is the only German auxiliaries chaplain to defect to an American pulpit, being received into the

---

97. Waldeck, *Eighteenth-Century America*, 170.

98. See the discussion on desertion in Wilson, "Switching Sides," 105–18. Chaplain Johannes Braunsdorf kept a "Death Register" in which he notes the causes of death in the Anhalt-Zerbst regiment and its civilian followers. The regiment was garrisoned in Quebec City from their arrival in 1778 through the duration of the war. On surviving the first year the overall drop in the death rate is steep for the acclimated soldiers; however, incidents of unnatural death increase, and suicide rates climb through to the end of the deployment in 1783. See Burgoyne, *Hessian Chaplains*, 66–109.

99. Burgoyne, *Hessian Chaplains*, 66–109.

100. Döhla, *Hessian Diary*, 234n6. The memoir by Karl Bauer inflates the promise to 3,000 acres for officers to settle in Nova Scotia or Canada (Bauer, *Journal*, 176).

Pietist-oriented Pennsylvania Ministerium, Triebner is the only Halle-vetted Pietist missionary in America to serve a chaplaincy in the royalist forces.

Once settled in London his published theological works rival Melsheimer's output, but Triebner wrote in English.[101] The focus of his writing was on apocalyptic interpretations of the times—a significant thread in Pietist literature—particularly with the French Revolution in view as a harbinger of the dooms and plagues of Revelation. These fancies were based on German authors which he translated for English readers, and are only laughable given the wisdom of hindsight. They are neither more nor less ludicrous than the literature that has been continually produced in that genre to the present time.

Significantly, Mühlenberg himself was not above such speculation. His doleful predictions for the future of the United States based on its spiritual condition in the 1780s might be seen as a fairly accurate prophecy of the Civil War. At the same time it must be said that he did not discern the coming of the Second Great Awakening. Melsheimer, in his book-length polemical response to Deism, draws on many of the same interpretive strategies as Triebner for understanding the shape of history as allegorically disclosed in the visions of the prophet Daniel.[102]

## Notoriety or Vindication

Triebner's notoriety in the historiography of Ebenezer is based on the role he played in a schism among pastors in his first call. With his early insubordination toward Rabenhorst and the resulting recriminations being so well documented, historiographers have been tempted to presume guilt on subsequent and far less grounded allegations. The series of events leading to the collapse of the Ebenezer cooperative have caused historiographers to find in Triebner a convenient scapegoat, and take it for granted that he sired a child out of wedlock. This is a harsh verdict. The impugning of Triebner fails to take into account, first, the comparative milieu of immigrant Lutheran pastors in America and their learning curves in the eighteenth century; second, the loyalty of a base of supporters who saw in him a champion for the vision that had brought them to

---

101. For example, see Triebner, *Essay*.

102. Melsheimer, *Warheit der Christlichen Religion*, 166–70; cf. Wilson, "Switching Sides," 244–47.

America under Boltzius; third, the testimonies *of the female victims* who insisted on Triebner's innocence in the sex scandal.

Triebner remained a steadfast loyalist even after the war turned irreversibly against the crown. He was the only missionary sent by the Halle Institutes to serve as a military chaplain in the Revolutionary War, and that was for the Hessians. It is true that, like thousands of others under duress, he abjured his oath to the king. When the pressure was removed, he recanted and proved consistent in his loyalism. After he served out his chaplaincy he removed to England where he exercised parish ministry as a seasoned Lutheran pastor to the end of his life.

Ebenezer as a cooperative community did not survive the war. Few people returned to live in the town. Jerusalem Church was served as a hub in a circuit of rural parishes by Johann Ernst Bergmann beginning in 1786. Along with J. F. Weiland who was sent to Pennsylvania, these two represent the last missionary pastors sent by the Halle Institutes to North America.[103] Bergmann served Jerusalem Church until 1824—a tenure longer than Boltzius's. His son effected the Jerusalem circuit's transition to the English language. Jerusalem Church itself continues its ministry as of 2019.

The pressures on the cooperative freeholder model had already subverted Boltzius's vision before the founder's death. It is unfair to assign the destruction of that vision to Triebner, when Rabenhorst himself hastened it along by his consolidation of private and glebe plantations and by shifting control of the millworks to an independent lease-holder.

Perhaps as the town dissolved, this allowed the animosities in the congregations to dissolve as well. In at least one of the personal dimensions of the conflict, a reconciliation of sorts was effected in the third generation: A granddaughter, Anne Mary Triebner, married Christian Treutlen, the grandson of the Ebenezer Magistrate-become-Governor of Georgia who had been the pastor's nemesis.[104]

---

103. Mühlenberg, *Journals*, 3:711, 715.
104. Melton, *Religion, Community, and Slavery*, 292.

# Conclusion

## *God on All Sides*

SEPTEMBER 27, 1777, WILL forever live in the memory of Lancaster, Pennsylvania, as the day it served as the capital of the United States. Congress convened in its courthouse for a brief session, before adjourning further west, across the Susquehanna River, to York. Others at the time found that day more or less memorable, more or less obscure, in their experiences of the War of Independence. On that Saturday the elderly German Lutheran missionary pastor Heinrich Mühlenberg was mocked as a Hessian in his own church in Providence, Pennsylvania, by members of Col. Dunlap's Cumberland County Militia, First Battalion. Meanwhile the pastor's son, Brigadier General Peter Mühlenberg, spent a tense and anxious day with George Washington's army at Whitehead, reviewing the details of the disposition of General Howe's royalist army force in and around Philadelphia.

The Brigadier General's sister and brother-in-law, Peggy and J. C. Kunze, woke up that Saturday to their first morning under British occupation. They could scarcely have imagined how their own lives would be changed. In short order the German Reformed pastor would be arrested under suspicion of fomenting rebellion. Zion Lutheran Church would soon be used as a hospital, and the parsonage would soon billet Chaplain Wagner of the German Auxiliaries from Ansbach-Bayreuth. That fall the Kunzes also became privy to the letter from Gottlieb Freylinghausen, the benefactor at the Halle Institutes. Freylinghausen's insinuations that the senior of the Pennsylvania Ministerium was falling short of his obligations to neutrality as a Lutheran pastor aroused the suspicion of the German officers in the city. Perhaps the letter was in the care of none other than Chaplain Wagner himself, who may have held on to it hoping to secure a personal meeting with Heinrich Mühlenberg. Perhaps Wagner was also in charge of reviewing Pennsylvania Ministerium correspondence passing through lines. This neat solution to the mystery of the German officer who kept the letter without ever delivering it is pure speculation.

J. C. Kunze ended up serving Philadelphia's German Lutherans alone during its occupation by the royalists, as his brother-in-law, Heinrich Ernst Mühlenberg, had already set about his flight from the city. Heinrich Ernst arrived safely at his father's home in Providence the evening of September 27, having spent several days in nervous travel.

Nerves were not as taut, perhaps, in Bethlehem, further removed from the lines, although Johann Ettwein had his own worries with his town having been taken over by the Continental Army to be used for prisons, hospitals, a garrison and a depot. Yet the Moravians had been conditioned to bear patiently with the impositions of the world; older members could recall how, twenty years earlier, the town had been overrun by refugees from the uprising of French-allied Native Nations. Some of their guests this time were celebrities and were expected to be treated as VIP's. By Saturday September 27 Major General the Marquis de Lafayette had been in Bethlehem nearly a week with a wounded leg. Based on Washington's personal interest, one imagines that Ettwein was particularly studious in his concern for the youthful dignitary's health and recuperation.

Far beyond the fronts of battle, back in Massachusetts, the German Lutheran Chaplain Melsheimer and his roommate Surgeon Wasmus were adjusting to their new home in Brimfield, Massachusetts. This may have involved doing what they could to clean and groom themselves, their wigs and their clothes for worship the next day. Having already met the town's young and friendly Congregationalist Pastor Nehemiah Williams and many of the people at a funeral, they were intent to cultivate such positive first impressions as they had made. There was also the matter of securing the trust of the dozen or so Hitchcock children in the house, who like their five year-old sister had no doubt heard the rumors that the hired German soldiers from Europe were cannibals.

Hundreds of miles to the west, beyond the Alleghenies and beyond effective patriot power, David Zeisberger held a delicate balance of influence in the Delaware Nation. On that day he journeyed from Lichtenau to meet with the nation's chiefs at their fire, troubled by the reports of war parties roaming with intent to kill patriot messengers from Fort Pitt, and urging the Delaware to be strong in their posture of neutrality.

Down south, by September 27, 1777, Christoph Triebner was *persona non grata* among the German Lutherans of the Halle-sponsored settlement of Ebenezer, Georgia. He kept himself busy with the affairs of his own plantation. Since his rival was dead, the pulpits of the community were empty. He remained in place, biding his time.

This day in history illustrates how the War of Independence put pressure on two distinct Pietist communities, the Moravian town of Bethlehem in Pennsylvania with its mission satellites, and the Halle-sponsored Lutheran Pietist clergy in the Pennsylvania Ministerium and in Georgia. These distinct ethnic German communities were in place in the colonies for decades before revolution erupted. Each had been planted in America with unique visions and assumptions during a time of relative peace on the frontiers. Each had grown during a period of aggressive recruitment for new colonists among ethnic Germans from the states of the Holy Roman Empire and elsewhere in central Europe. Overcoming challenges, and growing in competence, confidence, and numbers in their new settings governed by English law, ethnic Germans made informed choices regarding the partisan options set before them in the 1760s, 1770s, and 1780s. Those choices landed them, and the Holy Spirit of Christ whom they carried in their hearts, on all three sides of the War of Independence.

For laypeople it is manifestly the case that the opportunities or challenges that are part of one's social and economic status, combined with one's ambitions, are much more predictive of political alignment than is the faith one espouses at one's church. Ethnic German Lutheran merchants in New York City happily served the royalist occupation for most of the duration of the War of Independence. Ethnic German Lutherans on Virginia's Shenandoah frontier, *even though they were nominally aligned with the established Anglican Church*, flocked to join Peter Mühlenberg's patriot regiment by the hundreds. This study might well have chosen to compare the ethnic German Lutheran Pietist David Grimm, the loyalist Lutheran in New York City, with John Adam Treutlen, the patriot elder of the Halle-sponsored Lutheran Church in Ebenezer who became the first patriot governor of Georgia, while setting in the "neutral" position those Lutherans that J. C. Kunze and his wife Peggy served in Philadelphia during its occupation.

However, in the Lutheran Pietist case the focus of this study has been on clergy. Peter Mühlenberg left the pastoral vocation to become a patriot officer, though he remained committed to Halle-sponsored Pennsylvania Ministerium churches for the rest of his life. Moving in the opposite direction is Christoph Triebner, who became a royalist chaplain even after the issue of the war was decided. Among the neutrals are Heinrich Helmuth and J. C. Kunze, praised for their circumspection by the "Reverend Father" and Director of the Halle Institutes, G. A. Freylinghausen. Friedrich Melsheimer presents the case of someone who, in the personal experience of an army on campaign, came to the distinctive Pietist crisis of ethical awakening years after his ordination as an orthodox Lutheran. Taking a Moravian bride and later praising their community based on his internment with them, his desire was nevertheless to remain in the Lutheran fold. The German Lutheran church in Lebanon during his first, conflicted years of ministry, was nevertheless his path to escaping the war and engaging the issues in America from the standpoint of neutrality and nonviolence.

The pressures of the war resulted in diverse outcomes among the Halle-sponsored endeavors in America. The Pennsylvania Ministerium saw a few pastors move to Canada, but on the whole continued a vigorous ministry in the German language for several more decades after the death of its founder, Heinrich Melchior Mühlenberg. During the War of Independence the posture of neutrality among its clergy served the Pennsylvania Ministerium well, allowing for the new realities that followed the war to be absorbed into the continuity of community and identity among ethnic German Lutherans that had prevailed beforehand despite partisan differences. The correspondence between Grimm and the elder Muhlenberg over the winter of 1777–78 demonstrates the manner in which partisan conflicts could be viewed as temporary flare-ups rather than permanent alienations.

Ebenezer presents the opposite outcome. Only the church remained; the town around it dissolved under the partisan antipathies that had taken shape before the war, but which the war had served to crystallize and make irreconcilable. Healing took generations.

Among the Moravians the partisan choices were narrowed by the commitment to nonviolence. That commitment was understood differently among Moravian leaders. Zinzendorf had paid to have the men of Herrnhut exempted from conscription, but a generation later Ettwein refused to condone the practice of paying others to take one's own place under Pennsylvania's conscription law. In the 1750s August Spangenberg stepped into the vacuum of leadership in the failure of Pennsylvania's government, raised walls around Bethlehem and mobilized a watch. In the 1770s Ettwein enjoined the members of the Single Men's Choir not to report to the militia when it mustered for drills, and instead to apply to him if they needed help paying the fines. Peaceful engagement also meant accommodating the occupation of Bethlehem by the Continental Army, and the appropriation of its buildings. There was no passive resistance or effort to sabotage the war effort as took place among Quakers.

Even so, the ultimate non-resistance among Moravians was evinced among its Native American converts, who practiced the meekness and faith David Zeisberger had taught them as the condition for entering the communities of the converted. They sang psalms as they waited to be murdered by patriots in a militia that had mobilized with the express purpose of performing such a slaughter among them.

These ethnic German Pietists and their indigenous proselytes together manifest the paradox that through the spiritual power of "heart religion," God was personally present and active on all sides of America's partisan struggles in the eighteenth century. The stories of these ethnic German Pietists collectively are evidence that *shared faith does not predict shared agreement on social and political issues*.

The axiom that one's religion predicts one's politics is false; one might even go so far as to consider the axiom patently absurd. That the cases that falsify the axiom are based on extremely particular religious affinities, suggests that the axiom should have no place in popular discourse. This is turn infers certain ethical corollaries that apply across the broad horizons of discourse in religion, spirituality and politics today. Here are eight such corollaries that follow:

First, any adherent of any faith, no matter how fervent, should be cautious of hubris toward their co-religionists when there is disagreement on political matters. As noted by Heinrich Mühlenberg, neither side in the War of Independence could claim righteousness in their behaviors or inherent virtue in their cause to the exclusion of the other, and both sides were at enough fault to warrant divine chastisement.

Second, for a religious adherent to demonize, dehumanize, or alienate a co-adherent for disagreeing on a social or political issue, may be blasphemy, for it impugns that same divine principle, essence or Spirit who is at work in the other as well as in oneself. Socially and ethically, demonizing an enemy leads to depersonalizing and dehumanizing the enemy until shared humanity is no longer recognized. Crimes against humanity occur once a perspective of common humanity is lost.

Third, the use of violence to advance partisan social and political agendas can scarcely be condoned by the clerics of any global-scale religion, for these faiths represent millions or billions of adherents who will be found holding every kind of partisan opinion, social view and economic ideology. Coercion and violence dislocate community and make mere worldly concerns supreme over the life of one's co-adherents in faith. Pastor Christoph Triebner could never be bound in conscience by an oath he gave when a sword was held to his throat. The sword-to-the-throat strategy is counter-productive politically just as much as it is spiritually destructive of religious community.

Fourth, an ethical posture which promotes security and reduces violence overall may legitimately draw a religious advocate of non-violence into sympathy with, and even the support, of a partisan cause. In this posture Weiser's descendants among Lutheran Pietists shared his view that government had an obligation to provide order and security, so the claimants to government that could provide that were the ones to be obeyed. The principle for reducing violence was also motivating Spangenberg to mobilize a watch in Bethlehem, and Zeisberger twenty years later to pass information to the patriots at Fort Pitt.

Fifth, many advocates of non-violence may find objectionable that Spangenberg armed a watch in Bethlehem and Zeisberger spied for the patriots, and may find even Johann Ettwein too pliant in his reluctant acquiescence to Continental Army requisitions. The Moravian posture does stand in sharp contrast to the Quaker absolutists who did not allow for any material aid in support of a military establishment. The Quakers did not distinguish between aiding the armed soldier engaged in battle and aiding the wounded soldier, and in their view a campaigning army was in no degree different from a force raised specifically for deterrence alone. Thus a principled posture of non-violence is itself a continuum. Even then, Christian Pacifism is grounded on the premise that a functioning worldly government is holding the sword given it by God. Paul described this principle in Romans 13, when the Roman Empire was at the peak of its function. When social order breaks down and people are vulnerable, a pacifist may in good conscience broach new strategies to reduce violence overall, especially in defense of those who have no power to choose for themselves to turn the other cheek.

Sixth, although the stadial model is rooted in eighteenth-century Euro-ethnic chauvinism, it is an open-ended model by its nature. Its lineage obtains where ever people begin to engage those from cultures unlike their own on the premise of belonging to a shared humanity with common needs. Some who are actually stadial in their views may be accused of being racist when what is at issue may be a poor choice of words or a myopic cultural insensitivity (of which even the great Zinzendorf was guilty!), but these things can be cured by engagement, experience and education. Race-based thinking, on the other hand, is a closed system that admits no facts or evidence of common humanity and is premised on alienation; racism is couched, finally, on terms that justify genocide. Racism is insidious in political society and must be defeated; in religious community racism is a sin that must be repented and converted. Pains must be taken to understand racism, but racism must never be excused. The racist component that entered into the fiber of American patriotism must be repudiated completely and atoned where possible.

Seventh, it may be just as useful to study the War of Independence from another aspect, that the Abomination of Desolation is found on all three sides. Glimpses of the worst impulses in humankind have appeared in this study, most pointedly as it concerned patriot consciousness and hubris exhibited in the desecration of Augustus Church in Providence, Pennsylvania, and in the racist massacre of converted Moravian Native Americans. However one need not look far to find a parallel between the Augustus Church debacle, and the royalist use of Presbyterian churches to stable the horses of redcoat officers; or to find a parallel between the Washington County militia and the brutal tactics of Brandon Tarleton's royalist cavalry in the southern theater of the war; or to find a parallel between patriot ideological hubris and the proclamation of royalist General John Burgoyne who threatened "desolations" to New York's countryside, and in royalist Governor Dunmore's reduction to cinders of the town of Norfolk. Moreover, between the patriot and royalist poles were those "neutrals" who behaved in the opposite manner of the Moravians, Mennonites and Quakers: By taking oaths and abjuring them without scruple, or by paying and sending substitutes for themselves to the militia, or by seeing the war as an opportunity to profiteer or to settle personal scores.

Eighth, pietist faith as such did not predict which partisan causes would be supported, but because of pietist faith we find extraordinary examples of integrity and courage on all sides of the War of Independence. Each of these are examples to follow on their own terms spiritually, whether one agrees politically: The stadial-inspired peace-making of Conrad Weiser needs to be lifted up as an example of a useful deportment in polarized twenty-first century societies. The strategic thinking in the temporary but effective palisades at Bethlehem erected by Spangenberg to remove the opportunities for violence is an example to celebrate. We can be moved by the struggles of Peter Mühlenberg between duty to his commission and duty to his family, and by the silence of the confessional maintained by Christoph Triebner at great cost to himself and his reputation. Meanwhile the struggles in conscience that Heinrich Mühlenberg and Friedrich Melsheimer wrestled through should be a check on anyone's myopic ideology and triumphalism.

*God on Three Sides* has shown that sharers of a religious vocabulary and experience—even one that is narrow and particular—can find themselves at distinct, mutually-exclusive partisan poles. From these cases a religious person may posit that God was found on each of the three sides whenever someone suffered a manifest injustice for the sake of conscience: Triebner the loyalist was forced to abjure his oath to the King at swordpoint, the neutral town of Bethlehem was forced to aid and abet the Continental Army, the patriot Brigadier General John Peter Mühlenberg was ready to quit in 1778 after slights to his honor. In Christian parlance to suffer injustice for the sake of one's conscience or religious conviction, is to "bear the cross." This was the key to the faith of the Moravian Native Americans, who experienced the worst injustice of all. To say that God is found on all sides of a partisan issue must take into account the manner in which God is found: It is to confess an ethical application of the Christian doctrine that in and through Christ, God is found *on the cross*.

These cases have furthermore proven a dark corollary: Whatever one's claims to religious faith, it is the Abomination of Desolation who lurks in the boasts of partisan political ideology, who fosters alienation, and raises the specter of racial genocide. Where God is truly found is in the quieter whispers of the conscience by which the believer is reminded that there are alternatives to alienation and the resort to violence. Any partisan issue that divides devout believers of a shared faith is going to find, on every side of that issue, co-adherents of that faith who are suffering for their convictions. No matter what religion is in view, the devout adherent should approach partisan political divides with an attitude of humility and the goal of peace.

# Bibliography

Adams, John. "John Adams to Abigail Adams, September 30, 1777." In *The American Revolution: Writings from the War of Independence*, edited by John Rhodehamel, 351–52. New York: Literary Classics of the United States, 2001.

Ahrendt, Theodore G. *The Lutherans in Georgia*. Chicago, IL: Adams, 1979.

Ahrens, Sabine. *Die Lehrkräfte der Universität Helmstedt (1576–1810)*. Vol. 7 of *Veröffentlichungen der Kreismuseum Helmstedt*. Wolfenbüttel, Germany: Roco, 2004.

Algeo, John. "The Effects of the Revolution on Language." In *A Companion to the American Revolution*, edited by Jack P. Green and J. R. Pole, 595–99. Malden, MA: Blackwell, 2004.

Allen, Thomas B. *Tories: Fighting for the King in America's First Civil War*. New York: HarperCollins, 2010.

American Council of Learned Societies, ed. *Dictionary of American Biography*. 22 Vols. New York: Scribner's Sons, 1928–37.

Anderson, Phil. *Lord of the Ring*. Ventura, CA: Regal, 2007.

André, John. "Journal, August 31–October 4, 1777." In *The American Revolution: Writings from the War of Independence*, edited by John Rhodehamel, 334–47. New York: Literary Classics of the United States, 2001.

———. "Journal, June 16–July 5, 1778." In *The American Revolution: Writings from the War of Independence*, edited by John Rhodehamel, 452–58. New York: Literary Classics of the United States, 2001.

Anonymous. "To The Virginia Gazette: Response to Lord Dunmore's Proclamation." In *The American Revolution: Writings from the War of Independence*, edited by John Rhodehamel, 81–86. New York: Literary Classics of the United States, 2001.

———. "A Whig: To the Public." In *The American Revolution: Writings from the War of Independence*, edited by John Rhodehamel, 530–33. New York: Literary Classics of the United States, 2001.

Asprey, Robert B. *Frederick the Great: The Magnificent Enigma*. New York: Houghton Mifflin, 1986.

Atwood, Craig D. "The Union of Masculine and Feminine in Zinzendorfian Piety." In *Masculinity, Senses, Spirit*, edited by Katherine M. Faull, 11–38. Lanham, MD: Bucknell University Press, 2011.

Atwood, Rodney. *The Hessians: Mercenaries from Hessen-Kassel*. Cambridge, UK: Cambridge University Press, 1980.

Aurand, A. Monroe. *Early Life of the Pennsylvania Germans*. 1945. Reprint, Lexington KY: Forgotten Books, 2007.

Bach, Jeff. *Voices of Ephrata: The Sacred World of Ephrata*. University Park, PA: Pennsylvania State University Press, 2003.

Bach, Tom. "The Halle Testimonial System: Conflicts and Controversies." *The Covenant Quarterly* 65.4 (2006) 39–55.

Baglyos, Paul. "From Pietism to Virtue: Frederick Augustus Conrad Mühlenberg in Halle and Philadelphia." In *Halle Pietism, Colonial North America, and the Young United States*, edited by Hans-Jürgen Grabbe, 225–32. Stuttgart: Franz Steiner Verlag, 2008.

———. "The Mühlenbergs Become Americans." *Lutheran Quarterly* 19 (2005) 43–62.

Bailyn, Bernard. *The Ideological Origins of the American Revolution*. Cambridge, MA: Harvard University Press, 1967, 2017.

Balmer, Randall, and Lauren F. Winner. *Protestantism in America*. New York: Columbia University Press, 2002.

Barba, Preston A. "Frederick Valentine Melsheimer: Father of American Entomology, Part I." *American German Review* 11.3 (1945) 17–19.

———. "Frederick Valentine Melsheimer: Father of American Entomology, Part II." *American German Review* 11.4 (1945) 17–20.

Barone, Michael. *Our First Revolution: The Remarkable British Upheaval that Inspired America's Founding Fathers*. New York: Crown, 2007.

Bartel, Klaus J. "Germany and the Germans at the Time of the American Revolution." *The Modern Language Journal* 60.3 (1976) 96–100.

Barton, William. "Journal, August 27–September 14, 1779." In *The American Revolution: Writings from the War of Independence*, edited by John Rhodehamel, 534–42. New York: Literary Classics of the United States, 2001.

Bauer, Karl. *Journal of Hessian Grenadier Battalion*. Edited and translated by Bruce E. Burgoyne. Westminster, MD: Heritage, 2008.

Beard, Eva. "The Beetles of Pastor Melsheimer." *Frontiers: A Magazine of Natural History* 22.5 (1958) 144–55.

Bergen, Doris L., ed. *The Sword of the Lord: Military Chaplains from the First to the Twenty-First Century*. Notre Dame, IN: University of Notre Dame Press, 2004.

*The Bethlehem Diary*. Vol. 1. Edited and translated by Kenneth G. Hamilton. Bethlehem, PA: Archives of the Moravian Church, 1971.

"Bild des Menschen." *Evangelisches Magazin* 4.1 (1815) 55–63.

Black, Jeremy. *Tools of War: The Weapons that Changed the World*. London, UK: Quercus, 2007.

Brecht, Martin. *Geschichte des Pietismus*. Vols. 1–2. Göttingen, Germany: Vandenhoeck & Ruprecht, 1993–95.

Brekus, Catherine A. *Sarah Osborne's Word: The Rise of Evangelical Christianity in Early America*. New Haven, CT: Yale University Press, 2013.

Brock, Peter. *Pacifism in the United States: From the Colonial Era to the First World War*. Princeton, NJ: Princeton University Press, 1968.

Burgoyne, Bruce E., ed. *Hessian Chaplains: Their Diaries and Duties*. Translated by Bruce E. Burgoyne. Westminster, MD: Heritage, 2007.

Burgoyne, John. "Proclamation." In *The American Revolution: Writings from the War of Independence*, edited by John Rhodehamel, 303–5. New York: Literary Classics of the United States, 2001.

Burke, Edmund. "Speech on Moving His Resolutions for Conciliation with the Colonies. March 22, 1775." In *The Works of the Right Honourable Edmund Burke*, by Edmund Burke, 99-186. Vol. 2. London: John C. Nimmo, 1887. http://www.gutenberg.org/files/15198/15198-h/15198-h.htm.

Bussey. "Letter to Conrad Weiser, 1756." Conrad Weiser Papers, Historical Society of Pennsylvania, Philadelphia, PA.

Butler, John. "The Spiritual Importance of the Eighteenth Century." In *In Search of Peace and Prosperity: New German Settlements in Eighteenth-Century Europe and America*, edited by Hartmut Lehmann, et al., 101-14. University Park, PA: Pennsylvania State University Press, 2000.

Calhoun, Robert M. "The Impact of the Revolution on Church and State." In *A Companion to the American Revolution*, edited by Jack P. Green and J. R. Pole, 444-51. Malden, MA: Blackwell, 2004.

———. "Loyalism and Neutrality." In *A Companion to the American Revolution*, edited by Jack P. Green and J. R. Pole, 235-47. Malden, MA: Blackwell, 2004.

———. "The Religious Consequences of the Revolution." In *A Companion to the American Revolution*, edited by Jack P. Green and J. R. Pole, 579-85. Malden, MA: Blackwell, 2004.

Calloway, Colin G. *The Indian World of George Washington: The First President, the First Americans, and the Birth of the Nation*. Oxford: Oxford University Press, 2018.

Camenzind, Krista, "Violence, Race, and the Paxton Boys." In *Friends and Enemies in Penn's Woods*, edited by William A. Pencak and Daniel K. Richter, 201-20. University Park, PA: Penn State University Press, 2004.

Campell, Archibald. *Journal of an expedition against the rebels of Georgia in North America under the orders of Archibald Campbell, Esquire, Lieut. Colol. of His Majesty's 71st Regimt., 1778*. Augusta, GA: Richmond County Historical Society, 1981.

Carter, Landon. "Diary: June 26-July 16, 1776." In *The American Revolution: Writings from the War of Independence*, edited by John Rhodchamel, 133-41. New York: Literary Classics of the United States, 2001.

Cassara, Ernest. *The Enlightenment in America*. New York: Twayne, 1975.

Clark, George Rogers. "Narrative of the March to Vincennes." In *The American Revolution: Writings from the War of Independence*, edited by John Rhodehamel, 502-22. New York: Literary Classics of the United States, 2001.

Clifton-Soderstrom, Michelle. *Angels, Worms, and Bogeys: The Christian Ethic of Pietism*. Eugene, OR: Cascade, 2010.

The Continental Congress. "Address to the Six Nations, July 13, 1775." In *The American Revolution: Writings from the War of Independence*, edited by John Rhodehamel, 54-60. New York: Literary Classics of the United States, 2001.

Crumrine, Boyd, et al. *History of Washington County, Pennsylvania*. Philadelphia: H. L. Everts and Co., 1882.

*The Declaration of Independence and the Constitution of the United States of America*. Washington, DC: Cato Institute, 2002.

DeLancey, Stephen. "Stephen DeLancey to Cornelia Barclay DeLancey, January 14, 1779." In *The American Revolution: Writings from the War of Independence*, edited by John Rhodehamel, 498-501. New York: Literary Classics of the United States, 2001.

Diamond, Jared. *Guns, Germs, and Steel: The Fate of Human Societies*. New York: W. W. Norton and Co., 1999.

Dickinson, John. "A Pennsylvanian Reacts to Lexington and Concord: April 1775." In *The American Revolution: Writings from the War of Independence*, edited by John Rhodehamel, 21–24. New York: Literary Classics of the United States, 2001.

Digby, William. "Journal, July 24–October 13, 1777." In *The American Revolution: Writings from the War of Independence*, edited by John Rhodehamel, 306–33. New York: Literary Classics of the United States, 2001.

Dippel, Horst. *Die Amerikanische Revolution 1763-1787*. Frankfurt Am Main, Germany: Suhrkamp Verlag, 1985.

———. *Germany and the American Revolution 1770–1800*. Translated by Bernhard A. Uhlendorf. Chapel Hill, NC: University of North Carolina Press, 1977.

———. *Geschichte Der USA*. 1996. Reprint, München, Germany: C. H. Beck, 2003.

———. "The Influence of the American Revolution in Germany." In *A Companion to the American Revolution*, edited by Jack P. Green and J. R. Pole, 550–53. Malden, MA: Blackwell, 2004.

Doering, Heinrich. *Die Gelehrten Theologen Deutchlands im achtzehnten und neunzehnten jahrhundert*. Vol. 2. Neustadt a.b. Orla, Germany: Johann Karl Gottfried Wagner, 1832.

Döhla, Johann Conrad. *A Hessian Diary of the American Revolution*. Edited and translated by Bruce E. Burgoyne. Norman, OK: University of Oklahoma Press, 2011.

Dubbs, J. H. *History of Franklin and Marshall College*. Lancaster, PA: Franklin Marshall Alumni Association, 1903.

Dudley, William, ed. *The American Revolution: Opposing Viewpoints*. San Diego, CA: Greenhaven, 1992.

Ellis, Joseph J. *His Excellency, George Washington*. New York: Alfred K. Knopf, 2004.

Emanuel Lutheran Church. "Our History." https://www.emanuelwoodstock.org/our-history.

Engel, Katherine Carte. *Religion and Profit: Moravians in Early America*. Philadelphia: University of Pennsylvania Press, 2009.

———. "The SPCK and the American Revolution: The Limits of International Protestantism." *Church History* 81.1 (2012) 77–103.

Epstein, Klaus. *The Genesis of German Conservatism*. Princeton, NJ: Princeton University Press, 2015.

Erb, Peter C., ed. *Pietists: Selected Writings*. New York: Paulist, 1983.

Ernst, Patrick, ed. *Die Direktoren der Franckeschen Stiftungen*. Halle A.S., Germany: Freundeskreis der Franckeschen Stiftungen e.V. Halle, 2006.

Ewald, Johann. *Diary of the American War*. Edited and translated by Joseph P. Tustin. New Haven, CT: Yale University Press, 1979.

Ferling, John. *Almost a Miracle: The American Victory in the War of Independence*. Oxford: Oxford University Press, 2007.

Finck, William J. *Lutheran Landmarks and Pioneers in America: A Series of Sketches of Colonial Times*. Philadelphia: United Lutheran, 1913.

Fitz, Jabez. "Narrative." In *The American Revolution: Writings from the War of Independence*, edited by John Rhodehamel, 266–94. New York: Literary Classics of the United States, 2001.

Fogleman, Aaron Spencer. *Hopeful Journeys: German Immigration, Settlement, and Culture in Colonial America, 1717–1775*. Philadelphia: University of Pennsylvania Press, 1996.

———. *Jesus is Female: Moravians and Radical Religion in Early America*. Philadelphia: University of Pennsylvania Press, 2007.
Fortenbaugh, Robert. *The Development of the Synodical Polity of the Lutheran Church in America, to 1829*. Philadelphia: University of Pennsylvania, 1926.
Francke, August Hermann. *Faith's Work Perfected; or, Francke's Orphan House at Halle*. Edited and translated by William L. Gage. 1867. Reprint, Lexington, KY: University of Michigan, 2014.
———. "From the Autobiography." In *Pietists: Selected Writings*, edited by Peter C. Erb, 99-107. New York: Paulist, 1983.
———. *A Guide to the Reading and Study of the Holy Scriptures*. Edited and translated by William Jacques. 1823. Reprint, n.p.: Nabu Public Domain Reprints, 2014.
Franklin, Benjamin. *The American Revolution: Writings from the War of Independence*. Edited by John Rhodehamel. New York: Literary Classics of the United States, 2001.
———. *The Completed Autogiography by Benjamin Franklin*. Edited by Mark Skousen. Washington, DC: Regnery, 2006.
———. *Essays, Articles, Bagatelles, and Letters, Poor Richard's Almanack, Autobiography*. New York: Library of America, 1987.
Fraser, David. *Frederick the Great*. New York: Fromm International, 2000.
Frederick, George William, III. "His Majesty's Most Gracious Speech to Both Houses of Parliament." October 27, 1775. Library of Congress. https://www.loc.gov/item/rbpe.10803800.
Freeman, Alan, and Elizabeth Mensch. "Property." In *A Companion to the American Revolution*, edited by Jack P. Green and J. R. Pole, 638-44. Malden, MA: Blackwell, 2004.
Freylinghausen, Gottlieb Anastasius. "Brief Den 1 Jun. 1776. An H. Pastor und Rector Mühlenberg zu Philadelphia." June 1, 1776. M 4 C15:46, 143-46. Franckesche Stiftungen, Halle, Germany.
———. *Wohlverdientes Ehrengedächtnis: gestift dem weiland Hochwürdiger und Hochgelährten Herrn D. Johann George Knapp*. Halle, Germany: In der Buchhandlung des Waisenhauses, 1771.
Froom, LeRoy Edwin. *The Prophetic Faith of our Fathers*. Vol. 1. Washington, DC: Review and Herald, 1950.
Frostin, Per. *Luther's Two Kingdoms Doctrine: A Critical Study*. Lund, Sweden: Lund University Press, 1994.
Fry, H. C., et al., eds. *The History of the Lancaster Conference of the Evangelical Lutheran Ministerium of Pennsylvania and the Adjacent States, together with the Histories of the Congregations*. Lebanon, PA: Lancaster Conference, 1942.
Gaustad, Edwin S. "Religion Before the Revolution." In *A Companion to the American Revolution*, edited by Jack P. Green and J. R. Pole, 60-64. Malden, MA: Blackwell, 2004.
Germann, William. "The Crisis in the Early Life of General Peter Mühlenberg." *The Pennsylvania Magazine of History and Biography* 37.4 (1913) 298-329, 450-70.
Gillespie, Michele, and Robert Beachy, eds. *Pious Pursuits: German Moravians in the Atlantic World*. New York: Berghahn, 2007.
Glatfelter, Charles H. *Pastors and People: German Lutheran and Reformed Churches in the Pennsylvania Field, 1717-1793*. Vol. 2. Breinigsville, PA: Pennsylvania German Society, 1981.

Glover, John. "John Glover to Jonathan Glover and Azor Orne, September 21 and 29, 1777." In *The American Revolution: Writings from the War of Independence*, edited by John Rhodehamel, 348–50. New York: Literary Classics of the United States, 2001.

Gnadenhuetten Monument Society. *A True History of the Massacre of Ninety-Six Christian Indians at Gnadenhuetten, Ohio, March 8th, 1782.* New Philadelphia, OH: Ohio Democrat Office, 1870. http://cdm16007.contentdm.oclc.org/cdm/ref/collection/p16007coll17/id/465.

Gollin, Gillian Lindt. *Moravians in Two Worlds: A Study of Changing Communities.* New York: Columbia University Press, 1967.

Good, James I. *History of the Reformed Church in the United States, 1725–1792.* Reading, PA: Daniel Miller, 1899. https://archive.org/details/historyofreformedusa00good.

Gordon, Scott Paul, and Robert Paul Lienemann. "The Gunmaking Trade in Bethlehem, Christiansbrunn, and Nazareth, Opportunity and Constraint in Managed Moravian Economies, 1750–1800." *Journal of Moravian History* 16.1 (2016) 1–44.

Grabo, Norman S. "The Cultural Effects of the Revolution." In *A Companion to the American Revolution*, edited by Jack P. Green and J. R. Pole, 586–94. Malden, MA: Blackwell, 2004.

Griffin, Patrick. *American Leviathan: Empire, Nation, and Revolutionary Frontier.* New York: Hill and Wang, 2007.

———. *America's Revolution.* Oxford: Oxford University Press, 2013.

Haeberlein, Mark. *The Practice of Pluralism: Congregational Life and Religious Diversity in Lancaster, Pennsylvania, 1730–1820.* University Park, PA: Penn State University Press, 2009.

Hagen, H. A. "The Melsheimer Family and the Melsheimer Collection." *The Canadian Entomologist* 15 (1883) 191–97.

Haller, Albrecht von. *Briefe über die wichtigsten Wahrheiten der Offenbarung.* Bern: In Verlag der neuen Buchhandlung, 1773.

Hamilton, Alexander. "Hamilton to La Fayette, October 15, 1781." Alexander Hamilton Papers: General Correspondence, 1734–1804; 1781. Manuscript/Mixed Material. https://www.loc.gov/item/mss246120006.

Hamilton, J. Taylor. *A History of the Moravian Church.* Bethlehem, PA: Times, 1900.

Hamilton, Keith. *John Ettwein and the Moravian Church During the Revolutionary Period.* Bethlehem, PA: Times, 1940.

Harper, Steven C. "Delawares and Pennsylvanians After the Walking Purchase." In *Friends and Enemies in Penn's Woods*, edited by William A. Pencack and Daniel K. Richter, 167–79. University Park, PA: Penn State University Press, 2004.

Herman, Arthur: *How the Scots Invented the Modern World.* New York: Three Rivers, 2001.

Hibbert, Christopher. *Redcoats and Rebels: The American Revolution Through British Eyes.* New York: W. W. Norton and Co., 1990.

Hinderaker, Eric. "The Amerindian Population in 1763." In *A Companion to the American Revolution*, edited by Jack P. Green and J. R. Pole, 94–98. Malden, MA: Blackwell, 2004.

Hinderaker, Eric, and Peter C. Mancall. *At the Edge of Empire: The Backcountry in British North America.* Baltimore, MD: John Hopkins University Press, 2003.

Hirschfeld, Fritz. *Washington and Slavery: A Documentary Portrayal.* Columbia, MO: University of Missouri Press, 1997.

Hocker, Edward H. *The Fighting Parson in the American Revolution.* Philadelphia: Self-published, 1936.
Hurt, R. Douglas. *The Ohio Frontier: Crucible of the Old Northwest, 1720–1830.* Bloomington, IN: Indiana University Press, 1996.
Ingrao, Charles. *The Hessian Mercenary State: Ideas, Institutions and Reform under Frederick II, 1760–1785.* Cambridge, UK: Cambridge University Press, 1987.
"Instructions on Raising a Militia." Conrad Weiser Papers, Historical Society of Pennsylvania, Philadelphia, PA.
Ireland, Owen S. *Religion, Ethnicity, and Politics: Ratifying the Constitution in Pennsylvania.* University Park, PA: Penn State University Press, 1995.
Jefferson, Thomas. *Writings: Autobiography, Notes on the State of Virginia, Public and Private Papers, Addresses, Letters.* Edited by Merrill D. Peterson. New York: Library of America, 1984.
Johnson, Richard R. "Intra-imperial Communication, 1689–1775." In *A Companion to the American Revolution,* edited by Jack P. Green and J. R. Pole, 14–18. Malden, MA: Blackwell, 2004.
Jones, George Fenwick. *The Salzburger Saga: Religious Exiles and Other Germans Along the Savannah.* Athens, GA: University of Georgia Press, 1984.
Jones, George Fenwick, and Shirley Exley, eds. *Ebenezer Church Record Book, 1754–1781.* Translated by George F. Jones and Shirley Exley. Baltimore, MD: Genealogical, 1991.
Kathgasser, Archbishop Alois. "Statement of Regret." https://web.archive.org/web/20101216094901/http://www.kirchen.net/portal/page.asp?id=14640.
Kennedy, Michael V. "The Home Front during the War for Independence: The Effect of Labor Shortages on Commercial Production." In *A Companion to the American Revolution,* edited by Jack P. Green and J. R. Pole, 332–41. Malden, MA: Blackwell, 2004.
Ketchum, Richard M. *Saratoga: Turning Point of America's Revolutionary War.* New York: Henry Holt and Co., 1997.
———. *Victory at Yorktown: The Campaign that Won the Revolution.* New York: Henry Holt and Co., 2004.
Kidd, Thomas. *God of Liberty: A Religious History of the American Revolution.* New York: Basic, 2010.
Kiernan, V. G. "Foreign Mercenaries and Absolute Monarchy." *Past & Present* 11 (1957) 66–86.
Kirk, Linda. "The Matter of Enlightenment." *The Historical Journal* 43.4 (2000) 1129–43.
Kloppenberg, James T. "Virtue." In *A Companion to the American Revolution,* edited by Jack P. Green and J. R. Pole, 696–700. Malden, MA: Blackwell, 2004.
Knittle, Walter Allen. *Early Eighteenth-Century Palatine Emigration: A British Government Redemptioner Project to Manufacture Naval Stores.* Philadelphia: Durrance and Co., 1937.
Knouff, Gregory T. "Whiteness and Warfare on a Revolutionary Frontier." In *Friends and Enemies in Penn's Woods,* edited by William A. Pencak and Daniel K. Richter, 238–58. University Park, PA: Penn State University Press, 2004.
Kolb, Robert, and Timothy J. Wengert, eds. *The Book of Concord: The Confessions of the Evangelical Lutheran Church.* Translated by Robert Kolb and Timothy J. Wengert. Minneapolis: Fortress, 2000.

Koller, J. C. "Historical Discourse." *The Memorial Volume of the Sesqui-centennial Services in St. Matthew's Evangelical Lutheran Church*. York, PA: York Daily, 1893.

Köppen, Daniel Jaochim. *Die Bibel ein Werk der göttlichen Weisheit*. Leipzig: im Verlage der Koppenschen Buchhandlung, 1787.

Kramnick, Isaac. "Ideological Background." In *A Companion to the American Revolution*, edited by Jack P. Green and J. R. Pole, 88–93. Malden, MA: Blackwell, 2004.

Kurt, Johann Heinrich. *History of the Christian Church*. Vol. 2. London: Hodder and Stoughton, 1868.

La Vopa, Anthony J. "Vocations, Careers, and Talent: Lutheran Pietism and Sponsored Mobility in Eighteenth-Century Germany." *Comparative Studies in Society and History* 28.2 (1986) 255–86.

Langton, Edward. *History of the Moravian Church: The Story of the First International Protestant Church*. London, UK: George Allen and Unwin Ltd., 1956.

Laurens, Henry. "Henry Laurens to Horatio Gates, June 17, 1778." In *The American Revolution: Writings from the War of Independence*, edited by John Rhodehamel, 171–75. New York: Literary Classics of the United States, 2001.

———. "Henry Laurens to John Laurens, August 14, 1776." In *The American Revolution: Writings from the War of Independence*, edited by John Rhodehamel, 159–70. New York: Literary Classics of the United States, 2001.

Learned, M. D. "The Pennsylvania German Dialect." *The American Journal of Philology* 9.1 (1888) 64–83.

LeConte, John L. *List of the Coleoptera of North America*. Vol. 1. Washington, DC: Smithsonian Institution, 1866.

Lehmann, Hartmut. "Transatlantic Migration, Transatlantic Networks, Transatlantic Transfer: Concluding Remarks." In *In Search of Peace and Prosperity: New German Settlements in Eighteenth-Century Europe and America*, edited by Hartmut Lehmann, et al., 307–30. University Park, PA: Pennsylvania State University Press, 2000.

Lehmann, Helmut. "Henry Melchior Mühlenberg: A Bibliographic Essay." *Lutheran Quarterly* 1.34 (1987) 457–67.

———. "Pietism and Nationalism: The Relationship between Protestant Revivalism and National Renewal in Nineteenth-Century Germany." *Church History* 51.1 (1982) 39–53.

LeMay, J. A. Leo. *Soldier, Scientist, and Politician*. Vol. 3 of *The Life of Benjamin Franklin*. Philadelphia: University of Pennsylvania Press, 2009.

Levering, Joseph Mortimer. *A History of Bethlehem, Pennsylvania, 1741–1892*. Reprint, n.p.: Andesite, 2017.

Locke, John. *An Essay Concerning Human Understanding*. 1690. Reprint, University Park, PA: Penn State University Press, 1999. ftp://ftp.dca.fee.unicamp.br/pub/docs/ia005/humanund.pdf.

———. *Second Treatise of Government*. 1689. Reprint, Bowen Island, British Columbia: Jonathan Bennett, 2017. https://www.earlymoderntexts.com/assets/pdfs/locke1689a.pdf.

Lockhart, Paul. *The Drill Master of Valley Forge: The Baron de Steuben and the Making of the American Army*. New York: HarperCollins, 2008.

Longenecker, Stephen. *Piety and Tolerance*. Washington, DC: Scarecrow, 1994.

Luebke, Frederick C. "German Immigrants and American Politics: Problems of Leadership, Parties, and Issues." In *Germans in America, Retrospect and Prospect: Tricentennial Lectures Delivered at the German Society of Pennsylvania in 1983*, edited by Randall M. Miller, 57–74. Philadelphia: German Society of Pennsylvania, 1984.

Luther, Martin. "Temporal Authority: The Extent to Which it should Be Obeyed." In *Martin Luther's Basic Theological Writings*, edited by Timothy F. Lull, 655–703. Minneapolis, MN: Augsburg Fortress, 1989.

Mann, Barbara Alice. *George Washington's War on Native Americans*. Westport, CT: Praeger, 2005.

Marienstras, Elise. "Liberty." In *A Companion to the American Revolution*, edited by Jack P. Green and J. R. Pole, 627–32. Malden, MA: Blackwell, 2004.

———. "Nationality and Citizenship." In *A Companion to the American Revolution*, edited by Jack P. Green and J. R. Pole, 680–86. Malden, MA: Blackwell, 2004.

Marschke, Benjamin. *Absolutely Pietist: Patronage, Factionalism, and State-building in the Early Eighteenth-Century Prussian Army Chaplaincy*. Tübingen: Max Niemeyer, 2005.

———. "Lutheran Jesuits: Halle Pietist Communication Networks at the Court of Frederick William I of Prussia." *The Covenant Quarterly* 65.4 (2006) 19–38.

Marshall, Peter. "The West and the Amerindians." In *A Companion to the American Revolution*, edited by Jack P. Green and J. R. Pole, 157–64. Malden, MA: Blackwell, 2004.

Marshall, Robert J. "The Church Still Being Planted: A Survey History of Muhlenberg's Ministerium." In *Muhlenberg's Ministerium, Ben Franklin's Deism, and the Churches of the Twenty-First Century*, edited by John Reumann, 5–34. Grand Rapids: Eerdmans, 2011.

McDonnel, Forrest. *Alexander Hamilton, A Biography*. New York: W. W. Norton & Co., 1979.

McHenry, James. "Journal, June 18–July 23, 1778." In *The American Revolution: Writings from the War of Independence*, edited by John Rhodehamel, 459–69. New York: Literary Classics of the United States, 2001.

Melsheimer, Frederick Valentine. "Autobiography." Translated and typed manuscript. November 27, 1935. Hanover, PA. https://www.ancestry.com/mediaui-viewer/tree/14925746/person/184600570/media/119a4838-5c11-4037-bd8a-6df9dfc113b4.

———. "A Candid and Unbiased Account of the Reputation, Life, and Community of the Moravian Brethren [Freymuthig, und unparteische Untersuchung der Ehre, des Lebens, und der Gewohnheiten der Mohrischen Brüder!]." 1789. Moravian Archives, Bethlehem, PA.

———. *A Catalogue of Insects of Pennsylvania*. 1806. Reprint, n.p.: Nabu Public Domain, 2014.

———. "Correspondence, 1790: Payment of back salary, with creditor letter enclosed." Franklin College Records, Trustees, Archives, and Special Collections, Franklin and Marshall College, Lancaster, PA.

———. *Eine Controversia oder Disputations-Schreiben Zwischen einem Lutherischen Prediger und etlichen Handwerksleute welche die Lehre der Wiederbringung aller Dinge glauben*. Hanover: PA, Heinrich Willcocks, 1793.

———. *Gespräche zwischen einem Protestanten und Römischen, über eine Schmähschrift des römischen Priesters, Herrn Brosius; gegen die Protestanten überhaupt, und den Pfarrer Melsheimer besonders.* Hanover, PA: Lepper and Stettinius, 1797.

———. "Letter of Resignation." May 26, 1789. Franklin College Records, Trustees, Archives and Special Collections, Franklin and Marshall College, Lancaster, PA.

———. "Letters to John Ettwein." April 29, 1779; May 11, 1779; May 14, 1779; 1789. John Ettwein Papers, 400–405. Moravian Archives, Bethlehem, PA.

———. "Probe einer neuen Beschreibung von Pensylvanien." *Schleswigisches ehemals Braunschweigisches Journal* 3 (1792) 443–71. http://adw.sub.uni-goettingen.de/idrz/pages/sub/statisch/Bedienung.jsf.

———. "Scholars. 1788 Oct 17–1789 Jan 17." Archives and Special Collections, Franklin and Marshall College, Lancaster, PA.

———. *Journal of the Voyage of the Brunswick Auxiliaries from Wolfenbüttel to Quebec.* Montreal, Canada: Morning Chronicle, 1891. http://www.journalofvoyageooomelsuoft.pdf.

———. *Wahrheit der Christlichen Religion für Unstudirte.* 1811. Reprint, n.p.: Nabu Public Domain Reprints, 2014.

Melton, James Van Horn. *Religion, Community, and Slavery on the Colonial Southern Frontier.* New York: Cambridge University Press, 2015.

Miller, Randall M., and William Pencak. *Pennsylvania: A History of the Commonwealth.* University Park, PA: Pennsylvania State University Press, 2002.

Mills, Frederick V., Sr. "Bishops and other Ecclesiastical Issues, to 1776." In *A Companion to the American Revolution,* edited by Jack P. Green and J. R. Pole, 179–83. Malden, MA: Blackwell, 2004.

Minardi, Lisa. *Pastors and Patriots: The Muhlenberg Family of Pennsylvania.* Collegeville, PA: Philip and Muriel Berman Museum of Art, Ursinus College, 2011.

Morton, Robert. "Diary, September 16–December 14, 1777." In *The American Revolution: Writings from the War of Independence,* edited by John Rhodehamel, 359–82. New York: Literary Classics of the United States, 2001.

Moultrie, William. "Journal, April 2–May 12, 1779." In *The American Revolution: Writings from the War of Independence,* edited by John Rhodehamel, 559–74. New York: Literary Classics of the United States, 2001.

Mühlenberg, Heinrich Melchior. *The Journals of Henry Melchior Muhlenberg.* Translated and edited by Theodore G. Tappert and John W. Doberstein. 3 vols. Philadelphia: Muhlenberg, 1942–58.

———. *Notebook of a Colonial Clergyman: Condensed from the Journals of Henry Melchior Muhlenberg.* Edited and translated by Theodore G. Tappert and John W. Doberstein. 1959. Reprint, Minneapolis, MN: Fortress, 1998.

Mühlenberg, Heinrich Melchior, et al. *Die Korrespondenz Heinrich Melchior Mühlenbergs.* Edited by Kurt Aland. 5 Vols. Berlin: de Gruyter, 1986–2002.

Muhlenberg, Henry A. *The Life of Major-General Peter Muhlenberg.* Philadelphia: Carey and Hart, 1849. Reprint: Forgotten Books, 2012.

Muhlenberg, John Peter, et al. "The Address of the State Committee of Republicans." Philadelphia: William Duane, 1802.

———. "Diary of a Journey Over the Alleghenies to the Ohio River." 1784. Gilder Lehrman Institute of American History. https://www.gilderlehrman.org/content/diary-journey-over-alleghenies-ohio-river.

———. "Minutes of the Meeting at the Home of Richard Campbell, Woodstock." January 10, 1775. MSS.3D9Z17.a1. Virginia Historical Society, Richmond, VA.

Müller-Bahlke, Thomas. "Communication at Risk: The Beginnings of the Halle Correspondence with the Pennsylvania Lutherans." In *In Search of Peace and Prosperity: New German Settlements in Eighteenth-Century Europe and America*, edited by Hartmut Lehmann, et al., 139–55. University Park, PA: Pennsylvania State University Press, 2000.

———. *Kirche zwischen zwei Welten: Die Obrigkeitsproblematik bei Heinrich Melchior Mühlenberg und die Kirchengründung der deutschen Lutheraner in Pennsylvania.* Stuttgart: Franz Steiner Verlag, 1994.

Mundhenke, Herbert, ed. *Die Matrikel der Universität Helmstedt.* Vol. 3. Hildesheim, Germany: August Lax, 1979.

Murphy, Andrew R. *William Penn, A Life.* Oxford: Oxford University Press, 2019.

Murray, John. "The Indian Expedition: Official report of Affairs in Virginia." Letter to Lord Dartmouth, Williamsburg, December 24, 1774. West Virginia Archives and History. http://www.wvculture.org/history/dunmore/dunmore.html.

Niemeyer, August Hermann. *Leben und Charakter des Gottlieb Anastasius Freylinghausens.* 1786. Reprint, n.p.: Nabu Public Domain Reprints.

Noll, Mark. "American Lutherans Yesterday and Today." In *Lutherans Today: American Lutheran Identity in the Twenty-First Century*, edited by Richard Cimino, 3–25. Grand Rapids: Eerdmans, 2003.

Nussbaum, Stanley. *Reader's Guide to Transforming Mission.* Maryknoll, NY: Orbis, 2005.

Nygren, Anders. "Luther's Doctrine of the Two Kingdoms." *The Ecumenical Review* 1.3 (1949) 301–10.

Oliver, Peter. "A Tory View of Frontier Warfare." In *The American Revolution: Writings from the War of Independence*, edited by John Rhodehamel, 487–89. New York: Literary Classics of the United States, 2001.

Olmstead, Earl P. *Blackcoats Among the Delaware: David Zeisberger on the Ohio Frontier.* Kent, OH: Kent State University Press, 1991.

O'Neill, Lindsay. *The Opened Letter: Networking in the Early Modern British World.* Philadelphia: University of Pennsylvania Press, 2015.

O'Toole, Fintan. *White Savage: William Johnson and the Invention of America.* Albany, NY: State University of New York Press, 2005.

Otterness, Philip. *Becoming German: The 1709 Palatine Migration to New York.* Ithaca, NY: Cornell University Press, 2004.

———. "The Palatine Immigrants of 1710 and the Native Americans." In *A Peculiar Mixture: German-Language Cultures and Identities in Eighteenth Century North America*, edited by Jan Stieverman and Oliver Scheiding, 58–82. University Park, PA: Pennsylvania State University Press, 2013.

Paine, Thomas. *The Age of Reason.* Vol. 2. Paris: Barrois, 1795.

———. "The American Crisis, Number I, December 19, 1776." In *The American Revolution: Writings from the War of Independence*, edited by John Rhodehamel, New York: Literary Classics of the United States, 2001.

———. *Common Sense, Rights of Man, and other Essential Writings.* New York: Signet Classics, 2003.

Pasche, William. "Brief von Kensington an Herrn Inspector Fabricius zu Halle, 15ten Juni 17(79)." June 15, 1779. M4C19:11, 35. Franckesche Stiftungen, Halle an der Saale, Germany.

Paulson, Steven D. *Lutheran Theology*. New York: T&T Clark, 2011.

Peterson, Harold L. *The Book of the Continental Soldier*. Harrisburg, PA: Stackpole Co., 1968.

Phillips, Kevin. *The Cousins' Wars: Religion, Politics, and the Triumph of Anglo-America*. New York: Basic, 1999.

Popp, Stephan. *A Hessian Soldier in the American Revolution*. Translated and edited by Reinhart J. Pope. n.p., 1953.

Post, Christian Frederick, and John Hays. *Journey on the Forbidden Path: Chronicles of a Diplomatic Mission to the Allegheny Country*. Edited by Robert S. Grumet. Philadelphia: American Philosophical Society, 1999.

Purvis, Thomas L. "The Seven Years' War and its Political Legacy." In *A Companion to the American Revolution*, edited by Jack P. Green and J. R. Pole, 112–117. Malden, MA: Blackwell, 2004.

Qualben, Lars P. *The Lutheran Church in Colonial America*. New York: Thomas Nelson and Sons, 1940.

Ratcliffe, Donald. "The Right to Vote and the Rise of Democracy, 1787–1828." *Journal of the Early Republic* 33.2 (2013) 219–54.

Reed, T.J. "Talking to Tyrants: Dialogues with Power in Eighteenth-Century Germany." *The Historical Journal* 33.1 (1990) 63–79.

Reumann, John. "Muhlenberg's Ministerium and the Churches of Today and Tomorrow, in the Setting of the Deism of the Founding Fathers, Especially Benjamin Franklin." In *Muhlenberg's Ministerium, Ben Franklin's Deism, and the Churches of the Twenty-First Century*, edited by John Reumann, 217–227. Grand Rapids: Eerdmans, 2011.

Richards, Henry Melchior Muhlenberg. *The Pennsylvania-German in the Revolutionary War*. Philadelphia: Pennsylvania-German Society, 1908.

Riedesel, Friederike Charlotte. *Letters and Journals Relating to the War of the American Revolution and the Capture of the German Troops at Saratoga*. Translated by William L. Stone. 1867. Reprint, n.p.: Kessinger, 2012.

Riedesel, Friedrich Adolf. *Memoirs, Letters, and Journals of Major General Riedesel During His Residence in America*. 2. vols. Edited by Max von Eelking. Translated by William Leete Stone. 1868. Reprint, n.p.: Forgotten Books, 2012.

Rightmyer, Thomas Nelson. "The Holy Orders of Peter Muhlenberg." *Historical Magazine of the Protestant Episcopal Church* 30 (1961) 183–97.

Rodney, Thomas. "Diary, December 18–25, 1776." In *The American Revolution: Writings from the War of Independence*, edited by John Rhodehamel, 247–53. New York: Literary Classics of the United States, 2001.

———. "Diary, January 2–4, 1777." In *The American Revolution: Writings from the War of Independence*, edited by John Rhodehamel, 257–63. New York: Literary Classics of the United States, 2001.

Roeber, A. Gregg. *Palatines, Liberty, and Property: German Lutherans in Colonial British America*. Baltimore, MD: John Hopkins University Press, 1993.

———. "The Problem of the Eighteenth Century in Transatlantic Religious History." In *In Search of Peace and Prosperity: New German Settlements in Eighteenth-Century*

*Europe and America*, edited by Hartmut Lehmann, et al., 115–38. University Park, PA: Pennsylvania State University Press, 2000.

Rohrbough, Faith E. "The Political Maturation of Henry Melchior Mühlenberg." In *Henry Melchior Mühlenberg: The Roots of 250 Years of Organized Lutheranism in North America*, edited by John W. Kleiner, 35–52. Lewiston, NY: Edwin Mellen, 1998.

Rosengarten, Joseph G. "American History from German Archives." *Proceedings of the American Philosophical Society* 39.162 (1900) 129–54.

———. "A Defense of the Hessians." *The Pennsylvania Magazine of History and Biography* 23.2 (1899) 157–83.

Rousseau, Jean-Jacques. "Discourse on the Origin of Inequality." In *The Basic Political Writings*, edited and translated by Donald A. Cress, 25–109. Indianapolis, IN: Hackett, 1988.

Scaer, David P. "The Concept of *Anfechtungen* in Luther's Thought." *Concordia Theological Quarterly* 47.1 (1983) 15–30. http://www.ctsfw.net/media/pdfs/scaeranfechtung.pdf downloaded 11/10/2014.

Schicketanz, Peter. *Der Pietismus von 1675 bis 1800*. Leipzig, Germany: Evangelische Verlagsanstalt, 2001.

Schierenbeck, J. H. C. *Lebens-Beschreibungen, oder, Nachrichten von dem Leben und den Schriften aller evangelisch-lutherischen Prediger, welche seit Dr. Heinrich Melchior Mühlenberg's Zeit im Staate Pennsylvanien Gemeinded bedient haben*. Selingsgrove, PA: Kirchenbeten, 1863.

Schlesinger, Arthur M., Sr. "New Viewpoints in American History Revisited." *The New England Quarterly* 61.4 (1988) 483–501.

Schmucker, George W. "Letters of General Daniel Morgan and Peter Muhlenberg." *Pennsylvania Magazine of History and Biography* 21.4 (1897) 488–92.

Schmucker, Samuel Simon. *The American Lutheran Church*. 5th ed. 1852. Reprint, Lexington, KY: Bibliolife, 2014.

Scholz, Robert F. "The Confessional Stance of Henry Melchior Mühlenberg and the Early Pennsylvania Ministerium." *Lutheran Quarterly* 1.4 (1987) 439–557.

———. "Personal Experience in the Muhlenberg Tradition." In *Muhlenberg's Ministerium, Ben Franklin's Deism, and the Churches of the Twenty-First Century*, edited by John Reumann, 53–59. Grand Rapids: Eerdmans, 2011.

Schroder, Walter K. *The Hessian Occupation of Newport and Rhode Island, 1776–1779*. Westminster, MD: Heritage, 2009.

Schutt, Amy C. "Female Relationships and Intercultural Bonds in Moravian Indian Missions." In *Friends and Enemies in Penn's Woods*, edited by William A. Pencak and Daniel K. Richter, 87–103. University Park, PA: Pennsylvania State Press, 2004.

Schwarz, E. A. "Some Notes on Melsheimer's Catalogue of the Coleoptera of Pennsylvania." *Entomological Society of Washington*. n.p. 134–39.

Schweitzer, Mary M. "The Economic and Demographic Consequences of the American Revolution." *A Companion to the American Revolution*, edited by Jack P. Green and J. R. Pole, 559–78. Malden, MA: Blackwell, 2004.

Seidel, Nathaniel. "Supplement for the Month of May 1782 to the Diary from Bethlehem containing the Personalia of our dear venerable Brother Nathanael Seidel." May 1782. Introduced, transcribed, and translated by Katherine Carté Engel.

Bethlehem Digital History Project. February 9, 2006. http://bdhp.moravian.edu/personal_papers/memoirs/seidel/seidel.pdf.

Serle, Ambrose. "Journal, March 9–June 19, 1778." In *The American Revolution: Writings from the War of Independence*, edited by John Rhodehamel, 416–43. New York: Literary Classics of the United States, 2001.

Shalhope, Robert E. "Republicanism." In *A Companion to the American Revolution*, edited by Jack P. Green and J. R. Pole, 668–73. Malden, MA: Blackwell, 2004.

Shaw, Samuel. "Samuel Shaw to Francis and Sarah Shaw, June 28, 1779." In *The American Revolution: Writings from the War of Independence*, edited by John Rhodehamel, 528–29. New York: Literary Classics of the United States, 2001.

———. "Samuel Shaw to Francis Shaw, September 30, October 3, 13, and 15, 1777." In *The American Revolution: Writings from the War of Independence*, edited by John Rhodehamel, 353–58. New York: Literary Classics of the United States, 2001.

Shenandoah County Library. "Emmanuel Episcopal Church." http://shenandoahstories.org/items/show/54.

Shy, John. *A People Numerous and Armed: Reflections on the Military Struggle for Independence*. Ann Arbor, MI: University of Michigan Press, 1990.

Smaby, Beverly Prior. *The Transformation of Moravian Bethlehem: From Communal Mission to Family Economy*. Philadelphia: University of Pennsylvania Press, 1988.

Smith, Adam. *The Wealth of Nations*. 1937. Reprint, New York: Random House, 1965.

Smylie, James H. "Protestant Clergymen and American Destiny: I. Promise and Judgment, 1781–1800." *The Harvard Theological Review* 56.3 (1963) 217–31.

Spaeth, Adolph, et al., ed. *Documentary History of the Evangelical Lutheran Ministerium of Pennsylvania, Proceedings of the Annual Conventions from 1748 to 1821*. Translated by A. Spaeth, et al. Philadelphia: General Council of the Evangelical Lutheran Church in North America, 1898.

Spangenberg, August Gottlieb. *The Life of Nicholas Lewis Count Zinzendorf*. Translated by Samuel Jackson. London, UK: Samuel Holdsworth, 1838.

Speck, W. A. "The Structure of British Politics in the Mid-Eighteenth Century." *A Companion to the American Revolution*, edited by Jack P. Green and J. R. Pole, 3–7. Malden, MA: Blackwell, 2004.

Spener, Philip Jacob. *Pia Desideria*. Translated by Theodore G. Tappert. Philadelphia: Fortress, 1964.

Splitter, Wolfgang. "*Divide et Impera*: Some Critical Remarks on Halle Missionaries' Formation of a Lutheran Church in Pennsylvania." In *Halle Pietism, Colonial North America, and the Young United States*, edited by Hans-Jürgen Grabbe, 45–92. Stuttgart: Franz Steiner Verlag, 2008.

———. "The Germans in Pennsylvania Politics: A Quantitative Analysis." *The Pennsylvania Magazine of History and Biography* 122.1/2 (1998) 39–76.

———. "The 'Unknown' Henry Melchior Mühlenberg." *Lutheran Quarterly* 21 (2007) 78–94.

Spycker, Peter. "Letter to the Governor of Pennsylvania, 1757." Conrad Weiser Papers, Historical Society of Pennsylvania, Philadelphia, PA.

Starna, William A. "The Diplomatic Career of Canasatego." In *Friends and Enemies in Penn's Woods*, edited by William A. Pencak and Daniel K. Richter, 144–66. University Park, PA: Penn State University Press, 2004.

Stein, K. James. *Philipp Jakob Spener: Pietist Patriarch*. Chicago, IL: Covenant, 1986.

Stein, Stephen J. "Some Thoughts on Pietism in American Religious History." In *Pietism in Germany and North America 1680–1820*, edited by Jonathan Strom, et al., 23–32. Farnham, England: Ashgate, 2008.

Stephenson, Michael. *Patriot Battles: How the War of Independence was Fought*. New York: HarperCollins, 2007.

Stieverman, Jan. "Defining the Limits of American Liberty: Pennsylvania's German Peace Churches During the Revolution." In *A Peculiar Mixture: German-Language Cultures and Identities in Eighteenth Century North America*, edited by Jan Stieverman and Oliver Scheiding, 207–45. University Park, PA: Pennsylvania State University Press, 2013.

Stott, John. *Basic Christianity*. Grand Rapids: Eerdmans, 1959.

Strobel, P. A. *The Salzburgers and Their Descendants*. Athens, GA: University of Georgia Press, 1953.

Stump, Adam, and Henry Anstadt, eds. *The History of the Evangelical Lutheran Synod of West Pennsylvania 1825–1925*. Chambersburg, PA: J. R. Kerr and Bro., 1925.

Tappert, Theodore G. "Henry Melchior Mühlenberg and the American Revolution." *Church History* 11.4 (1942) 284–301.

Thompson, Parker C. *The United States Army Chaplaincy, Vol. 1: From its European Antecedents to 1791*. Washington, DC: Department of the Army, 1978.

Thwaites, Reuben Gold, and Louise Phelps Kellogg, eds. *Documentary History of Dunmore's War*. Madison, WI: Wisconsin Historical Society, 1905.

Tice, Terrence. *Abingdon Pillars of Theology: Schleiermacher*. Nashville, TN: Abingdon, 2006.

Triebner, Christopher Frederick. *Cursory and Introductory Thoughts on Richard Brothers's Prophecies*. 1795. Reprint, n.p.: Gale ECCO, 2014.

———. *An Essay to Lay Open the Gospel in its Original Purity*. 1788. Reprint, n.p.: Gale ECCO, 2014.

———. *A Key to the French Revolution, or, an Account of Modern Jesuitism, to which is added, an Essay to Reduce the Principles of Unity, Indivisibility, Liberty, Equality, Social Guarantee, and Resistance of Oppression*. 1794. Reprint, n.p.: Gale ECCO, 2014.

———. "Letter to the Governor of Georgia, February 1781." Digital Library of Georgia, Hagrett Library, University of Georgia, Athens, GA. https://dlg.galileo.usg.edu/hargrett/1170/pdfs/hargl170-038e-016.pdf.

Trump, John P. "A Twisted Cord: A Drama Involving Muhlenberg and Johann Caspar Stoever, Jr." In *Muhlenberg's Ministerium, Ben Franklin's Deism, and the Churches of the Twenty-First Century*, edited by John Reumann, 158–79. Grand Rapids: Eerdmans, 2011.

Tully, Alan. "The Political Development of the Colonies After the Glorious Revolution." In *A Companion to the American Revolution*, edited by Jack P. Green and J. R. Pole, 29–38. Malden, MA: Blackwell, 2004.

Turdo, Mark A. "A Different Kind of Indian Conversion Account: The Financial Record of Abraham in Gnadenhütten." In *The Distinctiveness of Moravian Culture*, edited by Craig D. Atwood and Peter Vogt, 141–53. Nazareth, PA: Moravian Historical Society, 2003.

Veltmann, Claus, ed. *Freiheit, Fortschritt und Verheißung: Blickwechsel zwischen Europa und Nordamerika seit der fruhen Neuzeit*. Halle, Germany: Franckeschen Stiftungen, 2011.

Vethanayagamony, Peter. *It Begun in Madras: The Eighteenth Century Lutheran-Anglican Ecumenical Ventures in Mission and Benjamine Schultze*. Dehli, India: ISPCK, 2010.
Volo, Dorothy Deneen, and James M. Volo. *Daily Life During the American Revolution*. Westport, CT: Greenwood, 2003.
Waldeck, Philipp. *Eighteenth-Century America: A Hessian Report on the People, the Land, the War as Noted in the Diary of Chaplain Philipp Waldeck*. Edited and translated by Bruce E Burgoyne. Westminster, MD: Heritage, 2008.
Walker, Mack. "The Salzburger Migration to Prussia: Causes and Choices." In *In Search of Peace and Prosperity: New German Settlements in Eighteenth-Century Europe and America*, edited by Hartmut Lehmann, et al., 69–76. University Park, PA: Pennsylvania State University Press, 2000.
Walker, Williston. *Great Men of the Christian Church*. Freeport, NY: Books for Libraries, 1968.
Wallace, Paul A. W. *Conrad Weiser, 1696–1760: Friend of Colonist & Mohawk*. Philadelphia: Wennawoods, 1945, 1996.
———. *The Muhlenbergs of Pennsylvania*. Philadelphia: University of Pennsylvania Press.
Walton, Joseph Solomon. *Conrad Weiser and the Indian Policy of Colonial Pennsylvania*. Philadelphia: George W. Jacobs & Co., 1900.
Walz, John A. "The American Revolution and German Literature." *Modern Language Notes* 16.8 (1901) 225–31.
Ward, Harry M. *Between the Lines: Banditti of the American Revolution*. Westport, CT: Greenwood, 2002.
Washington, George. "General Orders, December 17, 1777." In *The American Revolution: Writings from the War of Independence*, edited by John Rhodehamel, 398–99. New York: Literary Classics of the United States, 2001.
———. "To Robert Dinwiddie, May 29, 1754." In *Writings*, edited by John H. Rhodehamel, 40–46. New York: Library of America, 1997.
———. *Writings*. Edited by John H. Rhodehamel. New York: Library of America, 1997.
Wasmus, Julius. *An Eye-Witness Account of the American Revolution and New England Life: The Journal of J. F. Wasmus, German Company Surgeon, 1776–1783*. Edited by Mary C. Lynn. Translated by Helga Doblin. Westport, CT: Greenwood, 1990.
Weigley, Russel F., et al. *Philadelphia: A 300-Year History*. New York: Norton and Co., 1982.
Weiser, Conrad. "Letter to Richard Peters, 1746." Conrad Weiser Papers, Historical Society of Pennsylvania, Philadelphia, PA.
———. "Letter to William Johnson, 1751." Conrad Weiser Papers, Historical Society of Pennsylvania, Philadelphia, PA.
———. "On Serious Advice to the German People." 1741. No. 7633. Conrad Weiser Papers, Historical Society of Pennsylvania, Philadelphia, PA.
———. "Receipt of Purchase." 1756. Conrad Weiser Papers, Historical Society of Pennsylvania, Philadelphia, PA.
Weiser, Frederick C. *The Lutheran Church in New Holland, Pennsylvania, 1730–1980*. New Holland, PA: Trinity Lutheran Congregation, 1980.
———. *The Lutheran Church on the Conewago at Hanovertown: A History of St. Matthew Evangelical Lutheran Church, Hanover, Pennsylvania, 1735–1810*. York, PA: York Graphics, 1993.

Wellenreuther, Hermann. "Contexts for Migration in the Early Modern World: Public Policy, European Migrating Experiences, Transatlantic Migration, and the Genesis of American Culture." In *In Search of Peace and Prosperity: New German Settlements in Eighteenth-Century Europe and America*, edited by Hartmut Lehmann, et al., 3-35. University Park, PA: Pennsylvania State University Press, 2000.

———. *Heinrich Melchior Mühlenberg und die deutschen Lutheraner in Nordamerika: Wissentransfer und Wandel eines atlantischen zu einem amerikanischen Netzwerk*. Berlin, Germany: LIT Verlag, 2013.

———. "Recent Research on Migration." In *In Search of Peace and Prosperity: New German Settlements in Eighteenth-Century Europe and America*, edited by Hartmut Lehmann, et al., 265-306. University Park, PA: Pennsylvania State University Press, 2000.

Wentz, A. R. *Basic History of Lutheranism in America*. Rev. ed. Philadelphia: Fortress, 1964.

Wessel, Carola. "'We Do Not Want to Introduce Anything New': Transplanting the Communal Life from Herrnhut to the Upper Ohio Valley." In *In Search of Peace and Prosperity: New German Settlements in Eighteenth-Century Europe and America*, edited by Hartmut Lehmann, et al., 246-62. University Park, PA: Pennsylvania State University Press, 2000.

Williamson, Lanie. "Marquis de Lafayette Healed his Wounds in Bethlehem." *The Morning Call*, September 13, 2007. http://articles.mcall.com/2007-09-13/opinion/3771279_1_single-sisters-house-marquis-lafayette.

Wilson, Benjamin. "Letter to Peter Muhlenberg." January 23, 1776. MSS.3D921.7a 2-6. Virginia Historical Society, Virginia Historical Society, Richmond, VA.

Wilson, David K. *The Southern Strategy: Britain's Conquest of South Carolina and Georgia, 1775-1780*. Columbia, SC: University of South Carolina Press, 2005.

Wilson, Jonathan M. "Am I a Deserter? A Lutheran Pastor's 'Catch-22' from the Revolutionary War." In *Subject to None, Servant of All: Essays in Christian Scholarship in Honor of Kurt Karl Hendel*, edited by Peter Vethanayagamony and Kenneth Sawyer, 139-51. Minneapolis, MN: Lutheran University Press, 2016.

———. "Civil Unrest and the Pastoral Vocation: Halle's Encyclical of 1776 to the Pennsylvania Ministerium." *Journal of the Lutheran Historical Conference* 6 (2016) 7-17.

———. "Keeping the Synod German. How a Hessian Chaplain Steered the Pennsylvania Ministerium." *Journal of the Lutheran Historical Conference* 5 (2015) 108-26.

———. "The Moravian Pietist Martyrs of the American Revolution." *The Covenant Quarterly*. Forthcoming.

———. "The Pietist Chaplains of the American Revolution." *The Covenant Quarterly* 76.1-2 (2018) 3-23.

———. "Switching Sides: A Hessian Chaplain in the Pennsylvania Ministerium." PhD diss., Lutheran School of Theology at Chicago, 2015.

Wilson, Renate. "Halle and Ebenezer: Pietism, Agriculture, and Commerce in Colonial Georgia." PhD diss., University of Maryland, 1988.

———. "Land, Population, and Labor: Lutheran Immigrants in Colonial Georgia." In *In Search of Peace and Prosperity: New German Settlements in Eighteenth-Century Europe and America*, edited by Hartmut Lehmann, et al., 217-45. University Park, PA: Pennsylvania State University Press, 2000.

Wister, Sarah. "Journal, October 19–December 12, 1777." *The American Revolution: Writings from the War of Independence,* edited by John Rhodehamel, 383–97. New York: Literary Classics of the United States, 2001.

Withuhn, William L. "Salzburgers and Slavery, A Problem of Mentalite." *Georgia Historical Quarterly* 68.2 (1984) 173–92.

Wokeck, Marianne S. "German Settlements in the British North American Colonies: A Patchwork of Cultural Assimilation and Persistence." In *In Search of Peace and Prosperity: New German Settlements in Eighteenth-Century Europe and America,* edited by Hartmut Lehmann, et al., 191–216. University Park, PA: Pennsylvania State University Press, 2000.

*Wolfenbütteler Digitale Bibliothek.* Wolfenbüttel, Germany: Herzog August Bibliothek. http://www.hab.de/en/home.html.

Wood, W. J. *Battles of the Revolutionary War.* Chapel Hill, NC: Algonquin, 1990.

Woodford, William. "William Woodford to Edmund Pendleton, December 5, 1775." In *The American Revolution: Writings from the War of Independence,* edited by John Rhodehamel, 87–90. New York: Literary Classics of the United States, 2001.

Zall, Paul M. *Franklin on Franklin.* Lexington, KY: University Press of Kentucky, 2000.

Zeisberger, David. *The Moravian Mission Diaries of David Zeisberger, 1772–1781.* Edited by Hermann Wellenreuther and Carola Wessel. Translated by Julie Tomberlin Weber. University Park, PA: Penn State University Press, 2005.

Zinzendorf, Nikolaus Ludwig von. *Christian Life and Witness: Count Zinzendorf's 1738 Berlin Speeches.* Edited and translated by Gary S. Kinkel. Eugene, OR: Pickwick, 2010.

———. *Nine Public Lectures.* Edited and translated by George W. Forrell. Eugene, OR: Wipf and Stock, 1998.

# Index of Names and Locations

Abercrombie, John, 81
Adams, John, 30, 35, 135, 218, 287
Albany, NY, 71, 73–75, 106, 156, 201
   royalist campaign toward
      108n79, 153, 153n58, 156,
      201, 222
   Albany Purchase 73–77, 82
Allen, Chaplain Thomas, 140, 154,
      159, 160
Amherst, Jeffrey 21, 22, 27, 93, 233
André, John, 205
Anhalt-Zerbst (Germany), 144, 172,
      276n98
Anne, Queen of United Kingdom,
      53, 190, 252
Ansbach-Bayreuth (Germany), 164,
      168, 172, 210, 276, 279
Arnold, Benedict, 150, 156, 162,
      204–6, 219
Augsburg (Germany), 252–53,
      267–68

Baltimore, Lord *see* Calvert, Cecil
Bauer, Karl, 168n142, 276n100
Beissel, Conrad, 64–66, 97, 134,
      256, 258
Bengel, J. Albrecht, 4n5
Bennington, Battle of, 140–41,
      146n32, 151, 157–60,
      160n97, 162, 163, 184
Berlin (Germany), 116
Bethlehem, PA, 11, 115, 133–38,
      139, 161, 165, 166, 172, 174,
      201, 283, 286
Böhme, Jakob, 119

Boltzius, F. Michael, 119, 188, 189,
      248, 249, 254–64, 267, 273,
      278
Bonnie Prince Charlie *see* Stuart,
   Charles
Boston, MA, 38, 40, 46, 62, 153,
      161–63, 167, 193
   Tea Party, 193
   Intolerable Acts, 12, 28, 193, 269
Braddock, Edward, 76, 77, 81, 92,
      128, 229
Brandywine, Battle of, 52, 103, 134,
      181–184, 199–202, 210
Braunsdorff, Johannes S., 144,
      146n29, 172, 275, 276n98
Braunschweig, Lüneburg–Hanover
   (Germany), 87, 179
Braunschweig-Wolfenbüttel
   (Germany), 10, 15n23,
      108n79, 140, 143–50, 163–
      67, 172, 178, 204n77
Brimfield, MA, 12, 161, 163, 166–
      68, 172, 280
Burgoyne, John, 41, 43, 106, 116,
      140, 150–58, 162, 164, 181,
      201–4, 222, 285
Burke, Edmund, 43

Calvert, Cecil (Lord Baltimore), 29
Campbell, Archibald, 246–7, 270–71
Campbell, John, 71
Canada, 13, 18, 106, 137–38, 142,
      146–49, 153, 156, 162,
      168, 222, 227–28, 236, 244,
      275–76, 282

305

Captain Pipe, 232–39
Carleton, Guy, 148–53
Carlisle, PA, 12, 29, 72–73, 76, 82, 128
Canasetoga, 22, 59–60, 69, 71, 81, 224
Champlain, Lake 150, 152–53
  Battle of, 150
Charles I, King of Scotland and England, 44
Charles II, King of Scotland and England, 32
Charleston, SC, 38, 88, 265–66, 272
  First Battle of, 197
  Second Battle of, 198, 210, 272
Clinton, George, 63, 71
Clinton, Henry, 43, 113, 164, 197, 203, 207, 246
Concord, Battle of, *see* Lexington and Concord, Battle of
Cornwallis, Charles, 199, 205–7, 210, 237, 274
Cowpens, Battle of, 206
Croghan, George, 25, 25n14, 63, 70
Cromwell, Oliver, 31, 42, 44

De Kalb, Johannes, 8, 135
Delaware River, 32, 57–58, 185
Detroit, Fort, 222, 232, 235, 237–38, 240
Dorchester, Lord *see* Carleton, Sir Guy
Dunlap, James, 12–13, 114, 279
Dunmore, Earl of *see* Murray, John
Duquesne, Fort, 20, 73, 76, 82, 128

Easton, PA, 59, 75, 81–84, 171, 201
  Treaty of, 74, 229
Ebenezer, New Ebenezer, GA, 18, 39, 88, 101, 111, 119, 185, 189, 205, 246–50, 254–82
Ephrata, PA, 64–66, 97, 134, 256, 258
d'Estaing, Charles H., 272
Ettwein, Johann, 6, 16n28, 17, 115, 115n1, 116n2, 131–39, 151, 165n124, 166, 169, 169–70n146, 170–76, 280, 282, 284
Ettwein, Johanetta, 133

Fallen Timbers, Battle of, 218
Florida, 246, 250, 274–76
Francke, August H., 4,5. 14. 16n30, 87, 107, 116, 252
Francke, Gotthilf A., 70, 87–88, 107, 184–85, 261
Franklin, Benjamin, 1, 6, 34–35, 64, 72–74, 78, 113, 130, 130n41–42, 132n42
  and German voters, 72, 97–98, 113, 215–16
  and Native Nations, 73, 78, 129, 242–43
  and Pennsylvania Politics, 52, 73, 78, 94–96, 99, 129
  and Pennsylvania statehood, 188, 213
Franklin College, 216
Franklin, William, 1, 113
Frederick II "The Great," King of Prussia (Germany), 12, 92, 107
Freylinghausen, Gottlieb A. 6, 7n7, 101, 107–13, 171, 175, 275, 282
Friedenshütten, Delaware Nation, (Pennsylvania), 229–30, 232

Gage, Thomas, 22, 27, 76, 233
Gates, Horatio, 135, 162, 204–5, 219
Gekelemükpechünk, Delaware Nation (Ohio), 230, 232
Gelemind (John Killbuck), 221, 232, 234, 235, 237, 245
George I, King of United Kingdom, 42, 110
George II, King of United Kingdom, 9, 20, 61, 62, 67, 68, 70, 72, 86, 110, 227, 229
George III, King of United Kingdom, 13, 31, 34, 42, 43, 101, 110, 112, 168, 195, 243
George, Fort, 70

Georgia, 6, 20, 30, 37, 88, 100–101, 107, 111, 119, 185, 195, 198, 228, 248–60, 262, 263, 266, 278
  and transition to slavery, 188, 189, 250, 259–60
  in the War of Independence, 6, 12, 18, 39, 197, 205, 207n88, 246–47, 269–75, 281
Germaine, George, 150, 153
Germantown, Battle of, 134, 182, 182n3, 200–201
von Gersdorff, Henrietta, 87, 87n6, 119
Glaucha *see* Halle an der Saale
Gnadennhütten, Delaware Nation (Ohio), 222, 230, 234–44
Gnadenhütten, Wyoming River Reservation (Pennsylvania), 77, 92, 128, 227, 229
Goshachgünk, Delaware Nation (Ohio), 234
Göttingen, University of (Germany), 87
Greene, Nathaniel, 33, 199, 204–6, 219
Grimm (also Grim), David, 105–6, 106n70, 109–13, 172, 281, 282
Gronau, Israel Christian, 249, 250, 261
Gross Aspach (Germany), 52–53
Grosshenersdorff (Germany), 87, 87n6, 116, 119

Handschuh, Johann Friedrich, 100, 262n46
Halle an der Saale (Germany), x, 3–7, 11–17, 35, 63, 67, 70, 82, 86–92, 98–104, 107–9, 116–19, 175, 178, 182–86, 190, 192, 205, 248, 250, 254–63, 267, 268, 273–74, 277–82
Hamburg (Germany), 178
Hamilton, Alexander, 208–12, 218–19
Hancock, John, 135

Hanover, PA, 176
Hanover (Germany), 87, 110
Hanoverian Dynasty, 27, 41, 42, 44, 45, 110, 190, 191 *see* George I, George II, George III
Hartwick, Johann, 69, 167–68, 170
Helmstet, University of, 143–44
Helmuth, Heinrich, 101–2, 107–8, 174, 176, 177, 180, 185, 186, 217, 262, 282
Hesse-Hanau (Germany), 157, 159
Hesse-Kassel (Germany), also Hessen-Kassel, Hesse Cassel, 144, 167, 275
Hobbes, Thomas, 23–25
Holland, 44, 216
Holy Roman Empire (Germany), 47, 49, 86, 147n33, 281
Howe, Richard, 43
Howe, William, 1–2, 13, 34, 38, 41, 43, 45, 85, 108, 113, 150, 153, 156, 164, 181–82, 200, 203, 279
Hudson River, 152–53, 156, 201
Hunter, Robert, 54–55
Hutcheson, Francis, 23, 27

Illinois Country, 25n14
India, 108
Ireland, 29, 32, 40, 53 *see* Ulster County (Ireland)

James River, 204
Jamestown, VA, 254
Jefferson, Thomas, 32, 35, 39, 44, 42, 194, 204–6, 206n84, 211, 214–15, 218
John Killbuck *see* Gelemind
Johnson, William, 21, 25, 25n14, 26–28, 63, 70, 70n61, 71, 74, 230, 233

Karl, Duke of Braunschweig-Wolfenbüttel, 146, 149
Killbuck, John *see* Gelemind
Knapp, Johann Georg, 261

Kunze, J. Christian, 85, 100, 101, 107–9, 168, 175, 185, 186, 263, 266, 279–82
Kunze, Margaret "Peggy" nee Mühlenberg, 85, 101, 103, 168, 176, 266, 279, 281
Kurz, J. Daniel, 177
Kurz, J. Nicholas, 82, 177

Lafayette, Gilbert du Motier, Marquis de, 134–35, 135n48, 161, 206, 208, 211–12, 219, 280
Lancaster, PA, 11, 29, 48, 89, 91, 107, 137, 161, 174–77, 179–81, 201, 215, 217, 237, 263, 279
and Paxton Boys, 93–94
Lancaster County, PA, 97, 187
Lebanon, PA, 90n15, 175, 177–79, 282
Lee, Charles, 197
Lee, Richard Henry, 135
Lemke, Johanna, 267–68, 273
Lemke, Timotheus, 268
Lemke, Wilhelm Hermann, 248, 258, 260 261, 267
Lexington and Concord, Battle of, 193, 269
Lincoln, Benjamin, 204, 205, 208, 210, 271–72
Livingston Manor, NY, 41, 53–55, 61, 69, 77, 95, 146, 255, 258
Livingston, Robert, 56
Locke, John, 23–25
Loudon, Fourth Earl of see Campbell, John
Luther, Martin, 104, 104n62, 117, 253

Madison, James, 32
Mason, George, 47
Mau, Maria Agnes, 172–74
Mau, Samuel, 125, 126, 151, 172, 173
McCrae, Jane, 155, 155n69

Melsheimer, Friedrich, 6, 7, 12, 140–80, 216–17, 276–77, 280, 282, 286
Mohawk Valley, Mohawk Nation (New York), 55, 56, 106, 156, 235
Monmouth, Battle of, 202, 203
Montreal, QC, 41, 46, 148, 149, 150, 152, 154, 222
Morgan, Daniel, 206
Mühlenberg, Anna nee Meyer (Hanna), 187–90, 203, 219
Mühlenberg, Anna Maria nee Weiser, 67, 90, 99–104, 183, 190, 266
Mühlenberg, Charles Frederick, 187–88, 203
Mühlenberg, Friedrich A. C., 13, 178, 218
Mühlenberg, Enoch Samuel, 99
Mühlenberg, Gotthilf Heinrich (Henry) Ernst, 13–14, 83, 176, 177, 180, 217, 262, 263, 280
Mühlenberg, Heinrich Melchior, 6, 11, 12–17, 48, 51–52, 63, 66–67, 69, 82, 83, 85–114, 131, 147, 148, 161, 167, 168, 175–79, 217, 219, 226, 237, 248, 254, 261, 262, 263, 269, 274, 277, 279, 280, 282, 283, 286
in Georgia, 263, 264, 265–67
political views of, 91–99, 103–5, 109–14
relationship with Peter Mühlenberg, 6, 109, 201, 202–3
Mühlenberg, (John) Peter, 6, 13, 15, 37n34, 38, 83, 179, 181–219, 279, 281, 286
Mühlenberg, Sally, 266
Murray, John (Lord Dunmore), 39, 193, 233, 233n29, 285
Muskingum River, 230–32, 234, 239, 240, 245

Nazareth, PA, 59, 120, 128, 171

INDEX OF NAMES AND LOCATIONS    309

Netawatwees, 221, 231, 234, 237
New Hanover, PA, 89
New Jersey, 1, 57, 57n20, 89, 113,
    185, 206
  War of Independence battles in
    199, 203
  College of (Princeton
    University), 40
Newport, RI, 163–66, 169–70n146,
    172, 271,
New York, 37, 49, 51, 53–56, 81, 95,
    146, 147, 152, 153, 167, 204,
    206, 208, 227, 254, 285
  relations with Native Nations,
    20–21, 28, 57, 62–63, 70–71,
    73–74, 155, 235–36
  War of Independence battles in,
    12, 13, 156, 181, 199, 235
  partisan factions by region, 11,
    37, 106, 155
New York City 2, 16, 48, 102, 106,
    109, 152, 153, 165, 172, 176,
    203, 212, 218, 266, 273
  German Lutheran churches in,
    106, 114,
  royalist occupation of, 105–6,
    106n70, 108, 172, 179, 207,
    235, 275, 281
  Howe's use of churches in, 2,
    45, 273
Niagara, Fort, 21, 25n14
Niemeyer, Leonhard, 183–85
Norfolk, VA, 193–94, 196, 285
North Carolina, 271
Nyberg, Laurentius, 237


Ohio Country, Frontier, Valley, 12,
    20, 26, 35, 41, 44, 52, 77, 82,
    93, 193, 202, 230, 234, 235,
    239, 244
  Peter Mühlenberg's exploration,
    213
  Native Nations claims, 20, 26,
    27, 57, 60, 61, 67–68, 70, 74,
    77, 80, 82, 220, 229, 230, 236
Ohio River, 193, 233
Onondaga, Council Fire at, 57–59,
    62, 68, 69, 71, 75, 77, 81, 91

Ontario, 244
Oriskany, Battle of, 156

Paine, Thomas, 33, 44n42
Pasche, Wilhelm, 108, 108n79
Paxton Boys, 93–97, 104, 113, 128
Penn, John, 56–57, 64, 94, 98, 192
Penn, Thomas, 56–57, 71, 77, 78,
    98, 192
Penn, William, 20, 32–33, 56–57,
    57n18, 58, 59, 136
Pennsylvania x, 11, 32, 37, 49, 51,
    52, 55, 56, 63–65, 88, 89–90,
    100, 101, 111, 119, 120, 124–
    25, 125, 134, 137, 149, 167,
    169, 170, 171, 175, 181, 183,
    185, 186, 188, 194, 201, 216,
    217, 218, 220, 223, 227, 228,
    229, 239, 244, 248, 251, 254,
    257, 262, 264, 274, 278,
  militia, 14, 73, 75, 78, 136–38,
    219, 279, 281, 282, 285
  political factions, 10–11, 32, 33,
    42, 48, 60–61, 73, 81, 91, 97,
    98–99, 111, 113, 129, 131,
    136, 181, 195, 213–14, 218
  proprietary government, 32–33,
    38, 47, 51, 56, 64–65, 98,
    120, 192
  relations with Native Nations,
    28, 57–60, 62, 67, 68, 70–71,
    73, 77, 79, 81–82, 83, 84, 97,
    120, 229
  in the French and Indian War,
    19–21, 73–82, 126–31, 282
  in Pontiac's War 93, 97
  in the War of Independence, 11,
    12–14, 29, 37, 111, 112, 113,
    115, 136–38, 164–65, 170–
    72, 189, 196–97, 199–200,
    279, 282
Philadelphia 11, 34, 59, 67, 72, 76,
    79, 80, 86, 88, 97, 100, 102,
    135, 153, 170, 171, 177, 178,
    179, 180, 183, 185, 186, 215,
    216, 218, 224, 226, 254, 265
  ethnic Germans in 11, 48, 72,
    85, 89, 101, 102, 103, 107,

310  INDEX OF NAMES AND LOCATIONS

Philadelphia (*continued*)
  ethnic Germans in (*continued*)
    113, 119, 120, 172, 176, 187,
    189, 191, 216–17, 280, 281
  response to Paxton Boys alarm,
    93–96, 128
  royalist occupation during War
    of Independence, 12, 13–14,
    33, 34, 85, 107, 108–9, 110,
    153, 168, 176, 181, 200, 203,
    273, 279
  use of churches during War of
    Independence, 85, 103, 114,
    210
Pitt, Fort, 213, 221, 222, 234, 235,
  236, 237, 238, 239, 240, 241,
  242, 243, 280, 284
Pittsburgh, PA, University of, 244
Pittsfield, MA, 140, 154, 159
Princeton, Battle of, 199
Princeton University *see* College of
  New Jersey
Proclamation Line, 22–28, 38, 251
Providence (Trappe) PA, 12, 14, 85,
  88, 91, 102, 103, 161, 176,
  178, 179, 181, 183, 185, 188,
  189, 190, 200, 219, 279, 280,
  285

Quebec City, 82, 92, 113, 148,
  148n45, 150, 152, 172,
  205n82, 275
Quebec Territory (as encompassed
  by "Quebec Act"), 42,
  108n79, 148, 152, 153,
  204n77

Reid, Thomas, 44n42
Rhine River (Germany), 53,
Rhinebeck, NY, 69, 167
Rhode Island, 32, 163, 164, 166,
  207n88, 271
Riedesel, Friedrich zu, 108n79, 146,
  148, 150, 157, 163, 165, 166,
  170, 172, 174
Riedesel, Frederika Charlotte zu,
  108n79
Richmond, Battle of, 206

St. Augustine, FL, 246, 274
Sandusky River, Michigan, 232, 237,
  238, 239, 242
Saratoga, Battles of, 12, 162, 181,
  204
Savannah, GA, 205, 246, 247, 249,
  257, 259, 265, 269, 270, 271,
  272, 274
Savannah River, 246
Schönbrunn, Delaware Nation
  (Ohio), 230, 234, 237, 239,
  242
Schultze, Betsy (Elizabeth) nee
  Mühlenberg, 187
Schultze, C. Emmanuel, 175, 177,
  179
Shamokin, Oneida Nation
  (Pennsylvania), 58, 67, 68,
  79, 127, 224, 226, 227–28,
  229
Shenandoah Valley, 38, 101, 190,
  191, 194, 196, 197, 281
Smith, Adam, 23
South Carolina, 30, 51, 69, 125, 197,
  204, 246, 255, 257, 267, 270,
  271, 272, 273, 274
Spangenberg, August, 6, 17, 119,
  120, 123, 124, 125, 126, 129,
  130, 131, 132, 133, 136, 226,
  229, 282, 284, 285
Spener, Philipp Jakob, 87, 116
Stanwyx, Fort, 107, 153, 156, 162
  Treaty of, 27, 239
Stark, John, 140, 158, 159
Steuben, Friedrich von, 8, 204, 205,
  206, 213, 219
Streit, Christian, 109, 114, 180, 185,
  191
Sullivan, John, 235, 236, 239
Swaine, Francis, 197, 198
Swaine, Polly nee Mühlenberg, 190,
  198

Tarawachiagon *see* Weiser, Conrad
Tarleton, Brandon, 206, 285
Teedyuscung, 60, 81, 82, 229
Ticonderoga, Fort, 81, 154, 162
Trappe, PA *see* Providence, PA

## INDEX OF NAMES AND LOCATIONS   311

Treutlen, John Adams, 6, 247, 258, 264–70, 274, 278, 281
Trenton, Battle of, 199
Triebner, Christoph (Christopher), 6, 189, 247–48, 261–70, 272–78, 284, 286,
Tübingen, University of (Germany), 4n5, 89, 91
Tulpehocken, PA, 55, 56, 64, 65, 67, 78, 79, 82, 89, 90, 90n13, 103, 104, 175, 176, 177, 179, 180, 200, 224, 225

Urlsperger, August, 252, 253, 260n60, 266

Valcour Bay, *see* Lake Champlain, Battle of
Vermont. 140, 157 *see* Bennington, Battle of

Wagner, Chaplain Johann Christoph, 168, 276, 279, 280
Waldeck, Chaplain Philipp, 16n28, 106n70, 144, 147, 170, 171, 275, 276
Waloomsac River, 158, *see* Bennington, Battle of
Warner, Seth, 159
Washington County, PA, 238–42, 243–44, 285
Washington, George, 2, 6, 28, 31, 35, 39, 194, 218, 219, 239
  and French and Indian War, 52, 73–76, 78
  and War of Independence, 46–47, 105, 134, 135, 153, 164, 181, 199, 200, 205, 206–208, 209–12, 235–36, 272, 279, 280
  and Peter Mühlenberg, 6, 13, 37n34, 83, 182, 182n3, 193, 198, 200, 201, 202–3
Wasmus, Julius (Julian), 15n23, 140, 149, 155, 158, 160–64, 166, 167, 280

Watteville, Johannes de, 124, 132, 133
Wayne, Anthony, 200, 206
Weiser, Ann Eve (Feg), 56, 90n13
Weiser, Conrad, 6, 20, 21, 25, 51–84, 90, 91–93, 113, 120, 127, 183, 188, 217, 219, 223, 224–26, 227, 228, 229, 233, 251, 284, 285
Weiser, Johann, 52, 54, 55–56
Weiser, Peter, 199–200
Wesley, John, 4n6, 31, 147–48
West Point, 153
White Eye, 221, 234, 235, 237
Whitefield, George, 4n6, 6, 16, 30, 31, 120
William of Orange, King of England, 33
Williamson, Col. David, 239, 240–41
Wilson, Benjamin, 197
Wilson, James, 12, 40, 44n42
Witherspoon, John, 40, 44n42
Wolfe, James, 82
Wrangel, Karl, 96, 100, 183n6, 185
Württemberg (Germany), 52–53, 90, 91, 178
Wyoming River, 60, 75, 77, 81–82, 92, 120, 128, 130, 224–27, 229

Yorktown, VA, 106, 168, 182n4, 206, 207–10, 211, 22, 237, 239, 272, 274, 276

Zeisberger, David, 6, 12, 17, 68, 137, 220–22, 227–40, 244–45, 280, 283, 284
Ziegenhagen, Friedrich Michael, 88, 89, 108, 192, 257, 261, 265n60, 266
von Zinzendorf, Johann, 116
von Zinzendorf, Nicholas Ludwig, 4n5, 6, 48, 87, 88, 91, 116–20, 125, 132, 169, 228, 285
  confrontation with Heinrich Muhlenberg, 67, 67n49, 89, 226

## INDEX OF NAMES AND LOCATIONS

von Zinzendorf, Nicholas Ludwig (*continued*)
    ecumenical synod efforts, 65, 66, 120
    pacifism, 137, 256, 282
    response to "sifting time," 122–25, 132
    views of marriage, 121–22, 173, 230
    use of the lot, 66, 225–26
Wyoming Valley mission conference, 52, 66, 66n47, 120, 223, 224–26, 227

www.ingramcontent.com/pod-product-compliance
Lightning Source LLC
Chambersburg PA
CBHW050619300426
44112CB00012B/1576